# DISCOURSES OF

# PRESIDENT GORDON B. HINCKLEY

## VOLUME 2: 2000-2004

**DESERET BOOK**
SALT LAKE CITY, UTAH

**Library of Congress Cataloging-in-Publication Data**

Hinckley, Gordon Bitner, 1910-
  [Selections. 2005]
  Discourses of president Gordon B. Hinckley, vol. 2.
      p.    cm.
  Includes bibliographical references and index.
  ISBN 1-59038-518-7 (hardbound : alk. paper)
    1. Church of Jesus Christ of Latter-day Saints—Sermons.  2. Mormon Church—Sermons.  3. Sermons, American.  I. Title.
  BX8639.H56D572 2005
  252'.09332—dc22                                                                 2004025335

Printed in the United States of America                                          18961
R. R. Donnelley and Sons, Crawfordsville, IN

10   9   8   7   6   5   4   3   2   1

# CONTENTS

SECTION 1
GENERAL CONFERENCE AND OTHER
GENERAL MEETINGS

# CONTENTS

# CONTENTS

## SECTION 2
## MEMBER MEETINGS

CONTENTS

# CONTENTS

## SECTION 3
### MESSAGES TO THE GENERAL PUBLIC

## CONTENTS

# PREFACE

I N OCTOBER 2002, Thomas S. Monson, First Counselor in the First Presidency of The Church of Jesus Christ of Latter-day Saints, shared this tribute to President Gordon B. Hinckley:

"He has traversed frontiers not heretofore crossed and has visited with government leaders and with members the world over. His love for people transcends the barriers of language and culture. . . . He has the capacity to lift to a higher plane those from all walks of life, regardless of the faith to which they ascribe. He is a model of unfailing optimism, and we revere him as prophet, seer, and revelator" (in Conference Report, Oct. 2002, 69–70; or *Ensign*, Nov. 2002, 62).

These attributes are readily apparent in this collection of discourses delivered by President Hinckley between 2000 and 2004—a period marked by growth and advancement in the Church but also by terror and spiritual danger in the world generally. This volume contains 84 discourses, divided into three sections and arranged chronologically within each section. For the purposes of this collection, some of the discourses have received minor editing.

Section 1 contains all of President Hinckley's general conference addresses from 2000 to 2004. This includes the dedication of the Conference Center in October 2000 (see pages 54–58) and

President Hinckley's talk announcing the establishment of the Perpetual Education Fund (see pages 77–81). Section 1 also contains the addresses he gave at general meetings of the Young Women and the Relief Society.

Section 2, "Member Meetings," is a representative sample of President Hinckley's messages to gatherings of Latter-day Saints in many nations. The 24 discourses in this section were given at regional conferences, missionary meetings, devotionals, and other meetings in the United States, Singapore, Guam, Trinidad, Ukraine, Ghana, the Virgin Islands, and Spain. Section 2 also contains several discourses that were broadcast by satellite to Saints throughout the world.

Section 3, "Messages to the General Public," contains speeches President Hinckley gave at media gatherings, conventions of civic organizations, and community events. In many of these settings, President Hinckley was being honored for his leadership and acts of service with awards such as the Gold Good Citizenship Award from the Sons of the American Revolution (see pages 482–484), the 2004 Communicator of the Year Award from the National Forensic League (see pages 549–552), and the Presidential Medal of Freedom (see pages 553–555). Also of note in this section are President Hinckley's remarks during an impromptu memorial service on the evening of September 11, 2001 (see pages 502–503).

On that occasion, President Hinckley shared the source of his optimism during perilous times: "Dark as is this hour, there is shining through the heavy overcast of fear and anger the solemn and wonderful image of the Son of God, the Savior of the world, the Prince of Peace, the Exemplar of universal love, and it is to Him that we look in these circumstances. It was He who gave His life that all might enjoy eternal life" (page 503).

In these words, as in all of his discourses, President Hinckley's purpose has been to encourage all to draw "nearer to the Savior, with a more firm resolution to follow His teachings and His example" (page 60).

# SECTION 1

---

# GENERAL
# CONFERENCE
# AND OTHER
# GENERAL
# MEETINGS

# 170TH ANNUAL
# GENERAL CONFERENCE

# SATURDAY MORNING
# SESSION

APRIL 1, 2000

M Y DEARLY BELOVED brethren and sisters, what a magnificent sight you are, this vast congregation of Latter-day Saints gathered together in this new and wonderful hall.

The organ is not completed, and there are various construction details yet to be attended to. But fortunately the work is far enough along that we are able to use it for this conference. A year or so ago in speaking concerning it, I expressed the opinion that we may not be able to fill it initially. It seats three and a half times the capacity of the Tabernacle. But already we are in trouble. People are filling all of the seats.

During the four general sessions and the priesthood session, we will be able to accommodate about 100,000. We had requests for 370,000 tickets. The Tabernacle and Assembly Hall will serve as overflow. But with all of this, many, very many, will be disappointed. We apologize. We ask for your forgiveness. We are powerless to do anything about it. So many wanted to attend this first conference in the new hall. Unfortunately, that is impossible. I was somewhat shocked to learn that the people from my own ward, who are nearby and whom I love, have received no tickets.

But we are grateful for the enthusiasm of the Latter-day Saints concerning this new meeting place. I hope that enthusiasm will continue and that we shall have a full house at every conference in the future.

This is the newest in a series of meeting places constructed by our people. When first they came to this valley, they built a bowery. It shaded them from the sun but provided no warmth and very little comfort. Then they built the old Tabernacle. That was followed by the new Tabernacle, which has served us so very well for more than 130 years.

Now in this historic season, when we mark the birth of a new century and the beginning of a new millennium, we have built this new and wonderful Conference Center.

Each of the undertakings of the past was a bold venture, and particularly the Tabernacle. It was unique in its design. No one had constructed a building like that before. It is still unique. What a wonderful hall it has been and will continue to be. It will go on living, for I believe that buildings have lives of their own. It will go on serving long into the unforeseeable future.

The building of this structure has been a bold undertaking. We worried about it. We prayed about it. We listened for the whisperings of the Spirit concerning it. And only when we felt the confirming voice of the Lord did we determine to go forward.

At the general conference of April 1996, I said:

> I regret that many who wish to meet with us in the Tabernacle this morning are unable to get in. There are very many out on the grounds. This unique and remarkable hall, built by our pioneer forebears and dedicated to the worship of the Lord, comfortably seats about 6,000. Some of you seated on those hard benches for two hours may question the word *comfortably*.
>
> My heart reaches out to those who wish to get in and could not be accommodated. About a year ago I suggested to the Brethren that perhaps the time has come when we should study the feasibility of constructing another dedicated house of worship on a much larger scale that would accommodate

three or four times the number who can be seated in this building. [In Conference Report, Apr. 1996, 88–89; or *Ensign*, May 1996, 65]

The vision of a new hall was clearly in mind. Various architectural schemes were studied. One was finally selected. It included a massive structure to seat 21,000, with a theater accommodating another thousand. There would be no interior pillars to obstruct the view of the speaker. There would be trees and running water on the roof.

Ground was broken July 24, 1997, the 150th anniversary of the arrival of the first pioneers in this valley. That was a historic event.

We did not know it at the time, but in 1853 Brigham Young, in speaking of temples, said, "The time will come when . . . we shall build . . . on the top, groves and fish ponds" (*Deseret News*, Apr. 30, 1853, 46).

In 1924 Elder James E. Talmage of the Council of the Twelve wrote: "I have long seen the possible erection of a great pavilion on the north side of the Tabernacle, seating perhaps twenty thousand people or even double that number, with amplifiers capable of making all hear the addresses given from the Tabernacle stands, and in addition to this a connection with the broadcasting system, with receivers in the several chapels or other meeting houses throughout the intermountain region" (journal of James E. Talmage, Aug. 29, 1924, Special Collections and Manuscripts, Harold B. Lee Library, Brigham Young University, Provo, Utah).

In 1940 the First Presidency and the Twelve had their architect draw up a plan of a building that would seat 19,000 and would stand where this building stands. That was 60 years ago. They thought about it, they talked about it, but finally they dropped the idea entirely.

These statements and actions were wonderfully prophetic. We knew nothing about them. All of them have come to our attention since we began this construction.

We have not built a temple with trees and fishponds on the roof. But on this edifice we have many trees and running water. Brigham Young may have foreseen this structure very near the temple. We have what Brother Talmage thought of and much, much more. These services will not only be heard by all who are seated in the Conference Center, they will be carried by radio, television, and cable, and they will be transmitted by satellite to Europe, to Mexico, to South America. We reach far beyond the intermountain area of which Brother Talmage spoke. We reach beyond the confines of the United States and Canada. We essentially reach across the world.

This is truly a magnificent building. I know of no other comparable structure built primarily as a hall of worship that is so large and that will seat so many. It is beautiful in its design, in its appointments, and in its wonderful utility. It is built of reinforced concrete to the highest seismic codes required in this area. The concrete is faced with granite taken from the same quarry as was the stone for the temple. Both buildings even carry the blemishes of that granite.

The interior is beautiful and wonderfully impressive. It is huge, and it is constructed in such a way that nothing obstructs the view of the speaker. The carpets, the marble floors, the decorated walls, the handsome hardware, the wonderful wood all bespeak utility, with a touch of elegance.

It will prove to be a great addition to this city. Not only will our general conferences be held here, and some other religious meetings, but it will serve as a cultural center for the very best artistic presentations. We hope that those not of our faith will come here, experience the ambience of this beautiful place, and feel grateful for its presence. We thank all who have worked so hard to bring it to this stage—the architects, with whom we have had many meetings; the general contractors, three of whom have worked together; the subcontractors; the hundreds of craftsmen who have labored here; the construction supervisor; the city building inspectors; and everyone who has had a hand in this project. They have all joined in a herculean effort so that we might meet together this morning. Many of them are with us, I am happy to say.

And now, my brothers and sisters, I would like to tell you about another feature of this wonderful building. If I get a little personal and even a little sentimental, I hope you will forgive me.

I love trees. When I was a boy, we lived on a farm in the summer, a fruit farm. Every year at this season we planted trees. I think I have never missed a spring since I was married, except for two or three years when we were absent from the city, that I have not planted trees, at least one or two—fruit trees, shade trees, ornamental trees, and spruce, fir, and pine among the conifers. I love trees.

Well, some 36 years ago I planted a black walnut. It was in a crowded area where it grew straight and tall to get the sunlight. A year ago, for some reason it died. But walnut is a precious furniture wood. I called Brother Ben Banks of the Seventy, who, before giving his full time to the Church, was in the business of hardwood lumber. He brought his two sons, one a bishop and the other recently released from a bishopric and who now run the business, to look at the tree. From all they could tell it was solid, good, and beautiful wood. One of them suggested that it would make a pulpit for this hall. The idea excited me. The tree was cut down and then cut into two heavy logs. Then followed the long process of drying, first naturally and then kiln drying. The logs were cut into boards at a sawmill in Salem, Utah. The boards were then taken to Fetzer's woodworking plant, where expert craftsmen designed and built this magnificent pulpit with that wood.

The end product is beautiful. I wish all of you could examine it closely. It represents superb workmanship, and here I am speaking to you from the tree I grew in my backyard, where my children played and also grew.

It is an emotional thing for me. I have planted another black walnut or two. I will be long gone before they mature. When that day comes and this beautiful pulpit has grown old, perhaps one of them will do to make a replacement. To Elder Banks and his sons, Ben and Bradford, and to the skilled workers who have designed and built this, I offer my profound thanks for making it possible to have a small touch of mine in this great hall where the voices of prophets will go out to all the world in testimony of the Redeemer of mankind.

And so to all who have made this sacred edifice possible, and to all of you who are here assembled on this historic occasion, I express gratitude and appreciation, my love and my thanks for this day and this sacred and beautiful house of worship, in the name of Jesus Christ, amen.

# PRIESTHOOD
# SESSION

## APRIL 1, 2000

It now becomes my pleasure to share with you a few remarks. First, thank you for being here. I've never seen anything like this. I should have brought my binoculars to see how you in the upper balcony look. I've counted five empty seats in this entire hall. What a pleasure it is to be here.

My brethren, what a wonderful thing is the priesthood of God. There is nothing to compare with it. It is received only by the laying on of hands by those in authority to bestow it. In this dispensation, that bestowal goes back to John the Baptist and the Lord's Apostles Peter, James, and John. They came to earth and physically laid their hands on the heads of Joseph Smith and Oliver Cowdery and with audible voices spoke words of bestowal of this wondrous power. Since then every man who has received it has done so through the laying on of hands by one who received it in turn in the same manner, traced back to its original bestowal.

It is classless. Every worthy man, regardless of nationality, ethnic background, or any other factor, is eligible to receive the priesthood. His obedience to the commandments of God becomes the determining factor. Its bestowal is based only on worthiness before the Lord.

With it comes the right and the authority to govern in the

9

Church of Christ. I recall the experiences I had long ago when I was a member of the Council of the Twelve. I attended a stake conference where the president was a man of wealth and affluence. He was very successful by the standards of the world. He lived in a magnificent home. He met me at the airport in a beautiful car. We had lunch at a first-class restaurant. And yet he was humble in his office, anxious to learn, and ever willing to do the right thing in administering the affairs of his stake.

I subsequently went to another conference. The president met me in a car that had seen many seasons. We stopped at a fast-food place for a bite to eat. His home was extremely modest—neat and clean and quiet but not richly furnished. He was a carpenter by trade. He had none of the fancy things of the world. He too was a wonderful stake president doing his duty in a remarkable way. He was excellent in every respect.

Such is the wonder of this priesthood. Wealth is not a factor. Education is not a factor. The honors of men are not a factor. The controlling factor is acceptability unto the Lord.

All of the Authorities who are here tonight could testify that in the reorganization of stakes, they have had remarkable and inspiring experiences. I recall being assigned to reorganize a stake about 40 years ago. The president had suddenly died. The Brethren asked me to go down and speak at the funeral and reorganize the stake. I had never done this before. I was new as a General Authority. I was to be all alone.

When I arrived I was taken to another town, where I participated in the funeral service. I asked all of the stake officers and the bishops to remain after the service and announced that a reorganization of the stake would take place the next evening.

I asked the mission president to sit with me as I interviewed the brethren, none of whom I knew. We interviewed late into the evening. I soon discovered there were problems in the stake. There were divisive feelings. When we were all through, I said to the mission president, "I am not satisfied. Are there not others?" He said, "I know of only one man whom we have not interviewed. He moved here rather recently on a transfer in his company. He is the second counselor in a bishopric. I do not know him well. He resides in another city."

I said, "Let's go see him." We drove and went to the hotel where I would be staying for the night. Here I was, having interviewed all of these brethren and having not found one that I considered worthy to preside and having scheduled the reorganization for the next evening.

We arrived late at the hotel. I called the man; a sleepy voice answered the phone. I said that I wished to see him that evening. I apologized for calling him so late. He said, "I've just gone to bed, but I'll put on my clothes and come."

He came to the hotel. The conversation that followed was most interesting. He was a graduate of BYU in petroleum geology. He worked for a big oil company. He had served elsewhere in positions of responsibility in the Church. He knew the program of the Church. He had served a mission. He knew the gospel. He was mature in the Church. And the territory for which he was responsible as an employee of the oil company was exactly the same as the territory of the stake. I told him we would telephone him in the morning and excused him.

The mission president went on his way, and I went to bed.

At about three o'clock the next morning I awoke. Doubts began to flood my mind. This man was almost a total stranger to the people of the stake. I got out of bed and got on my knees and pleaded with the Lord for direction. I did not hear a voice, but I had a very distinct impression that said, "I told you who should be stake president. Why do you continue to ask?"

Ashamed of myself for troubling the Lord again, I went to bed and fell asleep. I phoned the man early the next morning and issued to him a call to serve as president of the stake. I asked him to select counselors.

That evening when people gathered for the meeting, there was much speculation as to who would be the stake president, but no one even thought of this man. When I announced his name, people looked at one another for a clue to discovering who he was. I had him come to the stand. I announced his counselors and had them come to the stand.

Even though they did not know him, the people sustained him. Things began to happen in that stake. The people had known for a long time that they needed a stake center, but they had been uncertain and argumentative as to where it should go. He went to work and within 18 months had a beautiful new stake center ready for dedication. He unified the stake. He traveled up and down, meeting the people and extending his love to them. That stake, which had grown tired, came to life and literally bubbled with new enthusiasm. It stands as a shining star in the large constellation of stakes in this Church.

Brethren, I can testify to you that revelation from the Lord is made manifest in the naming of a stake president. I once spoke in this meeting on bishops, and tonight I wish to say a few words about stake presidents.

The office came into the Church in 1832. Joseph Smith, the President of the Church, was also stake president. When a new stake was organized in Missouri in 1834, this pattern was changed, with officers drawn from the ranks of the priesthood.

This is an office that came of revelation. The organization of a stake represents the creation of a family of wards and branches. The program of the Church has become increasingly complex, and the demands upon stake presidencies have grown. Smaller stakes have been created. We now have 2,550 stakes in the Church, with more approved for organization.

The president of the stake is the officer called under revelation to stand between the bishops of wards and the General Authorities of the Church. It is a most important responsibility. He is trained by the General Authorities, and in turn he trains the bishops.

It is most interesting to me that we have 17,789 wards in the Church, with a bishop in each. They are scattered over the earth. Their members speak various languages. And yet they are all alike. You may attend Sunday meetings in Singapore or Stockholm, and the service will be the same. Think of the confusion we would have if every bishop followed his own inclinations. The Church would literally fall apart in a very short time.

The stake president serves as an adviser to the bishops. Every bishop knows that when he has to deal with a difficult problem, there is one readily available to whom he may go to share his burden and receive counsel.

He provides a secondary measure of safety in determining those worthy to go to the house of the Lord. Bishops are very close to their people. They live with them as neighbors. Sometimes they do not have the heart to refuse to grant a recommend even though the patron's worthiness may be somewhat in question. But the stake president also interviews. Until Wilford Woodruff's time, the President of the Church signed all temple recommends. But the burden became too heavy, and stake presidents were given the responsibility. They have done a tremendous work in this regard.

The president likewise becomes a second screen in determining the worthiness of those who go out to represent the Church in the mission field. He too interviews the candidate, and only when he is satisfied of his or her worthiness does he endorse the recommendation. He likewise has been given authority to set apart those called on missions and to extend releases when they have completed their service.

Most importantly, he is the principal disciplinary officer of the stake. The duties of a teacher in the Aaronic Priesthood might be applied to the president of the stake. He "is to watch over the [entire stake], and be with and strengthen [the members];

"And see that there is no iniquity in the church, neither hardness with each other, neither lying, backbiting, nor evil speaking;

"And see that the church meet together often, and also see that all the members do their duty" (D&C 20:53–55).

He carries the very heavy responsibility of seeing that the doctrine taught in the stake is kept pure and unsullied. It is his duty to see that there is no false doctrine that is taught nor false practice that occurs. If there be any Melchizedek Priesthood holder out of line, or any other person for that matter, under some circumstances, he is to counsel with them, and if the individual persists in his or her practice, then the president is obliged to take action. He will summon the offender to appear before a disciplinary council, where action may be taken to assign a probationary period or to disfellowship or excommunicate him or her from the Church.

This is a most onerous and unwelcome task, but the president must face up to it without fear or favor. All of this is done in harmony with the direction of the Spirit and as set forth in section 102 of the Doctrine and Covenants.

Then subsequently he must do all he can to labor with and bring back in due time the one who was disciplined.

All of this and much more compose his responsibilities. It follows, therefore, that his own life must be exemplary before his people.

What a wonderful body of men comprise the stake presidents of this Church. Chosen by inspiration, they are most diligent in the pursuit of their duties. They are men of ability. They are men well schooled in the doctrines and practices of the Church. They are men of great faith. They are men who are called of the Lord to preside in the areas of their jurisdiction.

I think I know a little about the office of stake president. My grandfather was one when there were only 25 stakes in the Church.

My father presided for years over the largest stake in the Church. I served as a stake president before being called as a General Authority. And one of my sons has just been released after nine years of service as a stake president. This represents four generations serving in this capacity.

I have total confidence in the men who fill this office. Their duties are numerous, their responsibilities great. They recognize their own inadequacy, and I know that they pray for guidance and help. I know they study the scriptures to find answers. I know they place this work first in their lives. Because we have such confidence in them, we urge local members that they not seek out General Authorities to counsel with and bless them. Their stake presidents have been called under the same inspiration under which the General Authorities were called.

I pray for these, my beloved brethren, that the Spirit of the Lord will rest upon them. I pray that they may be inspired in their words, in their thoughts, in their actions. I hope their homes will be places of peace and love and harmony where they will draw inspiration for their work. I pray they will magnify and bless their wives and children, being the kind of husbands and fathers who will stand as examples for all of the people of their stakes. I hope that whatever their vocations, they may pursue them with honor and integrity, that they may be workmen worthy of their hire. I hope they will so live that they will merit the respect of those not only of our faith but of others with whom they may be associated. And when they have served well over a period of years and led their people in honor and love, the time will come that they are to be released. Their only reward will be the love of the people and the confidence of their brethren.

There is no other office in the Church quite like this office. The president of the stake is close enough to the people to know them and love them. And yet, with his counselors, he stands aloof enough to deal objectively according to the will and pattern of the Lord.

I pray that the rich and wondrous blessings of the Lord may be poured out upon these devoted brethren that they may be men of faith, men of inspired judgment, men of patience, men who love the Lord and who love His people. May they be happy, and may they find their reward in the satisfaction of having served well is my humble prayer in the name of Jesus Christ, amen.

# SUNDAY MORNING SESSION

APRIL 2, 2000

Now it becomes my opportunity to say a few words, my brothers and sisters. I am overwhelmed with feelings of thanksgiving this morning. I feel so richly blessed of the Lord. As I look into the faces of the thousands upon thousands who are gathered in this new and beautiful hall and then think of the hundreds of thousands who are assembled across the world listening to this conference, I am almost overcome with feelings of gratitude for the great unity that exists among us. If I may speak personally for a little while, I think no man has been blessed so richly as I have been blessed. I cannot understand it. I so much appreciate your many expressions of kindness and love.

Through the great goodness of others I have traveled far and wide across the earth in the interest of this Church. I have had remarkable opportunities to speak to the world through the generosity of the media. I have lifted my voice in testimony in the great halls of this nation, from Madison Square Garden in New York to the Astrodome in Houston. Men and women of high station have received me and spoken with great respect concerning our work.

On the other hand, during these years I have come to know of the mean and contemptuous ways of our critics. I think the Lord had them in mind when He declared:

"Cursed are all those that shall lift up the heel against mine anointed, saith the Lord, and cry they have sinned when they have not sinned before me, . . . but have done that which was meet in mine eyes, and which I commanded them.

" . . . Those who cry transgression do it because they are the servants of sin, and are the children of disobedience themselves. . . .

"Wo unto them. . . .

"Their basket shall not be full, their houses and their barns shall perish, and they themselves shall be despised by those that flattered them" (D&C 121:16–17, 19–20).

We leave to Him, whose right it is, judgments that may come to those who oppose His work.

I return to my expressions of gratitude. Thank you, brothers and sisters, for your prayers. Thank you for your support in the great work we are all trying to accomplish. Thank you for your obedience to the commandments of God. He is pleased and loves you. Thank you for your faithfulness in carrying forward the great responsibilities which you have. Thank you for your ready response to every call which is made upon you. Thank you for bringing up your children in the way of light and truth. Thank you for the unfailing testimonies which you carry in your hearts concerning God, our Eternal Father, and His Beloved Son, the Lord Jesus Christ.

I am so grateful for the youth of the Church. There is so much of evil everywhere. Temptation, with all its titillating influences, is about us everywhere. We lose some to these destructive forces, unfortunately. We sorrow over every one who is lost. We reach out to help them, to save them, but in too many cases our entreaties are spurned. Tragic is the course they are following. It is the way which leads down to destruction.

But there are so many, many hundreds of thousands of our young people who are faithful and true, who are straight as an arrow and as strong as a great wave of the sea in following the course they have mapped out for themselves. It is a course of righteousness and goodness, a course of accomplishment and achievement. They are making something of their lives, and the world will be so much the better for them.

I am profoundly grateful for this wonderful season of history in which we live. There has never been another like it. We, of all people who have walked the earth, are so richly and abundantly blessed.

But of all the things for which I feel grateful this morning, one stands out preeminently. That is a living testimony of Jesus Christ, the Son of the Almighty God, the Prince of Peace, the Holy One.

On one occasion at a missionary meeting in Europe, an elder raised his hand and said, "Give us your testimony, and tell us how you gained it."

I feel I might try saying a few words this morning on the evolution of my testimony. This is a personal area, of course. I hope you will excuse that.

The earliest instance of which I have recollection of spiritual feelings was when I was about five years of age, a very small boy. I was crying from the pain of an earache. There were no wonder drugs at the time. That was 85 years ago. My mother prepared a bag of table salt and put it on the stove to warm. My father softly put his hands upon my head and gave me a blessing, rebuking the pain and the illness by authority of the holy priesthood and in the name of Jesus Christ. He then took me tenderly in his arms and placed the bag of warm salt at my ear. The pain subsided and left. I fell asleep in my father's secure embrace. As I was falling asleep, the words of his administration floated through my mind. That is the earliest remembrance I have of the exercise of the authority of the priesthood in the name of the Lord.

Later in my youth, my brother and I slept in an unheated bedroom in the winter. People thought that was good for you. Before falling into a warm bed, we knelt to say our prayers. There were expressions of simple gratitude. They concluded in the name of Jesus. The distinctive title of Christ was not used very much when we prayed in those days.

I recall jumping into my bed after I had said amen, pulling the covers up around my neck, and thinking of what I had just done in speaking to my Father in Heaven in the name of His Son. I did not have great knowledge of the gospel. But there was some kind of lingering peace and security in communing with the heavens in and through the Lord Jesus.

When I went on a mission to the British Isles, that testimony quickened. Each morning my companion and I read the Gospel of John together, commenting on each verse. It was a wonderful, illuminating experience. That marvelous testament opens with a declaration of the divinity of the Son of God. It states:

"In the beginning was the Word, and the Word was with God, and the Word was God.

"The same was in the beginning with God.

"All things were made by him; and without him was not any thing made that was made. . . .

"And the Word was made flesh, and dwelt among us, (and we beheld his glory, the glory as of the only begotten of the Father,) full of grace and truth" (John 1:1–3, 14).

I thought of that declaration much then, and I have thought of it much since. It leaves no doubt concerning the individuality of the Father and the Son. To the Son, the Father gave the great responsibility of creating the earth, "and without him was not any thing made that was made."

I have seen much of ugliness in this world. Most of it is the work of man. But I think I have seen much more of beauty. I marvel at the majestic works of the Creator. How magnificent they are. And they are all the work of the Son of God.

"And the Word was made flesh, and dwelt among us." He, the Son of the Father, came to earth. He condescended to leave His royal courts on high—where He stood as Prince, the Firstborn of the Father—to take upon Himself mortality, to be born in a manger, the humblest of all places, in a vassal state ruled by the centurions of Rome.

How could He have condescended further?

He was baptized of John in Jordan "to fulfil all righteousness" (Matthew 3:15). His earthly ministry was preceded by the clever temptations of the adversary. He withstood, saying, "Get thee behind me, Satan" (Luke 4:8).

He went about Galilee, Samaria, and Judea preaching the gospel of salvation, causing the blind to see, the lame to walk, the dead to rise to life again. And then, to fulfill His Father's plan of happiness for His children, He gave His life as a price for the sins of each of us.

That testimony grew in my heart as a missionary when I read the New Testament and the Book of Mormon, which further bore witness of Him. That knowledge became the foundation of my life, standing on the footings of the answered prayers of my childhood.

Since then my faith has grown much further. I have become His Apostle, appointed to do His will and teach His word. I have become His witness to the world. I repeat that witness of faith to you and to all who hear my voice this Sabbath morning.

*Jesus is my friend.* None other has given me so much. "Greater love hath no man than this, that a man lay down his life for his friends" (John 15:13). He gave His life for me. He opened the way to eternal life. Only a God could do this. I hope that I am deemed worthy of being a friend to Him.

*He is my exemplar.* His way of life, His absolutely selfless conduct, His outreach to those in need, His final sacrifice all stand as an example to me. I cannot measure up entirely, but I can try.

> *He marked the path and led the way,*
> *And ev'ry point defines*

21

*To light and life and endless day*
*Where God's full presence shines.*
*["How Great the Wisdom and*
*the Love," Hymns, no. 195]*

*He is my teacher.* No other voice ever spoke such wondrous language as that of the Beatitudes:

And seeing the multitudes, . . . he opened his mouth, and taught them, saying,
Blessed are the poor in spirit: for theirs is the kingdom of heaven.
Blessed are they that mourn: for they shall be comforted.
Blessed are the meek: for they shall inherit the earth.
Blessed are they which do hunger and thirst after righteousness: for they shall be filled.
Blessed are the merciful: for they shall obtain mercy.
Blessed are the pure in heart: for they shall see God.
Blessed are the peacemakers: for they shall be called the children of God.
Blessed are they which are persecuted for righteousness' sake: for theirs is the kingdom of heaven. [Matthew 5:1–10]

No other teacher has ever offered the matchless counsel given the multitude on the mount.

*He is my healer.* I stand in awe at His wondrous miracles. And yet I know they happened. I accept the truth of these things because I know that He is the Master of life and death. The miracles of His ministry bespeak compassion, love, and a sense of humanity wonderful to behold.

*He is my leader.* I am honored to be one in the long cavalcade of those who love Him and who have followed Him during the two millennia that have passed since His birth.

*Onward, Christian soldiers!*
*Marching as to war,*

*With the cross of Jesus*
*Going on before.*
*Christ, the royal Master,*
*Leads against the foe;*
*Forward into battle,*
*See his banners go!*
　　　　[*"Onward, Christian Soldiers,"*
　　　　Hymns, *no. 246]*

*He is my Savior and my Redeemer.* Through giving His life in pain and unspeakable suffering, He has reached down to lift me and each of us and all the sons and daughters of God from the abyss of eternal darkness following death. He has provided something better—a sphere of light and understanding, growth and beauty where we may go forward on the road that leads to eternal life. My gratitude knows no bounds. My thanks to my Lord has no conclusion.

*He is my God and my King.* From everlasting to everlasting, He will reign and rule as King of Kings and Lord of Lords. To His dominion there will be no end. To His glory there will be no night.

None other can take His place. None other ever will. Unblemished and without fault of any kind, He is the Lamb of God, to whom I bow and through whom I approach my Father in Heaven.

Isaiah foretold of His coming: "For unto us a child is born, unto us a son is given: and the government shall be upon his shoulder: and his name shall be called Wonderful, Counsellor, The mighty God, The everlasting Father, The Prince of Peace" (Isaiah 9:6).

Those who walked with Him in Palestine bore witness of His divinity. The centurion who watched Him die declared in solemnity, "Truly this was the Son of God" (Matthew 27:54).

Thomas, on seeing His resurrected body, cried out in wonder, "My Lord and my God" (John 20:28).

Those in this hemisphere to whom He appeared heard the voice of the Father introduce Him: "Behold my Beloved Son, in whom I am well pleased, in whom I have glorified my name" (3 Nephi 11:7).

And the Prophet Joseph, speaking in this dispensation, declared:

"And now, after the many testimonies which have been given of him, this is the testimony, last of all, which we give of him: That he lives!

"For we saw him, even on the right hand of God; and we heard the voice bearing record that he is the Only Begotten of the Father" (D&C 76:22–23).

To which I add my own witness that He is "the way, the truth, and the life" and that "no man cometh unto the Father, but by [Him]" (John 14:6).

Gratefully, and with love undiminished, I bear witness of these things in His Holy name, even the name of Jesus the Christ, amen.

# Sunday Afternoon Session

## April 2, 2000

I'M SURE YOU ARE RATHER weary of listening to me. I'll do my best.

What a wonderful conference this has been, my brethren and sisters. We have rejoiced in all that has occurred. The speakers have been inspired, every one of them. The music has been superb. The prayers have been beautiful and touching. We have been uplifted in every way as we have participated together.

There was a popular piece of music when I was young that said, "The song is ended but the melody lingers on" (Irving Berlin [1927]).

I pray that will be the case with this conference. When we leave, I hope we will have pleasant recollections and fond memories of this great occasion.

As we return to our homes, let us go with thanksgiving in our hearts. We have been present and have participated in the proceedings of the 170th general conference of the Church. We have for the first time used this great new building. We have been here April 1 and 2 of the year 2000, the opening of a new century and a great new millennium. There is something wonderfully significant about all of this. It is a time of new beginnings.

I hope that each of us will long remember what we have heard, but more importantly, what we have felt. May it become an anchor in our lives, a guide by which to live, a training time where we learned to shape our actions toward others and our attitudes toward ourselves.

I pray that the effects of this conference will be felt in our homes.

I hope that each one of us will be a better husband or wife, kinder to one another, more thoughtful, more restrained in criticism, and more generous with compliments. I hope that as fathers and mothers we will strive more fully to rear our children "in the nurture and admonition of the Lord" (Ephesians 6:4), treating them with respect and love, giving encouragement at every opportunity, and subduing our critical remarks. I hope that as sons and daughters we will be more respectful than we have been, that we will look to our parents with the knowledge that they love us, and that we will try to be more obedient in following their counsel.

Let us as Latter-day Saints reach out to others not of our faith. Let us never act in a spirit of arrogance or with a holier-than-thou attitude. Rather, may we show love and respect and helpfulness toward them. We are greatly misunderstood, and I fear that much of it is of our own making. We can be more tolerant, more neighborly, more friendly, more of an example than we have been in the past. Let us teach our children to treat others with friendship, respect, love, and admiration. That will yield a far better result than will an attitude of egotism and arrogance.

Let us study the ways of the Lord, reading His life and teachings in the sacred scripture He has given us. Let us take a little time to meditate, to think of what we can do to improve our lives and to become better examples of what a Latter-day Saint should be.

Let us reach out to the world in our missionary service, teaching all who will listen concerning the restoration of the gospel; speaking without fear, but also without self-righteousness, of the First Vision; testifying of the Book of Mormon and of the restoration of the priesthood. Let us, my brothers and sisters, get on our knees and pray for the opportunity to bring others into the joy of the gospel.

Now, in closing, may I give you just a very brief report on temples. As of today we have 76 in operation. That is many more than we had a few years ago. We will dedicate the Palmyra Temple this coming Thursday. That will be a great occasion. The temple overlooks the Sacred Grove. Then on Sunday—next Sunday—we will dedicate the Fresno California Temple. We plan on dedicating altogether 36 new temples in the year 2000. I think we will accomplish all we set out to do. Quite a number of others in construction or announced will not be completed until 2001 or 2002.

Now, additionally, we announce at this conference that we hope to build a house of the Lord in Aba, Nigeria. Brother Pace, we may be delayed in Ghana, but we hope there will be no delay in Nigeria. Others in Asunción, Paraguay; Helsinki, Finland; Lubbock, Texas; Snowflake, Arizona; and somewhere in the Tri-Cities area of the state of Washington.

So we shall go on in the process of bringing temples to the people.

Now, we have been on a great shakedown cruise, as it were. This building has been filled to capacity. I don't see an empty seat anywhere. It is a miracle! It is a tremendous and wonderful thing, for which we thank the Lord with all our hearts.

I leave with you my love and blessing and my testimony of this divine work. God, our Eternal Father, lives. You know that. I know that. His Beloved Son, the resurrected Redeemer of the world, stands at His side. You know that also, as do I. They appeared to the Prophet Joseph and ushered in this glorious work. How fortunate we are to be a part of it. Let us stand a little higher and let the nobility of good character shine through our lives, I humbly pray in the name of Him who is our great Redeemer, even the Lord Jesus Christ, amen.

God bless you, my beloved friends, my brothers, my sisters, my associates, in this great and holy work. Thank you.

# General Relief
# Society Meeting

I WOULD BE SATISFIED to close the meeting right now. We have been well taught. I commend the presidency on their excellent remarks. You may know that they have worried and prayed and pleaded with the Lord to help them in their preparation and in their presentation. We are all indebted to you, Sister Smoot, Sister Jensen, Sister Dew. You've done a great work.

I count it a precious opportunity to speak to you. There is no other congregation like this congregation. We speak from the Tabernacle on Temple Square in Salt Lake City. But you hear from almost everywhere. You are gathered across the United States and Canada, across the nations of Europe, and Mexico, Central America, and South America. You are as one in this great gathering even though you are in Asia, the South Pacific, and in other distant lands.

Your hearts are all of one kind. You are gathered together because you love the Lord. You have a testimony and conviction concerning His living reality. You pray unto the Father in Jesus's name. You understand the efficacy of prayer. You are wives and mothers. You are widows and single mothers carrying very heavy burdens. You are newly married women, and you are women who have not married. You are a vast concourse of women of The

Church of Jesus Christ of Latter-day Saints. You belong to this great organization, more than four million of you. No one can calculate the tremendous force for good that you can become. You are the keepers of the hearth. You are the managers of the home. Along with Sister Dew, I charge you to stand tall and be strong in defense of those great virtues which have been the backbone of our social progress. When you are united, your power is limitless. You can accomplish anything you wish to accomplish. And oh, how very, very great is the need for you in a world of crumbling values where the adversary seems so very much to be in control.

I have great respect and admiration for you young women who have come into the Society rather recently. You have largely weathered the storm that beat about you in your youth. You have kept yourself unsullied from the world. You have kept yourself free from the taints and stains of unrighteousness. You are the very flower of the good, maturing youth of the Church. You have made it thus far, clean and beautiful and virtuous. I compliment you most warmly.

I commend you women who are single. You have known much of loneliness. You have known anxiety and fear and desperate longing. But you have not let this overcome you. You have gone forward with your lives, making significant and wonderful contributions along the way. God bless you, my dear sisters and friends.

Tonight I cannot talk directly to all of you. I have singled out one segment of this vast congregation, and that is you who are mothers. I might include those who will become mothers. What a wonderful thing you have done as mothers. You have given birth and nurtured children. You have entered into a partnership with our Father in Heaven to give mortal experience to His sons and daughters. They are His children, and they are your children, flesh of your flesh, for whom He will hold you responsible. You have rejoiced over them, and in many cases you have sorrowed. They have brought you happiness as no one else could. They have brought you pain as none other could.

By and large, you have done a remarkable job in rearing them. I have said many times that I believe we have the finest generation of young people that this Church has ever known. They are better educated; they are better motivated; they know the scriptures; they live the Word of Wisdom; they pay their tithing; they pray. They try to do the right thing. They are bright and able, clean and fresh, attractive and smart. These are very substantial in number. More of them go on missions than ever before. More of them marry in the temple. They know what the gospel is about, and they are trying to live it, looking to the Lord for His guidance and help.

But I regret to say that so many of our young people fall between the cracks. They try one foolish thing after another, never evidently satisfied, until they are pulled down into a pit from which they cannot extricate themselves. Some of our own are among these, and it is you mothers who bear the burden of sorrow that flows therefrom. They are your sons and daughters. And so tonight with the hope that I may be helpful, I plead with you.

In some cases it may be too late, but in most cases you still have the opportunity to guide and persuade, to teach with love, to lead in paths that are fruitful and productive and away from those dead-end situations which bring no good.

You have nothing in this world more precious than your children. When you grow old, when your hair turns white and your body grows weary, when you are prone to sit in a rocker and meditate on the things of your life, nothing will be so important as the question of how your children have turned out. It will not be the money you have made. It will not be the cars you have owned. It will not be the large house in which you live. The searing question that will cross your mind again and again will be "How well have my children done?"

If the answer is that they have done very well, then your happiness will be complete. If they have done less than well, then no other satisfaction can compensate for your loss.

And so I plead with you tonight, my dear sisters. Sit down and quietly count the debits and the credits in your role as a mother. It is not too late. When all else fails, there is prayer and the promised help of the Lord to assist you in your trials. But do not delay. Start now, whether your child be 6 or 16.

I am told that there was recently held in this area a great gathering which attracted 10,000 young people. I am satisfied that some of those young people were our own.

It is reported that the acts of that evening's entertainment were lewd and evil. They were loathsome and downgrading. They were representative of the foulest aspects of life. There was no beauty in them. There was only ugliness and depravity. It was sleaze in its worst form.

These young people paid from $35 to $50 admission. In many cases that money came from their parents. Similar things are going on across the world. Some of your sons and daughters make it possible for the promoters of such filth to prosper in their evil undertakings.

Last Sunday the *Deseret News* carried a detailed feature story on underground drug parties that go by the name of *rave*. They run from 3:00 until 7:30 of a Sunday morning. Here young men and women, in their late teens to early twenties, dance to the metallic beat of so-called music pouring forth from stacks of amplifiers. "Some are wearing brightly colored beads; others are waving glow sticks. Some have pacifiers in their mouths, while others are wearing painter's masks" (Pat Reavy, "Rave: Secrecy Shrouds Underground Drug Parties," Sept. 17, 2000, B1). Drugs go back and forth from sellers to users at $20 to $25 a pill.

I know of no better answer to these foul practices that confront our young people than the teachings of a mother, given in love with an unmistakable warning. There will be failures, yes. There will be

31

heartbreaking disappointments. There will be tragedies, bleak and hopeless. But in very many cases, if the process begins early and continues, there will be success and happiness and love and much of gratitude. Opening your purse and handing a son or daughter money before you rush off to work will not do. It may only lead to more evil practice.

The proverb spoken of old said, "Train up a child in the way he should go: and when he is old, he will not depart from it" (Proverbs 22:6). Another wise saying reads, "As the twig is bent the tree's inclin'd" (Alexander Pope, *Moral Essays,* in *The Complete Poetical Works of Pope* [1903], 159).

Teach your children when they are very young and small, and never quit. As long as they are in your home, let them be your primary interest. I take the liberty tonight of suggesting several things that you might teach them. The list is not complete. You can add other items.

*Teach them to seek for good friends.* They are going to have friends, good or bad. Those friends will make a vast difference in their lives. It is important that they cultivate an attitude of tolerance toward all people, but it is more important that they gather around them those of their own kind who will bring out the best they have within them. Otherwise they may be infected with the ways of their associates.

I have never forgotten a story that Elder Robert Harbertson told at this Tabernacle pulpit. He spoke of an Indian boy who climbed a high mountain. It was cold up there. At his feet was a snake, a rattlesnake. The snake was cold and pleaded with the young man to pick it up and take it down where it was warmer.

The Indian boy listened to the enticings of the serpent. He gave in. He gathered it up into his arms and covered it with his shirt. He carried it down the mountain to where it was warm. He gently put it on the grass. When the snake was warm, it raised its head and struck the boy with its poisonous fangs.

The boy cursed at the snake for striking him as an answer to his kindness. The snake replied, "You knew what I was when you picked me up." (See "Restoration of the Aaronic Priesthood," *Ensign,* July 1989, 77.)

Warn your children against those with poisonous fangs who will entice them, seduce them with easy talk, then injure and possibly destroy them.

*Teach them to value education.* "The glory of God is intelligence, or, in other words, light and truth" (D&C 93:36).

There rests upon the people of this Church a mandate from the Lord to acquire learning. It will bless their lives now and through all the years to come.

With fascination I watched one evening on television the story of a family in the Midwest. It included the father and mother and three sons and one daughter.

The father and mother determined when they married that they would do all they could to see that their children were exposed to the very best educational experiences.

They lived in a modest home. They observed modest ways. But they nurtured their children with knowledge. Every one of those children achieved in a remarkable way. Every one was well educated. One became a university president; the others became heads of large business institutions, successful individuals by any measure.

*Teach them to respect their bodies.* The practice is growing among young people of tattooing and piercing their bodies. The time will come when they will regret it, but it will then be too late. The scriptures unequivocally declare:

"Know ye not that ye are the temple of God, and that the Spirit of God dwelleth in you?

"If any man defile the temple of God, him shall God destroy; for the temple of God is holy, which temple ye are" (1 Corinthians 3:16–17).

It is sad and regrettable that some young men and women have their bodies tattooed. What do they hope to gain by this painful process? Is there "anything virtuous, lovely, or of good report or praiseworthy" (Articles of Faith 1:13) in having unseemly so-called art impregnated into the skin to be carried throughout life, all the way down to old age and death? They must be counseled to shun it. They must be warned to avoid it. The time will come that they will regret it but will have no escape from the constant reminder of their foolishness except through another costly and painful procedure.

I submit that it is an uncomely thing, and yet a common thing, to see young men with ears pierced for earrings, not for one pair only, but for several.

They have no respect for their appearance. Do they think it clever or attractive to so adorn themselves?

I submit it is not adornment. It is making ugly that which was attractive. Not only are ears pierced, but other parts of the body as well, even the tongue. It is absurd.

We—the First Presidency and the Council of the Twelve—have taken the position, and I quote, that "the Church discourages tattoos. It also discourages the piercing of the body for other than medical purposes, although it takes no position on the minimal piercing of the ears by women for one pair of earrings."

*Teach your sons and daughters to avoid illegal drugs as they would the plague.* The use of these narcotics will destroy them. They cannot so abuse their bodies, they cannot so build within themselves vicious and enslaving appetites without doing incalculable injury. One habit calls for another, until the victim in so many cases is led down to a situation of utter helplessness, with loss of all self-control and habituated to a point where it cannot be broken.

A recent television program indicated that 20 percent of young people who are on drugs were introduced to their use by parents. What is wrong with people? The use of illegal drugs becomes a dead-end road. It takes one nowhere except to loss of self-control, to loss of self-respect, and to self-destruction. Teach your children to avoid them as they would a foul disease. Build within them an utter abhorrence of such.

*Teach them to be honest.* The jails of the world are filled with people who began their evil activities with small acts of dishonesty. A small lie so often leads to a greater lie. A small theft so often leads to a greater theft. Soon the individual has woven a web from which he cannot extricate himself. The broad road to prison begins as a small and attractive pathway.

*Teach them to be virtuous.* Teach young men to respect young women as daughters of God endowed with something very precious and beautiful. Teach your daughters to have respect for young men, for boys who hold the priesthood, boys who should and do stand above the tawdry evils of the world.

*Teach them to pray.* None of us is wise enough to make it on our own. We need the help, the wisdom, the guidance of the Almighty in reaching those decisions that are so tremendously important in our lives. There is no substitute for prayer. There is no greater resource.

My dear mothers, these things I have mentioned are of course not new. They are as old as Adam and Eve. But they are as certain in their cause and effect as the sunrise in the morning, and the list is not complete.

With all there is to avoid, there can be much of fun and pleasure. With good friends there can be much of happiness. They need not be prudes. They can, and they have shown that they do, have a good time.

God bless you, dear friends. Do not trade your birthright as a mother for some bauble of passing value. Let your first interest be in your home. The baby you hold in your arms will grow quickly as the sunrise and the sunset of the rushing days. I hope that when that occurs you will not be led to exclaim as did King Lear, "How sharper than a serpent's tooth it is to have a thankless child!"

(William Shakespeare, *King Lear*, act 1, scene 4). Rather, I hope that you will have every reason to be proud concerning your children, to have love for them, to have faith in them, to see them grow in righteousness and virtue before the Lord, to see them become useful and productive members of society. If with all you have done there is an occasional failure, you can still say, "At least I did the very best of which I was capable. I tried as hard as I knew how. I let nothing stand in the way of my role as a mother." Failures will be few under such circumstances.

Lest you think I am putting all of this responsibility on you, I may say that I intend to speak to the fathers concerning these matters in the general priesthood meeting two weeks from tonight.

May the blessings of heaven rest upon you, my dear sisters. May you not trade a present thing of transient value for the greater good of sons and daughters, boys and girls, young men and women for whose upbringing you have an inescapable responsibility.

May the virtue of your children's lives sanctify and hallow your old age. May you be led to exclaim with gratitude as did John, "I have no greater joy than to hear that my children walk in truth" (3 John 1:4). For this I pray, and pray most earnestly, in the sacred name of Jesus Christ, amen.

# 170TH SEMIANNUAL GENERAL CONFERENCE

# SATURDAY MORNING SESSION

OCTOBER 7, 2000

Mᴀ BROTHERS AND SISTERS, what a wonderful occasion this is! I know of nothing else like it in all the world. We are gathered this morning as a great family in reverence and worship of the Lord our God. We are of one faith and one doctrine. We speak words of testimony concerning God, our Eternal Father, and His Beloved Son. We declare with conviction and certainty that They have restored in this last dispensation The Church of Jesus Christ of Latter-day Saints.

The great voices of radio, television, and cable are now joined by the Internet to carry our words literally to the ends of the earth. To meetinghouses scattered far and wide, the satellite will beam our signal to congregations large and small. And Saints across the earth will listen in their own homes to the proceedings of this great conference by means of the Internet.

Workmen have labored long and hard in preparing for this great occasion. We thank each one of them for his devoted service. Tomorrow we shall dedicate this magnificent Conference Center and other facilities. An important chapter in the history of our people will then have been written.

Welcome to each of you, wherever you may be. May we all be touched by the Holy Spirit as we meet together in solemn worship is my humble prayer. In the name of Jesus Christ, amen.

# Priesthood Session

OCTOBER 7, 2000

I<small>T NOW BECOMES MY PLEASURE</small> to speak to you, and I hope I get through on time. I haven't timed this. The young men here tonight have received some wonderful counsel. I hope they have listened well and that their lives will be touched for good as a result.

I have chosen to speak to the fathers. You already know what I am going to talk about. Your wives have reminded you that this will be my subject tonight. I told them so at the Relief Society conference two weeks ago. I may say some of the same things to you that I said to them. I remind you that repetition is a law of learning.

Now, this is a subject which I take very seriously. It is a matter with which I am deeply concerned. I hope you will not take it lightly. It concerns the most precious asset you have. In terms of your happiness, in terms of the matters that make you proud or sad, nothing—I repeat, nothing—will have so profound an effect on you as the way your children turn out.

You will either rejoice and boast of their accomplishments, or you will weep, head in hands, bereft and forlorn, if they become a disappointment or an embarrassment to you.

Many of you are in this meeting with your sons. I compliment you most warmly. I also compliment them. Both of you are in the very best of company. I am so proud of so many of our youth—

both boys and girls. They are bright. They are self-disciplined. They take the long view. They have their heads on straight. Tonight they are in the place where they ought to be. Some are singing in this choir. They are seated in congregations across the world. They are serving missions. They are struggling through school, forgoing present pleasures for future opportunities. I admire them. I love them. And so do you. They are our sons and daughters.

I hope, I pray, I plead that they will continue on the path they are now following.

But sad to say, I am confident there are some of our young men who have slipped and are slipping into the foggy swamp of immorality, drugs, pornography, and failure. I hope they are a minority among their peers, but even the loss of one is too many.

Fathers, you and their mothers have a responsibility you cannot escape. You are the fathers of your children. Your genetic pattern is forever etched in their genetic code.

While we are in this meeting, some of them, I am satisfied, are out cruising the town. They or their friends have cars to drive. In many cases their fathers bought them. They have handed them the keys and told them to have a good time.

They want to do something exciting. They think that wish is not satisfied with wholesome entertainment. They are drifters, looking to do something that will make them feel macho.

My officer friend told me recently of two young men in the backseat of a police car, handcuffs about their wrists. They had started out innocently enough that evening. Four of them in a car went about looking for excitement. They found it. Soon there was a fight. Then the police cars converged. The boys were detained and handcuffed.

These were good young men. They were not of the kind that go to the jailhouse periodically. The mother of one of them had said to him before he left home, "Bad things happen after 11 o'clock."

He had quickly learned the meaning of that statement. He was embarrassed. He was ashamed to face his mother.

I told the Relief Society of secret underground drug parties that go by the name of *rave*. Here, with flashing lights and noisy music, if it can be called that, young men and women dance and sway. They sell and buy drugs. The drugs are called Ecstasy. They are a derivative of methamphetamine. The dancers suck on babies' pacifiers because the drug makes them grind their teeth. The hot music and the sultry dancing go on until 7:30 of a Sunday morning. What does it all lead to? Nowhere. It is a dead end.

Now there has developed another practice in this search for something new and different and riskier. They choke one another. Boys choke girls until they pass out. At a local school the other day a girl with a health problem was choked until she was unconscious. Only the speedy action of paramedics saved her life.

Are boys involved in such ridiculous practices aware of the fact that their prank may lead to a charge of manslaughter? If that should happen, their lives would be ruined forever.

If they want to get involved in pornography, they can do so very easily. They can pick up the phone and dial a number with which they are familiar. They can sit at a computer and revel in cyberspace filth.

I fear this may be going on in some of your homes. It is vicious. It is lewd and filthy. It is enticing and habit forming. It will take a young man or woman down to destruction as surely as anything in this world. It is foul sleaze that makes its exploiters wealthy, its victims impoverished.

I regret to say that many fathers themselves like to hear the siren song of those who peddle filth. Some of them also work the Internet for that which is lewd and lascivious. If there be any man within the sound of my voice who is involved in this or who is moving in this direction, I plead with you to get it out of your life. Get away from it. Stay away from it. Otherwise it will become an obsession. It will destroy your home life. It will destroy your marriage. It will take the good and beautiful out of your family relationships and replace these with ugliness and suspicion.

To you young men, and to the young women who are your associates, I plead with you not to befoul your minds with this ugly and vicious stuff. It is designed to titillate you, to absorb you into its net. It will take the beautiful out of your life. It will lead you into the dark and ugly.

A recent magazine article contains the story of a 12-year-old girl who got hooked on the Internet. In a chat room she met an admirer. One thing led to another until the discussion became sexually explicit. As she conversed with him, she thought he was a boy of about her own age.

When she met him, she found "a tall, overweight gray-haired man." He was a vicious predator, a scheming pedophile. Her mother, with the help of the FBI, saved her from what might have been a tragedy of the worst kind. (See Stephanie Mansfield, "The Avengers Online," *Reader's Digest,* Jan. 2000, 100–102.)

Our youth find this tempting stuff all about them. They need the help of their parents in resisting it. They need a tremendous amount of self-control. They need the strength of good friends. They need prayer to fortify them against this flood tide of filth.

The problem of parental direction of sons and daughters is not new. It is perhaps more acute than it has ever been, but every generation has faced some aspect of it.

In 1833 the Lord Himself rebuked Joseph Smith and his counselors and the Presiding Bishop. To the Prophet Joseph He said in language clear and unmistakable, as He had said to others:

"You have not kept the commandments, and must needs stand rebuked before the Lord;

"Your family must needs repent and forsake some things, and give more earnest heed unto your sayings, or be removed out of their place" (D&C 93:47–48).

Specifically what brought about these rebukes, I do not know. But I do know that the situation was serious enough and its future fraught with sufficient danger for the Lord Himself to speak with clarity and warning.

I think He likewise speaks to us with clarity and warning. My heart reaches out to our youth, who in many cases must walk a very lonely road. They find themselves in the midst of these evils. I hope they can share their burden with you, their fathers and mothers. I hope that you will listen, that you will be patient and understanding, that you will draw them to you and comfort and sustain them in their loneliness. Pray for direction. Pray for patience. Pray for the strength to love even though the offense may have been serious. Pray for understanding and kindness and, above all, for wisdom and inspiration.

I believe this to be the most marvelous age in all the history of the world. For some reason you and I have been permitted to come on the scene at this time when there is such a great flowering of knowledge. What a tragedy it is, what a bleak and terrible thing to witness a son or daughter on whom you counted so much walk the tortuous path that leads down to hell. On the other hand, what a glorious and beautiful thing it is to see the child of your dreams walk with head up, standing tall, unafraid, and with confidence, taking advantage of the tremendous opportunities that open around him or her. Isaiah said, "All thy children shall be taught of the Lord; and great shall be the peace of thy children" (Isaiah 54:13).

So lead your sons and daughters, so guide and direct them from the time they are very small, so teach them in the ways of the Lord, that peace will be their companion throughout life.

I mentioned to the Relief Society women several specific things that they ought to teach their sons and daughters. I repeat them briefly, perhaps in different language.

*The first is to encourage them to develop good friendships.* Every boy or girl longs for friends. No one wishes to walk alone. The warmth, the comfort, the camaraderie of a friend mean everything to a boy or girl. That friend can be either an influence for good or an influence for evil. The street gangs which are so vicious are an example of friendships gone afoul. Conversely, the association of young people in church and their mingling in school with those of their own kind will lead them to do well and to excel in their endeavors. Open your homes to the friends of your children. If you find they have big appetites, close your eyes and let them eat. Make your children's friends your friends.

*Teach them the importance of education.* The Lord has enjoined upon this people the responsibility to train their minds that they may be equipped to serve in the society of which they will become a part. The Church will be blessed by reason of their excellence. Furthermore, they will be amply rewarded for the effort they make.

I read from a clipping I made the other day:

"The latest Census information . . . indicated the annual wage for someone without a degree and no high school diploma stood at little more than $16,000 nationally [in 1997]. The jump wasn't much higher for a high school diploma—$22,895 annual average income. As the level of education increases, however, so does the span. The holder of a bachelor's degree earned, on average, $40,478 that year. Finally, the holder of an advanced degree typically bumped up their annual earnings by more than $20,000 to a nationwide average of $63,229, according to [these] Census figures" (Nicole A. Bonham, "Does an Advanced Degree Pay Off?" *Utah Business,* Sept. 2000, 37).

*Teach your children self-respect.* Teach them that their bodies are the creation of the Almighty. What a miraculous, wonderful, and beautiful thing is the human body.

As has been said here tonight, Paul, in writing to the Corinthians, declared:

"Know ye not that ye are the temple of God, and that the Spirit of God dwelleth in you?

43

"If any man defile the temple of God, him shall God destroy; for the temple of God is holy, which temple ye are" (1 Corinthians 3:16–17).

Now comes the craze of tattooing one's body. I cannot understand why any young man—or young woman, for that matter—would wish to undergo the painful process of disfiguring the skin with various multicolored representations of people, animals, and various symbols. With tattoos the process is permanent unless there is another painful and costly undertaking to remove it. Fathers, caution your sons against having their bodies tattooed. They may resist your talk now, but the time will come when they will thank you. A tattoo is graffiti on the temple of the body.

Likewise the piercing of the body for multiple rings in the ears, in the nose, even in the tongue. Can they possibly think that is beautiful? It is a passing fancy, but its effects can be permanent. Some have gone to such extremes that the ring had to be removed by surgery. The First Presidency and the Quorum of the Twelve have declared that we discourage tattoos and also "the piercing of the body for other than medical purposes." We do not, however, take any position "on the minimal piercing of the ears by women for one pair of earrings"—one pair.

*Teach them to stay away from drugs.* That's been spoken of eloquently here. I have already spoken about Ecstasy. Do you wish your children to have the peace of which Isaiah spoke? They will not know peace if they get involved with drugs. These illegal substances will take away their self-control, will seize upon them to a point where they will do anything, within or outside the law, to get another dose.

*Teach them the virtue of honesty.* There is no substitute under the heavens for the man or woman, the boy or girl who is honest. No false words besmirch his or her reputation. No act of duplicity colors his or her conscience. He or she can walk with head high, standing above the crowd of lesser folk who constantly indulge in lying and cheating and who excuse themselves with statements that a little lying hurts no one. It does hurt, because small lying leads to large lying, and the prisons of the nation are the best proof of that fact.

*Teach them to be virtuous.* There is no peace to be had through sexual impurity. Our Heavenly Father placed within us the desires that make us attractive to one another—boys and girls, men and women. But with that urge must be self-discipline, rigid and strong and unbending.

*Teach them to look forward to the time when they may be married in the house of the Lord* as those who come to the altar free from taint or evil of any kind. They will be grateful all of the days of their lives that they were married in the temple, worthily, under the authority of the holy priesthood.

Parenthetically, a word to you men.

Watch the tides of your lives, that you do not become enmeshed in situations which lead to sorrow, regret, and, eventually, divorce. Divorce has become so common all around us. There are so many who violate the solemn covenants they have made before God in His holy house.

Brigham Young once said: "When people are married, instead of trying to get rid of each other, reflect that you have made your choice, and strive to honor and keep it, do not manifest that you have acted unwisely and say that you have made a bad choice, nor let any body know that you think you have. You made your choice, stick to it, and strive to comfort and assist each other" (*Deseret News,* May 29, 1861, 98).

A divorce, when all is said and done, represents a failed marriage.

So many men become chronic critics. Rather, if they would look for the virtues in their wives instead of looking for their failings, love would bloom and the home would be secure.

*Teach your children to pray.* There is no other resource to compare

45

with prayer. To think that each of us may approach our Father in Heaven, who is the great God of the universe, for individual help and guidance, for strength and faith is a miracle in and of itself. We come to Him by invitation. Let us not shun the opportunity which He has afforded us.

God bless you, dear fathers. May He bless you with wisdom and judgment, with understanding, with self-discipline and self-control, with faith and kindness and love. And may He bless the sons and daughters who have come into your homes, that yours may be a fortifying, strengthening, guiding hand as they walk the treacherous path of life. As the years pass—and they will pass ever so quickly—may you know that "peace . . . which passeth all understanding" (Philippians 4:7) as you look upon your sons and daughters, who likewise have known that sacred and wonderful peace. Such is my humble prayer in the name of the Lord Jesus Christ, amen.

# SUNDAY MORNING SESSION

OCTOBER 8, 2000

MY BROTHERS AND SISTERS, what a great inspiration you are. As I look into the faces of this vast congregation and realize that there are many more assembled across the world, I am overwhelmed with a great sense of love for each of you. What wonderful people you are. I pray that the Holy Spirit may guide me as I speak to you.

Before coming into the building this morning, we sealed the cover stone of the cornerstone of the structure, this great new structure. That marks the completion of this building.

We preserve the symbolism of the cornerstone in remembrance of the Son of God, upon whose life and mission this Church is established. He, and He alone, is the chief cornerstone. There is built upon Him a strong foundation of apostles and prophets and, above this, "all the building fitly framed together" to constitute The Church of Jesus Christ of Latter-day Saints (see Ephesians 2:20–21).

As I reminded the group at the cornerstone this morning, let this symbol be recognized as representing the Redeemer of the world, the Son of God, the Lord Jesus Christ, whose name this Church carries.

I am so grateful that this building is now complete. We occupied it for our April conference and on one other occasion last

June. It was not entirely finished then. It is now declared complete with a permanent occupancy permit.

This millennial year of 2000 has been a remarkable year for the Church. We have expanded on every front across the world. We have passed the 11 million membership mark. What a significant thing that is.

I was around in 1947, when the Church celebrated the centennial of the arrival of the pioneers. At that time, the This Is the Place Monument was dedicated. A great celebration was held, with a pageant in the Tabernacle representing the worldwide mission of the Church. The grand theme running through all of this was that the Church had reached a million members in its growth. Approximately one-half of them lived in Utah. Now only about 15 percent live here, and yet we have more members here than we have ever had. To think that today we have a membership of 11 million is a tremendous and wonderful thing that brings with it the promise of the future.

We have reached out across the world, wherever we are permitted to go. We have taught the gospel as revealed in this, the dispensation of the fulness of times. We are now going into areas whose names were seldom heard back in 1947. Our missionary work has expanded in a miraculous manner.

I think I have been in most of the places where the Church is organized. I have found wonderful people everywhere. They are Latter-day Saints in the truest sense of the word. They are seeking to live the commandments.

As I have met with them and talked with them, I have learned the real meaning of the words of Paul:

"And [God] hath made of one blood all nations of men for to dwell on all the face of the earth, and hath determined the times before appointed, and the bounds of their habitation;

"That they should seek the Lord, if haply they might feel after him, and find him, though he be not far from every one of us:

"For in him we live, and move, and have our being; . . . for we are also his offspring" (Acts 17:26–28).

We have become a great, cosmopolitan society, a vast family of brothers and sisters in the Lord. In the movement of this great concourse of men and women, boys and girls, all Saints of the Most High, we sing as we march forward:

Mine eyes have seen the glory of the coming of the Lord;

He is trampling out the vintage where the grapes of wrath are stored.

He hath loosed the fateful lightning of his terrible, swift sword;

His truth is marching on.

["Battle Hymn of the Republic," *Hymns,* no. 60]

This work is possessed of a vitality which has never been evidenced before to such a degree.

In the field of education, we have established the seminary and institute program wherever the Church has gone. It is touching for good the lives of students across the world. In the institutes, young college-age students find happy association; they find learning, social experience, and even husbands and wives within the faith.

In the past few months we have announced that Ricks College, a great pioneer educational institution, hitherto providing a two-year degree, will be expanded to provide four years of education and will carry the name BYU—Idaho. This in no way disparages the name of the great man for whom the school was named. This will enlarge the educational opportunities for many young men and women. It will make of what has been a great school an even greater one. It is an effort on the part of the Church to extend the opportunity of secular education within the framework of a Church school, where is taught faith in the living God and in His divine Son, our Lord.

Another item of remarkable consequence, emphasized in this millennial year, is the building of temples. It has been a miracle.

Last Sunday we dedicated in Boston, Massachusetts, the 100th working temple of the Church.

I came into the First Presidency in July of 1981 as a counselor to President Kimball. Since that time, 81 of these 100 temples have been dedicated. Only 19 were operating before then.

Fifty-three new temples, more than half of the 100 now in operation, have been dedicated since I was ordained President of the Church five years ago. I mention this only to remind you of the acceleration of this dramatic expansion.

When I announced in conference that I hoped we would see the dedication of the 100th operating temple before the end of the year 2000, I wondered if it were possible. I cannot say enough of thanks to the many men and women who have worked so long and so hard to bring this miracle to pass. Some of these new temples are smaller. But every ordinance that can be performed in the Salt Lake Temple, the largest in the Church, can be performed in these smaller temples. They are devoted exclusively to ordinance work. They are beautiful structures, well built in every respect. And they have made possible a much easier journey to the house of the Lord for thousands upon thousands of our people.

We shall go on building them. We will dedicate three more before the end of the year. We will continue to build in the future, perhaps not at the scale we have worked on during the past year, but there will be a steady construction of these sacred houses to accommodate the needs of the people.

How deeply grateful are our people. I hope and believe that the Lord is pleased.

And now today, as another significant accomplishment of this millennial year, we dedicate this great Conference Center. It is a unique and remarkable building. When it was first envisioned and planned, we were not concerned with building the largest house of worship to be found anywhere. We were concerned with a plan to accommodate the needs of our people. The Tabernacle, which has served us so well for more than a century, simply became inadequate for our needs.

It was a great and serious thing to undertake the building of this structure. We were, of course, aware of all of the electronic means for carrying far and wide the message spoken from the pulpit. However, we were also aware of the desire of so very many to sit in the same hall with the speaker, as evidenced this morning. As I said when [explaining] the decision to move forward:

"The building of this structure has been a bold undertaking. We worried about it. . . . We listened for the whisperings of the Spirit [as we prayed about] it. And only when we felt the confirming voice of the Lord did we determine to go forward" (in Conference Report, Apr. 2000, 3; or *Ensign,* May 2000, 4–5).

Announcement of our decision was made in the April 1996 general conference. I said on that occasion:

"I regret that many who wish to meet with us in the Tabernacle this morning are unable to get in. There are very many out on the grounds. . . .

"My heart reaches out to those who [wished] to get in and could not be accommodated. About a year ago I suggested to the Brethren that perhaps the time has come when we should study the feasibility of constructing another dedicated house of worship on a much larger scale that would accommodate three or four times the number who can be seated in this building" (in Conference Report, Apr. 1996, 88–89; or *Ensign,* May 1996, 65).

It was a little more than a year later when ground was broken. This occurred on the 24th of July, 1997, the 150th anniversary of the arrival of our forebears in this valley.

At the conclusion of the groundbreaking services, President Packer offered the benediction. In that prayer, he asked the Lord that He might preserve my life to be present for the dedication of the new building. I am grateful for the evident answer to that request.

Today we shall dedicate it as a house in which to worship God the Eternal Father and His Only Begotten Son, the Lord Jesus Christ. We hope and we pray that there will continue to go forth to the world from this pulpit declarations of testimony and doctrine, of faith in the living God, and of gratitude for the great atoning sacrifice of our Redeemer.

We will also dedicate it as a house in which artistic performances of a dignified nature will be presented.

Here this glorious Tabernacle Choir will sing anthems of praise. Here other musical groups will perform for the entertaining of large numbers of people. Here will be presented pageants depicting in a beautiful and artistic way the history of this movement, as well as many other things.

This structure has been built of the finest materials by the ablest of craftsmen. We are indebted to all who have contributed to make of this a magnificent center for conferences of the Church and other purposes.

We anticipate that there will be requests from other groups to use this hall. We will make it available under regulations that will ensure that its use will be in harmony with the purposes for which it will be dedicated today.

It is not a museum piece, although the architecture is superb. It is a place to be used in honor to the Almighty and for the accomplishment of His eternal purposes.

I am so grateful that we have it. I am so grateful that it is completed. There is a little work of tuning up the organ, which will go on for some time. I commend to your attention the excellent articles appearing in the October *Ensign* dealing with this subject.

As I contemplate this marvelous structure adjacent to the temple, there comes to mind the great prophetic utterance of Isaiah:

"And it shall come to pass in the last days, that the mountain of the Lord's house shall be established in the top of the mountains, and shall be exalted above the hills; and all nations shall flow unto it.

"And many people shall go and say, Come ye, and let us go up to the mountain of the Lord, to the house of the God of Jacob; and he will teach us of his ways, and we will walk in his paths: for out of Zion shall go forth the law, and the word of the Lord from Jerusalem. . . .

"O house of Jacob, come ye, and let us walk in the light of the Lord" (Isaiah 2:2–3, 5).

I believe that prophecy applies to the historic and wonderful Salt Lake Temple. But I believe also that it is related to this magnificent hall. For it is from this pulpit that the law of God shall go forth, together with the word and testimony of the Lord.

May God bless us as a people. We have found a new stride in this great millennial year. May we walk in the footsteps of the great Jehovah, the God of Abraham, Isaac, and Jacob. May we walk in the light of Him who was the Messiah of the world, the Son of God, who said of Himself, "I am the way, the truth, and the life: no man cometh unto the Father, but by me" (John 14:6), is my humble prayer in the name of Jesus Christ, amen.

Now, my brothers and sisters, in a moment I shall offer the dedicatory prayer, in which all of you are invited to join. Immediately at the close of the dedicatory prayer, we invite each one of you who may wish to participate to stand and join with us in the Hosanna Shout. This sacred salute to the Father and the Son is given at the dedication of each of the temples. It has also been given on a few occasions of historic importance, such as the laying of the capstone on the Salt Lake Temple and the celebration of the centennial of the Church in the 1930 general conference. We feel it is appropriate to give the shout here, as we dedicate this great building, the likes of which we may never undertake again. Any mention of this by the media should recognize that for us this is a very sacred and personal thing. We request that it be treated with deference and respect.

I will now demonstrate the shout. Each one takes a clean white handkerchief, holding it by one corner, and waves it while saying in unison, "Hosanna, Hosanna, Hosanna to God and the Lamb," repeated three times, followed by "Amen, Amen, and Amen."

Again, those wishing to participate are invited to stand and give the Hosanna Shout immediately following the dedicatory prayer. Those desiring to remain seated are at liberty to do so. If you do not have a white handkerchief, you may simply wave your hand. Those in other areas may join in giving the shout if their circumstances are appropriate.

At the conclusion of the shout, the Tabernacle Choir, without announcement, will sing the "Hosannah Anthem," which was written by Evan Stephens for the dedication of the Salt Lake Temple in 1893. On a signal from the conductor, the congregation will join in singing "The Spirit of God like a Fire Is Burning," which was written by W. W. Phelps and sung at the dedication of the Kirtland Temple in 1836. . . .

Now, my beloved brethren and sisters, if you will bow your heads and close your eyes, we will join in a prayer of dedication.

O God, our Eternal Father, with thankful hearts we approach Thee in prayer on this historic Sabbath when we dedicate this magnificent Conference Center.

It has been erected to Thine honor and Thy glory. It is another in a complex of great structures dedicated to the accomplishment of Thy purposes and the onrolling of Thy work. It is neighbor to the sacred temple which our forebears labored in building over a period of 40 years. It looks upon the historic Tabernacle, which has served Thy people so well for more than a century of time. Nearby is the Assembly Hall, whose uses are many and varied. Not far away are the Church Office Building, the Administration Building, and the Joseph Smith Memorial Building. Also nearby are the Lion House and the Beehive House, both of which are historic in character. In the other direction are the Museum of Church History and Art and the Family History Library.

This great new structure overlooks them all and complements their variety, utility, and beauty. Together they become a testimony of the strength and vitality of Thy work, the headquarters of Thy Church, and the fountain from which truth rolls forth to fill the earth.

We thank Thee for the very many dedicated and highly skilled men and women who have worked long and hard to bring it to completion. May they have a sense of pride in their accomplishment.

As we are assembled in this great general conference of Thy Church, with these services carried to people across the earth, we bow our heads in reverence before Thee.

Acting in the authority of the holy priesthood, which comes from Thee, and in the name of Thine Only Begotten Son, the Lord Jesus Christ, we dedicate and consecrate this, the Conference Center of The Church of Jesus Christ of Latter-day Saints. We dedicate it unto Thee, our Father and our God, and unto Thy Beloved Son, our Redeemer, whose name Thy Church bears.

We dedicate it as a gathering place for Thy people, where they may assemble to hear the word of the Lord as it is spoken by Thy servants who stand as prophets, seers, and revelators and as witnesses unto the world of the living reality of the Lord Jesus Christ, whose name is the only name given among men whereby they may be saved.

We dedicate it from the footings on which it rests to the top of its tower. We dedicate this magnificent hall, unique in its design and size, constructed to house the thousands who through the years will gather here to worship Thee and to be entertained in a wholesome and wonderful way.

From this pulpit may Thy name be spoken with reverence and love. May the name of Thy Son be constantly remembered with sacred declaration. May testimony of Thy divine work ring forth from here to all the world. May righteousness be proclaimed and evil denounced. May words of faith be spoken with boldness and conviction. May proclamations and declarations of doctrine ring forth to the nations.

Though the earth tremble, may this magnificent edifice stand solid and safe under Thy watchful care. May no evil voice ever be lifted in this hall in derogation of Thee, of Thy Son, of Thy restored Church, or of its prophets and leaders who have presided through the years. Protect it from the storms of nature and the desecrating hand of the vandal and destroyer. Preserve it from conflict and acts of terrorism. May all who pass this way, whatever their religious persuasion, look upon this structure with respect and admiration.

May this great hall be a place of dignified entertainment, a home to those arts which are uplifting and which amplify the culture of the people. May there never be anything presented here which is lacking in dignity and which does not portray that beauty which is of Thy divine nature.

We dedicate the great organ, the beautiful halls and other rooms, the parking area, and all other features and facilities pertaining to this structure. May it be a thing of beauty to the beholder both inside and out. May it be a house of many uses, a house of culture, a house of art, a house of worship, a house of faith, a house of God.

May it give expression to the declaration of Thy people that "if there is anything virtuous, lovely, or of good report or praiseworthy, we seek after these things" (Articles of Faith 1:13).

Now Father, as we dedicate this Conference Center, we also dedicate the theater which adjoins it. It is a beautiful structure, designed to serve as a meeting place, as a home for the performing arts, and for a variety of uses, all dignified and created to cultivate the beautiful and ennobling. Protect it and bless it as we have prayed concerning the Conference Center.

We likewise on this day dedicate the parking facility built under Main Street and all the improvements made to the area immediately in the front of the house of the Lord, the temple of our God.

May this area be looked upon as a place of peace, an oasis in the midst of this bustling city. May it be a place where the weary may sit and contemplate the things of God and the beauties of nature. It is adorned with trees and shrubs, flowers and water, all combined to create an island of quiet beauty in the midst of this great, thriving community. May the desire of the people of Thy Church to improve and beautify this area be appreciated by all who pass this way.

We pray that favorable expressions may prevail and grow until there is universal acceptance and appreciation for what has been done. We invoke Thy blessings upon this community and this state. This is the area to which Thy people came seeking asylum from the oppression they had known. Now this has become a great cosmopolitan society to which people from all over the nation and the entire world have gathered. May all who live here and all who come here recognize a community environment that is unique and attractive. May we of Thy Church be hospitable and gracious. May we maintain the standards and practices for which we are known and accord to others the privilege of worshipping who, "where, or what they may" (Articles of Faith 1:11).

Bless us to reach out as good neighbors and be helpful to all. May we lift up the hands and strengthen the faltering knees of any in distress. May we all live together in peace with appreciation and respect one for another.

Almighty God, how thankful we are for Thy wondrous blessings upon us. Accept of our gratitude. Keep Thine ancient promises concerning those who contribute their tithes and offerings, which have made all of this possible. Open the windows of heaven and shower down blessings upon them.

We love Thee and Thy divine Son. We seek to do Thy will. We praise Thy holy name. We lift our voices in anthems of worship. We testify of Thee and of our Redeemer, Thy matchless Son. Majestic is Thy way, glorious the tapestry of Thine eternal plan for all who walk in obedience unto Thee.

Wilt Thou smile with favor upon us, we pray in the sacred name of our Lord Jesus Christ, amen.

# SUNDAY AFTERNOON SESSION

OCTOBER 8, 2000

*The tumult and the shouting dies;*
*The captains and the kings depart.*
*Still stands thine ancient sacrifice,*
*An humble and a contrite heart.*
*Lord God of Hosts, be with us yet,*
*Lest we forget, lest we forget.*
                    *["God of Our Fathers, Known*
                    *of Old," Hymns, no. 80]*

These immortal words of Rudyard Kipling express my feelings as we bring to a conclusion this wonderful conference of the Church.

Following the benediction we shall depart this great hall, turn off the lights, and lock the doors. You who are listening across the world will switch off your television set or the radio or shut down the Internet. As we do so, I would hope that we will remember that when all is over, "still stands thine ancient sacrifice, an humble and a contrite heart."

I hope that we shall ponder with subdued feelings the talks to which we have listened. I hope that we will quietly reflect on the wonderful things we have heard. I hope that we will feel a little more contrite and humble.

All of us have been edified. The test will come in the application of the teachings given. If, hereafter, we are a little more kind, if we are a little more neighborly, if we have drawn nearer to the Savior, with a more firm resolution to follow His teachings and His example, then this conference will have been a wonderful success. If, on the other hand, there is no improvement in our lives, then those who have spoken will have in large measure failed.

Those changes may not be measurable in a day or a week or a month. Resolutions are quickly made and quickly forgotten. But in a year from now, if we are doing better than we have done in the past, then the efforts of these days will not have been in vain.

We will not remember all that has been said, but there will arise from all of this a spiritual uplift. It may be indefinable, but it will be real. As the Lord said to Nicodemus, "The wind bloweth where it listeth, and thou hearest the sound thereof, but canst not tell whence it cometh, and whither it goeth: so is every one that is born of the Spirit" (John 3:8).

So it will be with the experience we have enjoyed. And perhaps out of all we have heard, there may be a phrase or a paragraph that will stand out and possess our attention. If this occurs, I hope we will write it down and reflect on it until we savor the depth of its meaning and have made it a part of our own lives.

In our family home evenings I hope we will discuss with our children these things and let them taste the sweetness of the truths we have enjoyed. And when the *Ensign* magazine comes out in November, with all of the conference messages, please don't just throw it aside with the comment that you have heard it all, but read and ponder the various messages. You will find many things that you missed when you listened to the speakers.

I have only one regret concerning the conference. That is that so few of the Brethren and sisters have opportunity to speak. It is simply a matter of the constraints of time.

Tomorrow morning we will be back at our jobs, back to our

studies, back to whatever constitutes the busy regimen of our lives. But we can have the memories of this great occasion to sustain us.

We can draw nearer to the Lord in our prayers. These can become conversations of thanksgiving. I can never fully understand how the great God of the universe, the Almighty, invites us as His children to speak with Him individually. How precious an opportunity is this. How wonderful that it actually happens. I testify that our prayers, offered in humility and sincerity, are heard and answered. It is a miraculous thing, but it is real.

Let us lower our voices in our homes. Let love abound and find expression in our actions. May we walk the quiet ways of the Lord, and may prosperity crown our labors.

The great "Hosanna" salutation in which we participated this morning should remain an unforgettable experience. From time to time, we can repeat quietly in our minds, when we are alone, those beautiful words of worship.

I bear witness of the truth of this work and of the living reality of God, our Eternal Father, and of His Only Begotten Son, whose Church this is. I extend my love to every one of you. God be with you, my dear, dear friends. I invoke the blessings of heaven upon you as we bid you good-bye for a season, in the name of Him who is our Master, our Redeemer, and our King, even the Lord Jesus Christ, amen.

# GENERAL YOUNG WOMEN MEETING

## MARCH 24, 2001

THANK YOU FOR THAT beautiful hymn. Thank you for your prayers; thank you for your faith; thank you for what you are. Young women of the Church, thank you so much. And thanks to you, Sister Nadauld, Sister Thomas, Sister Larsen, for the wonderful talks that you have given to these young women tonight.

What a wonderful sight you are in this great hall. Hundreds of thousands of others are assembled across the world. They will hear us in more than a score of languages. Our speech will be translated into their native tongues.

It is an overwhelming responsibility to speak to you. And at the same time it is a tremendous opportunity. I pray for the direction of the Spirit, the Holy Ghost, of which we have heard so much this night.

Though of various nationalities, you are all of one great family. You are daughters of God. You are members of The Church of Jesus Christ of Latter-day Saints. In your youth you speak of the future, and it is bright with promise. You speak of hope and faith and achievement. You speak of goodness and love and peace. You speak of a better world than we have ever known.

You are creatures of divinity; you are daughters of the Almighty. Limitless is your potential. Magnificent is your future, if you will take control of it. Do not let your lives drift in a fruitless and worth-less manner.

Someone gave me a copy of my high school yearbook the other day. It seems that when people get tired of old books, they send them to me. I spent an hour thumbing through it, looking at the pictures of my friends of 73 years ago, my high school class of 1928. Most of those in that yearbook have now lived their lives and gone beyond. Some seem to have lived almost without purpose, while others lived with great achievements.

I looked at the faces of the boys who were my friends and asso-ciates. Once they were youthful and bright and energetic. Now those who are left are wrinkled and slow in their walk. Their lives still have meaning, but they are not as vital as they once were. I looked in that old yearbook at the faces of the girls I knew. Many of them have passed on, and the remainder live in the shadows of life. But they are still beautiful and fascinating.

My thoughts go back to those young men and women of my youth, back to where you are today. By and large, we were a happy lot. We enjoyed life. I think we were ambitious. The dark and terrible Depression which swept over the earth would not come for another year. Nineteen twenty-eight was a season of high hopes and splendid dreams.

In our quieter moments we were all dreamers. The boys dreamed of mountains yet to climb and careers yet to be lived. The girls dreamed of becoming the kind of woman that most of them saw in their mothers.

As I have thought of this, I have concluded to title my talk for tonight "How Can I Become the Woman of Whom I Dream?"

Some months ago I spoke to you and the young men of the Church. I suggested six B's that you ought to pursue. Do you think we could name them together? Let's try: Be Grateful. Be Smart. Be Clean. Be True. Be Humble. Be Prayerful.

I have not the slightest doubt that these patterns of behavior will yield success and happiness and peace. I recommend them to you again, with a promise that if you will follow them, your lives will be fruitful of great good. I believe you will be successful in your endeavors. As you grow old, I am satisfied that you will look back with appreciation for the manner in which you chose to live.

Tonight, in speaking to you young women, I may touch on some of these same things without repeating the same language. They are worthy of repetition, and I again commend them to you.

In the yearbook of which I have spoken is the picture of a young woman. She was bright and effervescent and beautiful. She was a charmer. Life for her could be summed up in one short word—*fun*. She dated the boys and danced away the days and nights, studying a little but not too much, just enough to get grades that would take her through graduation. She married a boy of her own kind. Alcohol took possession of her life. She could not leave it alone. She was a slave to it. Her body succumbed to its treacherous grip. Sadly, her life faded without achievement.

There is a picture of another girl in that yearbook. She was not particularly beautiful. But she had a wholesome look about her, a sparkle in her eyes, and a smile on her face. She knew why she was in school. She was there to learn. She dreamed of the kind of woman she wanted to be and patterned her life accordingly.

She also knew how to have fun but knew when to stop and put her mind on other things.

There was a boy in school at the time. He had come from a small rural town. He had very little money. He brought lunch in a brown paper bag. He looked a little like the farm from which he had come. There was nothing especially handsome or dashing about him. He was a good student. He had set a goal for himself. It was lofty and, at times, appeared almost impossible of attainment.

These two fell in love. People said, "What does he see in her?" Or, "What does she see in him?" They each saw something wonderful which no one else saw.

Upon graduating from the university, they married. They scrimped and worked. Money was hard to come by. He went on to graduate school. She continued to work for a time, and then their children came. She gave her attention to them.

A few years ago, I was riding a plane home from the East. It was late at night. I walked down the aisle in the semidarkness. I saw a woman asleep with her head on the shoulder of her husband. She awakened as I approached. I immediately recognized the girl I had known in high school so long before. I recognized the boy I had also known. They were now approaching old age. As we talked, she explained that their children were grown, that they were grandparents. She proudly told me that they were returning from the East, where he had gone to deliver a paper. There at a great convention he had been honored by his peers from across the nation.

I learned that they had been active in the Church, serving in whatever capacity they were asked to serve. By every measure, they were successful. They had accomplished the goals which they had set for themselves. They had been honored and respected and had made a tremendous contribution to the society of which they were a part. She had become the woman of whom she had dreamed. She had exceeded that dream.

As I returned to my seat on the plane, I thought of those two girls of whom I have spoken to you tonight. The life of the one had been spelled out in a three-letter word: *F-U-N*. It had been lived aimlessly, without stability, without contribution to society, without ambition. It had ended in misery and pain and early death.

The life of the other had been difficult. It had meant scrimping and saving. It had meant working and struggling to keep going. It had meant simple food and plain clothing and a very modest apartment in the years of her husband's initial effort to get started in his profession. But out of that seemingly sterile soil there had grown a plant—yes, two plants, side by side—that blossomed and bloomed in a beautiful and wonderful way. Those beautiful blossoms spoke of service to fellowmen, of unselfishness one to another, of love and respect and faith in one's companion, of happiness as they met the needs of others in the various activities which they pursued.

As I pondered the conversation with these two, I determined within myself to do a little better, to be a little more dedicated, to set my sights a little higher, to love my wife a little more dearly, to help her and treasure her and look after her.

And so, my dear, dear young friends, I feel so earnest, so sincere, so anxious to say something to you this night which will help you become the woman of whom you dream.

As a starter, there must be cleanliness, for immorality will blight your life and leave a scar that will never entirely leave you. There must be purpose. We are here to accomplish something, to bless society with our talents and our learning. There can be fun, yes. But there must be recognition of the fact that life is serious, that the risks are great, but that you can overcome them if you will discipline yourselves and seek the unfailing strength of the Lord.

Let me first assure you that if you have made a mistake, if you have become involved in any immoral behavior, all is not lost. Memory of that mistake will likely linger, but the deed can be forgiven, and you can rise above the past to live a life fully acceptable unto the Lord where there has been repentance. He has promised that He will forgive your sins and remember them no more against you (see D&C 58:42).

He has set up the machinery with helpful parents and Church leaders to assist you in your difficulty. You can put behind you any evil with which you have been involved. You can go forward with a renewal of hope and acceptability to a far better way of life.

But there will be scars that will remain. The best way, the only way for you, is to avoid any entrapment with evil. President George Albert Smith used to say, "Stay on the Lord's side of the line" (*Sharing the Gospel with Others*, sel. Preston Nibley [1948], 42). You have within you instincts, powerful and terribly persuasive, urging you at times to let go and experience a little fling. You must not do it. You cannot do it. You are daughters of God with tremendous potential. He has great expectations concerning you, as do others. You cannot let down for a minute. You cannot give in to an impulse. There must be discipline, strong and unbending. Flee from temptation, as Joseph fled from the wiles of Potiphar's wife.

There is nothing in all this world as magnificent as virtue. It glows without tarnish. It is precious and beautiful. It is above price. It cannot be bought or sold. It is the fruit of self-mastery.

You young women spend a lot of time thinking of the boys. You can have a good time with them, but never overstep the line of virtue. Any young man who invites or encourages you or demands that you indulge in any kind of sexual behavior is unworthy of your company. Get him out of your life before both yours and his are blighted. If you can thus discipline yourselves, you will be grateful for as long as you live. Most of you will marry, and your marriage will be much the happier for your earlier restraint. You will be worthy to go to the house of the Lord. There is no adequate substitute for this marvelous blessing. The Lord has given a wonderful mandate. He has said, "Let virtue garnish thy thoughts unceasingly" (D&C 121:45). This becomes a commandment to be observed with diligence and discipline. And there is attached to it the promise of marvelous and wonderful blessings. He has said to those who live with virtue:

"Then shall thy confidence wax strong in the presence of God. . . .

"The Holy Ghost"—of which we have spoken tonight—"shall be thy constant companion, and thy scepter an unchanging scepter of righteousness and truth; and thy dominion shall be an everlasting dominion, and without compulsory means it shall flow unto thee forever and ever" (D&C 121:45–46).

Could there be a greater or more beautiful promise than this?

Find purpose in your life. Choose the things you would like to do, and educate yourselves to be effective in their pursuit. For most it is very difficult to settle on a vocation. You are hopeful that you will marry and that all will be taken care of. In this day and time, a girl needs an education. She needs the means and skills by which to earn a living should she find herself in a situation where it becomes necessary to do so.

Study your options. Pray to the Lord earnestly for direction. Then pursue your course with resolution.

The whole gamut of human endeavor is now open to women. There is not anything that you cannot do if you will set your mind to it. You can include in the dream of the woman you would like to be a picture of one qualified to serve society and make a significant contribution to the world of which she will be a part.

I was in the hospital the other day for a few hours. I became acquainted with my very cheerful and expert nurse. She is the kind of woman of whom you girls could dream. When she was young she decided she wished to be a nurse. She received the necessary education to qualify for the highest rank in the field. She worked at her vocation and became expert at it. She decided she wanted to serve a mission and did so. She married. She has three children. She works now as little or as much as she wishes. There is such a demand for people with her skills that she can do almost anything she pleases. She serves in the Church. She has a good marriage. She has a good life. She is the kind of woman of whom you might dream as you look to the future.

For you, my dear friends, the sky is the limit. You can be excellent in every way. You can be first class. There is no need for you to be a scrub. Respect yourself. Do not feel sorry for yourself. Do not dwell on unkind things others may say about you. Particularly, pay no attention to what some boy might say to demean you. He is no better than you. In fact, he has already belittled himself by his actions. Polish and refine whatever talents the Lord has given you. Go forward in life with a twinkle in your eye and a smile on your face, but with great and strong purpose in your heart. Love life and look for its opportunities, and forever and always be loyal to the Church.

Never forget that you came to earth as a child of the divine Father, with something of divinity in your very makeup. The Lord did not send you here to fail. He did not give you life to waste it. He bestowed upon you the gift of mortality that you might gain experience—positive, wonderful, purposeful experience—that will lead to life eternal. He has given you this glorious Church, His Church, to guide you and direct you, to give you opportunity for growth and experience, to teach you and lead you and encourage you, to bless you with eternal marriage, to seal upon you a covenant between you and Him that will make of you His chosen daughter, one upon whom He may look with love and with a desire to help. May God bless you richly and abundantly, my dear young friends, His wonderful daughters.

Of course there will be some problems along the way. There will be difficulties to overcome. But they will not last forever. He will not forsake you.

> *When upon life's billows you are tempest-tossed,*
> *When you are discouraged, thinking all is lost,*
> *Count your many blessings; name them one by one,*
> *And it will surprise you what the Lord has done. . . .*
> *So amid the conflict, whether great or small,*
> *Do not be discouraged; God is over all.*
> *Count your many blessings; angels will attend,*
> *Help and comfort give you to your journey's end.*
> *["Count Your Blessings,"*
> Hymns, *no. 241]*

Look to the positive. Know that He is watching over you, that He hears your prayers and will answer them, that He loves you and will make that love manifest. Let the Holy Spirit guide you in all that you do as you look to become the kind of woman of whom you dream. You can do it. You will have friends and loved ones to help. And God will bless you as you pursue your course. This, girls, is my humble promise and prayer in your behalf, in the name of the Lord Jesus Christ, amen.

# Saturday Morning Session

$M$Y BROTHERS AND SISTERS, my heart is filled with gratitude this morning as we gather in this great conference. I am grateful that the Lord has spared my life to see this day. As I reminded the young women to whom I spoke a week ago, someone recently gave me a copy of my old high school yearbook. It was the year of my graduation. It was 73 years ago. I was part of the class of 1928. It was an intriguing experience to thumb through it. Most of those who were so young and energetic at that time have passed on. A few are left, but they are wrinkled and somewhat feeble in their movements. Now and again when I complain of some little ailment, my wife will say, "It's your age, boy."

I repeat, I am deeply grateful to be alive. I am excited with this wonderful age in which we live. I thank the Lord for men and women of great dedication and great capacity who are doing so much to extend human life and to make it more comfortable and pleasant. I am grateful for good doctors who help us with our infirmities.

I am thankful for wonderful friends, among whom I include the great and faithful Saints across the world whom I have come to know. Thank you for all that you do for me, for the letters you send, for flowers and books and various expressions of your thoughtfulness and love. I am thankful for generous friends through whose kindness it has been possible for me to get out among the Saints in the nations of the earth, to meet with them, to share testimony and love with them.

I am grateful for my dear wife, with whom I have shared these nearly 64 years of companionship. I feel grateful for a faithful posterity. The Lord has blessed me in a marvelous way.

I am thankful for my Brethren of the General Authorities, who are so kind and deferential toward me. I am thankful for every one of you in this great family, more than 11 million strong, which constitutes The Church of Jesus Christ of Latter-day Saints.

In opening the conference I simply want to very briefly give a report on the Church.

It is stronger than it has ever been. It is not only larger in numbers, but I believe there is greater faithfulness among the Saints generally. During the past six months, we have had the opportunity of dedicating temples scattered over the earth, far and wide. We have heard testimony of the truth of this work spoken in various languages. We have seen the overwhelming faith of our people who have traveled long distances to get to these dedications. We have witnessed a marvelous increase in the growth of temple activity. We are experiencing slow but steady improvement in most of our fields of activity.

I am so grateful that we live in an era of comparative peace. There are no great wars raging across the world. There is trouble here and there but not a great worldwide conflict. We are able to carry the gospel to so many nations of the earth and bless the lives of the people wherever it goes.

We are well on our way to enlarging the educational opportunity for our youth. We have announced that Ricks College will become a four-year school to be known as BYU—Idaho. We are grateful to learn that the school has now received an endorsement from the accrediting body. It is remarkable to have this in so short a time.

We are constructing new buildings on a scale of which we never have dreamed before. We must do so if we are to accommodate the growth of the Church.

The welfare program moves forward. We are particularly grateful that we have been able to extend humanitarian aid of a very substantial volume in many parts of the earth. We have distributed food, medicine, clothing, bedding, and other necessities to assist those who have suddenly found themselves victims of catastrophe.

I will speak this evening to the priesthood brethren concerning another program which I think will be of great interest to all of you.

One of the bellwether marks of the growth and vitality of the Church is the construction of temples. I have spoken of this before, but I am so deeply grateful that since we last met in general conference we were able to reach our goal of 100 operating temples by the end of the year 2000; in fact, we exceeded it. We have just come from dedicating a temple in Uruguay, the 103rd working temple of the Church.

The great work of temple building goes on throughout the world. I looked the other day at a list of all the temples which are now in operation or have been announced—121 of them. I was amazed at the length of the list and the incredible diversity of the areas in which they are located. It is wonderful, but we are not satisfied. We will keep on working to bring the temples to the people, making it more convenient for Latter-day Saints everywhere to receive the blessings which can be had only in these holy houses.

I have said before that the blessings of the temple represent that fulness of the priesthood of which the Lord spoke when He revealed His will unto the Prophet Joseph Smith (see D&C 124:28). With the location of temples much nearer to the homes of our people, there is made more available to them all of the

73

ordinances to be had in the Lord's house for both the living and the dead.

Temples will soon be dedicated in Winter Quarters, Nebraska; Guadalajara, Mexico; and Perth, Australia. They are under construction in Asunción, Paraguay; Campinas, Brazil; the Tri-Cities area of Washington; Copenhagen, Denmark; Lubbock, Texas; Monterrey, Mexico; Nauvoo, Illinois; Snowflake, Arizona; and The Hague, Netherlands. Another six temples have been announced, and groundbreaking services will soon be held for these. In addition, we have visited and are giving consideration to a significant number of potential temple sites in the United States, Central and South America, Europe, and the isles of the sea. I will not mention their names because this would only create excitement when we do not yet have the ground on which to build them.

The construction of each temple represents a maturing of the Church. We will continue to build these sacred houses of the Lord as rapidly as energy and resources will allow. We are grateful for the faithful Latter-day Saints who pay their tithing and make possible this important program.

We are not without critics, some of whom are mean and vicious. We have always had them, and I suppose we will have them all through the future. But we shall go forward, returning good for evil, being helpful and kind and generous. I remind you of the teachings of our Lord concerning these matters. You are all acquainted with them. Let us be good people. Let us be friendly people. Let us be neighborly people. Let us be what members of The Church of Jesus Christ of Latter-day Saints ought to be.

My dearly beloved brethren and sisters, how much I appreciate your prayers and your love. I extend my love to each of you. May the heavens open, and may blessings come down upon you in abundance as you walk in faithfulness before the Lord.

We shall now be pleased to go forward with the proceedings of this great gathering.

God bless you, my beloved associates, I pray in the name of Jesus Christ, amen.

# PRIESTHOOD SESSION

## MARCH 31, 2001

Brethren, before I begin my talk I want to congratulate very warmly this Melchizedek Priesthood choir, composed of men from many walks of life, all singing together out of their hearts filled with testimony of the hymns of Zion. Brethren, thank you very, very much.

Now, I seek the inspiration of the Lord as I speak briefly on what I consider to be a very important subject.

I begin by taking you back 150 years and more. In 1849 our forebears faced a serious problem. Our people had then been in the Salt Lake Valley for two years. Missionaries in the British Isles and Europe continued to gather converts. They came into the Church by the hundreds. When they were baptized, they desired to gather to Zion. Their strength and their skills were needed here, and their wish to come was very strong. But many of them were distressingly poor, and they had no money with which to buy passage. How were they to get here?

Under the inspiration of the Lord, a plan was devised. What was known as the Perpetual Emigration Fund was established. Under this plan, funded by the Church, notwithstanding its serious poverty at that time, money was loaned to those members who had little or nothing. Loans were made with the understanding that when the converts arrived here, they would find employment, and as they were able to do so, they would pay off the loan. The money repaid would then be loaned to others to make it possible for them to emigrate. It was a revolving resource. It was truly a Perpetual Emigration Fund.

With the help of this fund, it is estimated that some 30,000 converts to the Church were enabled to gather to Zion. They became a great strength to the work here. Some of them came with needed skills, such as stone masonry, and others developed skills. They were able to perform a tremendous service in constructing buildings, including the Salt Lake Temple and Tabernacle, and doing other work which required expertise. They came here by wagons and by handcarts. Notwithstanding the terrible handcart tragedy of 1856, when approximately 200 of them died from cold and sickness on the plains of Wyoming, they traveled safely and became an important part of the family of the Church in these mountain valleys.

For instance, James Moyle was a stonecutter in Plymouth, England, when he was baptized at the age of 17. Of that occasion he wrote: "I then covenanted with the Lord that I would serve Him through good and evil report. It was the turning point in my life, as it kept me from evil company" (in Gordon B. Hinckley, *James Henry Moyle* [1951], 18).

Notwithstanding his skill as a mason, he had little money. He borrowed from the Perpetual Emigration Fund and left England in 1854, sailed to America, crossed the plains, and almost immediately secured employment as a stonemason on the Lion House at $3 a day. He saved his money, and when he had $70, the amount of his indebtedness, he promptly repaid the Emigration Fund. He said, "I then considered that I was a free man" (see *Moyle*, 19–24).

When the Perpetual Emigration Fund was no longer needed, it was dissolved. I believe that many within the sound of my voice are descendants of those who were blessed by reason of this fund. You are today prosperous and secure because of what was done for your forebears.

Now, my brethren, we face another problem in the Church. We have many missionaries, both young men and young women, who are called locally and serve with honor in Mexico, Central America, South America, the Philippines, and other places. They have very little money, but they make a contribution with what they have. They are largely supported from the General Missionary Fund, to which many of you contribute, and for these contributions we are very deeply grateful.

They become excellent missionaries, working side by side with elders and sisters sent from the United States and Canada. While in this service, they come to know how the Church operates. They develop a broadened understanding of the gospel. They learn to speak some English. They work with faith and devotion. Then comes the day of their release. They return to their homes. Their hopes are high. But many of them have great difficulty finding employment because they have no skills. They sink right back into the pit of poverty from which they came.

Because of limited abilities, they are unlikely to become leaders in the Church. They are more likely to find themselves in need of welfare help. They will marry and rear families who will continue in the same cycle that they have known. Their future is bleak indeed. There are some others who have not gone on missions who find themselves in similar circumstances in development of skills to lift them from the ranks of the poor.

In an effort to remedy this situation, we propose a plan—a plan which we believe is inspired by the Lord. The Church is establishing a fund, largely from the contributions of faithful Latter-day Saints who have and will contribute for this purpose. We are deeply grateful to them. Based on similar principles to those underlying the Perpetual Emigration Fund, we shall call it the Perpetual Education Fund.

From the earnings of this fund, loans will be made to ambitious young men and women, for the most part returned missionaries, so that they may borrow money to attend school. Then when they qualify for employment, it is anticipated that they will return that which they have borrowed, together with a small amount of interest designed as an incentive to repay the loan.

It is expected that they will attend school in their own communities. They can live at home. We have an excellent institute program established in these countries, where they can be kept close to the Church. The directors of these institutes are familiar with the educational opportunities in their own cities. Initially, most of these students will attend technical schools, where they will learn such things as computer science, refrigeration engineering, and other skills which are in demand and for which they can become qualified. The plan may later be extended to training for the professions.

It is expected that these young men and women will attend institute, where the director can keep track of their progress. Those desiring to participate in the program will make application to the institute director. He will clear them through their local bishops and stake presidents to determine that they are worthy and in need of help. Their names and the prescribed amount of their loans will then be sent to Salt Lake City, where funds will be issued, payable not to the individual but to the institution where they will receive their schooling. There will be no temptation to use the money for other purposes.

We shall have a strong oversight board here in Salt Lake and a director of the program who will be an emeritus General Authority, a man with demonstrated business and technical skills and who has agreed to accept this responsibility as a volunteer.

It entails no new organization, no new personnel except a volunteer director and secretary. It will cost essentially nothing to administer.

We shall begin modestly, commencing this fall. We can envision the time when this program will benefit a very substantial number.

With good employment skills, these young men and women can rise out of the poverty they and generations before them have known. They will better provide for their families. They will serve in the Church and grow in leadership and responsibility. They will repay their loans to make it possible for others to be blessed as they have been blessed. It will become a revolving fund. As faithful members of the Church, they will pay their tithes and offerings, and the Church will be much the stronger for their presence in the areas where they live.

There is an old saying that if you give a man a fish, he will have a meal for a day, but if you teach him how to fish, he will eat for the remainder of his life.

Now, this is a bold initiative, but we believe in the need for it and in the success that it will enjoy. It will be carried forward as an official program of the Church, with all that this implies. It will become a blessing to all whose lives it touches—to the young men and women, to their future families, to the Church that will be blessed with their strong local leadership.

It is affordable. We have enough money, already contributed, to fund the initial operation. It will work because it will follow priesthood lines and because it will function on a local basis. It will deal with down-to-earth skills and needed fields of expertise. Participation in the program will carry with it no stigma of any kind but rather a sense of pride in what is happening. It will not be a welfare effort, commendable as those efforts are, but rather an education opportunity. The beneficiaries will repay the money, and when they do so they will enjoy a wonderful sense of freedom because they have improved their lives not through a grant or gift but through borrowing and then repaying. They can hold their heads high in a spirit of independence. The likelihood of their remaining faithful and active throughout their lives will be very high.

We are already carrying forward in limited areas an employment service under the welfare program of the Church. This consists primarily of offices of referral. The matter of education will rest with the Perpetual Education Fund. The operation of employment centers will rest with the welfare program. These employment centers deal with men and women who are seeking employment and have skills but lack proper referrals. The one is a rotating education fund to make possible the development of skills. The other is the placing of men and women in improved employment who already have some marketable skills.

President Clark used to tell us in these general priesthood meetings that there is nothing that the priesthood cannot accomplish if we will work unitedly together in moving forward a program designed to bless the people (see J. Reuben Clark Jr., in Conference Report, Apr. 1950, 180).

May the Lord grant us vision and understanding to do those things which will help our members not only spiritually but also temporally. We have resting upon us a very serious obligation. President Joseph F. Smith said nearly a hundred years ago that a religion which will not help a man in this life will not likely do much for him in the life to come (see "The Truth about Mormonism," *Out West* magazine, Sept. 1905, 242).

Where there is widespread poverty among our people, we must do all we can to help them to lift themselves, to establish their lives upon a foundation of self-reliance that can come of training. Education is the key to opportunity. This training must be done in the areas where they live. It will then be suited to the opportunities of those areas. And it will cost much less in such places than it would if it were done in the United States or Canada or Europe.

Now, this is not an idle dream. We have the resources through the goodness and kindness of wonderful and generous friends. We have the organization. We have the manpower and dedicated servants of the Lord to make it succeed. It is an all-volunteer effort that will cost the Church practically nothing. We pray humbly and gratefully that God will prosper this effort and that it will bring blessings, rich and wonderful, upon the heads of thousands, just as its predecessor organization, the Perpetual Emigration Fund, brought untold blessings upon the lives of those who partook of its opportunities.

As I have said, some have already given very substantial amounts to fund the corpus whose earnings will be used to meet the need. But we will need considerably more. We invite others who wish to contribute to do so.

We anticipate there may be some failures in the repayment of loans. But we are confident that most will do what is expected of them, and generations will be blessed. We may anticipate that future generations will also be in need, for as Jesus said, "The poor always ye have with you" (John 12:8). It must, therefore, be a revolving fund.

It is our solemn obligation, it is our certain responsibility, my brethren, to "succor the weak, lift up the hands which hang down, and strengthen the feeble knees" (D&C 81:5). We must help them to become self-reliant and successful.

I believe the Lord does not wish to see His people condemned to live in poverty. I believe He would have the faithful enjoy the good things of the earth. He would have us do these things to help them. And He will bless us as we do so. For the success of this undertaking I humbly pray, while soliciting your interest, your faith, your prayers, your concerns in its behalf. I do so in the name of the Lord Jesus Christ, amen.

# SUNDAY MORNING
# SESSION

APRIL 1, 2001

M Y DEAR BROTHERS AND SISTERS, my heart reaches out to you wherever you may be this Sabbath morning. I feel a kinship with all of you who are members of The Church of Jesus Christ of Latter-day Saints. I love this work and marvel at its strength and growth, for the manner in which it touches the lives of people throughout the world. I feel extremely humble in speaking to you. I have pleaded with the Lord to direct my thoughts and words.

We have just returned from a long journey from Salt Lake City to Montevideo, Uruguay, to dedicate a temple, the 103rd working temple of the Church. It was a time of great rejoicing for our members there. Thousands gathered in that beautiful and sacred building and in surrounding chapels.

One of the speakers, a woman, told a story, the likes of which you have heard many times. As I remember it, she recounted a time in their lives when the missionaries knocked on their door. She had not the remotest idea of what they were teaching. However, she invited them in, and she and her husband listened to their message.

It was, for them, an unbelievable story. They told of a boy who lived in the state of New York. He was 14 years of age when he read in the book of James, "If any of you lack wisdom, let him ask of

God, that giveth to all men liberally, and upbraideth not; and it shall be given him" (James 1:5).

Desiring wisdom, because various creeds each claimed to have the truth, young Joseph determined to go into the woods and pray to the Lord.

This he did, and he experienced a vision in response to his prayer. God the Eternal Father and His Son, Jesus Christ, the resurrected Lord, appeared before him and spoke with him. Other manifestations followed. Among these was securing from a hill near his home golden plates which he translated by the gift and power of God. Heavenly messengers appeared to him, bestowing upon him keys of the priesthood and the authority to speak in the name of God.

How could anyone believe such a story? It seemed preposterous. And yet these people believed as they were instructed. Faith came into their hearts to accept that which they had been taught. It was a miracle. It was a gift from God. They could not believe it, and yet they did.

Following their baptism, their knowledge of the Church grew. They learned more of temple marriage, of families united for eternity under the authority of the holy priesthood. They were determined to have this blessing. But there was no temple anywhere near them. They scrimped and saved. When they had enough, they traveled all the way from Uruguay to Utah with their children, here to be sealed together as a family in the bonds of eternal marriage. She is today an assistant to the matron in the new Montevideo Uruguay Temple. Her husband is a counselor in the temple presidency.

I am not surprised that comparatively few people join the Church from among the large number on whom the missionaries call. There's no faith. On the other hand, I am amazed that so many do. It is a marvelous and wonderful thing that thousands are touched by the miracle of the Holy Spirit, that they believe and accept and become members. They are baptized. Their lives are forever touched for good. Miracles occur. A seed of faith comes into their hearts. It enlarges as they learn. And they accept principle upon principle until they have every one of the marvelous blessings that come to those who walk with faith in this, The Church of Jesus Christ of Latter-day Saints.

It is faith that is the converter. It is faith that is the teacher. Thus it has been from the beginning.

I marvel at the quality of the men and women who accepted Joseph Smith's testimony and came into the Church. They included such men as Brigham Young, the Pratt brothers, Willard Richards, John Taylor, Wilford Woodruff, Lorenzo Snow, the wives of these men, and a host of others. They were people of substance. Many of them were well educated. They were blessed of the Lord with the faith to accept the story which they heard. When they received the message, when the gift of faith touched their lives, they were baptized. The brethren gladly gave up what they had been doing and, with the support of their families, responded to calls to go across the sea to teach that which they had accepted on faith.

I read again the other day Parley P. Pratt's account of his reading the Book of Mormon and coming into the Church. Said he:

"I opened it with eagerness, and read its title page. I then read the testimony of several witnesses in relation to the manner of its being found and translated. After this I commenced its contents by course. I read all day; eating was a burden, I had no desire for food; sleep was a burden when the night came, for I preferred reading to sleep.

"As I read, the spirit of the Lord was upon me, and I knew and comprehended that the book was true, as plainly and manifestly as a man comprehends and knows that he exists" (*Autobiography of Parley P. Pratt*, ed. Parley P. Pratt Jr. [1938], 37).

The gift of faith touched his life. He could not do enough to repay the Lord for what had come to him. He spent the remainder of his days in missionary service. He died a martyr to this great work and kingdom.

Beautiful new temples are now being constructed in Nauvoo, Illinois, and Winter Quarters, Nebraska. They will stand as testimonies to the faith and faithfulness of the thousands of Latter-day Saints who built and later forsook Nauvoo to move with great suffering across what is now the state of Iowa to their temporary abode in Council Bluffs and in Winter Quarters, just north of Omaha.

The Winter Quarters Temple property adjoins the burial ground of many who gave their lives for this cause, which they regarded as more precious than life itself. Their journey to the valley of the Great Salt Lake is an epic without parallel. The suffering they endured, the sacrifices they made became the cost of what they believed.

I have in my office a small statue of my own pioneer grandfather burying beside the trail his wife and half-brother, who died on the same day. He then picked up his infant child and carried her to this valley.

Faith? There can be no doubt about it. When doubts arose, when tragedies struck, the quiet voice of faith was heard in the stillness of the night as certain and reassuring as was the place of the polar star in the heavens above.

It was this mysterious and wonderful manifestation of faith that brought reassurance, that spoke with certainty, that came as a gift from God concerning this great latter-day work. Countless, literally countless, are the stories of its expression in the pioneer period of the Church. But it does not stop there.

As it was then, so it is today. This precious and marvelous gift of faith, this gift from God, our Eternal Father, is still the strength of this work and the quiet vibrancy of its message. Faith underlies it all. Faith is the substance of it all. Whether it be going into the mission field, living the Word of Wisdom, or paying one's tithing, it is all the same. It is the faith within us that is evidenced in all we do.

Our critics cannot understand it. Because they do not understand, they attack. A quiet inquiry, an anxious desire to grasp the principle behind the result could bring greater understanding and appreciation.

I was asked at a news conference on one occasion how we get men to leave their vocations, to leave home, and serve the Church. I responded that we simply ask them, and we know what their answer will be.

What a marvelous and wonderful thing it is, this powerful conviction that the Church is true. It is God's holy work. He overrules in the things of His kingdom and in the lives of His sons and daughters. This is the reason for the growth of the Church. The strength of this cause and kingdom is not found in its temporal assets, impressive as they may be. It is found in the hearts of its people. That is why it is successful. That is why it is strong and growing. That is why it is able to accomplish the wonderful things that it does. It all comes of the gift of faith, bestowed by the Almighty upon His children who doubt not and fear not but go forward.

I sat in a meeting in Aruba the other evening. I daresay that most of those who hear me do not know where Aruba is or that there is even such a place. It is an island off the coast of Venezuela. It is a protectorate of the Netherlands. It is an inconspicuous place in this vast world. There were about 180 in the meeting. On the front row were eight missionaries: six elders and two sisters. The congregation consisted of men and women, boys and girls of various racial strains. A little English was spoken, much of Spanish, and some expressions of other languages.

As I looked into the faces of that congregation, I thought of the faith there represented. They love this Church. They appreciate all that it does. They stand and testify of the reality of God the

Eternal Father and of His resurrected Beloved Son, the Lord Jesus Christ. They testify of the Prophet Joseph Smith and of the Book of Mormon. They serve where they are called to serve. They are men and women of faith who have embraced the true and living gospel of the Master, and in their midst are these eight missionaries. I am sure that it is a lonely place for them. But they are doing what they have been asked to do because of their faith. The two young women are beautiful and happy. As I looked at them, I said to myself, "Eighteen months is a long time to be in this faraway place." But they do not complain. They speak of the great experience they are having and of the wonderful people they meet. Shining through all of their service is the reassuring faith that the work in which they are engaged is true and that the service they are giving is given unto God.

It is so with our missionaries wherever they might serve, whether it be here in Salt Lake City or in Mongolia. They go and serve with faith in their hearts. It is a phenomenon of great power that quietly whispers, "This cause is true, and to you there is an obligation to serve it regardless of the cost."

Again, people cannot understand it, these thousands of bright and able young men and women who forgo social life, leave school, and selflessly go wherever they are sent to teach the gospel. They go by the power of faith, and they teach by the power of faith, planting a seed of faith here and another there which grow and mature into converts of strength and capacity.

Faith is the basis of testimony. Faith underlies loyalty to the Church. Faith represents sacrifice, gladly given in moving forward the work of the Lord.

The Lord has commanded us to take upon ourselves "the shield of faith wherewith ye shall be able to quench all the fiery darts of the wicked" (D&C 27:17).

In the spirit of faith of which I have spoken, I testify that this is the work of the Lord, that this is His kingdom, restored to the earth in our time to bless the sons and daughters of God of all generations.

O Father, help us to be faithful unto Thee and unto our glorious Redeemer, to serve Thee in truth, to make that service an expression of our love is my humble prayer, in the name of Jesus Christ, amen.

# SUNDAY AFTERNOON SESSION

## APRIL 1, 2001

BRETHREN AND SISTERS, we've had a wonderful conference. The talks have been inspirational. The prayers of the speakers who prepared them and of those of us who heard them have been answered. We've all been edified.

Now, before I give my concluding words, I would like to make a little explanation. People are talking about why in the world I'm walking with a cane. That's become the topic of conversation these days. Well, I saw that Brigham Young used a cane. John Taylor had a cane, and Wilford Woodruff had a cane, and President Grant had a cane in his old age. And I've seen President McKay with a cane and Spencer Kimball with a cane, and I'm just trying to get in style.

The fact of the matter is, I have a little vertigo. I'm a little unsteady on my feet, and the doctors don't know why it is. But they're still working on me, and I hope it'll be over in a day or two.

Now, we've all been edified in this great conference. We should all be standing a little taller as we adjourn today than we were when we came together yesterday morning.

I constantly marvel at these great semiannual gatherings. We have heard 26 speakers during these two days. That's a very large number. Each is told how much time he or she will have. But none is told what to speak about. And yet all of the talks seem to harmonize, one with another, each a thread in the tapestry of a grand and beautiful pattern. I think nearly everyone in this vast worldwide audience can now say of one or more of the talks, "That was intended just for me. That is just what I needed to hear."

This is the reason, I may say, why these conferences are held—to strengthen our testimonies of this work, to fortify us against temptation and sin, to lift our sights, to receive instruction concerning the programs of the Church and the pattern of our lives.

Many churches, of course, have large gatherings, but I know of none to compare with these conferences held every six months, year after year. They are truly world conferences.

This work is alive and vital as it moves across the world in communities both large and small. The genius of this work lies with the missionaries who teach in faraway places with strange-sounding names, and with the converts who come of these teachings. As I have occasion to travel, these are the places I like to visit—the small and largely unknown and scattered branches where a great pioneer work is going forward.

Now, brothers and sisters, let us go forth from this conference with a stronger resolve to live the gospel, to be more faithful, to be better fathers and mothers and sons and daughters, to be absolutely loyal to one another as families, and absolutely loyal to the Church as members.

This is God's holy work. It is divine in its origin and in its doctrine. Jesus Christ stands as its head. He is our immortal Savior and Redeemer. His revelation is the source of our doctrine, our faith, our teaching, in fact the underlying pattern of our lives. Joseph Smith was an instrument in the hands of the Almighty in bringing to pass this Restoration. And that basic element of revelation is with the Church today as it was in Joseph's day.

Our individual testimonies of these truths are the basis of our faith. We must nurture them. We must cultivate them. We can never forsake them. We can never lay them aside. Without them we have nothing. With them we have everything.

As we return to our homes, may we experience a strengthening of our faith in these eternal and unchanging truths. May there be peace and love in our homes and an abundance of the good things of heaven and earth, I humbly pray as I bid you good-bye for another season, in the sacred name of Jesus Christ, amen.

# 171ST SEMIANNUAL GENERAL CONFERENCE

# SATURDAY MORNING SESSION

OCTOBER 6, 2001

MY BELOVED BRETHREN AND SISTERS, wherever you may be, welcome to this great world conference of The Church of Jesus Christ of Latter-day Saints. We are assembled in our wonderful new Conference Center in Salt Lake City. This building is filled or soon will be. I am so glad that we have it. I am so thankful for the inspiration to build it. What a remarkable structure it is. I wish all of us could be assembled under one roof. But that is not possible. I am so deeply thankful that we have the wonders of television, radio, cable, satellite transmission, and the Internet. We have become a great worldwide Church, and it is now possible for the vast majority of our members to participate in these meetings as one great family, speaking many languages, found in many lands, but all of one faith and one doctrine and one baptism.

This morning I can scarcely restrain my emotions as I think of what the Lord has done for us.

I do not know what we did in the preexistence to merit the wonderful blessings we enjoy. We have come to earth in this great season in the long history of mankind. It is a marvelous age, the best of all. As we reflect on the plodding course of mankind, from the time of our first parents, we cannot help feeling grateful.

The era in which we live is the fulness of times spoken of in the scriptures, when God has brought together all of the elements of previous dispensations. From the day that He and His Beloved Son manifested themselves to the boy Joseph, there has been a tremendous cascade of enlightenment poured out upon the world. The hearts of men have turned to their fathers in fulfillment of the words of Malachi. The vision of Joel has been fulfilled wherein the Lord declared:

> And it shall come to pass afterward, that I will pour out my spirit upon all flesh; and your sons and your daughters shall prophesy, your old men shall dream dreams, your young men shall see visions:
>
> And also upon the servants and upon the handmaids in those days will I pour out my spirit.
>
> And I will shew wonders in the heavens and in the earth, blood, and fire, and pillars of smoke.
>
> The sun shall be turned into darkness, and the moon into blood, before the great and the terrible day of the Lord come.
>
> And it shall come to pass, that whosoever shall call on the name of the Lord shall be delivered: for in mount Zion and in Jerusalem shall be deliverance, as the Lord hath said, and in the remnant whom the Lord shall call. [Joel 2:28–32]

There has been more of scientific discovery during these years than during all of the previous history of mankind. Transportation, communication, medicine, public hygiene, the unlocking of the atom, the miracle of the computer, with all of its ramifications, have blossomed forth, particularly in our own era. During my own lifetime, I have witnessed miracle after wondrous miracle come to pass. We take it for granted.

And with all of this, the Lord has restored His ancient priesthood. He has organized His Church and kingdom during the past century and a half. He has led His people. They have been tempered in the crucible of terrible persecution. He has brought to pass the wondrous time in which we now live.

We have seen only the foreshadowing of the mighty force for good that this Church will become. And yet I marvel at what has been accomplished.

Our membership has grown. I believe it has grown in faithfulness. We lose too many, but the faithful are so strong. Those who observe us say that we are moving into the mainstream of religion. We are not changing. The world's perception of us is changing. We teach the same doctrine. We have the same organization. We labor to perform the same good works. But the old hatred is disappearing; the old persecution is dying. People are better informed. They are coming to realize what we stand for and what we do.

But wonderful as this time is, it is fraught with peril. Evil is all about us. It is attractive and tempting and in so many cases successful. Paul declared:

"This know also, that in the last days perilous times shall come.

"For men shall be lovers of their own selves, covetous, boasters, proud, blasphemers, disobedient to parents, unthankful, unholy,

"Without natural affection, trucebreakers, false accusers, incontinent, fierce, despisers of those that are good,

"Traitors, heady, highminded, lovers of pleasures more than lovers of God;

"Having a form of godliness, but denying the power thereof: from such turn away" (2 Timothy 3:1–5).

We see today all of these evils, more commonly and generally, than they have ever been seen before, as we have so recently been reminded by what has occurred in New York City, Washington, and Pennsylvania, of which I shall speak tomorrow morning. We live in a season when fierce men do terrible and despicable things. We live in a season of war. We live in a season of arrogance. We live in a season of wickedness, pornography, immorality. All of the sins of Sodom and Gomorrah haunt our society. Our young people have never faced a greater challenge. We have never seen more clearly the lecherous face of evil.

And so, my brothers and sisters, we are met together in this great conference to fortify and strengthen one another, to help and lift one another, to give encouragement and build faith, to reflect on the wonderful things the Lord has made available to us, and to strengthen our resolve to oppose evil in whatever form it may take.

We have become as a great army. We are now a people of consequence. Our voice is heard when we speak up. We have demonstrated our strength in meeting adversity. Our strength is our faith in the Almighty. No cause under the heavens can stop the work of God. Adversity may raise its ugly head. The world may be troubled with wars and rumors of wars, but this cause will go forward.

You are familiar with these great words written by the Prophet Joseph: "No unhallowed hand can stop the work from progressing; persecutions may rage, mobs may combine, armies may assemble, calumny may defame, but the truth of God will go forth boldly, nobly, and independent, till it has penetrated every continent, visited every clime, swept every country, and sounded in every ear, till the purposes of God shall be accomplished, and the Great Jehovah shall say the work is done" (*History of the Church,* 4:540).

The Lord has given us the goal toward which we work. That goal is to build His kingdom, which is a mighty cause of great numbers of men and women of faith, of integrity, of love and concern for mankind, marching forward to create a better society, bringing blessings upon ourselves and upon the heads of others.

As we recognize our place and our goal, we cannot become arrogant. We cannot become self-righteous. We cannot become smug or egotistical. We must reach out to all mankind. They are all sons and daughters of God, our Eternal Father, and He will hold us accountable for what we do concerning them.

May the Lord bless us. May He make us strong and mighty in good works. May our faith shine forth as the sunlight of the morning.

May we walk in obedience to His divine commandments. May He smile with favor upon us.

As we go forward, may we bless humanity with an outreach to all, lifting those who are downtrodden and oppressed, feeding and clothing the hungry and the needy, extending love and neighborliness to those about us who may not be part of this Church. The Lord has shown us the way. He has given us His word, His counsel, His guidance, yea, His commandments. We have done well. We have much to be grateful for and much to be proud of. But we can do better, so much better.

How I love you, my brothers and sisters of this great cause. I love you for what you have become and for what you can become. Notwithstanding the afflictions about us, notwithstanding the sordid things we see almost everywhere, notwithstanding the conflict that sweeps across the world, we can be better.

I invoke the blessings of heaven upon you as I express my love for you and commend to you the great messages you will hear from this pulpit during the next two days, and do so in the sacred name of our Lord, Jesus Christ, amen.

# PRIESTHOOD SESSION

OCTOBER 6, 2001

Now, MY DEAR BRETHREN, as I face this great body of men in this hall and realize there are tens of thousands more scattered across the world, all of one mind and of one heart and all carrying the authority of the priesthood of the living God, I am subdued and humbled. I seek the guidance of the Holy Spirit.

This body is unique in all the world. There is nothing else like it. You compose the legions of the Lord, men ready to do battle with the adversary of truth, men willing to stand up and be counted, men who carry testimonies of the truth, men who have sacrificed and given much for this great cause. May the Lord bless you and sustain you and magnify you. "Ye are a chosen generation, a royal priesthood" (1 Peter 2:9).

Brethren, let us be worthy of the priesthood which we hold. Let us live nearer to the Lord. Let us be good husbands and fathers.

Any man who is a tyrant in his own home is unworthy of the priesthood. He cannot be a fit instrument in the hands of the Lord when he does not show respect and kindness and love toward the companion of his choice. Likewise, any man who is a bad example for his children, who cannot control his temper, or who is involved in dishonest or immoral practices will find the power of his priesthood nullified.

I remind you "that the rights of the priesthood are inseparably connected with the powers of heaven, and that the powers of heaven cannot be controlled nor handled only upon the principles of righteousness.

"That they may be conferred upon us, it is true; but when we undertake to cover our sins, or to gratify our pride, our vain ambition, or to exercise control or dominion or compulsion upon the souls of the children of men, in any degree of unrighteousness, behold, the heavens withdraw themselves; the Spirit of the Lord is grieved; and when it is withdrawn, Amen to the priesthood or the authority of that man" (D&C 121:36–37).

Brethren, let us be good men as those favored of the Lord with a bestowal of His divine power upon us.

Now, to a different but related matter. Last April in our priesthood meeting, I announced a new program. I spoke of the large numbers of our missionaries from South America, Mexico, the Philippines, and other areas. They respond to calls and serve with their North American brothers and sisters. They develop strong testimonies. They learn a new way of life. They are highly effective because they speak their native tongues and know the cultures of their native lands. They enjoy a wonderful season of hard and dedicated work.

Then they are released to go back home. Their families are living in poverty, and many of them fall back into the same situation from which they came, unable to move because of a lack of skills and the consequent difficulty in finding good employment.

I spoke to you of the Perpetual Emigration Fund, which was established in the pioneer era of the Church to assist the poor in coming from England and Europe. A revolving fund was established from which small loans were made, which made it possible for 30,000 to emigrate from their native lands and gather in Zion.

I told you we would apply the same principle and create what would be known as the Perpetual Education Fund. Out of the funds which would be donated by our people, and not from tithing funds, we would create a corpus, the earnings from which would be used to assist our young brethren and sisters in attending school to qualify themselves for better employment. They would develop skills whereby they could earn sufficient to take good care of their families and rise above the poverty level that they and their prior generations had known.

We had nothing in the fund at the time it was planned. But moving forward in faith, we established an organization, modest in its dimensions, to implement that which we felt was necessary. I am pleased to report that the money has come in, tens of thousands of dollars, hundreds of thousands of dollars, even millions. This has come from generous members of the Church who love the Lord and wish to assist the less fortunate of His people in rising in the economic world. We now have a substantial sum. It is not all that we need. We hope that these contributions will continue. The size of the corpus will determine the number who can be helped.

Now, six months later, I wish to give you a report of what has been accomplished. First, we called Elder John K. Carmack, who served so well in the First Quorum of the Seventy and who became an emeritus Seventy with this conference. He is an accomplished attorney, a man of sound judgment in business, a man of great ability. He has been appointed managing director, and though he is retired from the work of the Seventy, he will give his full time to the prosecution of this endeavor.

Elder Richard E. Cook of the Seventy, who likewise has become emeritus, will join him in looking after the finances. Elder Cook was formerly assistant controller of the Ford Motor Company, a man experienced in worldwide finance, a most capable executive, and a man who loves the Lord and the Lord's children.

We have worn out these brethren on one side, and now have turned them over to wear them out on the other side.

They have associated with them Brother Rex Allen, an expert

in organization and training, and Brother Chad Evans, who has vast experience in programs of advanced education.

All contribute their time and expertise without compensation.

The program is up and running. These brethren have been very careful to get it off to a proper start with sound governing principles. We have restricted the area in which it will operate initially, but this area will be expanded as we have the means to do so.

These brethren have gone to work to utilize the existing organization of the Church. The program is priesthood based, and that is why it will succeed. It begins with the bishops and the stake presidents. It involves the Church Educational System, the Employment Services offices, and others who work together in a marvelous spirit of cooperation.

The program was first implemented in Peru, Chile, and Mexico—areas where the number of returned missionaries is large and the need is great. The local leaders have been enthusiastic and committed. The beneficiaries are learning true principles of self-reliance. Their vision of their potential is greatly broadened. They are selecting good local schools for training and are using, to the extent possible, their personal, family, and other local resources. They are appreciative and willing and deeply grateful for the opportunity afforded them. Let me give you two or three vignettes.

The first is that of a young man who served in the Bolivia Cochabamba Mission. He lives with his faithful mother and nieces in a poor neighborhood. Their little home has a concrete floor and one lightbulb; the roof leaks, and the window is broken. He was a successful missionary. He says:

> My mission was the best thing that I have been able to do in my life. I learned to be obedient to the commandments and to be patient in my afflictions. I also learned some English and to manage my money, my time, and my skills better.
>
> Then, when I finished my mission, going home was difficult. My American companions went back to a university. But

there is a lot of poverty in our country. It is very difficult to get an education. My mother does her best, but she can't help us. She has suffered so much, and I am her hope.

When I learned of the Perpetual Education Fund, I felt so happy. The prophet recognized our efforts. I was filled with joy. . . . There was a possibility I could study, become self-reliant, have a family, help my mother.

I will study accounting at a local school where I can study and work. It is a short course, just three years long. I have to keep working as a janitor, but that is OK. Once I graduate and get a job in accounting, I will work toward higher education in international business.

This is our opportunity, and we cannot fail. The Lord trusts us. I have read many times in the Book of Mormon the words the Lord told the prophets, that as we keep the commandments, we would prosper in the land. This is being fulfilled. I am so grateful to God for this great opportunity to receive what my brothers and sisters did not have, to help my family, to accomplish my goals. And I am excited to repay the loan to see others be so blessed. I know the Lord will bless me as I do it.

Now, isn't that wonderful? Now another. A young man in Mexico City was approved to receive a loan of approximately $1,000 to make it possible for him to attend school to become a diesel mechanic. He has said: "My promise is to give my best in order to feel satisfied with my efforts. I know this program is valuable and important. Because of this, I am trying to take maximum advantage of this for the future. I will be able to serve and help the poor and help counsel my family members. I thank my Father in Heaven for this beautiful and inspired program."

A loan was recently approved for another young man from Mexico City, who served in the Nevada Las Vegas Mission. He desires to become a dental technician. His training will require 15 months of dedicated work. He says, "My promise upon finishing my studies at the technical school with the help of the Perpetual Education Fund is to repay the loan so that other returned missionaries can enjoy these blessings."

And so we have begun this work of making it possible for our faithful and able young men and women to climb the ladder which will assure them of economic success. With greatly improved opportunities, they will step out of the cycle of poverty which they and those before them have known for so long. They have served missions, and they will continue to serve in the Church. They will become leaders in this great work in their native lands. They will pay their tithes and offerings, which will make it possible for the Church to expand its work across the world.

We anticipate that by the end of this year we will have about 1,200 in the program. Three years from now, we estimate there will be more than 3,000. The opportunities are there. The need is urgent. We may fail in a few cases. But the vast majority will perform as we expect, both young men and young women.

Our only limitation will be the amount we have in the fund. We again invite all who wish to participate to make a contribution, large or small. We can then extend this great work which will make it possible for those of faith and latent ability to rise to economic independence as faithful members of The Church of Jesus Christ of Latter-day Saints.

Can you grasp the meaning of the tremendous work of this Church? Let me paint you a scenario. A pair of missionaries knock on the door of a little home somewhere in Peru. A woman answers. She does not quite understand what the missionaries want. But she invites them in. They arrange to come when her husband and other members of the family are there.

The missionaries teach them. Touched by the power of the Spirit, they respond to the message of eternal truth. They are baptized.

The family is active in the Church. They pay an honest but very meager tithing. They have a son or daughter in that family who is in his or her late teens. At the right time, the son or the daughter is called to serve a mission. The family does all it can to support him or her, and the remainder is made up from the missionary fund, which comes of the contributions of the Saints.

The son or daughter works with a companion from the United States or Canada. He or she learns English, while the companion's Spanish is greatly improved. They work together with love and appreciation and respect, one for another, representatives of two great divergent cultures.

Upon completion of their missions, the North American returns home and goes back to school. The Peruvian returns home and is hopeful only of finding work of a menial nature. The pay is ever so small. The future is dismal. He or she does not have the needed skills to rise above such employment. And then comes this bright ray of hope. Well, brethren, you know the picture. I need not labor it further. The way before us is clear, the need is tremendous, and the Lord has pointed the way.

Elder Carmack recently came across an old account book. He brought it to me. We discovered that way back in 1903, a small fund was established to help aspiring schoolteachers qualify for greater opportunities through small loans to assist them while going to school.

It was continued for 30 years until it was finally dropped during the Depression.

I was amazed at the names contained in that old ledger book. Two became university presidents. Others became well-known and highly qualified educators. The ledger shows repayments of $10.00, of $25.00, of $3.10 interest, and such things. One of the beneficiaries of that program became a bishop, then a stake president, then an Apostle, and eventually a counselor in the First Presidency.

Brethren, we need to care for one another more diligently. We need to make a little more effort to assist those who are down at the bottom of the ladder. We need to give encouragement and a lifting hand to men and women of faith and integrity and ability, who can climb that ladder with a little help.

That principle applies not only with reference to our present undertaking in this fund, but in a more general way. Let us open our hearts; let us reach down and lift up; let us open our purses; let us show a greater love for our fellowmen.

The Lord has blessed us so abundantly. And the needs are so great. He has said, "Inasmuch as ye have done it unto one of the least of these my brethren, ye have done it unto me" (Matthew 25:40).

I read from the book of Acts:

> And a certain man lame from his mother's womb was carried, whom they laid daily at the gate of the temple which is called Beautiful, to ask alms of them that entered into the temple;
>
> Who seeing Peter and John about to go into the temple asked an alms.
>
> And Peter, fastening his eyes upon him with John, said, Look on us.
>
> And he gave heed unto them, expecting to receive something of them.
>
> Then Peter said, Silver and gold have I none; but such as I have give I thee: In the name of Jesus Christ of Nazareth rise up and walk.
>
> And he took him by the right hand, and lifted him up: and immediately his feet and ankle bones received strength.
>
> And he leaping up stood, and walked, and entered with them into the temple, walking, and leaping, and praising God. [Acts 3:2–8]

Now, note that Peter took him by the right hand and lifted him up. Peter had to reach down to lift the lame man. We must also reach down.

God bless you, my dear brethren, young and old. Keep the faith. Minister with love. Rear your families in the way of the Lord. "Look to God and live" (Alma 37:47).

I so pray in the name of Jesus Christ, amen.

# SUNDAY MORNING SESSION

OCTOBER 7, 2001

$M$Y BELOVED BRETHREN AND SISTERS, I accept this opportunity in humility. I pray that I may be guided by the Spirit of the Lord in that which I say.

I have just been handed a note that says that a U.S. missile attack is under way. I need not remind you that we live in perilous times. I desire to speak concerning these times and our circumstances as members of this Church.

You are acutely aware of the events of September 11, less than a month ago. Out of that vicious and ugly attack we are plunged into a state of war. It is the first war of the 21st century. The last century has been described as the most war torn in human history. Now we are off on another dangerous undertaking, the unfolding of which and the end thereof we do not know. For the first time since we became a nation, the United States has been seriously attacked on its mainland soil. But this was not an attack on the United States alone. It was an attack on men and nations of goodwill everywhere. It was well planned, boldly executed, and the results were disastrous. It is estimated that more than 5,000 innocent people died. Among these were many from other nations. It was cruel and cunning, an act of consummate evil.

Recently, in company with a few national religious leaders, I was invited to the White House to meet with the president. In talking to us he was frank and straightforward.

That same evening he spoke to the Congress and the nation in unmistakable language concerning the resolve of America and its friends to hunt down the terrorists who were responsible for the planning of this terrible thing and any who harbored such.

Now we are at war. Great forces have been mobilized and will continue to be. Political alliances are being forged. We do not know how long this conflict will last. We do not know what it will cost in lives and treasure. We do not know the manner in which it will be carried out. It could impact the work of the Church in various ways.

Our national economy has been made to suffer. It was already in trouble, and this has compounded the problem. Many are losing their employment. Among our own people, this could affect welfare needs and also the tithing of the Church. It could affect our missionary program.

We are now a global organization. We have members in more than 150 nations. Administering this vast worldwide program could conceivably become more difficult.

Those of us who are American citizens stand solidly with the president of our nation. The terrible forces of evil must be confronted and held accountable for their actions. This is not a matter of Christian against Muslim. I am pleased that food is being dropped to the hungry people of a targeted nation. We value our Muslim neighbors across the world and hope that those who live by the tenets of their faith will not suffer. I ask particularly that our own people do not become a party in any way to the persecution of the innocent. Rather, let us be friendly and helpful, protective and supportive. It is the terrorist organizations that must be ferreted out and brought down.

We of this Church know something of such groups. The Book of Mormon speaks of the Gadianton robbers, a vicious, oath-bound, and secret organization bent on evil and destruction. In their day they did all in their power, by whatever means available, to bring down the Church, to woo the people with sophistry, and to take control of the society. We see the same thing in the present situation.

We are people of peace. We are followers of the Christ, who was and is the Prince of Peace. But there are times when we must stand up for right and decency, for freedom and civilization, just as Moroni rallied his people in his day to the defense of their wives, their children, and the cause of liberty (see Alma 48:10).

On the Larry King television broadcast the other night, I was asked what I think of those who, in the name of their religion, carry out such infamous activities. I replied: "Religion offers no shield for wickedness, for evil, for those kinds of things. The God in whom I believe does not foster this kind of action. He is a God of mercy. He is a God of love. He is a God of peace and reassurance, and I look to Him in times such as this as a comfort and a source of strength."

Members of the Church in this and other nations are now involved with many others in a great international undertaking. On television we see those of the military leaving their loved ones, knowing not whether they will return. It is affecting the homes of our people. Unitedly, as a Church, we must get on our knees and invoke the powers of the Almighty in behalf of those who will carry the burdens of this campaign.

No one knows how long it will last. No one knows precisely where it will be fought. No one knows what it may entail before it is over. We have launched an undertaking the size and nature of which we cannot see at this time.

Occasions of this kind pull us up sharply to a realization that life is fragile, peace is fragile, civilization itself is fragile. The economy is particularly vulnerable. We have been counseled again and again concerning self-reliance, concerning debt, concerning thrift.

So many of our people are heavily in debt for things that are not entirely necessary. When I was a young man, my father counseled me to build a modest home, sufficient for the needs of my family, and to make it beautiful and attractive and pleasant and secure. He counseled me to pay off the mortgage as quickly as I could so that, come what may, there would be a roof over the heads of my wife and children. I was reared on that kind of doctrine. I urge you as members of this Church to get free of debt where possible and to have a little laid aside against a rainy day.

We cannot provide against every contingency. But we can provide against many contingencies. Let the present situation remind us that this we should do.

As we have been continuously counseled for more than 60 years, let us have some food set aside that would sustain us for a time in case of need. But let us not panic or go to extremes. Let us be prudent in every respect. And, above all, my brothers and sisters, let us move forward with faith in the living God and His Beloved Son.

Great are the promises concerning this land of America. We are told unequivocally that it "is a choice land, and whatsoever nation shall possess it shall be free from bondage, and from captivity, and from all other nations under heaven, if they will but serve the God of the land, who is Jesus Christ" (Ether 2:12). This is the crux of the entire matter—obedience to the commandments of God.

The Constitution under which we live, and which has not only blessed us but has become a model for other constitutions, is our God-inspired national safeguard ensuring freedom and liberty, justice and equality before the law.

I do not know what the future holds. I do not wish to sound negative, but I wish to remind you of the warnings of scripture and the teachings of the prophets which we have had constantly before us.

I cannot forget the great lesson of Pharaoh's dream of the fat and lean kine and of the full and withered stalks of corn (see Genesis 41:14–36).

I cannot dismiss from my mind the grim warnings of the Lord as set forth in the 24th chapter of Matthew.

I am familiar, as are you, with the declarations of modern revelation that the time will come when the earth will be cleansed and there will be indescribable distress, with weeping and mourning and lamentation (see D&C 112:24).

Now, I do not wish to be an alarmist. I do not wish to be a prophet of doom. I am optimistic. I do not believe the time is here when an all-consuming calamity will overtake us. I earnestly pray that it may not. There is so much of the Lord's work yet to be done. We, and our children after us, must do it.

I can assure you that we who are responsible for the management of the affairs of the Church will be prudent and careful, as we have tried to be in the past. The tithes of the Church are sacred. They are appropriated in the manner set forth by the Lord Himself. We have become a very large and complex organization. We carry on many extensive and costly programs. But I can assure you that we will not exceed our income. We will not place the Church in debt. We will tailor what we do to the resources that are available.

How grateful I am for the law of tithing. It is the Lord's law of finance. It is set forth in a few words in the 119th section of the Doctrine and Covenants. It comes of His wisdom. To every man and woman, to every boy and girl, to every child in this Church who pays an honest tithing, be it large or small, I express gratitude for the faith that is in your hearts. I remind you, and those who do not pay tithing but who should, that the Lord has promised marvelous blessings (see Malachi 3:10–12). He has also promised that "he that is tithed shall not be burned at his coming" (D&C 64:23).

I express appreciation to those who pay a fast offering. This costs the giver nothing other than going without two meals a

110

month. It becomes the backbone of our welfare program, designed to assist those in distress.

Now, all of us know that war, contention, hatred, suffering of the worst kind are not new. The conflict we see today is but another expression of the conflict that began with the War in Heaven. I quote from the book of Revelation:

"And there was war in heaven: Michael and his angels fought against the dragon; and the dragon fought and his angels,

"And prevailed not; neither was their place found any more in heaven.

"And the great dragon was cast out, that old serpent, called the Devil, and Satan, which deceiveth the whole world: he was cast out into the earth, and his angels were cast out with him.

"And I heard a loud voice saying in heaven, Now is come salvation, and strength, and the kingdom of our God, and the power of his Christ" (Revelation 12:7–10).

That must have been a terrible conflict. The forces of evil were pitted against the forces of good. The great deceiver, the son of the morning, was defeated and banished, and took with him a third of the hosts of heaven.

The book of Moses and the book of Abraham shed further light concerning this great contest. Satan would have taken from man his agency and taken unto himself all credit and honor and glory. Opposed to this was the plan of the Father, which the Son said He would fulfill, under which He came to earth and gave His life to atone for the sins of mankind.

From the day of Cain to the present, the adversary has been the great mastermind of the terrible conflicts that have brought so much suffering. Treachery and terrorism began with him. And they will continue until the Son of God returns to rule and reign with peace and righteousness among the sons and daughters of God.

Through centuries of time, men and women, so very, very many, have lived and died. Some may die in the conflict that lies ahead. To us, and we bear solemn testimony of this, death will not be the end. There is life beyond this as surely as there is life here. Through the great plan which became the very essence of the War in Heaven, men shall go on living.

Job asked, "If a man die, shall he live again?" (Job 14:14). He replied:

"For I know that my redeemer liveth, and that he shall stand at the latter day upon the earth:

"And though after my skin worms destroy this body, yet in my flesh shall I see God:

"Whom I shall see for myself, and mine eyes shall behold, and not another" (Job 19:25–27).

Now, brothers and sisters, we must do our duty, whatever that duty might be. Peace may be denied for a season. Some of our liberties may be curtailed. We may be inconvenienced. We may even be called on to suffer in one way or another. But God, our Eternal Father, will watch over this nation and all of the civilized world who look to Him. He has declared, "Blessed is the nation whose God is the Lord" (Psalm 33:12). Our safety lies in repentance. Our strength comes of obedience to the commandments of God.

Let us be prayerful. Let us pray for righteousness. Let us pray for the forces of good. Let us reach out to help men and women of goodwill, whatever their religious persuasion and wherever they live. Let us stand firm against evil, both at home and abroad. Let us live worthy of the blessings of heaven, reforming our lives where necessary and looking to Him, the Father of us all. He has said, "Be still, and know that I am God" (Psalm 46:10).

Are these perilous times? They are. But there is no need to fear. We can have peace in our hearts and peace in our homes. We can be an influence for good in this world, every one of us.

May the God of heaven, the Almighty, bless us, help us, as we walk our various ways in the uncertain days that lie ahead. May we look to Him with unfailing faith. May we worthily place our reliance on His Beloved Son, who is our great Redeemer, whether it be in life or in death, is my prayer in His holy name, even the name of Jesus Christ, amen.

# Sunday Afternoon
# Session

OCTOBER 7, 2001

My dear brothers and sisters, I'm glad we've had with us, today and yesterday, Sister Inis Hunter, the widow of President Howard W. Hunter. We very much appreciate her presence.

Now we come to the close of this great conference. The choir will sing "God Be with You Till We Meet Again." I'm grateful for that song. It says:

> *God be with you till we meet again;*
> *By his counsels guide, uphold you;*
> *With his sheep securely fold you. . . .*
> *When life's perils thick confound you,*
> *Put his arms unfailing round you. . . .*
> *Keep love's banner floating o'er you;*
> *Smite death's threat'ning wave before you.*
> *God be with you till we meet again.*
> [Hymns, *no. 152]*

I have sung those words in English when others sang them in a score of languages. I have lifted my voice with those wonderful and simple words on memorable occasions on all the continents of the earth. I have sung them in bidding farewell to missionaries, with tears in my eyes. I have sung them with men in battle dress during the war in Vietnam. In a thousand places and in many circumstances

114

over these almost numberless years, I have raised my voice with so many others in these words of parting, sung by people who love one another.

We were strangers when we met. We were brothers and sisters when we said good-bye.

These simple words became a prayer offered to the throne of heaven in behalf of one another. And in that spirit we bid good-bye as we close what has been a most remarkable and historic conference.

I hope that as we have heard the brethren and the sisters speak, our hearts have been touched and our resolutions lifted. I hope that every married man has said to himself, "I will be more kind and generous toward my companion and children. I will control my temper." I hope that kindness will replace harshness in our conversations one with another.

I hope that every wife will look to her husband as her dear companion, the star of her life, her supporter, her protector, her companion with whom she walks hand in hand, equally yoked (see 2 Corinthians 6:14). I hope that she will look to her children as sons and daughters of God, the most significant contribution she has made to the world, her greatest concern with regard to their achievements, and more precious than any other thing she has or could hope for.

I hope that boys and girls will leave this conference with a greater appreciation for their parents, with more fervent love in their hearts for those who have brought them into the world, for those who love them most and are most anxious concerning them.

I hope that the noise of our homes will drop a few decibels, that we will subdue our voices and speak to one another with greater appreciation and respect.

I hope that all of us who are members of this Church will be absolutely loyal to the Church. The Church needs your loyal support, and you need the loyal support of the Church.

I hope that prayer will take on a new luster in our lives. None of us knows what lies ahead. We may speculate, but we do not know. Sickness may strike us. Misfortune may overtake us. Fears may afflict us. Death may place his cold and solemn hand upon us or a loved one.

Regardless of what may come, may faith, immovable and constant, shine above us as the polar star.

Now, today, we are faced with particular problems, serious and consuming and difficult and of great concern to us. Surely we have need for the Lord.

When I went home for lunch, I turned on the television, looked at the news for a moment, and paraphrased in my mind the words of the Psalms: "Why do the nations so furiously rage together?" (see Psalm 2:1). I've lived through all of the wars of the 20th century. My eldest brother lies buried in the soil of France, a victim of the First World War. I have lived through the Second World War, the Korean War, the Vietnam War, the Gulf War, and lesser conflicts. We have been a very quarrelsome and difficult people in our conflicts one with another. We so need to turn to the Lord and look to Him. I think of the great words of Kipling:

> Far-called, our navies melt away;
> On dune and headland sinks the fire.
> Lo, all our pomp of yesterday
> Is one with Nineveh and Tyre!
> Judge of the nations, spare us yet,
> Lest we forget, lest we forget.
> ["God of Our Fathers,
> Known of Old," Hymns, no. 80]

Our safety lies in the virtue of our lives. Our strength lies in our righteousness. God has made it clear that if we will not forsake Him, He will not forsake us. He, watching over Israel, slumbers not nor sleeps (see Psalm 121:4).

And now as we close this conference, even though we shall have a benediction, I should like to offer a brief prayer in these circumstances:

O God, our Eternal Father, Thou great Judge of the nations, Thou who art the Governor of the universe, Thou who art our Father and our God, whose children we are, we look to Thee in faith in this dark and solemn time. Please, dear Father, bless us with faith. Bless us with love. Bless us with charity in our hearts. Bless us with a spirit of perseverance to root out the terrible evils that are in this world. Give protection and guidance to those who are engaged actively in carrying forth the things of battle. Bless them; preserve their lives; save them from harm and evil. Hear the prayers of their loved ones for their safety. We pray for the great democracies of the earth which Thou hast overseen in creating their governments, where peace and liberty and democratic processes obtain.

O Father, look with mercy upon this, our own nation, and its friends in this time of need. Spare us and help us to walk with faith ever in Thee and ever in Thy Beloved Son, on whose mercy we count and to whom we look as our Savior and our Lord. Bless the cause of peace and bring it quickly to us again, we humbly plead with Thee, asking that Thou wilt forgive our arrogance, pass by our sins, be kind and gracious to us, and cause our hearts to turn with love toward Thee. We humbly pray in the name of Him who loves us all, even the Lord Jesus Christ, our Redeemer and our Savior, amen.

# 172ND ANNUAL GENERAL CONFERENCE

# SATURDAY MORNING SESSION

APRIL 6, 2002

$M$Y BELOVED BROTHERS AND SISTERS, it is wonderful to meet with you again in a great world conference of the Church.

One hundred and seventy-two years ago today, Joseph Smith and his associates met in the inconspicuous log house on the Peter Whitmer farm in the quiet village of Fayette, New York, and organized the Church of Christ.

From that modest beginning something truly remarkable has happened. Great has been the history of this work. Our people have endured every kind of suffering. Indescribable have been their sacrifices. Immense beyond belief have been their labors. But out of all of this fiery crucible has come something glorious. Today we stand on the summit of the years and look about us.

From the original 6 members has grown a vast family of worshippers, 11 million-plus strong. From that quiet village has grown a movement that today is scattered through some 160 nations of the earth. This has become the fifth largest church in the United States. That is a remarkable development. More members of the Church reside out of this nation than in it. That too is a remarkable thing. No other church to come out of the soil of America has grown so fast or spread so widely. Within its vast embrace are members from many nations who speak many tongues. It is a phenomenon without precedent. As the tapestry of its past has unrolled, a beautiful pattern has come to view. It finds expression in the lives of a happy and wonderful people. It portends marvelous things yet to come.

When our people first arrived in this valley 155 years ago, they saw with prophetic vision a great future. But I sometimes wonder if they really sensed the magnitude of that dream as it would unfold.

The headquarters of the Church are in this city, which recently hosted the 19th Winter Olympics. We made a deliberate decision that we would not use this as a time or place to proselytize, but we were confident that out of this significant event would come a wonderful thing for the Church. The great buildings we have here— the temple, the Tabernacle, this magnificent Conference Center, the Joseph Smith Memorial Building, the family history facilities, the Church Administration Building, the Church Office Building, our welfare facilities, together with scores of chapels in this valley— could not be overlooked by those who walked the streets of this and neighboring cities. As Mike Wallace once remarked to me, "These structures all denote something solid."

And beyond this, we had total confidence in our people, many thousands of them, who would serve as volunteers in this great undertaking. They would be dependable; they would be pleasant; they would be knowledgeable; they would be accommodating. The unique and distinctive capacity of our people in speaking the languages of the world would prove to be a tremendous asset beyond anything to be found elsewhere.

Well, it all worked out. The visitors came by the hundreds of thousands. Some came with suspicion and hesitancy, old and false images persisting in their minds. They came feeling they might get trapped in some unwanted situation by religious zealots. But they found something they never expected. They discovered not only the scenic wonder of this area, with its magnificent mountains and valleys, they found not only the wonderful spirit of the international games at their best, but they found beauty in this city. They found hosts who were gracious and accommodating and anxious to assist them. I do not wish to imply that such hospitality was limited to our people. The entire community joined together in a great expression of hospitality.

Out of all of this came something wonderful for this Church. Representatives of the media, so often a tough and calloused group, with very few exceptions spoke and wrote in language both complimentary and accurately descriptive of a unique culture they found here, of the people they met and dealt with, of the spirit of hospitality which they felt. Television carried the picture to billions of people across the earth. Newspapers and magazines ran story after story.

Thousands upon tens of thousands walked through Temple Square, admired the majestic house of the Lord, sat in the Tabernacle and listened to the matchless music of the choir. More thousands filled this great Conference Center to watch a wonderful production dealing with the Church and its worldwide mission. Other thousands visited the family history center. The media were hosted in the Joseph Smith Memorial Building. We were interviewed for television, radio, and the press by correspondents from many parts of this nation and from across the world. I am told that nearly 4,000 stories about the Church appeared in the German press alone.

Georgie Anne Geyer, prominent syndicated writer whose column appears in many newspapers, wrote as follows:

"How on Earth could a largely Mormon state do something so daring as hosting an international celebrity meeting? Would the world come gladly to a state whose dominant religion asks members to abstain from alcohol, tobacco and even caffeine, three staples of international conferences?"

And then she went on to quote Raymond T. Grant, artistic director of the Olympic Arts Festival. He talked of the opening ceremony and said:

" 'You know, 98 percent of the entire cast were volunteers, and that's huge. In fact, most were not paid at all. This is an extraordinary story, and I'd link it directly to Mormon culture. As a Catholic boy from New York, I found it interesting that Brigham Young, the founder of the Utah settlement of the Mormons, built a theater before anything else.'

"He went on to tally up: The state has six dance companies; more pianos and harps are sold in Utah than anywhere in the United States; the Mormon Tabernacle Choir has [360] members; and the oldest Steinway dealership in Utah . . . was started as early as 1862. In Utah, their per capita spending on students is one of the lowest—yet they boast high test scores. 'It has been fascinating for me, having to tap into this culture.' "

Miss Geyer concluded her story by writing: "It is simply the mix of a serious and upright religion, of families who foster and insist upon providing the highest levels of culture right along with the highest modern technology, and of generally sensible organizing and governing. In short, it is a modern mix of the old America" ("Salt Lake City and State of Utah Reveal Themselves to the World," *Salt Lake Tribune,* Feb. 15, 2002, A15).

If there were time, I could give you many quotations from the seasoned journalists of the world, who wrote in a most laudatory fashion.

Was there anything negative? Of course. But it was minimal. We had private interviews with presidents of nations, with ambassadors, with leaders in business and other fields.

In 1849, two years after our people first arrived here and following the discovery of gold in California, many were discouraged. They had struggled to wrest a living from the arid soil. Crickets had devoured their crops. The winters were cold. Many thought they would go to California and get rich. President Young stood before them and encouraged them to remain, promising that "God will temper the climate, and we shall build a city and a temple to the

Most High God in this place. We will extend our settlements to the east and west, to the north and to the south, and we will build towns and cities by the hundreds, and thousands of the Saints will gather in from the nations of the earth. This will become the great highway of the nations. Kings and emperors and the noble and wise of the earth will visit us here" (in James S. Brown, *Life of a Pioneer: Being the Autobiography of James S. Brown* [1900], 122).

We have witnessed the fulfillment of that prophecy in these recent days. Needless to say, I am happy with what has happened. Those visitors tasted the distinctive culture of this community. We believe that culture is worth preserving. I compliment and thank our people who participated in such numbers and so generously, and I compliment and thank all others who worked together to make of this a wonderful and most significant event.

Now I wish to speak rather quickly of one or two other matters.

Speaking of Brigham Young has reminded me of the Perpetual Education Fund which we have established. It was only a year ago that I first spoke of this in our general conference. The contributions of generous Latter-day Saints have come in to assure us that this endeavor is now on a solid foundation. We will need more yet, but already it has been demonstrated that vast good will come of this undertaking. Young men and women in the underprivileged areas of the world, young men and women who for the most part are returned missionaries, will be enabled to get a good education that will lift them out of the slough of poverty in which their forebears for generations have struggled. They will marry and go forward with skills that will qualify them to earn well and take their places in society where they can make a substantial contribution. They will likewise grow in the Church, filling positions of responsibility and rearing families who will continue in the faith.

I have time to read only one testimonial. It comes from a young man who has been blessed by this program. He says:

It is so wonderful that I do not have to just dream anymore about my education or my future. The Lord has cleared the way, and I am doing it!

I am currently attending a great technical institute in our country, where I am studying to become a computer technician. . . . By going to school, I am discovering my abilities. The discipline I developed on my mission helps me to succeed. . . . Never before has any young man felt more blessed than I do. The PEF has strengthened my faith in the Lord Jesus Christ. Now, more than ever, I feel the responsibility the gospel places upon me to prepare myself to be a better member, a better leader, and a better father. . . .

My dear mother, who has sacrificed so much, gets so emotional that she cries when she prays at night because of her gratitude to the Lord. . . .

Now I envision my town being blessed because of me. I envision the Church with leaders who have financial stability and who can support the Lord's work with all their might, mind, and strength. I see the Church prospering. I am excited to start my own family and teach them that we can be self-sufficient. So I must finish my education. I will then repay the loan quickly to help my fellowmen. . . . I am grateful for the Savior's mercy. He truly sustains us with His love.

And so it goes, my brothers and sisters. As this great work moves across the earth, we are blessing now some 2,400 young people. Others will be blessed.

May the Lord bless you, and each of us, as we rejoice in our opportunity to be a part of this great cause in this wonderful season of the Lord's work is my humble prayer in the name of Jesus Christ, amen.

# PRIESTHOOD
# SESSION

## APRIL 6, 2002

MY DEAR BRETHREN, I wish to speak very plainly this evening about a matter that I feel deeply concerned over. What a great pleasure and a worrisome challenge it is to speak to you. What a tremendous brotherhood we are as those who hold this precious and wonderful priesthood. It comes from God, our Eternal Father, who in this glorious dispensation has, with His Beloved Son, spoken again from the heavens. They have sent Their authorized servants to bestow this divine authority upon men.

Personal worthiness becomes the standard of eligibility to receive and exercise this sacred power. It is of this that I wish to speak tonight.

I begin by reading to you from the Doctrine and Covenants, section 121:

"The rights of the priesthood are inseparably connected with the powers of heaven, and . . . the powers of heaven cannot be controlled nor handled only upon the principles of righteousness.

"That they may be conferred upon us, it is true; but when we undertake to cover our sins, or to gratify our pride, our vain ambition, or to exercise control or dominion or compulsion upon the souls of the children of men, in any degree of unrighteousness, behold, the heavens withdraw themselves; the Spirit of the Lord is grieved; and when it is withdrawn, Amen to the priesthood or the authority of that man" (D&C 121:36–37).

That is the unequivocal word of the Lord concerning His divine authority. What a tremendous obligation this places upon each of us. We who hold the priesthood of God must stand above the ways of the world. We must discipline ourselves. We cannot be self-righteous, but we can and must be decent, honorable men.

Our behavior in public must be above reproach. Our behavior in private is even more important. It must clear the standard set by the Lord. We cannot indulge in sin, let alone try to cover our sins. We cannot gratify our pride. We cannot partake of the vanity of unrighteous ambition. We cannot exercise control or dominion or compulsion upon our wives or children or any others in any degree of unrighteousness.

If we do any of these things, the powers of heaven are withdrawn. The Spirit of the Lord is grieved. The very virtue of our priesthood is nullified. Its authority is lost.

The manner of our living, the words we speak, and our everyday behavior have a bearing upon our effectiveness as men and boys holding the priesthood.

Our fifth article of faith states, "We believe that a man must be called of God, by prophecy, and by the laying on of hands by those who are in authority, to preach the Gospel and administer in the ordinances thereof."

Even though those in authority lay hands upon our heads and we are ordained, we may through our behavior nullify and forfeit any right to exercise this divine authority.

Section 121 goes on to say:

"No power or influence can or ought to be maintained by virtue of the priesthood, only by persuasion, by long-suffering, by gentleness and meekness, and by love unfeigned;

"By kindness, and pure knowledge, which shall greatly enlarge the soul without hypocrisy, and without guile" (D&C 121:41–42).

Now, my brethren, those are the parameters within which this priesthood must find expression. It is not as a cloak that we put on and take off at will. It is, when exercised in righteousness, as the very tissue of our bodies, a part of us at all times and in all circumstances.

And so, to you young men who hold the Aaronic Priesthood, you have had conferred upon you that power which holds the keys to the ministering of angels. Think of that for a minute.

You cannot afford to do anything that would place a curtain between you and the ministering of angels in your behalf. You cannot be immoral in any sense. You cannot be dishonest. You cannot cheat or lie. You cannot take the name of God in vain or use filthy language and still have the right to the ministering of angels.

I do not want you to be self-righteous. I want you to be manly, to be vibrant and strong and happy. To those who are athletically inclined, I want you to be good athletes and strive to become champions. But in doing so, you do not have to indulge in unseemly behavior or profane or filthy language.

To you young men who look forward to going on missions, please do not cloud your lives with anything that would cast a doubt upon your worthiness to go forth as servants of the living God.

You who are missionaries must not, you cannot under any circumstances compromise the divine power which you carry within you as ordained ministers of the gospel. By way of warning and forewarning, the First Presidency and the Quorum of the Twelve Apostles have set forth the following statement directed to you:

"As missionaries, you are expected to maintain the highest standards of conduct, including strict observance of the law of chastity. . . .

" . . . You should never be alone with anyone else, male or female, adult or child [other than your assigned companion].

"Even false accusations against an innocent missionary can take many months to investigate and may result in disruption or termination of missionary service. Protect yourselves from such accusations by never being separated from your companion, even in the homes you visit" (First Presidency statement on missionary conduct, Mar. 22, 2002).

You need not worry about these things if you will at all times observe the rules of missionary service. If you do so, you will have a wonderful experience, and you will return in honor to those you love without taint or suspicion or regret.

When you return home, never forget that you are still an elder of The Church of Jesus Christ of Latter-day Saints.

You will become involved in the search for an eternal companion. You will wish to marry in the house of the Lord. For you there should be no alternative. Be careful, lest you destroy your eligibility to be so married. Have a wonderful time. But keep your courtship within the bounds of rigid self-discipline. The Lord has given a mandate and a promise. He has said, "Let virtue garnish thy thoughts unceasingly." Then there follows the promise that "thy confidence [shall] wax strong in the presence of God; and . . . the Holy Ghost shall be thy constant companion" (D&C 121:45–46).

The wife you choose will be your equal. Paul declared, "Neither is the man without the woman, neither the woman without the man, in the Lord" (1 Corinthians 11:11).

In the marriage companionship there is neither inferiority nor superiority. The woman does not walk ahead of the man; neither does the man walk ahead of the woman. They walk side by side as a son and daughter of God on an eternal journey.

She is not your servant, your chattel, nor anything of the kind.

How tragic and utterly disgusting a phenomenon is wife abuse. Any man in this Church who abuses his wife, who demeans her, who insults her, who exercises unrighteous dominion over her is unworthy to hold the priesthood. Though he may have been ordained, the heavens will withdraw, the Spirit of the Lord will be grieved, and it will be amen to the authority of the priesthood of that man.

Any man who engages in this practice is unworthy to hold a temple recommend.

I regret to say that I see too much of this ugly phenomenon. There are men who cuff their wives about, both verbally and physically. What a tragedy when a man demeans the mother of his children.

It is true that there are a few women who abuse their husbands. But I am not speaking to them tonight. I am speaking to the men of this Church, men upon whom the Almighty has bestowed His holy priesthood.

My brethren, if there be any within the sound of my voice who are guilty of such behavior, I call upon you to repent. Get on your knees and ask the Lord to forgive you. Pray to Him for the power to control your tongue and your heavy hand. Ask for the forgiveness of your wife and your children.

President McKay was wont to say, "No other success can compensate for failure in the home" (quoting J. E. McCulloch, *Home: The Savior of Civilization* [1924], 42; in Conference Report, Apr. 1935, 116).

And President Lee said, "The most important part of the Lord's work that you will do, is the work that you do within the walls of your own home" (*Doing the Right Things for the Right Reasons,* Brigham Young University Speeches of the Year [April 16, 1961], 5).

I am confident that when we stand before the bar of God, there will be little mention of how much wealth we accumulated in life or of any honors which we may have achieved. But there will be searching questions about our domestic relations. And I am convinced that only those who have walked through life with love and respect and appreciation for their companions and children will receive from our Eternal Judge the words, "Well done, thou good and faithful servant: . . . enter thou into the joy of thy lord" (Matthew 25:21).

I mention another type of abuse. It is of the elderly. I think it is not common among us. I hope it is not. I pray that it is not. I believe our people, almost all of them, observe the ancient commandment, "Honour thy father and thy mother: that thy days may be long upon the land which the Lord thy God giveth thee" (Exodus 20:12). But how tragic it is. How absolutely revolting is abuse of the elderly.

More and more we are living longer, thanks to the miracle of modern science and medical practice. But with old age comes a deterioration of physical capacity and sometimes mental capacity. I have said before that I have discovered that there is much of lead in the years that are called golden. I am so profoundly grateful for the love and solicitude of our children toward their mother and their father. How beautiful is the picture of a son or daughter going out of his or her way to assist with kindness and benevolence and love an aged parent.

Now I wish to mention another form of abuse that has been much publicized in the media. It is the sordid and evil abuse of children by adults, usually men. Such abuse is not new. There is evidence to indicate that it goes back through the ages. It is a most despicable and tragic and terrible thing. I regret to say that there has been some very limited expression of this monstrous evil among us. It is something that cannot be countenanced or tolerated. The Lord Himself said, "But whoso shall offend one of these little ones which believe in me, it were better for him that a millstone were hanged about his neck, and that he were drowned in the depth of the sea" (Matthew 18:6).

That is very strong language from the Prince of Peace, the Son of God.

I quote from our *Church Handbook of Instructions:*

"The Church's position is that abuse cannot be tolerated in any form. Those who abuse . . . are subject to Church discipline. They should not be given Church callings and may not have a temple recommend. Even if a person who abused a child sexually or physically receives Church discipline and is later restored to full fellowship or readmitted by baptism, leaders should not call the person to any position working with children or youth unless the First Presidency authorizes removal of the annotation on the person's membership record.

"In instances of abuse, the first responsibility of the Church is to help those who have been abused and to protect those who may be vulnerable to future abuse" (*Book 1: Stake Presidencies and Bishoprics* [1998], 157–58).

For a long period now we have worked on this problem. We have urged bishops, stake presidents, and others to reach out to victims, to comfort them, to strengthen them, to let them know that what happened was wrong, that the experience was not their fault, and that it need never happen again.

We have issued publications, established a telephone line where Church officers may receive counsel in handling cases, and offered professional help through LDS Family Services.

These acts are often criminal in their nature. They are punishable under the law. Professional counselors, including lawyers and social workers, are available on this help line to advise bishops and stake presidents concerning their obligations in these circumstances. Those in other nations should call their respective Area Presidents.

Now, the work of the Church is a work of salvation. I want to emphasize that. It is a work of saving souls. We desire to help both the victim and the offender. Our hearts reach out to the victim, and we must act to assist him or her. Our hearts reach out to the offender, but we cannot tolerate the sin of which he may be guilty. Where there has been offense, there is a penalty. The process of the civil law will work its way. And the ecclesiastical process will work its way, often resulting in excommunication. This is both a delicate and a serious matter.

Nevertheless, we recognize, and must always recognize, that when the penalty has been paid and the demands of justice have been met, there will be a helpful and kindly hand reaching out to assist. There may be continuing restrictions, but there will also be kindness.

Now brethren, I suppose that I have sounded negative as I have spoken to you this evening. I do not wish to. But I do wish to raise a warning voice to the priesthood of this Church throughout the world.

God has bestowed upon us a gift most precious and wonderful. It carries with it the authority to govern the Church, to administer in its affairs, to speak with authority in the name of the Lord Jesus Christ, to act as His dedicated servants, to bless the sick, to bless our families and many others. It serves as a guide by which to live our lives. In its fulness, its authority reaches beyond the veil of death into the eternities that lie ahead.

There is nothing else to compare with it in all this world. Safeguard it, cherish it, love it, live worthy of it.

"Let your light so shine before men, that they may see your good works, and glorify your Father which is in heaven" (Matthew 5:16) is my humble prayer as I leave my blessing upon you and extend my love, in the name of Jesus Christ, amen.

# SUNDAY MORNING SESSION

APRIL 7, 2002

Fʀᴏᴍ ᴡʜᴇʀᴇ ᴡᴇ sᴘᴇᴀᴋ, it is a beautiful April Sabbath morning. The tulips are well out of the ground and will soon be bursting into flowering beauty. In the winter of our doubt there came the hope of spring. We knew it would come. Such was our faith, based on the experiences of earlier years.

And so it is with matters of the spirit and soul. As each man or woman walks the way of life, there come dark seasons of doubt, of discouragement, of disillusionment. In such circumstances, a few see ahead by the light of faith, but many stumble along in the darkness and even become lost.

My call to you this morning is a call to faith, that faith which is "the substance of things hoped for, the evidence of things not seen" (Hebrews 11:1), as Paul described it.

In the process of conversion, the investigator of the Church hears a little. He may read a little. He does not, he cannot comprehend the wonder of it all. But if he is earnest in his search, if he is willing to get on his knees and pray about it, the Spirit touches his heart, perhaps ever so lightly. It points him in the right direction. He sees a little of what he has never seen before. And with faith, whether it be recognized or not, he takes a few guarded steps. Then another, brighter vista opens before him.

Long ago I worked for one of our railroads whose tracks threaded the passes through these western mountains. I frequently rode the trains. It was in the days when there were steam locomotives. Those great monsters of the rails were huge and fast and dangerous. I often wondered how the engineer dared the long journey through the night. Then I came to realize that it was not one long journey but rather a constant continuation of a short journey. The engine had a powerful headlight that made bright the way for a distance of 400 or 500 yards. The engineer saw only that distance, and that was enough, because it was constantly before him all through the night into the dawn of the new day.

The Lord has spoken of this process. He said:

"That which doth not edify is not of God, and is darkness.

"That which is of God is light; and he that receiveth light, and continueth in God, receiveth more light; and that light groweth brighter and brighter until the perfect day" (D&C 50:23–24).

And so it is with our eternal journey. We take one step at a time. In doing so we reach toward the unknown, but faith lights the way. If we will cultivate that faith, we shall never walk in darkness.

Let me tell you of a man I know. I will not mention his name lest he feel embarrassed. His wife felt there was something missing in their lives. She spoke with a relative one day who was a member of the Church. The relative suggested that she call the missionaries. She did so. But the husband was rude to them and told them not to come again.

Months passed. One day another missionary, finding the record of this visit, decided that he and his companion would try again. He was a tall elder from California who carried a big smile on his face.

They knocked on the door; the man answered. Could they come in for a few minutes? they asked. He consented.

The missionary said, in effect, "I wonder if you know how to pray." The man answered that he knew the Lord's Prayer. The missionary said, "That is good, but let me tell you how to give a personal prayer." He went on to explain that we get on our knees in an attitude of humility before the God of heaven. The man did so. The missionary then went on to say, "We address God as our Father in Heaven. We then thank Him for His blessings, such as our health, our friends, our food. We then ask for His blessings. We express our innermost hopes and desires. We ask Him to bless those in need. We do it all in the name of His Beloved Son, the Lord Jesus Christ, concluding with 'amen.'"

It was a pleasant experience for the man. He had gleaned a little light and understanding, a touch of faith. He was ready to try another step.

Line upon line, the missionaries patiently taught him. He responded as his faith grew into a dim light of understanding. Friends from his branch gathered around to reassure him and answer his questions. The men played tennis with him, and he and his family were invited to their homes for dinner.

He was baptized, and that was a giant step of faith. The branch president asked him to be a Scoutmaster to four boys. That led to other responsibilities, and the light of faith strengthened in his life with each new opportunity and experience.

That has continued. Today he stands as a capable and loved stake president, a leader of great wisdom and understanding, and, above all, a man of great faith.

The challenge which faces every member of this Church is to take the next step, to accept that responsibility to which he is called, even though he does not feel equal to it, and to do so in faith with the full expectation that the Lord will light the way before him.

Let me give you a story of a woman in São Paulo, Brazil. She worked while going to school to provide for her family. I use her own words in telling this story. She says:

> The university in which I studied had a regulation that pro-
> hibited the students that were in debt from taking tests. For

this reason, when I received my salary I would first separate the money for tithing and offerings, and the remainder was allotted for the payment of the school and other expenses.

I remember a time when I . . . faced serious financial difficulties. It was a Thursday when I received my salary. When I figured the monthly budget, I noticed that there wouldn't be enough to pay [both] my tithing and my university. I would have to choose between them. The bimonthly tests would start the following week, and if I didn't take them I could lose the school year. I felt great agony. . . . My heart ached. I had a painful decision before me, and I didn't know what to decide. I pondered between the two choices: to pay tithing or to risk the possibility of not obtaining the necessary credits to be approved in school.

This feeling consumed my soul and remained with me up to Saturday. It was then that I remembered that when I was baptized I had agreed to live the law of tithing. I had taken upon myself an obligation, not with the missionaries, but with my Heavenly Father. At that moment the anguish started to disappear, giving place to a pleasant sensation of tranquility and determination. . . .

That night when I prayed, I asked the Lord to forgive me for my indecision. On Sunday, before the beginning of sacrament meeting, I contacted the bishop, and with great pleasure I paid my tithing and offerings. That was a special day. I felt happy and peaceful within myself and with Heavenly Father.

The next day I was in my office; I tried to find a way to be able to take the tests that would begin on Wednesday. The more I thought, the further I felt from a solution. At that time I worked in an attorney's office, and my employer was the most strict and austere person I had ever met.

The working period was ending when my employer approached and gave the last orders of the day. When he had done so, with his briefcase in his hand he bid farewell. . . . Suddenly he halted, and looking at me he asked, "How is your college?" I was surprised, and I couldn't believe what I was hearing. The only thing I could answer with a trembling voice was, "Everything is all right!" He looked thoughtfully at me and bid farewell again. . . .

Suddenly the secretary entered the room, saying that I was a very fortunate person! When I asked her why, she simply answered, "The employer has just said that from today on the company is going to pay fully for your college and your books. Before you leave, stop at my desk and inform me of the costs so that tomorrow I can give you the check."

After she left, crying and feeling very humble, I knelt exactly where I was and thanked the Lord for His generosity. I . . . said to Heavenly Father that He didn't have to bless me so much. I only needed the cost of one month's installment, and the tithing I had paid on Sunday was very small compared to the amount I was receiving! During that prayer the words in Malachi came to my mind: "Prove me now herewith, saith the Lord of hosts, if I will not open you the windows of heaven, and pour you out a blessing, that there shall not be room enough to receive it" (Malachi 3:10). Up to that moment I had never felt the magnitude of the promise contained in that scripture and that this commandment was truly a witness of the love that God, our Heavenly Father, gives to His children here on earth.

Faith is the very fiber that gives strength to this work. Wherever this Church is established across this broad world, it is evident. It is not limited to one country or one nation or one language or one people. It is found everywhere. We are a people of faith. We walk by faith. We move forward on our eternal journey, one step at a time.

Great is the promise of the Lord to the faithful everywhere. He has said:

I, the Lord, am merciful and gracious unto those who fear me, and delight to honor those who serve me in righteousness and in truth unto the end.

Great shall be their reward and eternal shall be their glory.

And to them will I reveal all mysteries, yea, all the hidden mysteries of my kingdom from days of old, and for ages to come. . . .

Yea, even the wonders of eternity shall they know. . . .

And their wisdom shall be great, and their understanding reach to heaven; and before them the wisdom of the wise shall perish, and the understanding of the prudent shall come to naught.

For by my Spirit will I enlighten them, and by my power will I make known unto them the secrets of my will—yea, even those things which eye has not seen, nor ear heard, nor yet entered into the heart of man. [D&C 76:5–10]

How could anyone ask for more? How glorious is this work in which we are engaged. How wondrous are the ways of the Almighty when we walk in faith before Him.

The faith of an investigator is like a piece of green wood, thrown on a blazing fire. Warmed by the flames, it dries and begins to burn. But if it is pulled away, it cannot sustain itself. Its flickering flame dies. But if left with the fire, it gradually begins to burn with brightness. Soon it is part of the flaming fire and will light other, greener wood.

And so goes, my brothers and sisters, this great work of faith, lifting people across this broad earth to increased understanding of the ways of the Lord and greater happiness in following His pattern.

May God, our Eternal Father, continue to smile upon this, His Kingdom, and cause it to prosper as we, His children, walk in faith is my humble prayer in the name of the Lord Jesus Christ, amen.

# Sunday Afternoon Session

APRIL 7, 2002

My beloved brethren and sisters, I too would like to express deep appreciation for the tremendous service of Sister Smoot, Sister Jensen, Sister Dew, and their board, who have served so very faithfully and well in this great and tremendous organization for women. It is a marvelous society, 4,900,000 strong. There is nothing like it, I think, in all the world, and it touches for such tremendous good the lives of women everywhere across the earth. Thank you, dear sisters, for what you've done. Welcome to you, Sister Parkin and your counselors, and the board which you will select.

We now conclude this great conference. We have enjoyed a wonderful feast at the table of the Lord. We have been instructed in His ways after His pattern.

Each of us should be a little better for this rich experience. Otherwise, our gathering has been largely in vain.

When I conclude, the choir will sing:

*Abide with me; 'tis eventide.*
*The day is past and gone;*
*The shadows of the evening fall;*
*The night is coming on.*

*Within my heart a welcome guest,*
*Within my home abide.*
*O Savior, stay this night with me;*
*Behold, 'tis eventide.*
                *["Abide with Me; 'Tis*
                *Eventide," Hymns, no. 165]*

That pretty well sums up the feelings of our hearts as we return to our homes.

May the Spirit of our Lord accompany us and remain with us. We know not what lies ahead of us. We know not what the coming days will bring. We live in a world of uncertainty. For some, there will be great accomplishment. For others, disappointment. For some, much of rejoicing and gladness, good health, and gracious living. For others, perhaps sickness and a measure of sorrow. We do not know. But one thing we do know. Like the polar star in the heavens, regardless of what the future holds, there stands the Redeemer of the world, the Son of God, certain and sure as the anchor of our immortal lives. He is the rock of our salvation, our strength, our comfort, the very focus of our faith.

In sunshine and in shadow we look to Him, and He is there to assure and smile upon us.

He is the central focus of our worship. He is the Son of the living God, the Firstborn of the Father, the Only Begotten in the flesh, who left the royal courts on high to be born as a mortal in the most humble of circumstances. Of the loneliness of His living He said, "The foxes have holes, and the birds of the air have nests; but the Son of man hath not where to lay his head" (Matthew 8:20). He "went about doing good" (Acts 10:38).

He was a man of miracles. He reached out to those in distress. He healed the sick and raised the dead. Yet for all of the love He brought into the world, He was "despised and rejected of men; a man of sorrows, and acquainted with grief: . . . he was despised," and was esteemed not (Isaiah 53:3).

We look upon His matchless life and say with the prophet Isaiah:

"He hath borne our griefs, and carried our sorrows. . . .

" . . . He was wounded for our transgressions, he was bruised for our iniquities: the chastisement of our peace was upon him; and with his stripes we are healed" (Isaiah 53:4–5).

When the great War in Heaven was fought, Lucifer, the son of the morning, came forth with a plan that was rejected. The Father of us all, with love for us, His children, offered a better plan under which we would have freedom to choose the course of our lives. His Firstborn Son, our Elder Brother, was the key to that plan. Man would have his agency, and with that agency would go accountability. Man would walk the ways of the world and sin and stumble. But the Son of God would take upon Himself flesh and offer Himself a sacrifice to atone for the sins of all men. Through unspeakable suffering He would become the great Redeemer, the Savior of all mankind.

With some small understanding of that incomparable gift, that marvelous gift of redemption, we bow in reverent love before Him.

As a Church we have critics, many of them. They say we do not believe in the traditional Christ of Christianity. There is some substance to what they say. Our faith, our knowledge is not based on ancient tradition, the creeds which came of a finite understanding and out of the almost infinite discussions of men trying to arrive at a definition of the risen Christ. Our faith, our knowledge comes of the witness of a prophet in this dispensation who saw before him the great God of the universe and His Beloved Son, the resurrected Lord Jesus Christ. They spoke to him. He spoke with Them. He testified openly, unequivocally, and unabashedly of that great vision. It was a vision of the Almighty and of the Redeemer of the world, glorious beyond our understanding but certain and unequivocating in the knowledge which it brought. It is out of that knowledge, rooted deep in the soil of modern revelation, that we, in the words of Nephi, "talk of Christ, we rejoice in Christ, we preach of Christ, we prophesy of Christ, and we write according to our prophecies, that [we and] our children may know to what source [we] may look for a remission of [our] sins" (2 Nephi 25:26).

And so, my brothers and sisters, as we bid you good-bye for a season, we repeat our firm and enduring testimony. We do it as individuals with a sure and certain knowledge. As I have said many times before, and as I now say again, I know that God, our Eternal Father, lives. He is the great God of the universe. He is the Father of our spirits, with whom we may speak in prayer.

I know that Jesus Christ is His Only Begotten Son, the Redeemer of the world, who gave His life that we might have eternal life and who rules and reigns with His Father. I know that They are individual beings, separate and distinct one from another and yet alike in form and substance and purpose. I know that it is the work of the Almighty "to bring to pass the immortality and eternal life of man" (Moses 1:39). I know that Joseph Smith was a prophet, the great prophet of this dispensation through whom these truths have come. I know that this Church is the work of God, presided over and directed by Jesus Christ, whose holy name it bears.

Of these things I testify in solemnity as I leave with you, my beloved associates, my love and blessing, in the sacred name of Jesus Christ, amen. "God be with you till we meet again" (*Hymns,* no. 152).

# SATURDAY MORNING SESSION

OCTOBER 5, 2002

M Y BELOVED BRETHREN AND SISTERS, we greet you again in a great worldwide conference of The Church of Jesus Christ of Latter-day Saints.

Alma declared, "O that I were an angel, and could have the wish of mine heart, that I might go forth and speak with the trump of God, with a voice to shake the earth, and cry repentance unto every people!" (Alma 29:1).

We have reached a point where we can almost do that. The proceedings of this conference will be carried across the world, and the speakers will be heard and seen by Latter-day Saints on every continent. We have come a very long way in realizing the fulfillment of the vision set forth in the book of Revelation:

"And I saw another angel fly in the midst of heaven, having the everlasting gospel to preach unto them that dwell on the earth, and to every nation, and kindred, and tongue, and people" (Revelation 14:6).

What a tremendous occasion this is, my brothers and sisters. It is difficult to comprehend. We speak from this marvelous Conference Center. I know of no other building to compare with it.

We are as one great family, representatives of the human family in this vast and beautiful world.

142

Many of you participated in the dedication of the Nauvoo Temple last June. It was a great and marvelous occasion, one to be long remembered. We not only dedicated a magnificent building, a house of the Lord, but we also dedicated a beautiful memorial to the Prophet Joseph Smith.

In 1841, two years after he came to Nauvoo, he broke ground for a house of the Lord that should stand as a crowning jewel to the work of God. It is difficult to believe that in those conditions and under those circumstances a structure of such magnificence was designed to stand on what was then the frontier of America. I doubt, I seriously doubt, that there was another structure of such design and magnificence in all the state of Illinois.

It was to be dedicated to the work of the Almighty, to accomplish His eternal purposes. No effort was spared. No sacrifice was too great. Through the next five years men chiseled stone and laid footings and foundation, walls and ornamentation. Hundreds went to the north, there to live for a time to cut lumber, vast quantities of it, and then bind it together to form rafts which were floated down the river to Nauvoo. Beautiful moldings were cut from that lumber. Pennies were gathered to buy nails. Unimaginable sacrifice was made to procure glass. They were building a temple to God, and it had to be the very best of which they were capable.

In the midst of all of this activity, the Prophet and his brother Hyrum were killed in Carthage on the 27th of June 1844. None of us living today can comprehend what a disastrous blow that was to the Saints. Their leader was gone—he, the man of visions and revelations. He was not only their leader. He was their prophet. Great was their sorrow, terrible their distress.

But Brigham Young, President of the Quorum of the Twelve, picked up the reins. Joseph had placed his authority on the shoulders of the Apostles. Brigham determined to finish the temple, and the work went on. By day and by night they pursued their objective, notwithstanding all of the threats hurled against them by

143

lawless mobs. In 1845 they knew they could not stay in the city they had built from the swamplands of the river. They knew they must leave. It became a time of feverish activity: first, to complete the temple, and secondly, to build wagons and gather supplies to move into the wilderness of the West.

Ordinance work was begun before the temple was entirely completed. It went on feverishly until, in the cold of the winter of 1846, the people began to close the doors of their homes and wagons moved slowly down Parley Street to the water's edge, then across the river and up the banks on the Iowa side.

Movement continued. The river froze over, it was so bitter cold. But it made it possible for them to move on the ice.

Back to the east they looked for the last time to the city of their dreams and the temple of their God. Then they looked to the west to a destiny they did not know.

The temple was subsequently dedicated, and those who dedicated it said amen and moved on. The building was later burned by an arsonist who almost lost his life in the evil process. A tornado finally toppled most of what was left. The house of the Lord, the great objective of their labors, was gone.

Nauvoo became almost a ghost city. It faded until it almost died. The site of the temple was plowed and planted. The years passed, and there slowly followed an awakening. Our people, descendants of those who once lived there, had stir within them the memories of their forebears, with a desire to honor those who had paid so terrible a price. Gradually the city came alive again, and there was a restoration of parts of Nauvoo.

Under the prompting of the Spirit, and motivated by the desires of my father, who had served as mission president in that area and who wished to rebuild the temple for the centennial of Nauvoo but was never able to do so, we announced in the April conference of 1999 that we would rebuild that historic edifice.

Excitement filled the air. Men and women came forth with a

desire to be helpful. Large contributions of money and skills were offered. Again, no expense was spared. We were to rebuild the house of the Lord as a memorial to the Prophet Joseph and as an offering to our God. On the recent 27th of June, in the afternoon at about the same time Joseph and Hyrum were shot in Carthage 158 years earlier, we held the dedication of the magnificent new structure. It is a place of great beauty. It stands on exactly the same site where the original temple stood. Its outside dimensions are those of the original. It is a fitting and appropriate memorial to the great prophet of this dispensation, Joseph the Seer.

How grateful I am, how profoundly grateful for what has happened. Today, facing west, on the high bluff overlooking the city of Nauvoo, thence across the Mississippi and over the plains of Iowa, there stands Joseph's temple, a magnificent house of God. Here in the Salt Lake Valley, facing east to that beautiful temple in Nauvoo, stands Brigham's temple, the Salt Lake Temple. They look toward one another as bookends between which there are volumes that speak of the suffering, the sorrow, the sacrifice, even the deaths of thousands who made the long journey from the Mississippi River to the valley of the Great Salt Lake.

Nauvoo became the 113th working temple. We have since dedicated another in The Hague, Netherlands, making 114 in all. These wonderful buildings of various sizes and architectural designs are now scattered through the nations of the earth. They have been constructed to accommodate our people in carrying forward the work of the Almighty, whose design it is to bring to pass the immortality and eternal life of man (see Moses 1:39). These temples have been constructed to be used. We honor our Father as we make use of them.

At the opening of the conference, I urge you, my brethren and sisters, to utilize the temples of the Church. Go there and carry forward the great and marvelous work which the God of heaven has outlined for us. There let us learn of His ways and His plans. There

145

let us make covenants that will lead us in paths of righteousness, unselfishness, and truth. There let us be joined as families under an eternal covenant administered under the authority of the priesthood of God. And there may we extend these same blessings to those of previous generations, even our own forebears who await the service which we can now give.

May the blessings of heaven rest upon you, my beloved brethren and sisters. May the Spirit of Elijah touch your hearts and prompt you to do that work for others who cannot move forward unless you do so. May we rejoice in the glorious privilege that is ours, I humbly pray in the name of Jesus Christ, amen.

# PRIESTHOOD SESSION

Now, MY BELOVED BRETHREN, I speak with a desire to be helpful. I pray for the Spirit of the Lord to guide me.

I need not tell you that we have become a very large and complex Church. Our program is so vast and our reach is so extensive that it is difficult to comprehend. We are a Church of lay leadership. What a remarkable and wonderful thing that is. It must ever remain so. It must never move in the direction of an extensive paid ministry. But we know that the administrative load is very heavy on our bishops and stake presidents, as well as some others. An awareness of that fact has led the Presidency and the Twelve to hold a number of meetings, some of them long and interesting, in which, in effect, we have taken the Church apart and then put it together again. Our objective has been to see whether there might be some programs we could do away with. But as we have analyzed these, we have not seen much that could be dropped. To drop one is like giving away one of your children. You haven't the heart to do it. But I wish to assure you that we are aware of the burdens you carry and the time you spend. In this priesthood meeting I wish to mention a few of the items we have discussed. I think you will note that we have made some progress, although it may be small.

I shall speak to you about a number of miscellaneous items.

We have determined, first, that effective November 1, temple recommends will remain valid for two years instead of one. This should cut the time that bishops and stake presidents and their counselors have to spend in interviews for temple recommends. Of course, if at any time the recommend holder becomes unworthy of going to the temple, then it will become the responsibility of the bishop or stake president to pick up the individual's recommend.

But experience has shown that there are very few such incidents. And so this will become the program, brethren. Beginning the first of November, regardless of the date written on the recommend, the term will be extended for one year. Recommends will then be renewed every two years rather than the present one year. We hope this will be beneficial. We are confident that it will.

Another item.

Elder Ballard has spoken to you concerning missionaries. I wish to endorse what he said. I hope that our young men, and our young women, will rise to the challenge he has set forth. We must raise the bar on the worthiness and qualifications of those who go into the world as ambassadors of the Lord Jesus Christ.

Now, we have an interesting custom in the Church. Departing missionaries are accorded a farewell. In some wards this has become a problem. Between outgoing missionaries and returning missionaries, most sacrament meetings are devoted to farewells and homecomings.

No one else in the Church has a farewell when entering a particular service. We never have a special farewell meeting for a newly called bishop, for a stake president, for a Relief Society president, for a General Authority, or anyone else of whom I can think. Why should we have missionary farewells?

The First Presidency and the Twelve, after most prayerful and careful consideration, have reached the decision that the present program of missionary farewells should be modified.

The departing missionary will be given the opportunity to

speak in a sacrament meeting for 15 or 20 minutes. But parents and siblings will not be invited to do so. There might be two or more departing missionaries who speak in the same service. The meeting will be entirely in the hands of the bishop and will not be arranged by the family. There will not be special music or anything of that kind.

We know this will be a great disappointment to many families. Mothers and fathers, brothers and sisters, and friends have participated in the past. We ask that you accept this decision. Where a farewell has already been arranged, it may go forward. But none in the traditional sense should be planned for the future. We are convinced that when all aspects of the situation are considered, this is a wise decision. Please accept it, my dear brethren. I extend this plea also to the sisters, particularly the mothers.

We hope also that holding elaborate open houses after the sacrament meeting at which the missionary speaks will not prevail. Members of the family may wish to get together. We have no objection to this. However, we ask that there be no public reception to which large numbers are invited.

Missionary service is such a wonderful experience that it brings with it its own generous reward. And when a missionary returns to his family and his ward, he may again be given opportunity to speak in a sacrament meeting.

The next item.

Let me give you a brief report on the Perpetual Education Fund, which was established a year and a half ago at the April conference. The program is now going forward on a sound footing. We have a substantial financial corpus contributed by faithful Latter-day Saints. We hope more will be forthcoming to make it possible to assist a larger number of those worthy of help.

Today some 5,000 men and women, most of them young, are being educated who otherwise might not have had the opportunity. Think of the consequences of this. These faithful Latter-day

Saints are offered a ladder by which they may climb out of the condition of poverty in which they and their forebears have lived. Their earning capacity is being greatly increased. Their power of leadership is being enhanced. They will become men and women of substance, members of the Church who will carry forward its program in a manner previously unimagined.

I give you one example. The first young woman to receive a loan has now completed a year of training and has applied for funds for her last year of training. She is studying to become a dental assistant.

Previous to this she worked in a restaurant earning $130 a month. It is anticipated that when she completes her training, in a short time she will receive $650 a month to begin with—an immediate 500 percent increase. That will grow through the years.

What a marvelous difference a few dollars make when they are properly applied. Now, you multiply her experience by 5,000. It is a most remarkable thing to contemplate. Students are receiving training to become mechanics, systems analysts, administrative consultants, nursing technicians, information systems technicians, nurses, hospital workers, computer programmers, computer engineers, fashion designers, accountants, electricians, English teachers, bakers, hotel administrators, and graphic designers, to name a few.

The possibilities are endless, and what is happening is indeed a wonderful and miraculous thing.

The next item I wish to mention is family home evening. We are fearful that this very important program is fading in too many areas. Brethren, there is nothing more important than your families. You know that. This program was begun back in 1915, 87 years ago, when President Joseph F. Smith urged the Latter-day Saints to set aside one evening a week devoted specifically to the family. It was to be a time of teaching, of reading the scriptures, of cultivating talents, of discussing family matters. It was not to be a time to attend athletic events or anything of the kind. Of course, if there is family activity of such a kind occasionally, that may be all right. But in the increasingly frantic rush of our lives, it is so important that fathers and mothers sit down with their children, pray together, instruct them in the ways of the Lord, consider their family problems, and let the children express their talents. I am satisfied that this program came under the revelations of the Lord in response to a need among the families of the Church.

If there was a need 87 years ago, that need is certainly much greater today.

The decision was made that Monday evening would be devoted to this family activity. In those areas where there are large numbers of Church members, school officials and others honored the program and did not schedule events on that evening.

Now there appears to be a growing tendency to schedule other events on Monday night. We respectfully request that our public school officials and others let us have this one evening a week to carry forward this important and traditional program. We ask that they not schedule events that will require the time of children on Monday evenings. We are confident that they will realize that it is most important that families have the opportunity, at least once a week, to be together without conflicting loyalties. We shall be grateful indeed if they will cooperate in this matter. And we urge, in the strongest terms possible, that fathers and mothers regard most seriously this opportunity and challenge to make of Monday evening a time sacred to the family.

I have received not a few invitations to participate in community Monday gatherings of one kind or another. I have uniformly turned down these invitations with appreciation but with the explanation that I have reserved Monday as family home evening time. I earnestly hope that each of you will do the same.

The next item.

Brethren, I wish to urge again the importance of self-reliance on the part of every individual Church member and family. None of us knows when a catastrophe might strike. Sickness, injury, unemployment may affect any of us.

We have a great welfare program, with facilities for such things as grain storage in various areas. It is important that we do this. But the best place to have some food set aside is within our homes, together with a little money in savings. The best welfare program is our own welfare program. Five or six cans of wheat in the home are better than a bushel in the welfare granary.

I do not predict any impending disaster. I hope that there will not be one. But prudence should govern our lives. Everyone who owns a home recognizes the need for fire insurance. We hope and pray that there will never be a fire. Nevertheless, we pay for insurance to cover such a catastrophe, should it occur. We ought to do the same with reference to family welfare.

We can begin ever so modestly. We can begin with one week's food supply and gradually build it to a month and then to three months. I am speaking now of food to cover basic needs. As all of you recognize, this counsel is not new. But I fear that so many feel that a long-term food supply is so far beyond their reach that they make no effort at all.

Begin in a small way, my brethren, and gradually build toward a reasonable objective. Save a little money regularly, and you will be surprised how it accumulates.

Get out of debt, and rid yourself of the terrible bondage that debt brings. We hear much about second mortgages. Now I am told there are third mortgages. Discipline yourselves in matters of spending, in matters of borrowing, in practices that lead to bankruptcy and the agony that comes therewith.

Now, finally, my brethren, I wish to return briefly to a matter I have spoken on before and which has been dealt with by Elder Ballard and President Monson in this meeting. I hope that they will not object to my trying to emphasize again what they have said. I refer to the moral discipline of members of the Church.

Too many are being caught in the web of immorality and all of the bitter fruit that flows from it. To the boys who are here tonight—the young men—I wish to say in the strongest language of which I am capable, stay away from moral iniquity. You know what is right and wrong. You cannot use ignorance as an excuse for unacceptable behavior.

How can you possibly think that you can become involved in immoral practices and then go into the mission field as a representative of the Lord Jesus Christ? Do you suppose that you can be worthy to go to the house of the Lord, there to be married for time and eternity, if you have indulged in such practices?

I beg of you, my dear young friends, to avoid such behavior. It will not be easy. It will require self-discipline. The forces you confront are powerful and inviting. They are the forces of a clever adversary. You need the strength that comes of prayer.

Stay away from the erotic stuff of the Internet. It can only pull you down. It can lead to your destruction.

Never lose sight of the fact that you hold the priesthood of God. When John the Baptist conferred the Aaronic Priesthood upon Joseph Smith and Oliver Cowdery, he stated that this priesthood "holds the keys of the ministering of angels, and of the gospel of repentance, and of baptism by immersion for the remission of sins" (D&C 13).

Do you wish for the ministering of angels? That ministering will bring with it incomparable rewards. Take the high road in your lives, and God will bless you and nurture you and "lead [you] by the hand, and give [you] answer to [your] prayers" (D&C 112:10).

To you mature men I extend the same plea and the same warning. Small beginnings lead to great tragedies. We deal with them constantly. There is so much of heartache, resentment, disillusionment, and divorce among us.

May I again mention a matter with which I have dealt at length in the past. I speak of the evil and despicable sin of child abuse.

We cannot tolerate it. We will not tolerate it. Anyone who abuses a child may expect Church discipline as well as possible legal action.

Child abuse is an affront toward God. Jesus spoke of the beauty and innocence of children. To anyone who has an inclination that could lead to the abuse of children, I say in the strongest language of which I am capable, discipline yourself. Seek help before you do injury to a child and bring ruin upon yourself.

You men who hold this precious priesthood, bind it to your very souls. Be worthy of it at all times and in all circumstances. If you do so, you will enjoy that "peace of God, which passeth all understanding" (Philippians 4:7).

May God bless you, my dear brethren of the priesthood, young and old. Fathers, set an example for your children. Boys, look to your fathers for wisdom and guidance and understanding.

How great are the promises of the Lord to those who walk in faith. I leave with you my blessing, my love, and my testimony. What a great and marvelous force for good is in this priesthood if we are united and move forward as one. May the Lord bless us to do so, I humbly pray in the name of Jesus Christ, amen.

# SUNDAY MORNING SESSION

OCTOBER 6, 2002

MY DEAR BROTHERS AND SISTERS, I seek the inspiration of the Lord in addressing you. I never get over the tremendous responsibility of speaking to the Latter-day Saints. I am grateful for your kindness and for your forbearance. I constantly pray that I may be worthy of the confidence of the people.

I have recently come from a very long journey. It has been wearisome, but it has been wonderful to be out among the Saints. If it were possible, I would turn all of the day-to-day administrative matters of the Church over to others, and then I would spend my time out among our people, visiting those in small branches as well as those in large stakes. I would wish to gather with the Saints wherever they may be. I feel that every member of this Church is deserving of a visit. I regret that because of physical limitations I can no longer shake hands with everybody. But I can look them in the eye with gladness in my heart and express my love and leave a blessing.

The occasion for this most recent journey was the rededication of the Freiberg Germany Temple and the dedication of The Hague Netherlands Temple. It was my opportunity to dedicate the Freiberg Temple 17 years ago. It was a rather modest building constructed in what was then the German Democratic Republic, the east zone of a divided Germany. Its construction was literally a miracle. President Monson, Hans Ringger, and others had won the goodwill of East German government officials who consented to it.

It has served marvelously well through these years. Now the infamous wall is gone. It is easier for our people to travel to Freiberg. The building was worn after these years and had become inadequate.

The temple has been enlarged and made much more beautiful and serviceable. We held just one session of dedication. Saints gathered from a vast area. In the large room where we sat, we could look into the faces of many of those rugged and solid and wonderful Latter-day Saints who through all of these years, in sunshine and in shadow, under government-imposed restraint and now in perfect freedom, have kept the faith, served the Lord, and stood like giants. I am so sorry that I could not throw my arms around these heroic brethren and sisters and tell them how much I love them. If they are now hearing me, I hope that they will know of that love and will pardon my hurried departure from their midst.

From there we flew to France to take care of Church business. We then flew to Rotterdam and drove to The Hague. Work in three nations in one day is a rather heavy schedule for an old man.

The following day we dedicated The Hague Netherlands Temple. Four sessions were held. What a touching and wonderful experience that was.

The temple is a beautiful structure in a good area. I am so grateful for the house of the Lord which will accommodate the Saints of the Netherlands, Belgium, and parts of France. Missionaries were first sent to that part of Europe way back in 1861. Thousands have joined the Church. Most of them emigrated to the States. But we have there now a wonderful body of precious and faithful Latter-day Saints who are deserving of a house of the Lord in their midst.

I determined that while in that part of the world we would go to other areas. We accordingly flew to Kiev in Ukraine. I was there 21 years ago. There is a new sense of freedom in the air. What an inspiration to meet with more than 3,000 Ukrainian Saints. The people gathered from far and near, enduring great discomfort and expense to get there.

One family could not afford to bring all of its members. The parents remained at home and sent their children so that they might have the opportunity to be with us.

From there we went to Moscow, Russia. I was there 21 years ago also, and there is a change. It is like electricity. You cannot see it. But you can feel it. Here again we had a wonderful meeting, with opportunity to converse with important government officials as we had done in Ukraine.

What a priceless and precious privilege to meet with these wonderful Saints who have been gathered "one of a city, and two of a family" into the fold of Zion in fulfillment of the prophecy of Jeremiah (see Jeremiah 3:14). Life is not easy for them. Their burdens are heavy. But their faith is secure, and their testimonies are vibrant.

In these faraway places, strange to most of the Church, the gospel flame burns brightly and lights the way for thousands.

We then flew to Iceland. It is a beautiful place with beautiful people. Here we had a long interview with the president of the nation, a very distinguished and able man who has been to Utah and speaks very generously of our people.

Again we met with the Saints. What an inspiration to look into their faces as they crowded our own meetinghouse in the city of Reykjavík.

In all these places and in all these opportunities to speak to so many, one thing constantly occupied my mind—the wonder of this work, the absolute wonder of it. The words of our great hymn just sung by the choir repeatedly came to mind:

*How firm a foundation, ye Saints of the Lord,*
*Is laid for your faith in his excellent word!*
*["How Firm a Foundation,"*
Hymns, *no. 85]*

Do we as Latter-day Saints really understand and appreciate the strength of our position? Among the religions of the world, it is unique and wonderful.

Is this Church an educational institution? Yes. We are constantly and endlessly teaching, teaching, teaching in a great variety of circumstances. Is it a social organization? Indeed. It is a great family of friends who mingle together and enjoy one another. Is it a mutual aid society? Yes. It has a remarkable program for building self-reliance and granting aid to those in distress. It is all of these and more. But beyond these it is the Church and kingdom of God, established and directed by our Eternal Father and His Beloved Son, the risen Lord Jesus Christ, to bless all who come within its fold.

We declare without equivocation that God the Father and His Son, the Lord Jesus Christ, appeared in person to the boy Joseph Smith.

When I was interviewed by Mike Wallace on the *60 Minutes* program, he asked me if I actually believed that. I replied, "Yes, sir. That's the miracle of it."

That is the way I feel about it. Our whole strength rests on the validity of that vision. It either occurred or it did not occur. If it did not, then this work is a fraud. If it did, then it is the most important and wonderful work under the heavens.

Reflect upon it, my brethren and sisters. For centuries the heavens remained sealed. Good men and women, not a few—really great and wonderful people—tried to correct, strengthen, and improve their systems of worship and their body of doctrine. To them I pay honor and respect. How much better the world is because of their bold action. While I believe their work was inspired, it was not favored with the opening of the heavens, with the appearance of Deity.

Then in 1820 came that glorious manifestation in answer to the prayer of a boy who had read in his family Bible the words of James: "If any of you lack wisdom, let him ask of God, that giveth to all men liberally, and upbraideth not; and it shall be given him" (James 1:5).

Upon that unique and wonderful experience stands the validity of this Church.

In all of recorded religious history there is nothing to compare with it. The New Testament recounts the baptism of Jesus, when the voice of God was heard and the Holy Ghost descended in the form of a dove. At the Mount of Transfiguration, Peter, James, and John saw the Lord transfigured before them. They heard the voice of the Father, but they did not see Him.

Why did both the Father and the Son come to a boy, a mere lad? For one thing, they came to usher in the greatest gospel dispensation of all time, when all of previous dispensations should be gathered and brought together in one.

Can anyone doubt that the age in which we live is the most wonderful in the history of the world? There has been a marvelous flowering of science, of medicine, of communication, of transportation unequaled in all the chronicles of mankind. Is it reasonable to submit that there should also be a flowering of spiritual knowledge as a part of this incomparable renaissance of light and understanding?

The instrument in this work of God was a boy whose mind was not cluttered by the philosophies of men. That mind was fresh and without schooling in the traditions of the day.

It is easy to see why people do not accept this account. It is almost beyond comprehension. And yet it is so reasonable. Those familiar with the Old Testament recognize the appearance of Jehovah to the prophets who lived in that comparatively simple time. Can they legitimately deny the need for an appearance of the God of heaven and His resurrected Son in this very complex period of the world's history?

That They came, both of Them, that Joseph saw Them in Their resplendent glory, that They spoke to him, and that he heard and recorded Their words—of these remarkable things we testify.

I knew a so-called intellectual who said the Church was trapped by its history. My response was that without that history we have nothing. The truth of that unique, singular, and remarkable event is the pivotal substance of our faith.

But this glorious vision was but the beginning of a series of manifestations that constitute the early history of this work.

As if that vision were not enough to certify to the personality and the reality of the Redeemer of mankind, there followed the coming forth of the Book of Mormon. Here is something that a man could hold in his hands, could "heft," as it were. He could read it. He could pray about it, for it contained a promise that the Holy Ghost would declare its truth if that witness were sought in prayer (see Moroni 10:4).

This remarkable book stands as a testimonial to the living reality of the Son of God. The Bible declares, "In the mouth of two or three witnesses every word may be established" (Matthew 18:16). The Bible, the testament of the Old World, is one witness. The Book of Mormon, the testament of the New World, is another witness.

I cannot understand why the Christian world does not accept this book. I would think they would be looking for anything and everything that would establish without question the reality and the divinity of the Savior of the world.

There followed the restoration of the priesthood—first, of the Aaronic under the hands of John the Baptist, who had baptized Jesus in Jordan. Then came Peter, James, and John, Apostles of the Lord, who conferred in this age that which they had received under the hands of the Master, with whom they walked, even "the keys of the kingdom of heaven," with authority to bind in the heavens that which they bound on earth (see Matthew 16:19). Subsequently came the bestowal of further priesthood keys under the hands of Moses, Elias, and Elijah.

Think of it, my brothers and sisters. Think of the wonder of it. This is the restored Church of Jesus Christ. We as a people are Latter-day Saints. We testify that the heavens have been opened, that the curtains have been parted, that God has spoken, and that Jesus Christ has manifested Himself, followed by a bestowal of divine authority.

Jesus Christ is the cornerstone of this work, and it is built upon a "foundation of . . . apostles and prophets" (Ephesians 2:20).

This wondrous Restoration should make of us a people of tolerance, of neighborliness, of appreciation and kindness toward others. We cannot be boastful. We cannot be proud. We can be thankful, as we must be. We can be humble, as we should be.

We love those of other churches. We work with them in good causes. We respect them. But we must never forget our roots. Those roots lie deep in the soil of the opening of this, the final dispensation, the dispensation of the fulness of times.

What an inspiration it has been to look into the faces of men and women across the world who carry in their hearts a solemn conviction of the truth of this foundation.

When it comes to divine authority, this is the sum and substance of the whole matter.

God be thanked for His marvelous bestowal of testimony, authority, and doctrine associated with this, the restored Church of Jesus Christ.

This must be our great and singular message to the world. We do not offer it with boasting. We testify in humility but with gravity and absolute sincerity. We invite all, the whole earth, to listen to this account and take measure of its truth. God bless us as those who believe in His divine manifestations and help us to extend the knowledge of these great and marvelous occurrences to all who will listen. To these we say in a spirit of love, bring with you all that you have of good and truth which you have received from whatever source, and come and let us see if we may add to it. This invitation I extend to men and women everywhere with my solemn testimony that this work is true, for I know the truth of it by the power of the Holy Ghost. In the name of Jesus Christ, amen.

# SUNDAY AFTERNOON SESSION

OCTOBER 6, 2002

WHAT A WONDERFUL CONFERENCE this has been, my brothers and sisters. As we return to our homes and to our daily activities, each of us should be a better individual than we were when the conference opened.

All who have spoken have done very well. The prayers have been inspirational. The music has been magnificent.

But what matters most is what may have occurred within each of us as a result of our experience. I, for one, have made a stronger resolution within myself to be a better person than I have been in the past. I hope that I will be a little kinder to any I meet who may be in distress. I hope that I will be a little more helpful to those who are in need. I hope that I will be a little more worthy of your confidence. I hope that I will be a better husband, a better father and grandfather. I hope that I will be a better neighbor and friend. I hope that I will be a better Latter-day Saint, with an increased understanding of the wonderful aspects of this glorious gospel.

I challenge every one of you who can hear me to rise to the divinity within you. Do we really realize what it means to be a child of God, to have within us something of the divine nature?

I believe with all my heart that the Latter-day Saints, generally speaking, are good people. If we live by the principles of the gospel, we must be good people, for we will be generous and kind, thoughtful and tolerant, helpful and outreaching to those in distress. We can either subdue the divine nature and hide it so that it finds no expression in our lives, or we can bring it to the front and let it shine through all that we do.

There is room for improvement in every life. Regardless of our occupations, regardless of our circumstances, we can improve ourselves and while so doing have an effect on the lives of those about us.

We do not need to wear our religion on our sleeves. We certainly do not need to be boastful about it or to be arrogant in any way. Such becomes a negation of the Spirit of the Christ, whom we ought to try to emulate. That Spirit finds expression in the heart and the soul, in the quiet and unboastful manner of our lives.

All of us have seen those we almost envy because they have cultivated a manner that, without even mentioning it, speaks of the beauty of the gospel they have incorporated in their behavior.

We can lower our voices a few decibels. We can return good for evil. We can smile when anger might be so much easier. We can exercise self-control and self-discipline and dismiss any affront levied against us.

Let us be a happy people. The Lord's plan is a plan of happiness. The way will be lighter, the worries will be fewer, the confrontations will be less difficult if we cultivate a spirit of happiness.

Let us work a little harder at the responsibility we have as parents. The home is the basic unit of society. The family is the basic organization of the Church. We are deeply concerned over the quality of the lives of our people as husbands and wives and as parents and children.

There is too much of criticism and faultfinding with anger and raised voices. The pressures we feel each day are tremendous. Husbands come home from their employment each day tired and short tempered. Unfortunately, most of the wives work. They too face a serious challenge that may be more costly than it is worth. Children are left to seek their own entertainment, and much of it is not good.

My brothers and sisters, we must work at our responsibility as parents as if everything in life counted on it, because in fact everything in life does count on it.

If we fail in our homes, we fail in our lives. No man is truly successful who has failed in his home. I ask you men, particularly, to pause and take stock of yourselves as husbands and fathers and heads of households. Pray for guidance, for help, for direction, and then follow the whisperings of the Spirit to guide you in the most serious of all responsibilities, for the consequences of your leadership in your home will be eternal and everlasting.

God bless you, my beloved associates. May a spirit of peace and love attend you wherever you may be. May there be harmony in your lives. As I've said to our youth in many areas, be smart, be clean, be true, be grateful, be humble, be prayerful. May you kneel in prayer before the Almighty with thanksgiving unto Him for His bounteous blessings. May you then stand on your feet and go forward as sons and daughters of God to bring to pass His eternal purposes, each in your own way, is my humble prayer as I leave my love and blessing with you, in the sacred name of the Lord Jesus Christ, amen.

# 173RD ANNUAL GENERAL CONFERENCE

# SATURDAY MORNING SESSION

APRIL 5, 2003

My BELOVED BRETHREN AND SISTERS, what a miracle it is that we are able to address you out across the world. We speak here in the Conference Center in Salt Lake City. We speak in our native tongue. But many thousands of you are assembled in Church facilities in many lands, and you hear us in 56 languages.

We are met again in a great world conference of the Church according to the will and instruction of the Lord.

As we do so, the world is in turmoil. There is war and contention. There is much of unrest. Members of the Church family are citizens of many nations. We find ourselves on both sides of a great debate. I intend to speak about this tomorrow morning.

But with all the troubles with which we are confronted, I am pleased to report that the work of the Church moves forward. We continue to grow across the world. Our missionary work goes on without serious impediment. Converts continue to come into the Church, and our numbers are constantly being increased.

Paralleling this activity is the need to solidly integrate all those who are baptized as converts. We call upon every member of the Church to reach out to new converts, to put your arms around them and make them feel at home. Bless them with your friendship. Encourage them with your faith. See that there are no losses among them. Every man, woman, or child who is worthy of baptism is worthy of a secure and friendly situation in which to grow in the Church and its many activities.

Our sacrament meeting attendance gradually edges up. There is room for improvement, and I urge you to work at it constantly. Even so, I do not know of another church with as high a percentage of consistent attendance at its meetings.

I am so grateful for the strength of the youth of the Church. Sadly enough, some fall between the cracks. But it is a miracle to witness the strength of our young people in the midst of all of the sordid temptation that is constantly around them. The sleaze and the filth of pornography, the temptation to partake of drugs, the titillating invitation to drop all bars on sexual behavior—these are among some of the enticing attractions they constantly face. Notwithstanding the allurement of the world in which they live, they remain true to the faith of their fathers and the gospel they love. I cannot say enough of good concerning our wonderful young people.

Faith in the payment of tithes and offerings increases despite the straitened economic circumstances in which we find ourselves. We are able to go forward with the building of meetinghouses and temples, with our vast education program, with the very many activities which are conditioned upon the tithing income of the Church. I promise you that we will not put the Church in debt. We will strictly tailor the program to the tithing income and use these sacred funds for the purposes designated by the Lord.

I call attention to that which has received much notice in the local press. This is our decision to purchase the shopping mall property immediately to the south of Temple Square. We feel that we have a compelling responsibility to protect the environment of the Salt Lake Temple. The Church owns most of the ground on which this mall stands. The owners of the buildings have expressed a desire to sell. The property needs very extensive and expensive renovation.

We have felt it imperative to do something to revitalize this area. But I wish to give the entire Church the assurance that tithing funds have not and will not be used to acquire this property. Nor will they be used in developing it for commercial purposes.

Funds for this have come and will come from the commercial entities owned by the Church. These resources, together with the earnings of invested reserve funds, will accommodate this program.

I am pleased to report that we are able to go forward with the building of chapels. We are constructing about 400 new chapels a year to accommodate the growth in the membership of the Church. This is a significant and wonderful thing for which we are deeply grateful. We are also continuing to build temples across the earth and are pleased to report an increase in temple activity. This very important work, in behalf of the living and the dead, is a fundamental part of the gospel of Jesus Christ.

We are pleased to note an increase in family preparedness among our people. This program, which has been advocated for more than 60 years, adds immeasurably to the security and well-being of the Latter-day Saints. Every family has a responsibility to provide for its own needs to the extent possible. We again urge our people to avoid unnecessary debt, to be modest in the financial obligations which they undertake, to set aside some cash against an emergency. We warn our people against "get rich" schemes and other entanglements which are nearly always designed to trap the gullible.

I am constantly amazed at the vast amount of volunteer service which our people give. I am convinced that volunteer service is the Lord's way of accomplishing His work. The operation of wards and stakes and quorums, and the functions of the auxiliary organizations, all move forward under the direction of volunteers. The vast missionary program is dependent on volunteer service. Additionally, we have a large number of older members who serve in a Church-service missionary capacity. More than 18,000 give all or a large part of their time to this work. We thank them for their dedicated service.

This conference marks the second anniversary of the establishment of the Perpetual Education Fund. I am pleased to report that this program is now going forward on a solid basis. Some 8,000 young men and women are now in training to improve their skills and their employment opportunities. On average, with the two years of education they are now receiving, they are increasing their income some four and a half times. It is a miracle!

And so I might go on. Suffice it to say, the Church is in good condition. I believe its affairs are prudently handled. Our people are growing in faith, in love for the Lord, and in adherence to His teachings.

These are difficult times. The economy is struggling. There is conflict in the world. But the Almighty is keeping His promise that He will bless those who walk in faith and righteousness before Him.

The gospel of Jesus Christ is the way of peace. To the extent we follow it and incorporate it in our lives—to this extent will we be blessed and prospered. What a wonderful thing it is to be involved in this glorious work. Let us rejoice in our great opportunity. Let us serve with gladness.

May heaven's richest blessings rest upon you, my beloved associates. May faith grow in your hearts. May there be love and peace in your homes. May there be food upon your tables and clothing on your backs. May the smiles of heaven warm your hearts and bring comfort in times of trial. This is my prayer this morning as we open this great conference, in the sacred name of Jesus Christ, amen.

# PRIESTHOOD
# SESSION

### APRIL 5, 2003

THERE IS NOT ANOTHER MEETING in all the world comparable to this meeting. Wherever we may be, whatever the language we speak, we are all men who have had hands laid upon our heads to receive the priesthood of God. Whether we be boys who have received the lesser or Aaronic Priesthood or men who have received the higher or Melchizedek Priesthood, we each have had bestowed upon us something wonderful and magnificent, something of the very essence of godhood.

I repeat, there is no gathering in all the world like this. We meet together in the bonds of brotherhood, in a vast assemblage of men who have been endowed with a certain power or authority, honored with the privilege of speaking and acting in the name of the Almighty. The Lord God of heaven has seen fit to confer upon us something of that which is uniquely His. I sometimes wonder if we are worthy of it. I wonder if we really appreciate it. I wonder about the infinity of this power and authority. It is concerned with life and death, with family and Church, with the great and transcendent nature of God Himself and His eternal work.

Brethren, I greet you as members of quorums of the holy priesthood. I greet you as servants of the living God, who has laid upon each of us a responsibility from which we must not and cannot shrink.

In harmony with that greeting, I have chosen to speak on various aspects of one word. That word is *loyalty*.

I think of loyalty in terms of being true to ourselves. I think of it in terms of being absolutely faithful to our chosen companions. I think of it in terms of being absolutely loyal to the Church and its many facets of activity. I think of it in terms of being unequivocally true to the God of heaven, our Eternal Father, and His Beloved Son, our Redeemer, the Lord Jesus Christ.

We must be true to the very best that is in us. We are sons of God, honored to hold His divine authority. But we live in a world of evil. There is a constant power pulling us down, inviting us to partake of those things which are totally inconsistent with the divine priesthood which we hold. It is interesting to observe how the father of lies, that wily son of the morning who was cast out of heaven, always has the means and capacity to entice, to invite, to gather to his ways those who are not strong and alert. Very recently a certain moving picture was acclaimed the best of the year. I have not seen it, nor do I anticipate doing so. But I am told that it is laden with sex, that the use of profanity runs throughout.

Pornography is one of the hallmarks of our time. Its producers grow rich on the gullibility of those who like to watch it. In the opening lines of the revelation which we call the Word of Wisdom, the Lord declares, "In consequence of evils and designs which do and will exist in the hearts of conspiring men in the last days, I have warned you, and forewarn you, by giving unto you this word of wisdom by revelation" (D&C 89:4). He then goes on to talk about the food we put into our mouths. The same language might be applied with reference to that which we take into our minds when we indulge in pornography.

Brethren, every man and boy within the sound of my voice knows what is degrading. You do not need a road map to foretell

171

where indulgence will take you. Contrast that with the beauty, the peace, the wonderful feeling that comes of living near to the Lord and rising above the insidious narcotic practices that are all about us.

This applies to you, my dear boys who are in this meeting. You are particular targets for the adversary. If he can get you now, he knows he may win you for a lifetime. There has been implanted within you wondrous powers and instincts for a divine purpose. However, when these are perverted, they become destroyers rather than builders.

I am profoundly grateful for the strength of our youth. But I know also that some slip away from us. Every loss is a tragedy. The kingdom of our Lord needs you. Be worthy of it. Be loyal to your best selves. Never stoop to anything that would take from you the strength to abstain.

To you men I issue a challenge. Run from the tide of sleaze that would overcome you. Flee the evils of the world. Be loyal to your better self. Be loyal to the best that is in you. Be faithful and true to the covenants that are associated with the priesthood of God. You cannot wallow about in lasciviousness, you cannot lie, you cannot cheat, you cannot take advantage of others in unrighteousness without denying that touch of divinity with which each of us came into this life. I would pray with all of my strength, brethren, that we would rise above it and be loyal to our best selves.

Be loyal in your family relationships. I have witnessed much of the best and much of the worst in marriage. Every week I have the responsibility of acting on requests for cancellation of temple sealings. Divorce has become a very common phenomenon throughout the world. Even where it is not legal, men and women simply step over the line and live together. I am grateful to be able to say that divorce is much less frequent with those married in the temple. But even among these there is far more divorce than there should be.

The bride and groom come to the house of the Lord professing their love one for another. They enter into solemn and eternal covenants with each other and with the Lord. Their relationship is sealed in an eternal compact. No one expects every marriage to work out perfectly. But one might expect that every marriage in the house of the Lord would carry with it a covenant of loyalty one to another.

I have long felt that the greatest factor in a happy marriage is an anxious concern for the comfort and well-being of one's companion. In most cases selfishness is the leading factor that causes argument, separation, divorce, and broken hearts.

Brethren, the Lord expects something better of us. He expects something better than is to be found in the world. Never forget that it was you who selected your companion. It was you who felt that there was no one else in all the world quite like her. It was you who wished to have her forever. But in too many cases the image of the temple experience fades. A lustful desire may be the cause. Faultfinding replaces praise. When we look for the worst in anyone, we will find it. But if we will concentrate on the best, that element will grow until it sparkles.

I am not without personal experience. Sister Hinckley and I will soon have been married for 66 years. I do not know how she has put up with me all this long time. Now we have grown old. But how grateful I am for her. How anxious I am to see that she is comfortable. How much I desire the very best for her. What a wonderful companion she has been. What a marvelous wife, and what a tremendous mother and grandmother and great-grandmother.

You, of course, have heard of the man who lived to a ripe old age and was asked by reporters to what he attributed his longevity. He replied that when he and his wife were married they determined that if they argued, one would leave the house and go outside. He said, "Gentlemen, I attribute my longevity to the fact that I have breathed so much fresh air during all these many years."

Brethren, be loyal to your companion. May your marriage be

blessed with an uncompromising loyalty one to another. Find your happiness with one another. Give your companion the opportunity to grow in her own interests, to develop her own talents, to fly in her own way, and to experience her own sense of accomplishment.

Now may I say a word concerning loyalty to the Church.

We see much indifference. There are those who say, "The Church won't dictate to me how to think about this, that, or the other, or how to live my life."

No, I reply, the Church will not dictate to any man how he should think or what he should do. The Church will point out the way and invite every member to live the gospel and enjoy the blessings that come of such living. The Church will not dictate to any man, but it will counsel, it will persuade, it will urge, and it will expect loyalty from those who profess membership therein.

When I was a university student, I said to my father on one occasion that I felt the General Authorities had overstepped their prerogatives when they advocated a certain thing. He was a very wise and good man. He said, "The President of the Church has instructed us, and I sustain him as prophet, seer, and revelator and intend to follow his counsel."

I have now served in the general councils of this Church for 45 years. I have served as an Assistant to the Twelve, as a member of the Twelve, as a counselor in the First Presidency, and now for eight years as President. I want to give you my testimony that although I have sat in literally thousands of meetings where Church policies and programs have been discussed, I have never been in one where the guidance of the Lord was not sought nor where there was any desire on the part of anyone present to advocate or do anything which would be injurious or coercive to anyone.

The book of Revelation declares:

"I know thy works, that thou art neither cold nor hot: I would thou wert cold or hot.

"So then because thou art lukewarm, and neither cold nor hot, I will spue thee out of my mouth" (Revelation 3:15–16).

I make you a promise, my dear brethren, that while I am serving in my present responsibility I will never consent to nor advocate any policy, any program, any doctrine that will be otherwise than beneficial to the membership of this, the Lord's Church.

This is His work. He established it. He has revealed its doctrine. He has outlined its practices. He created its government. It is His work and His kingdom, and He has said, "They who are not for me are against me" (2 Nephi 10:16).

In 1933 there was a movement in the United States to overturn the law which prohibited commerce in alcoholic beverages. When it came to a vote, Utah was the deciding state.

I was on a mission, working in London, England, when I read the newspaper headlines that screamed, "Utah Kills Prohibition."

President Heber J. Grant, then President of this Church, had pleaded with our people against voting to nullify Prohibition. It broke his heart when so many members of the Church in this state disregarded his counsel.

On this occasion I am not going to talk about the good or bad of Prohibition but rather about uncompromising loyalty to the Church.

How grateful, my brethren, I feel—how profoundly grateful for the tremendous faith of so many Latter-day Saints who, when facing a major decision on which the Church has taken a stand, align themselves with that position. And I am especially grateful to be able to say that among those who are loyal are men and women of achievement, of accomplishment, of education, of influence, of strength—highly intelligent and capable individuals.

Each of us has to face the matter—either the Church is true, or it is a fraud. There is no middle ground. It is the Church and kingdom of God, or it is nothing.

Thank you, my dear brethren—you men of great strength and great fidelity and great faith and great loyalty.

Finally, loyalty to God, our Eternal Father, and His Beloved Son, the Lord Jesus Christ.

Every man in this Church is entitled to the knowledge that God is our Eternal Father and His Beloved Son is our Redeemer. The Savior gave the key by which we may have such knowledge. He declared, "If any man will do his will, he shall know of the doctrine, whether it be of God, or whether I speak of myself" (John 7:17).

Judas Iscariot has gone down in history as the great betrayer, who sold his loyalty for 30 pieces of silver (see Matthew 26:14–15).

How many in our time, to quote the words of Paul, "crucify . . . the Son of God afresh, and put him to an open shame" with profane and blasphemous language? (Hebrews 6:6). You know of the profanity of the school grounds and the street. Avoid it. Never let it cross your lips. Show your loyalty to the God of heaven and to the Redeemer of the world by holding Their names sacred.

Pray to your Heavenly Father in the name of the Lord Jesus Christ, and always, under all circumstances, by the very nature of your lives show your loyalty and your love.

> *Who's on the Lord's side? Who?*
> *Now is the time to show.*
> *We ask it fearlessly:*
> *Who's on the Lord's side? Who?*
> *["Who's on the Lord's Side?"*
> Hymns, *no. 260]*

May the blessings of heaven rest upon you and your families, my dear brethren. May each of us always be found to be true and faithful, men and boys of integrity and absolute loyalty, I pray in the sacred name of Jesus Christ, amen.

# SUNDAY MORNING SESSION

APRIL 6, 2003

$M$Y BRETHREN AND SISTERS, last Sunday as I sat in my study thinking of what I might say on this occasion, I received a phone call telling me that Staff Sergeant James W. Cawley of the U.S. Marines had been killed somewhere in Iraq. He was 41 years of age, leaving behind a wife and two small children.

Twenty years ago Elder Cawley was a missionary of the Church in Japan. Like so many others, he had grown up in the Church, had played as a schoolboy, had passed the sacrament as a deacon, and had been found worthy to serve a mission to teach the gospel of peace to the people of Japan. He returned home, served in the Marines, married, became a policeman, and was then recalled to active military duty, to which he responded without hesitation.

His life, his mission, his military service, his death seem to represent the contradictions of the peace of the gospel and the tides of war.

And so I venture to say something about the war and the gospel we teach. I spoke of this somewhat in our October conference of 2001. When I came to this pulpit at that time, the war against terrorism had just begun. The present war is really an outgrowth and continuation of that conflict. Hopefully it is now drawing to a conclusion.

As I discuss the matter, I seek the direction of the Holy Spirit. I have prayed and pondered much concerning this. I recognize it is a very sensitive subject for an international congregation, including those not of our religious faith.

The nations of the earth have been divided over the present situation. Feelings have run strong. There have been demonstrations for and against. We are now a world Church with members in most of the nations which have argued this matter. Our people have had feelings. They have had concerns.

War, of course, is not new. The weapons change. The ability to kill and destroy is constantly refined. But there has been conflict throughout the ages over essentially the same issues.

The book of Revelation speaks briefly of what must have been a terrible conflict for the minds and loyalties of God's children. The account is worth repeating:

"And there was war in heaven: Michael and his angels fought against the dragon; and the dragon fought and his angels,

"And prevailed not; neither was their place found any more in heaven.

"And the great dragon was cast out, that old serpent, called the Devil, and Satan, which deceiveth the whole world: he was cast out into the earth, and his angels were cast out with him" (Revelation 12:7–9).

Isaiah speaks further concerning that great conflict (see Isaiah 14:12–20). Modern revelation gives additional light (see D&C 76:25–29), as does the book of Moses (see Moses 4:1–4), which tells of Satan's plan to destroy the agency of man.

We sometimes are prone to glorify the great empires of the past, such as the Ottoman Empire, the Roman and Byzantine Empires, and in more recent times, the vast British Empire. But there is a darker side to every one of them. There is a grim and tragic overlay of brutal conquest, of subjugation, of repression, and an astronomical cost in life and treasure.

The great English essayist Thomas Carlyle once ironically shared the observation, "God must needs laugh outright, could such a thing be, to see his wondrous Manikins here below" (quoted in *Sartor Resartus* [1896], 164). I think our Father in Heaven must have wept as He has looked down upon His children through the centuries as they have squandered their divine birthright in ruthlessly destroying one another.

In the course of history, tyrants have arisen from time to time who have oppressed their own people and threatened the world. Such is adjudged to be the case presently, and consequently great and terrifying forces with sophisticated and fearsome armaments have been engaged in battle.

Many of our own Church members have been involved in this conflict. We have seen on television and in the press tearful children clinging to their fathers in uniform, going to the battlefront.

In a touching letter I received just this week, a mother wrote of her Marine son who is serving for the second time in a Middle Eastern war. She says that at the time of his first deployment, "he came home on leave and asked me to go for a walk. . . . He had his arm around me, and he told me about going to war. He . . . said, 'Mom, I have to go so you and the family can be free, free to worship as you please. . . . And if it costs me my life, . . . then giving my life is worth it.'" He is now there again and has written to his family recently, saying, "I am proud to be here serving my nation and our way of life. . . . I feel a lot safer knowing our Heavenly Father is with me."

There are other mothers, innocent civilians, who cling to their children with fear and look heavenward with desperate pleadings as the earth shakes beneath their feet and deadly rockets scream through the dark sky.

There have been casualties in this terrible conflict, and there likely will be more. Public protests will likely continue. Leaders of other nations have, in no uncertain terms, condemned the coalition strategy.

The question arises, "Where does the Church stand in all of this?"

First, let it be understood that we have no quarrel with the Muslim people or with those of any other faith. We recognize and teach that all the people of the earth are of the family of God. And as He is our Father, so are we brothers and sisters with family obligations one to another.

But as citizens we are all under the direction of our respective national leaders. They have access to greater political and military intelligence than do the people generally. Those in the armed services are under obligation to their respective governments to execute the will of the sovereign. When they joined the military service, they entered into a contract by which they are presently bound and to which they have dutifully responded.

One of our Articles of Faith, which represent an expression of our doctrine, states, "We believe in being subject to kings, presidents, rulers, and magistrates, in obeying, honoring, and sustaining the law" (Articles of Faith 1:12).

But modern revelation states that we are to "renounce war and proclaim peace" (D&C 98:16). In a democracy we can renounce war and proclaim peace. There is opportunity for dissent. Many have been speaking out and doing so emphatically. That is their privilege. That is their right, so long as they do so legally. However, we all must also be mindful of another overriding responsibility, which I may add, governs my personal feelings and dictates my personal loyalties in the present situation.

When war raged between the Nephites and the Lamanites, the record states that "the Nephites were inspired by a better cause, for they were not fighting for . . . power but they were fighting for their homes and their liberties, their wives and their children, and their all, yea, for their rites of worship and their church.

"And they were doing that which they felt was the duty which they owed to their God" (Alma 43:45–46).

The Lord counseled them, "Defend your families even unto bloodshed" (Alma 43:47).

And Moroni "rent his coat; and he took a piece thereof, and wrote upon it—In memory of our God, our religion, and freedom, and our peace, our wives, and our children—and he fastened it upon the end of a pole.

"And he fastened on his headplate, and his breastplate, and his shields, and girded on his armor about his loins; and he took the pole, which had on the end thereof his rent coat, (and he called it the title of liberty) and he bowed himself to the earth, and he prayed mightily unto his God for the blessings of liberty to rest upon his brethren" (Alma 46:12–13).

It is clear from these and other writings that there are times and circumstances when nations are justified, in fact have an obligation, to fight for family, for liberty, and against tyranny, threat, and oppression.

When all is said and done, we of this Church are people of peace. We are followers of our Redeemer, the Lord Jesus Christ, who was the Prince of Peace. But even He said, "Think not that I am come to send peace on earth: I came not to send peace, but a sword" (Matthew 10:34).

This places us in the position of those who long for peace, who teach peace, who work for peace, but who also are citizens of nations and are subject to the laws of our governments. Furthermore, we are a freedom-loving people, committed to the defense of liberty wherever it is in jeopardy. I believe that God will not hold men and women in uniform responsible as agents of their government in carrying forward that which they are legally obligated to do. It may even be that He will hold us responsible if we try to impede or hedge up the way of those who are involved in a contest with forces of evil and repression.

Now, there is much that we can and must do in these perilous times. We can give our opinions on the merits of the situation as we see it, but never let us become a party to words or works of evil concerning our brothers and sisters in various nations on one side or the other. Political differences never justify hatred or ill will. I hope that the Lord's people may be at peace one with another during times of trouble, regardless of what loyalties they may have to different governments or parties.

Let us pray for those who are called upon to bear arms by their respective governments and plead for the protection of heaven upon them that they may return to their loved ones in safety.

To our brothers and sisters in harm's way, we say that we pray for you. We pray that the Lord will watch over you and preserve you from injury and that you may return home and pick up your lives again. We know that you are not in that land of blowing sand and brutal heat because you enjoy the games of war. The strength of your commitment is measured by your willingness to give your very lives for that in which you believe.

We know that some have died, and others may yet die in this hot and deadly contest. We can do all in our power to comfort and bless those who lose loved ones. May those who mourn be comforted with that comfort which comes alone from Christ, the Redeemer. It was He who said to His beloved disciples:

"Let not your heart be troubled: ye believe in God, believe also in me.

"In my Father's house are many mansions: if it were not so, I would have told you. I go to prepare a place for you, . . . that where I am, there ye may be also. . . .

"Peace I leave with you, my peace I give unto you: not as the world giveth, give I unto you. Let not your heart be troubled, neither let it be afraid" (John 14:1–3, 27).

We call upon the Lord, whose strength is mighty and whose powers are infinite, to bring an end to the conflict, an end that will result in a better life for all concerned. The Lord has declared, "For I, the Lord, rule in the heavens above, and among the armies of the earth" (D&C 60:4).

We can hope and pray for that glorious day foretold by the prophet Isaiah when men "shall beat their swords into plowshares, and their spears into pruninghooks: nation shall not lift up sword against nation, neither shall they learn war any more" (Isaiah 2:4).

Even in an evil world we can so live our lives as to merit the protecting care of our Father in Heaven. We can be as the righteous living among the evils of Sodom and Gomorrah. Abraham pleaded that these cities might be spared for the sake of the righteous. (See Genesis 18:20–32.)

And, above all, we can cultivate in our own hearts, and proclaim to the world, the salvation of the Lord Jesus Christ. Through His atoning sacrifice we are certain life will continue beyond the veil of death. We can teach that gospel which will lead to the exaltation of the obedient.

Even when the armaments of war ring out in deathly serenade and darkness and hatred reign in the hearts of some, there stands immovable, reassuring, comforting, and with great outreaching love the quiet figure of the Son of God, the Redeemer of the world. We can proclaim with Paul:

"For I am persuaded, that neither death, nor life, nor angels, nor principalities, nor powers, nor things present, nor things to come,

"Nor height, nor depth, nor any other creature, shall be able to separate us from the love of God, which is in Christ Jesus our Lord" (Romans 8:38–39).

This life is but a chapter in the eternal plan of our Father. It is full of conflict and seeming incongruities. Some die young. Some live to old age. We cannot explain it. But we accept it with the certain knowledge that through the atoning sacrifice of our Lord we shall all go on living, and this with the comforting assurance of His immeasurable love.

He has said, "Learn of me, and listen to my words; walk in the meekness of my Spirit, and you shall have peace in me" (D&C 19:23).

And there, my brothers and sisters, we rest our faith. Regardless of the circumstances, we have the comfort and peace of Christ, our Savior, our Redeemer, the living Son of the living God. I so testify in His holy name, even the name of Jesus Christ, amen.

# Sunday Afternoon Session

### APRIL 6, 2003

WELL, MY BELOVED brethren and sisters, it's all over but the work. How grateful we all ought to feel for this wonderful conference. We have met together in peace without disturbance of any kind. We have reflected much on the wonderful blessings of the Lord. Our appreciation for the tremendous blessings which we have in the gospel has been greatly strengthened. As we have heard the testimonies of the speakers, our own witness of the truth has been rekindled into a bright and burning flame. I hope that everyone who has participated in this great conference has been touched for good, that each of us is a better man or woman for our experience together these past two days. I speak for myself when I say that I feel closer to the Lord. I hope this has been your experience. I have a strengthened desire to obey His commandments, to live His teachings, and to commune with Him in prayer, thereby preserving a relationship with Him who is my Father and my God.

And so, as we conclude this great gathering of Latter-day Saints, I offer a plea that each of us will seek to live closer to the Lord and to commune with Him more frequently and with increased faith.

Fathers and mothers, pray over your children. Pray that they may be shielded from the evils of the world. Pray that they may grow in faith and knowledge. Pray that they may be directed toward lives that will be profitable and good. Husbands, pray for your wives. Express unto the Lord your gratitude for them, and plead with Him in their behalf. Wives, pray for your husbands. Many of them walk a very difficult road with countless problems and great perplexities. Plead with the Almighty that they may be guided, blessed, protected, and inspired in their righteous endeavors.

Pray for peace in the earth, that the Almighty, who governs the universe, will stretch forth His hand and let His Spirit brood upon the people, that the nations may not rage one against another.

Pray for the weather. We have floods in one area and drought in another. I am satisfied that if enough prayers ascend to heaven for moisture upon the land, the Lord will answer those prayers for the sake of the righteous.

Way back in 1969 I was in South America. I flew from Argentina to Santiago, Chile. The Andes mountains were dry. There was no snow. The grass was burned. Chile was in the midst of a devastating drought. The people pleaded for help in bringing moisture.

We dedicated two new buildings on that visit. In each of those dedicatory services we pleaded with the Lord for rain upon the land. I have the testimony of many who were in those meetings that the heavens were opened and the rains fell with such abundance that the people asked the Lord to shut them off.

Pray for wisdom and understanding as you walk the difficult paths of your lives. If you are determined to do foolish and imprudent things, I think the Lord will not prevent you. But if you seek His wisdom and follow the counsel of the impressions that come to you, I am confident that you will be blessed.

Let us be a prayerful people. Let us bring up our children "in the nurture and admonition of the Lord" (Enos 1:1).

May the blessings of heaven deservedly rest upon you. In the words of Deuteronomy, "And now, Israel, what doth the Lord thy God require of thee, but to fear the Lord thy God, to walk in all his ways, and to love him, and to serve the Lord thy God with all thy heart and with all thy soul" (Deuteronomy 10:12). Be assured, my dear brothers and sisters, that "He, watching over Israel, slumbers not, nor sleeps" (Felix Mendelssohn, *Elijah*).

For the blessings of heaven to rest upon you I humbly pray as I express to you my love for each of you. Thank you for your great kindness to me and your great faithfulness and energy in moving forward the work of the Almighty, in the name of the Lord Jesus Christ, amen.

# General Relief Society Meeting

SEPTEMBER 27, 2003

SOMEONE HAS SAID, "Be kind to the women. They constitute half the population and are mothers to the other half."

My dear sisters, you marvelous women who have chosen the better part, I stand in great admiration for all that you do. I see your hands in everything.

Many of you are mothers, and that is enough to occupy one's full time.

You are companions—the very best friends your husbands have or ever will have.

You are housekeepers. That doesn't sound like much, does it? But what a job it is to keep a house clean and tidy.

You are shoppers. Until I got older I never dreamed of what a demanding responsibility it is to keep food in the pantry, to keep clothing neat and presentable, to buy all that is needed to keep a home running.

You are nurses. With every illness that comes along, you are the first to be told about it and the first to respond with help. In cases of serious sickness, you are at the bedside day and night, comforting, encouraging, ministering, praying.

You are the family chauffeur. You are driving your children about on paper routes, taking them to athletic events, driving them on ward outings, hauling here, there, and everywhere as they pursue their busy lives.

And so I might go on. My children are now all grown. Some are in their sixties. But when they call and I answer the phone, they say, "How are you?" And before I can answer, they ask, "Is Mother there?"

She has been their strength all of their lives. Since they were babies they have looked to her, and she has always responded with affection, guidance, teaching, blessing their lives in every way.

Now we have granddaughters who are mothers. They visit us, and I marvel at their patience, at their capacity to calm their children, to stop them from crying, and it seems to me to do a thousand other things. They drive cars, they run computers, they attend the activities of their children, they cook and sew, they teach classes, and they speak in church.

I see their husbands, and I feel like saying to them, "Wake up. Carry your share of the load. Do you really appreciate your wife? Do you know how much she does? Do you ever compliment her? Do you ever say thanks to her?"

Well, you dear women, I say thanks to you. Thank you for being the kind of people you are and doing the things you do. May the blessings of heaven rest upon you. May your prayers be answered and your hopes and dreams become realities.

You serve so well in the Church. You think it is so demanding. It is. But with every responsibility fulfilled, there comes a great reward.

Many of you think you are failures. You feel you cannot do well, that with all of your effort it is not sufficient. We all feel that way. I feel that way as I speak to you tonight. I long for, I pray for the power and the capacity to lift you, to inspire you, to thank you, to praise you, and to bring a measure of gladness into your hearts. We all worry about our performance. We all wish we could do

189

better. But unfortunately we do not realize, we do not often see the results that come of what we do.

I remember going to a stake conference in the East many years ago. On the plane coming home, I felt that I had been a total failure. I felt I had not touched anyone for good. I was miserable with a sense of inadequacy.

Then, some years later, I was at another conference in California. At the conclusion of the meeting, a man came up to me and said, "You were at a conference a few years ago in such-and-such a place."

"Yes," I said, "I was there, and I remember the occasion."

The man said, "You touched my heart. I came to that meeting out of curiosity. I really had no interest. I was on the verge of leaving the Church. But when it was announced that one of the Twelve Apostles would be there, I decided to go.

"You said something that started me to think. It touched me and stayed with me and stirred me. I decided to alter my course. I turned my life around. I am now living here in California. I have a good job, for which I am grateful. I hope I am a good husband and father. And I am now serving as a counselor in the bishopric of my ward. I am happier than I have ever been at any time in my life."

I thanked him, and when I left him I said to myself, shaking my head, "You never know. You never know whether you do any good. You never know how much good you do."

Now, my dear sisters, that is the way with you. You are doing the best you can, and that best results in good to yourself and to others. Do not nag yourself with a sense of failure. Get on your knees and ask for the blessings of the Lord; then stand on your feet and do what you are asked to do. Then leave the matter in the hands of the Lord. You will discover that you have accomplished something beyond price.

Now, we have a very diverse group to whom I am speaking. This includes young women who are still in school or who are working. You are single. You are hoping to catch that perfect man. I have yet to see one who is perfect. Aim high, but do not aim so high that you totally miss the target. What really matters is that he will love you, that he will respect you, that he will honor you, that he will be absolutely true to you, that he will give you freedom of expression and let you fly in the development of your own talents. He is not going to be perfect, but if he is kind and thoughtful, if he knows how to work and earn a living, if he is honest and full of faith, the chances are that you will not go wrong, that you will be immensely happy.

Some of you, unfortunately, will never marry in this life. That turns out to be the case sometimes. If that happens, do not spend your life grieving over it. The world still needs your talents. It needs your contribution. The Church needs your faith. It needs your strong, helping hand. Life is never a failure until we call it such. There are so many who need your helping hands, your loving smile, your tender thoughtfulness. I see so many capable, attractive, wonderful women whom romance has passed by. I do not understand it, but I know that in the plan of the Almighty, the eternal plan which we call God's plan of happiness, there will be opportunity and reward for all who seek them.

To you young women with small children, yours is a tremendous challenge. So often there is not enough money. You must scrimp and save. You must be wise and careful in your expenditures. You must be strong and bold and brave and march forward with gladness in your eye and love in your heart. How blessed you are, my dear young mothers. You have children who will be yours forever. I hope that you have been sealed in the house of the Lord and that your family will be an everlasting family in the kingdom of our Father.

May you be given strength to carry your heavy load, to meet every obligation, to walk side by side with a good and faithful and caring man, and together with him rear and nurture and bring up your children in righteousness and truth. Nothing else you will ever own, no worldly thing you will ever acquire will be worth so much as the love of your children. God bless you, my dear, dear young mothers.

Then we have you older women who are neither young nor old. You are in the most wonderful season of your lives. Your children are in their teens. Possibly one or two are married. Some are on missions, and you are sacrificing to keep them in the field. You are hoping and praying for their success and happiness. To you dear women I offer some special counsel.

"Count your blessings; name them one by one" (*Hymns,* no. 241). You don't need a great big mansion of a house with an all-consuming mortgage that goes on forever. You do need a comfortable and pleasant home where love abides. Someone has said that there is no more beautiful picture than that of a good woman cooking a meal for those she loves. Weigh carefully that which you do. You do not need some of the extravagances that working outside the home might bring. Weigh carefully the importance of your being in the home when your children come from school.

Mothers, take good care of your daughters. Be close to them. Listen to them. Talk with them. Lead them from doing foolish things. Guide them into doing the right thing. See that they dress in a comely and modest fashion. Safeguard them from the terrible evils that are all about them.

Nurture your sons with love and counsel. Teach them the importance of personal cleanliness, of neatness in their dress. Sloppy ways lead to sloppy lives. Instill in them a sense of discipline. Keep them worthy of service to the Church as missionaries. Give them things to do so that they may learn to work. Teach them to be frugal. Labor and frugality lead to prosperity. Teach them that nothing really good happens after 11 o'clock at night. And do not spoil them. If they go on missions, they may be compelled to live in

192

circumstances that you would not wish for them. Do not worry about them. Give them encouragement.

Stir within your children the desire for education. This is the latchkey to success in life. And at the same time, teach them that as President David O. McKay was wont to remind us, "No other success can compensate for failure in the home" (quoting J. E. McCulloch, *Home: The Savior of Civilization* [1924], 42; in Conference Report, Apr. 1935, 116).

Now I speak to you single mothers whose burdens are so heavy because you have been abandoned or have been widowed. Yours is a terrible load. Bear it well. Seek the blessings of the Lord. Be grateful for any assistance that may come out of the quorums of the priesthood to help you in your home or with other matters. Pray silently in your closet, and let the tears flow if they must come. But put a smile on your face whenever you are before your children or others.

Now to you dear grandmothers, you older widows, and older lonely women. How beautiful you are. I look upon my dear wife, soon to be 92 years of age. Her hair is white; her frame is stooped. I take one of her hands in mine and look at it. Once it was so beautiful, the flesh firm and clear. Now it is wrinkled and a little bony and not very strong. But it speaks of love and constancy and faith, of hard work through the years. Her memory is not what it once was. She can remember things that happened half a century ago but may not remember what happened half an hour ago. I am like that too.

But I am so grateful for her. For 66 years we have walked together, hand in hand, with love and encouragement, with appreciation and respect. It cannot be very long before one of us will step through the veil. I hope the other will follow soon. I just would not know how to get along without her, even on the other side, and I would hope that she would not know how to get along without me.

My dear friends of the Relief Society, whatever your circumstances, wherever you may live, may the windows of heaven be opened and blessings come down upon you. May you live with love one for another. May you reach down to lift up those whose burdens are heavy. May you bring light and beauty to the world and particularly into your homes and into the lives of your children.

You know as I do that God, our Eternal Father, lives. He loves you. You know as I do that Jesus is the Christ, His immortal Son, our Redeemer. You know that the gospel is true and that heaven is near if we will cultivate it in our lives.

You are the Relief Society of The Church of Jesus Christ of Latter-day Saints. There is no other organization to equal it. Walk with pride. Hold your heads up. Work with diligence. Do whatever the Church asks you to do. Pray with faith. You may never know how much good you accomplish. Someone's life will be blessed by your effort. May you know the comforting, rewarding embrace of the Holy Spirit, I pray in the sacred name of Jesus Christ, amen.

# 173RD SEMIANNUAL GENERAL CONFERENCE

# SATURDAY MORNING SESSION

OCTOBER 4, 2003

M Y BELOVED BRETHREN AND SISTERS throughout the world, we send greetings in the name of our Redeemer. We send our love and our blessing. I commend you most warmly on what you are doing to move forward the work of the Lord.

Now and again I quietly reflect on the growth and impact of this work. I reflect on that meeting with a few present in the Peter Whitmer farmhouse on the 6th of April 1830. Here the Church was organized, and here began the long march which has brought it to its present stature.

Our people have passed through oppression and persecution; they have suffered drivings and every imaginable evil. And out of all of that has come something which today is glorious to behold.

In the opening of this work the Lord declared:

Hearken, O ye people of my church, saith the voice of him who dwells on high, and whose eyes are upon all men; yea, verily I say: Hearken ye people from afar; and ye that are upon the islands of the sea, listen together.

For verily the voice of the Lord is unto all men, and there is none to escape; and there is no eye that shall not see, neither ear that shall not hear, neither heart that shall not be penetrated. . . .

> And the voice of warning shall be unto all people, by the mouths of my disciples, whom I have chosen in these last days.
>
> And they shall go forth and none shall stay them, for I the Lord have commanded them. [D&C 1:1–2, 4–5]

There can be no doubt concerning our responsibility to the peoples of the earth. There can be no doubt that we are moving forward in pursuing that responsibility.

As I speak to you today, most members of the Church, regardless of where you live, can hear me. It is a miracle. Who in the earlier days could have dreamed of this season of opportunity in which we live?

We now have strong congregations in every state of the United States and in every province of Canada. We have such in every state of Mexico, in every nation of Central America, and throughout the nations of South America. We have strong congregations in Australia and New Zealand and the isles of the Pacific. We are well established in the nations of the Orient. We are in every nation of Western Europe and in much of Eastern Europe, and we are firmly established in Africa.

We are being recognized for the tremendous virtues of our programs and the vast good which they do. A California newspaper recently commented:

> The white shirts, backpacks and bicycles give them away, even before you spot the Book of Mormon.
>
> They're stereotyped, for good reason.
>
> These armies of young men—missionaries in the Church of Jesus Christ of Latter-day Saints—are strictly regimented while serving missions around the globe.
>
> For two years, they spend 60 hours a week doing ecclesiastical work, praying, studying, and telling others about the Gospel that drove them to leave families, friends and the comfort of home behind.

Contact with their loved ones is limited to letters and two calls a year.

They live frugally, in private homes and apartments with companion missionaries, rising at 6 A.M. to study and pray for guidance in the work they will do until long after the sun sets. . . .

This life, they say, is a sacrifice—and the most "fun" they can imagine. [Priscilla Nordyke Roden, "Answering the Call," *San Bernardino County Sun*, Aug. 26, 2003, B1]

That might have been written of our missionaries in the more than 120 nations in which they are found serving.

What a miracle it is that we should have some 60,000 of them, most of them young, giving of their time and their testimonies to the world.

I recently met with a group of missionaries who were to be released the next day to return home. They were from various nations across the earth, from Mongolia to Madagascar. They were clean and bright and enthusiastic. They bespoke love for the Church, for their mission president, for their companions. What a marvelous thing is this unique and tremendous program of the Church.

Likewise other programs.

We recently were applauded in the public press for giving three million dollars to vaccinate children against measles in Africa. This money did not come from tithing. It came from contributions of the faithful to the humanitarian work of the Church. We have joined the American Red Cross, the United Nations Foundation, the Centers for Disease Control and Prevention, the United Nations Children's Fund, the World Health Organization, and the Pan American Health Organization in an effort to immunize 200 million children and prevent 1.2 million deaths from measles over the next five years. Our contribution alone will provide vaccine for three million children. What a marvelous and wonderful thing that is. And so it is with each of our humanitarian programs.

One more item.

In March 2001 we announced that the Church was establishing a plan to assist our returned missionaries and other young adults in gaining education and training leading to better employment opportunities in countries with less abundance and fewer opportunities. We invited those who wished to help in this plan to contribute to a fund called the Perpetual Education Fund, patterned after the 19th-century Perpetual Emigration Fund. I offer a brief report on what is happening with that plan.

Because of your generous contributions, we have been able to keep current with the growing need for loans. To date the Church has granted about 10,000 loans to young men and women in Latin America, Asia, Africa, and other areas of the Church. These young people have committed to repay their loans so that others may enjoy the same opportunities they are experiencing.

Many have graduated and are experiencing the benefits of their training. To date, about 600 young men and women have completed their training. The majority of these have found good employment. Many more will graduate and enter the workforce in their own communities in the months ahead. They will make their mark in the world, rear families, and serve the Church. Many are already achieving these objectives.

For example, Patrick was the first Perpetual Education Fund student to complete school in Jamaica. His basic training in management earned him a well-paying job at the national airport, with a promising future. Repayment of his loan began immediately.

Flavia, a sister from a poorer part of South America, found little opportunity and means for training and regular employment until help came through the PEF to receive training in operating computers. With the help of LDS Employment Services, she found work in a good company after completing her training. She reports:

"Today I am responsible for the financial consulting area of one of the largest hospitals in Recife using [a sophisticated] computer system. I was among the crew that implemented this financial system in the company."

These examples could be multiplied. We are happy to report that the plan is working well and gradually expanding as we gain experience. Early reports of loan repayments are encouraging. Again, we thank you for your generosity, interest, and prayers in behalf of the Perpetual Education Fund.

It was said that at one time the sun never set on the British Empire. That empire has now been diminished. But it is true that the sun never sets on this work of the Lord as it is touching the lives of people across the earth.

And this is only the beginning. We have scarcely scratched the surface. We are engaged in a work for the souls of men and women everywhere. Our work knows no boundaries. Under the providence of the Lord it will continue. Those nations now closed to us will someday be open. That is my faith. That is my belief. That is my testimony.

The little stone which was cut out of the mountain without hands is rolling forth to fill the earth (see Daniel 2:31–45; D&C 65:2).

To the Latter-day Saints everywhere, as we gather in this great conference, I say, may God bless you. Keep the faith; be true to your covenants. Walk in the light of the gospel. Build the kingdom of God in the earth.

The Church is in wonderful condition and can and will improve. It will grow and strengthen.

We are ordinary people who are engaged in an extraordinary undertaking. We are men who hold the priesthood of the living God. Those who have gone before have accomplished wonders. It is our opportunity and our challenge to continue in this great undertaking, the future of which we can scarcely imagine.

Thank you, my brothers and sisters, for your faith and faithfulness. Thank you for the love you carry for this, the work of the Almighty. We live in the world. We work in the world. But we must rise above the world as we pursue the work of the Lord and seek to build His kingdom in the earth. Let us now join together in a great world conference of men and women who are indeed brothers and sisters as children of God.

During the next two days we shall hear from many of our number, not one of whom has been told what to speak about, but each one of whom has pleaded with the Lord to be able to say something that will help, inspire, and lift all who hear.

May the blessings of heaven attend you. May you be faithful and true to the great and glorious cause which you have embraced is my humble prayer, in the name of our Redeemer, even the Lord Jesus Christ, amen.

# PRIESTHOOD
# SESSION

OCTOBER 4, 2003

Brethren, tonight I am going to do something a little unusual. I am going to repeat some elements of a talk which I gave 15 years ago in our general priesthood meeting. I am going to speak of and to the bishops of the Church, this wonderful body of men who are in a very real sense the shepherds of Israel.

Everyone who participates in this conference is accountable to a bishop or a branch president. Tremendous are the burdens which they carry, and I invite every member of the Church to do all that he or she can to lift the burden under which our bishops and branch presidents labor.

We must pray for them. They need help as they carry their heavy loads. We can be more supportive and less dependent upon them. We can assist them in every way possible. We can thank them for all that they do for us. We are wearing them out in a short time by the burdens which we impose upon them.

We have more than 18,000 bishops in the Church. Every one is a man who has been called by the spirit of prophecy and revelation and set apart and ordained by the laying on of hands. Every one of them holds the keys of the presidency of his ward. Each is a high priest, the presiding high priest of his ward. Each carries tremendous responsibilities of stewardship. Each stands as a father to his people.

None receives money for his service. No ward bishop is compensated by the Church for his work as a bishop.

The requirements of a bishop today are as they were in the days of Paul, who wrote to Timothy:

> A bishop then must be blameless, the husband of one wife, vigilant, sober, of good behaviour, given to hospitality, apt to teach;
>
> Not given to wine, no striker [that is, not a bully or a violent person], . . . not a brawler, not covetous;
>
> One that ruleth well his own house, having his children in subjection with all gravity;
>
> (For if a man know not how to rule his own house, how shall he take care of the church of God?)
>
> Not a novice, lest being lifted up with pride he fall into the condemnation of the devil. [1 Timothy 3:2–6]

In his letter to Titus, Paul adds that "a bishop must be blameless, as the steward of God; . . . holding fast the faithful word as he hath been taught, that he may be able by sound doctrine both to exhort and to convince the gainsayers" (Titus 1:7, 9).

Those words aptly describe a bishop today in The Church of Jesus Christ of Latter-day Saints.

Let me now speak directly to the thousands of bishops who are in attendance tonight. Let me say first that I love you for your integrity and goodness. You must be men of integrity. You must stand as examples to the congregations over which you preside. You must stand on higher ground so that you can lift others. You must be absolutely honest, for you handle the funds of the Lord, the tithes of the people, the offerings that come of their fasting, and the contributions which they make from their own strained resources. How great is your trust as the keepers of the purse of the Lord!

Your goodness must be as an ensign to your people. Your morals must be impeccable. The wiles of the adversary may be held before you because he knows that if he can destroy you, he can injure an entire ward. You must exercise wisdom in all of your relationships lest someone read into your observed actions some taint of moral sin. You cannot succumb to the temptation to read pornographic literature or even in the secrecy of your own chamber to view pornographic films. Your moral strength must be such that if ever you are called on to sit in judgment on the questionable morals of others, you may do so without personal compromise or embarrassment.

You cannot use your office as bishop to further your own business interests lest through some ensuing financial mishap accusation be placed against you by those who succumbed to your persuasiveness.

You cannot compromise your qualifications to sit as a common judge in Israel. It is a fearsome and awesome responsibility to stand as a judge of the people. You must be their judge in some instances as to worthiness to hold membership in the Church, worthiness to enter the house of the Lord, worthiness to be baptized, worthiness to receive the priesthood, worthiness to serve missions, worthiness to teach and to serve as officers in the organizations. You must be the judge of their eligibility in times of distress to receive help from the fast offerings of the people and commodities from the storehouse of the Lord. None for whom you are responsible must go hungry or without clothing or shelter though they be reluctant to ask. You must know something of the circumstances of all of the flock over whom you preside.

You must be their counselor, their comforter, their anchor and strength in times of sorrow and trouble. You must be strong with that strength which comes from the Lord. You must be wise with that wisdom which comes from the Lord. Your door must be open to hear their cries and your back strong to carry their burdens, your heart sensitive to judge their needs, your godly love broad enough and strong enough to encompass even the wrongdoer and the critic. You must be a man of patience, willing to listen and striving to understand. You are the only one to whom some can turn. You must be there when every other source has failed. Permit me to read you a few lines from a letter sent to a bishop.

> Dear Bishop:
>
> It has been almost two years since I desperately called you asking for help. At that time I was ready to kill myself. I had no one else to turn to—no money, no job, no friends. My house had been taken, and I had no place to live. The Church was my last hope.
>
> As you know, I had left the Church at the age of 17 and had broken just about every rule and commandment that there was in my search for happiness and fulfillment. Instead of happiness, my life was filled with misery, anguish, and despair. There was no hope or future for me. I even pleaded with God to let me die, to take me out of my misery. Not even He wanted me. I felt that He had rejected me too.
>
> That's when I turned to you and the Church. . . .
>
> You listened with understanding, you counseled, you guided, you helped.
>
> I began to grow and develop in understanding and knowledge of the gospel. I found that I had to make certain basic changes in my life that were terribly difficult, but that within me I had the worth and strength to do so.
>
> I learned that as I lived the gospel and repented, I had no more fear. I was filled with an inner peace. The clouds of anguish and despair were gone. Because of the Atonement, my weaknesses and sins were forgiven through Jesus Christ and His love for me.
>
> He has blessed and strengthened me. He has opened pathways for me, given me direction, and kept me from harm. I have found that as I overcame each obstacle, my business began to grow, enabling my family to benefit and making me feel as though I had accomplished something.
>
> Bishop, you have given me understanding and support

through these past two years. I never would have reached this point if not for your love and patience. Thank you for being what you are as the servant of the Lord to help me, His wandering child.

Bishops, you stand as watchmen on the tower of the wards over which you preside. There are many teachers in each ward. But you must be the chief teacher among them. You must see that there is no false doctrine creeping in among the people. You must see that they grow in faith and testimony, in integrity and righteousness and a sense of service. You must see that their love for the Lord strengthens and manifests itself in greater love for one another.

You must be their confessor, privy to their deepest secrets, holding absolutely inviolate the confidences placed in you. Yours is a privileged communication that must be guarded and respected against all intruders. There may be temptations to tell. You cannot succumb.

Unless specifically mandated by legal requirement in cases of abuse, what is told to you in confidence must remain with you. The Church maintains a hotline which you should call concerning cases of abuse which may come to you.

You as an individual preside over the Aaronic Priesthood of the ward. You are their leader, their teacher, their example, whether you wish to be or not. You are the presiding high priest, the father to the ward family, to be called upon as arbiter in disagreements, as defender of the accused.

You preside in meetings where the doctrine is taught. You are accountable for the spiritual nature of those meetings and for the administration of the sacrament to the members, that all may be reminded of sacred covenants and obligations incumbent upon those who have taken upon them the name of the Lord.

You must stand as the strong friend of the widow and the orphan, the weak and the beleaguered, the attacked and the helpless.

The sound of your trumpet must be certain and unequivocal. In your ward you stand as the head of the army of the Lord, leading them on to victory in the conquest against sin, indifference, and apostasy.

I know that the work is hard at times. There are never enough hours to get it done. The calls are numerous and frequent. You have other things to do. That is true. You must not rob your employer of the time and energy that are rightfully his. You must not rob your family of time which belongs to them. But as most of you have come to know, as you seek for divine guidance, you are blessed with wisdom beyond your own and strength and capacity you did not know you had. It is possible to budget your time so that you neglect neither your employer, your family, nor your flock.

God bless the good bishops of The Church of Jesus Christ of Latter-day Saints. You may on occasion be inclined to complain about the burdens of your office. But you also know the joys of your service. Heavy as the load may be, you know this is the sweetest, the most rewarding, the most important thing you have ever done outside the walls of your own home.

I thank the Lord for you. I thank the Lord for the good bishops in this Church throughout the world. I pray for you—all 18,000 of you. I plead with you to be strong. I plead with you to be true. I plead with you to be uncompromising in your own lives and in the goals you set for others. Though your days be long and wearisome, may your rest be sweet and in your hearts may you know that peace which comes alone from God to those who serve Him.

I bear testimony of the strength and goodness of the bishops of this Church. I pay tribute to counselors who help them and to all who serve under their direction in response to the calls they make.

We do not expect the impossible from you. We ask that you do the very best you can. Delegate to others every aspect of the work that you legitimately can. And then leave matters in the hands of the Lord.

Someday you will be released. It will be a time of sadness for you. But there will be comfort as your people thank you. Nor will they ever forget you. They will remember you and speak with appreciation through years to come, for among all Church officers you are nearest to them. You have been called, ordained, and set apart as shepherds to the flock. You have been endowed with discernment, judgment, and love to bless their lives. In the process, you will bless your own.

I bear testimony of the divine nature of your calling and of the magnificent way in which you fulfill it. May you, your counselors, your wives, and your children be blessed as you serve the children of the Lord, I humbly pray, in the sacred name of Jesus Christ, amen.

# Sunday Morning
# Session

OCTOBER 5, 2003

My beloved brethren and sisters, I wish to acknowledge my gratitude for your sustaining faith and prayers. The Lord has imposed upon the leadership of this Church a great and serious trust, and you have supported us in that responsibility. We know that you pray for us, and we wish you to know that we pray for you. Not a day passes that I do not thank the Lord for faithful Latter-day Saints. No day passes that I do not pray that He will bless you wherever you are and whatever your needs.

I wish to remind you that we are all in this together. It is not a matter of the General Authorities on one hand and the membership of the Church on the other. We are all working as one in a great cause. We are all members of the Church of Jesus Christ.

Within your sphere of responsibility you have as serious an obligation as do I within my sphere of responsibility. Each of us should be determined to build the kingdom of God on the earth and to further the work of righteousness.

I think I can honestly say that we have no selfish desires with reference to this work other than that it succeed.

We of the First Presidency are constantly dealing with a great variety of problems. They come before us every day. At the close of one particularly difficult day, I looked up at a portrait of Brigham

Young that hangs on my wall. I asked, "Brother Brigham, what should we do?" I thought I saw him smile a little, and then he seemed to say, "In my day, I had problems enough of my own. Don't ask me what to do. This is your watch. Ask the Lord, whose work this really is." And this, I assure you, is what we do and must always do.

As I reflected on these matters that recent difficult day, I opened my Bible to the first chapter of Joshua and read these words: "Have not I commanded thee? Be strong and of a good courage; be not afraid, neither be thou dismayed: for the Lord thy God is with thee" (Joshua 1:9).

I said to myself, "There is never reason to despair. This is the work of God. Notwithstanding the efforts of all who oppose it, it will go forward as the God of heaven has designed it should do."

I turned the pages of the Old Testament to the second chapter of Isaiah and read these words:

"And it shall come to pass in the last days, that the mountain of the Lord's house shall be established in the top of the mountains, and shall be exalted above the hills; and all nations shall flow unto it.

"And many people shall go and say, Come ye, and let us go up to the mountain of the Lord, to the house of the God of Jacob; and he will teach us of his ways, and we will walk in his paths: for out of Zion shall go forth the law, and the word of the Lord from Jerusalem" (Isaiah 2:2–3).

Ever since the Salt Lake Temple was dedicated, we have interpreted that scripture from Isaiah, repeated again in Micah (see Micah 4:1–2), as applying to this sacred house of the Lord. And of this place, since the day of its dedication, an ever-increasing number from across the world have said in effect, "Come ye, and let us go up to the mountain of the Lord, to the house of the God of Jacob, that He might teach us of His ways, that we might walk in His paths."

I believe and testify that it is the mission of this Church to stand as an ensign to the nations and a light to the world. We have had placed upon us a great, all-encompassing mandate from which we cannot shrink nor turn aside. We accept that mandate and are determined to fulfill it, and with the help of God we shall do it.

There are forces all around us that would deter us from that effort. The world is constantly crowding in on us. From all sides we feel the pressure to soften our stance, to give in here a little and there a little.

We must never lose sight of our objective. We must ever keep before us the goal which the Lord has set for us.

To quote Paul:

"Finally, my brethren, be strong in the Lord, and in the power of his might.

"Put on the whole armour of God, that ye may be able to stand against the wiles of the devil.

"For we wrestle not against flesh and blood, but against principalities, against powers, against the rulers of the darkness of this world, against spiritual wickedness in high places" (Ephesians 6:10–12).

We must stand firm. We must hold back the world. If we do so, the Almighty will be our strength and our protector, our guide and our revelator. We shall have the comfort of knowing that we are doing what He would have us do. Others may not agree with us, but I am confident that they will respect us. We will not be left alone. There are many not of our faith but who feel as we do. They will support us. They will sustain us in our efforts.

We cannot be arrogant. We cannot be self-righteous. The very situation in which the Lord has placed us requires that we be humble as the beneficiaries of His direction.

While we cannot agree with others on certain matters, we must never be disagreeable. We must be friendly, soft-spoken, neighborly, and understanding.

Now I emphasize a theme already treated in this conference. To our young people, the glorious youth of this generation, I say, be true. Hold to the faith. Stand firmly for what you know to be right.

You face tremendous temptation. It comes at you in the halls of popular entertainment, on the Internet, in the movies, on television, in cheap literature, and in other ways—subtle, titillating, and difficult to resist. Peer pressure may be almost overpowering. But, my dear young friends, you must not give in. You must be strong. You must take the long look ahead rather than succumbing to the present seductive temptation.

Uncouth-looking entertainers draw big crowds of our youth. They grow rich from high admission prices. Their songs, so many of them, are suggestive in nature.

Pornography is everywhere with its seductive invitation. You must turn away from it. It can enslave you. It can destroy you. Recognize it for what it is—tawdry and sleazy stuff created and distributed by those who grow rich at the expense of those who see it.

The sanctity of sex is utterly destroyed in its salacious portrayal in the media. That which by its nature is inherently beautiful is corrupted in its popular presentation. I was pleased to note that our Church-owned television station here in Salt Lake City refused to carry a network program of a salacious nature. It was also interesting to note that the only other station belonging to this network to cancel the broadcast was one in South Bend, Indiana, the location of the University of Notre Dame. It is comforting to know that there are others who feel as strongly as we feel and are willing to do something about it.

Life is better than that which is so frequently portrayed. Nature is better than that. Love is better than that. This kind of entertainment is only an evil caricature of the good and the beautiful.

You young men and women who are hearing me today, you university students on many campuses realize that one of the great problems on these campuses is binge drinking. It diminishes abilities. It destroys lives. It wastes money and time and constructive effort. What a sorry sight it is to see bright young people damage themselves and ruin their opportunities with excessive drinking.

It was a great tribute to the students of Brigham Young University when the *Princeton Review* found them to be the most "stone-cold sober" student body in America. Most of you, of course, cannot attend BYU, but wherever you are you can live by the same standards required on the BYU campus.

I recently read in our *New Era* magazine an article on young Latter-day Saints in Memphis, Tennessee. In some instances they are the only Latter-day Saints on campus. One of them is quoted as saying, "I may be the only member in my school, but . . . even when I'm physically alone, I'm never spiritually alone" (in Arianne B. Cope, "Smiling in Memphis," *New Era*, Oct. 2003, 23–24).

Another is quoted: "I know a lot of teens wonder if they really know if the gospel is true. But . . . here you have to know one way or the other because people are asking you about it every day. Every time you answer a question, you share your testimony" (New Era, Oct. 2003, 25).

These young people, scattered through that big city, have learned to stand together, to bolster one another.

God bless you, my dear young friends. You are the best generation we have ever had. You know the gospel better. You are more faithful in your duties. You are stronger to face the temptations which come your way. Live by your standards. Pray for the guidance and protection of the Lord. He will never leave you alone. He will comfort you. He will sustain you. He will bless and magnify you and make your reward sweet and beautiful. And you will discover that your example will attract others who will take courage from your strength.

As it is with the youth, so it is with you adults. If we are to hold up this Church as an ensign to the nations and a light to the world, we must take on more of the luster of the life of Christ individually and in our own personal circumstances. In standing for the right, we must not be fearful of the consequences. We must never be afraid. Said Paul to Timothy:

"For God hath not given us the spirit of fear; but of power, and of love, and of a sound mind.

"Be not thou therefore ashamed of the testimony of our Lord" (2 Timothy 1:7–8).

This Church, I submit, is far more than a social organization where we gather together to enjoy one another's company. It is more than Sunday School and Relief Society and priesthood meeting. It is more than sacrament meeting, more even than temple service. It is the kingdom of God in the earth. It behooves us to act in a manner befitting membership in that kingdom.

You men who hold the priesthood have such a tremendous responsibility. You must avoid the sultry siren voice of the world. You must rise above it. You must stand in the stature of the priesthood of God. You must eschew evil in all of its forms and take on the nature of goodness and decency, letting the light, the divine light, shine through your actions.

There is no way that a home can be a place of refuge and peace if the man who resides there is not an understanding and helpful husband and father. The strength to be gained from our homes will make us better able to face the world, more acceptable to the society in which we move, more valuable to those who employ us— better men.

I know many such men. It is evident that they love their wives and their children. They are proud of them. And the marvelous thing is, they are tremendously successful in their chosen professions. They are magnified and honored and respected.

And to you women. I spoke at length to the women of the Relief Society a week ago. That talk represented my heartfelt views

213

concerning you. You too can take on the luster of Christ. You too can be strong and encouraging and beautiful and helpful.

I remind all of us that we are Latter-day Saints. We have made covenants with our Heavenly Father, sacred and binding. Those covenants, if we keep them, will make us better fathers and mothers, better sons and daughters.

I believe that others will rally around us if we will do so. We can stand for truth and goodness, and we will not stand alone. Moreover, we shall have the unseen forces of heaven to assist us.

I take you back to the Old Testament:

"And when the servant of the man of God was risen early, and gone forth, behold, an host compassed the city both with horses and chariots. And his servant said unto him, Alas, my master! how shall we do?

"And he answered, Fear not: for they that be with us are more than they that be with them.

"And Elisha prayed, and said, Lord, I pray thee, open his eyes, that he may see. And the Lord opened the eyes of the young man; and he saw: and, behold, the mountain was full of horses and chariots of fire round about Elisha" (2 Kings 6:15–17).

The Lord has said to us:

"Therefore, fear not, little flock; do good; let earth and hell combine against you, for if ye are built upon my rock, they cannot prevail. . . .

"Look unto me in every thought; doubt not, fear not" (D&C 6:34, 36).

In the name of Jesus Christ, amen.

# Sunday Afternoon
# Session

OCTOBER 5, 2003

WHAT A GLORIOUS TIME we have had together, my beloved brethren and sisters. It is truly a wonderful thing to step out of the world, as it were, and set aside two days to reflect on things divine.

We are all so busy with our mundane pursuits which pull us this way and that. We all need, the whole world needs, the opportunity to meditate and reflect on the things of God and to listen to words that inspire and help.

Our testimonies have been strengthened, and it is good, for as President Harold B. Lee once said, our testimonies need renewing every day (see regional representatives' seminar, Dec. 12, 1970).

I am satisfied that the Latter-day Saints have within their hearts a desire to do the right thing, to live after the manner which the Lord has outlined for us. We have been reminded of many of these things during this conference.

I hope that when we return to our homes, before retiring for the night, we each will get on our knees and express our appreciation and ask for the strength to live the gospel more fully as a result of this conference.

I am so grateful for the beautiful music of the choir; they have sung so wonderfully. This is such a great and dedicated organization, and we thank all who give so generously of their time and

215

talents to this great effort. I am grateful for the music yesterday of the singles choir; they were an inspiration. And the great singing last night of the young men in the Missionary Training Center, who came and sang to us with great power, thank you so very much for what you have given us.

Now I would like to read in conclusion just a few words from Moroni:

"And awake, and arise from the dust, O Jerusalem; yea, and put on thy beautiful garments, O daughter of Zion; and strengthen thy stakes and enlarge thy borders forever, that thou mayest no more be confounded, that the covenants of the Eternal Father which he hath made unto thee, O house of Israel, may be fulfilled.

"Yea, come unto Christ, and be perfected in him, and deny yourselves of all ungodliness; and if ye shall deny yourselves of all ungodliness, and love God with all your might, mind and strength, then is his grace sufficient for you, that by his grace ye may be perfect in Christ; and if by the grace of God ye are perfect in Christ, ye can in nowise deny the power of [Christ]" (Moroni 10:31–32).

As a result of this great conference, each of us should be a better man or a better woman, a better boy or a better girl. Thank you so much, my brothers and sisters, for your great service in moving this work forward. What a tremendous work you are doing, you faithful Latter-day Saints all across the world, who carry in your hearts a firm and unswerving testimony of the reality of the living God and of the Lord Jesus Christ, our Savior and our Redeemer, and of Their appearance in this dispensation to begin anew a great era in the history of the world in preparation for that time when the Son of God shall come to reign as Lord of lords and King of Kings.

May the blessings of heaven rest upon you, my dear friends. I pray that what you have heard and seen may make a difference in your lives. I pray that each of us will be a little more kind, a little more thoughtful, a little more courteous. I pray that we will keep our tongues in check and not let anger prompt words which we would later regret. I pray that we may have the strength and the will to turn the other cheek, to walk the extra mile in lifting up the feeble knees of those in distress.

This gospel is an intimate thing. It is not some distant concept. It is applicable in our lives. It can change our very natures.

May God bless you, my wonderful, faithful associates, in this great work. May His peace and His love be upon you and enshrine your lives with an essence of godliness.

As we return to our homes, I pray that in our hearts there will be a resolution to live together more fully as we should do as Latter-day Saints. I leave my love and my blessing with you in the sacred name of the Lord Jesus Christ. God be with you till we meet again. Thank you, and amen.

# GENERAL YOUNG
# WOMEN MEETING

MARCH 27, 2004

M Y DEAR YOUNG FRIENDS, you beautiful young women, we have heard stirring testimonies and wonderful talks from this presidency of the Young Women. What gifted and able leaders they are. Behind them stands a general board of the same quality, and these give leadership to this great program for young women that extends throughout the world.

It is now my turn to speak to you, and I scarcely know what to say. You overwhelm me with your numbers. This great Conference Center contains thousands. There are overflow buildings nearby. These services are reaching into meetinghouses in many nations of this great, broad earth. There are so many of you.

My heart reaches out to you. I appreciate you. I honor you. I respect you. What a tremendous force for good you are. You are the strength of the present, the hope of the future. You are the sum of all the generations that have gone before, the promise of all that will come hereafter.

You must know, as you've been told, that you are not alone in this world. There are hundreds of thousands of you. You live in many lands. You speak various languages. And every one of you has something divine within you.

You are second to none. You are daughters of God. There has

come to you as your birthright something beautiful and sacred and divine. Never forget that. Your Eternal Father is the great Master of the universe. He rules over all, but He also will listen to your prayers as His daughter and hear you as you speak with Him. He will answer your prayers. He will not leave you alone.

In my quiet moments, I think of the future with all of its wonderful possibilities and with all of its terrible temptations. I wonder what will happen to you in the next 10 years. Where will you be? What will you be doing? That will depend on the choices you make, some of which may seem unimportant at the time but which will have tremendous consequences. Someone has said, "It may make a difference to all eternity whether we do right or wrong today" (James Freeman Clarke, in *Elbert Hubbard's Scrap Book* [1923], 95).

You have the potential to become anything to which you set your mind. You have a mind and a body and a spirit. With these three working together, you can walk the high road that leads to achievement and happiness. But this will require effort and sacrifice and faith.

Among other things, I must remind you that you must get all of the education that you possibly can. Life has become so complex and competitive. You cannot assume that you have entitlements due you. You will be expected to put forth great effort and to use your best talents to make your way to the most wonderful future of which you are capable. Occasionally, there will likely be serious disappointments. But there will be helping hands along the way, many such, to give you encouragement and strength to move forward.

I visited the hospital the other day to see a dear friend. I observed the various nurses who were on duty. They were extremely able. They impressed me as knowing everything that was going on and what to do about it. They had been well schooled, and it showed. A framed motto was on the wall of each room. It read, "We strive for excellence."

What a tremendous difference training makes. Training is the key to opportunity. It brings with it the challenge of increasing knowledge and the strength and power of discipline. Perhaps you do not have the funds to get all the schooling you would desire. Make your money go as far as you can, and take advantage of scholarships, grants, and loans within your capacity to repay.

It is for this reason that the Perpetual Education Fund was established. We recognized that a few dollars could make a world of difference in the opportunities for young men and young women to secure needed training. The beneficiary secures the training and repays the loan so someone else can have the same opportunity. Thus far our experience indicates that the training results in compensation three or four times what it was without training. Think of that!

While this program is not available everywhere, it is now in place where some of you live, and if available, it could prove to be a great blessing in your life.

As you walk the road of life, be careful of your friends. They can make you or break you. Be generous in helping the unfortunate and those in distress. But bind to you friends of your own kind, friends who will encourage you, stand with you, live as you desire to live; who will enjoy the same kind of entertainment; and who will resist the evil that you determine to resist.

To accomplish His plan of happiness, the great Creator planted within us an instinct that makes boys interested in girls and girls interested in boys. That powerful inclination can lead to beautiful experiences, or it can lead to terribly ugly experiences. As we look out over the world, it seems that morality has been cast aside. The violation of old standards has become common. Studies, one after another, show that there has been an abandonment of time-tested principles. Self-discipline has been forgotten, and promiscuous indulgence has become widespread. But, my dear friends, we cannot accept that which has become common in the world. Yours, as members of this Church, is a higher standard and more demanding. It declares as a voice from Sinai that thou shalt not indulge. You must keep control of your desires. For you there is no future in any other course. I should modify that to say that the Lord has provided for repentance and forgiveness. Nonetheless, yielding to temptation can become like a wound that seems never to heal and always to leave an ugly scar.

Modesty in dress and manner will assist in protecting against temptation. It may be difficult to find modest clothing, but it can be found with enough effort. I sometimes wish every girl had access to a sewing machine and training in how to use it. She could then make her own attractive clothing. I suppose this is an unrealistic wish. But I do not hesitate to say that you can be attractive without being immodest. You can be refreshing and buoyant and beautiful in your dress and in your behavior. Your appeal to others will come of your personality, which is the sum of your individual characteristics. Be happy. Wear a smile. Have fun. But draw some rigid parameters, a line in the sand, as it were, beyond which you will not go.

The Lord speaks of those who refuse counsel and who "stumble and fall when the storms descend, and the winds blow, and the rains descend, and beat upon their house" (D&C 90:5).

Stay away from sleazy entertainment. It may be attractive, but in all too many cases it is degrading. I do not wish to be prudish about this. I do not wish to be regarded as a killjoy. I do not wish to be thought of as an old man who knows nothing about youth and their problems. I think I do know something about these things, and it is out of my heart and my love that I plead with you to stay on the high road. Create fun with your good friends. Sing and dance, swim and hike, become involved in projects together, and live life with zest and excitement.

Respect your bodies. The Lord has described them as temples. So many these days disfigure their bodies with tattoos. How

221

shortsighted. These markings last for life. Once in place, they cannot be removed except through a difficult and costly process. I cannot understand why any girl would subject herself to such a thing. I plead with you to avoid disfigurement of this kind.

And while I am speaking of things to avoid, I again mention drugs. Please do not experiment with them. Stay away from them as if they were a foul disease, for such they really are.

Never assume that you can make it alone. You need the help of the Lord. Never hesitate to get on your knees in some private place and speak with Him. What a marvelous and wonderful thing is prayer. Think of it. We can actually speak with our Father in Heaven. He will hear and respond, but we need to listen to that response. Nothing is too serious and nothing too unimportant to share with Him. He has said, "Come unto me, all ye that labour and are heavy laden, and I will give you rest" (Matthew 11:28). He continues, "For my yoke is easy, and my burden is light" (Matthew 11:30). That simply means that when all is said and done, His way is easy to bear and His path is easy to trod. Paul wrote to the Romans, "For the kingdom of God is not meat and drink; but righteousness, and peace, and joy in the Holy Ghost" (Romans 14:17).

Faith in the Lord Jesus Christ must be a beacon light before you, a polar star in your sky.

President George Albert Smith used to talk of staying on the Lord's side of the line. How very important that is.

Many years ago I told a story in conference that I think I will repeat. It is a story about a baseball player. I realize that some of you in various parts of the world do not know much about baseball. You do not even care about it. But this story brings with it a tremendous lesson.

The event occurred in 1912. The World Series was being played, and this was the final game to determine the winner of the series. The score was 2–1 in favor of the New York Giants, who were in the field. The Boston Red Sox were at bat. The man at bat knocked a high, arching fly. Two New York players ran for it. Fred Snodgrass in center field signaled to his associate that he would take it. He came squarely under the ball, which fell into his glove. But he did not hold it there. The ball went right through his grasp and fell to the ground. A howl went up in the stands. The fans could not believe that Snodgrass had dropped the ball. He had caught hundreds of fly balls before. But now, at this most crucial moment, he had failed to hold the ball, and the Red Sox went on to win the world championship.

Snodgrass came back the following season and played brilliant ball for nine years. He lived to be 86 years of age, dying in 1974. But after that one slip, for 62 years, whenever he was introduced to anybody, the expected response was, "Oh, yes, you're the one who dropped the ball."

Unfortunately, we see people dropping the ball all the time. There is the student who thinks she is doing well enough and then, under the stress of the final exam, fails. There is the driver who is extremely careful. But, in one single moment of carelessness, he becomes involved in a tragic accident. There is the employee who is trusted and who does well. Then, in an instant, he is faced with a temptation he cannot resist. A mark is placed upon him which never seems entirely to disappear.

There is the outburst of anger that destroys in a single moment a long-standing friendship. There is the little sin that somehow grows and eventually leads to separation from the Church. There is the life lived with decency; then comes the one destructive, ever-haunting, one-time moral breakdown, the memory of which seems never to fade.

On all such occasions, someone dropped the ball. A person may have had plenty of self-confidence. He or she may have been a bit arrogant, thinking, "I do not really have to try." But when he or she reached for the ball, it passed through the glove and fell to the ground. There is repentance, yes. There is forgiveness, of course.

There is a desire to forget. But somehow, the time the ball was dropped is long remembered.

Now, you dear, wonderful girls, I speak with a father's love for you. I thank you that you have traveled so well so far. I plead with you to never let down, to establish a purpose and hold to the line and move forward undeterred by any opposing temptation or force that may cross your path.

I pray that your lives will not be wasted but that they may be fruitful of great and everlasting good. The years will pass, and I will not be here to see what you have done with your lives. But there will be many others, oh so many others, who will be counting on you, whose very peace and happiness will depend upon what you do. And above them all will be your Father in Heaven, who will ever love you as His daughter.

I wish to emphasize that if you make a mistake, it can be forgiven, it can be overcome, it can be lived above. You can go on to success and happiness. But I hope that such an experience will not come your way, and I am confident it will not if you will set your mind and pray for the strength to walk the high road, which at times may be lonely but which will lead to peace and happiness and joy supernal in this life and everlastingly hereafter.

For this I pray in the sacred name of Him who gave His life to make it possible for us to live eternally, even the Lord Jesus Christ, amen.

# 174TH ANNUAL GENERAL CONFERENCE

# SATURDAY MORNING SESSION

APRIL 3, 2004

$M$Y BELOVED BRETHREN AND SISTERS, we warmly welcome you to another worldwide conference of the Church. We are now a great international family, living in many nations and speaking many languages. To me it is a marvelous and miraculous thing that you are able to see us and hear us across the globe.

During my life as a General Authority, we have moved from the time when we thought it a remarkable thing that we could speak in the Salt Lake Tabernacle and be heard by radio throughout the state of Utah. Now we are assembled in this great and magnificent Conference Center, and our images and words are available to 95 percent of the membership of the Church.

New technology has become available as the Church has grown larger and stronger. Our membership now reaches almost 12 million, with more members outside the United States than within. Once we were recognized as a Utah church. Now we have become a great international body. We have made a very long journey in reaching out to the nations of the world. There is much more yet to be done, but what has been accomplished is truly phenomenal.

It is a fact that we lose some—far too many. Every organization of which I am aware does so. But I am satisfied that we retain and keep active a higher percentage of our members than does any other major church of which I know.

Everywhere there is great activity and great enthusiasm. We have strong and able leaders across the world who give of their time and means to move the work forward.

It is wonderfully refreshing to see the faith and faithfulness of our young people. They live at a time when a great tide of evil is washing over the earth. It seems to be everywhere. Old standards are discarded. Principles of virtue and integrity are cast aside. But we find literally hundreds of thousands of our young people holding to the high standards of the gospel. They find happy and uplifting association with those of their own kind. They are improving their minds with education and their skills with discipline, and their influence for good is felt ever more widely.

I am pleased to report, my brothers and sisters, that the Church is in good condition. We continue to build temples, to construct houses of worship, to carry forward many projects of construction and improvement, all made possible because of the faith of our people.

We are carrying on a great humanitarian effort, which is blessing the lives of many of the less fortunate of the earth and those who are the victims of the catastrophes of nature.

We are pleased to note that on April 1 of this year, the Illinois House of Representatives unanimously passed a resolution of regret for the forced expulsion of our people from Nauvoo in 1846. This magnanimous gesture may be coupled with action taken by then Governor Christopher S. Bond of Missouri, who in 1976 revoked the cruel and unconstitutional extermination order issued against our people by Governor Lilburn W. Boggs in 1838. These and other developments represent a most significant change of attitude toward the Latter-day Saints.

How deeply grateful I feel to each of you and all of you for your dedicated and consecrated service. I thank you for your many kindnesses to me wherever I go. I stand as your servant, ready and willing to assist you in any way that I can.

God bless you, my dear associates. How I love you. How I pray for you. How I thank you.

May heaven smile upon you. May there be love and harmony, peace and goodness in your homes. May you be preserved from harm and evil. May our Father's "great plan of happiness" (Alma 42:8) become the standard by which you live. I ask it humbly and gratefully in the sacred name of Jesus Christ, amen.

# PRIESTHOOD
# SESSION

## APRIL 3, 2004

In 1936, 68 YEARS AGO, one of the secretaries to the Quorum of the Twelve told me what a member of the Twelve had told her. She said that in the coming general conference there would be announced a program which would come to be recognized as even more noteworthy than the coming of our people to these valleys as pioneers.

Now, parenthetically, you should not tell your secretary what you should keep confidential, and she should not tell anyone else when she is given confidential information. But that was what happened back then. It never happens today. Oh, no! I should add that my able secretaries are never guilty of such a breach of confidentiality.

As you who are acquainted with the history know, there was announced at that time the Church security plan, the name of which was subsequently changed to the Church welfare program.

I wondered back in those days how anything the Church did could eclipse in anyone's judgment the historic gathering of our people to these western valleys of the United States. That was a movement of such epic proportions that I felt nothing could ever be so noteworthy. But I have discovered something of interest in the last short while.

We receive many prominent visitors in the office of the First

Presidency. They include heads of state and ambassadors of nations. A few weeks ago we entertained the mayor of one of the great cities of the world. We have likewise recently entertained the vice president and the ambassador of Ecuador, the ambassador from Lithuania, the ambassador from Belarus, and others. In our conversations, not one of these visitors mentioned the great pioneer journey of our forebears. But each of them, independently, spoke in high praise of our welfare program and our humanitarian efforts.

And so as I speak in this great priesthood meeting, I wish to say a few words concerning our efforts in behalf of those in need, be they members of the Church or otherwise, in various parts of the world.

When the modern welfare program was put in motion, it was designed to take care of the needs of our own people. In the years that have followed, thousands upon thousands have been served. Bishops and Relief Society presidents have had available to them food and clothing and other supplies for those in need. Numberless members of the Church have worked in volunteer capacities in producing that which was required. We now operate 113 storehouses, 63 farms, 105 canneries and home storage centers, 18 food processing and distribution plants, as well as many other facilities.

Not only have the needs of Church members been met, but aid has been extended to countless others. Right here in this Salt Lake City community, many of the hungry are fed daily by non-LDS agencies utilizing LDS welfare supplies.

Here, in this city, and in a number of other places, we operate beautiful stores where there is no cash register, where no money changes hands, where food, clothing, and other necessities are provided to those in distress. I believe that no better milk, no better meat, and no better flour is found on any grocery shelf than that which is distributed from the bishops' storehouses.

The principles on which these establishments operate are essentially what they were at the beginning. Those in need are expected

229

to do all they can to provide for themselves. Then families are expected to assist in taking care of their less-fortunate members. And then the resources of the Church are made available.

We believe in and take very seriously the words of our Lord:

"Come, ye blessed of my Father, inherit the kingdom prepared for you from the foundation of the world:

"For I was an hungred, and ye gave me meat: I was thirsty, and ye gave me drink: I was a stranger, and ye took me in:

"Naked, and ye clothed me: I was sick, and ye visited me: I was in prison, and ye came unto me" (Matthew 25:34–36).

This is the Lord's way of caring for those in need, which, He declared, "ye have . . . always with you" (Matthew 26:11).

Those who are able voluntarily work to provide for those who are not able. Last year there were 563,000 days of donated labor in welfare facilities. That is the equivalent of a man working eight hours a day for 1,542 years.

A recent issue of the *Church News* carried the story of a group of farmers in a small Idaho community. May I read briefly from that account?

"It is 6 A.M. in late October, and frost already hangs in the air over the sugar beet fields of Rupert, Idaho.

"The long arms of the 'beeters' stretch out over twelve rows, slicing the tops off sugar beets. Behind them, the harvesters thrust their steel fingers into the soil and scoop up the beets, pulling them up toward a belt and into a waiting truck.

" . . . This is the Rupert Idaho Welfare Farm, and those who are working here today are volunteers. . . . At times more than 60 machines [are] working in harmony together—. . . all owned by local farmers."

The work goes on throughout the day.

"[At] 7 P.M. . . . the sun has set, leaving the land dark and cold once again. The farmers head home, exhausted and happy.

"They have finished well another day.

"They have harvested the Lord's sugar beets" (Neil K. Newell, "A Harvest in Idaho," *Church News,* Mar. 20, 2004, 16).

Such remarkable volunteer service goes on constantly to assure supplies for the storehouses of the Lord.

Since the early beginnings, the program has moved beyond caring for the needy to the encouragement of preparedness on the part of families of the Church. No one knows when catastrophe might strike—or sickness or unemployment or a disabling accident.

Last year the program helped families store 18 million pounds of basic foods against a possible time of need. Hopefully that time will never come. But the good, wholesome, basic food so stored brings peace of mind and also the satisfaction of obedience to counsel.

Now there has been added another element. It began some years ago when drought in Africa brought hunger and death to uncounted numbers. Members of the Church were invited to contribute to a great humanitarian effort to meet the needs of those terribly impoverished people. Your contributions were numerous and generous. The work has continued because there are other serious needs in many places. The outreach of this aid has become a miracle. Millions of pounds of food, medical supplies, blankets, tents, clothing, and other materials have staved off famine and desolation in various parts of the world. Wells have been dug; crops have been planted; lives have been saved. Let me give you an example.

Neil Darlington is a chemical engineer who worked for a large industrial company in Ghana. Eventually he retired. He and his wife were then called as a missionary couple. They were sent to Ghana. Brother Darlington says, "In areas of famine, disease, and social unrest, we were there as representatives of the Church, extending a helping hand to the destitute, the hungry, the distressed."

In small villages they drilled new wells and repaired old ones.

231

Those of us who have fresh, clean water in abundance can scarcely appreciate the circumstances of those who are without.

Can you picture this couple, devoted Latter-day Saint missionaries? They drill into the dry earth. Their drill reaches the water table below, and the miracle liquid comes to the surface and spills over the dry and thirsty soil. There is rejoicing. There are tears. There is now water to drink, water with which to wash, water to grow crops. There is nothing more treasured in a dry land than water. How absolutely beautiful is water pouring from a new well.

On one occasion, when the tribal chiefs and the elders of the village gathered to thank them, Brother Darlington asked the chief if he and Sister Darlington could sing a song for them. They looked into the eyes of the dark-skinned men and women before them and sang "I Am a Child of God" as an expression of their common brotherhood.

This one couple, through their efforts, have provided water for an estimated 190,000 people in remote villages and refugee camps. Contemplate, if you will, the miracle of this accomplishment.

And now, literally thousands of their kind—married couples, couples who otherwise might simply have lived out their lives in largely idle pursuits—have served and are serving in scores of ways and in scores of places. They have worked and continue to work in the impoverished areas of America. They have worked, and still do so, in India and Indonesia, in Thailand and Cambodia, in Russia and the Baltic nations. And so the work expands.

Joining with others, the Church has recently provided wheelchairs for some 42,000 disabled persons. Think of what this means to people who literally have had to crawl to get about.

With the aid of selfless doctors and nurses, neonatal resuscitation training was provided to nearly 19,000 professionals in the year 2003 alone. The lives of thousands of babies will be spared as a consequence.

Last year some 2,700 individuals were treated for eye problems, and 300 local practitioners were trained in sight-saving procedures. The blind have literally been made to see.

Where devastating floods have come, where earthquakes have created disaster, where hunger has stalked the land, wherever want has been created by whatever cause, representatives of the Church have been there. Some $98 million in cash and in-kind assistance have been distributed in the past year, bringing such aid to a total of $643 million in just 18 years.

I have been a firsthand witness to the effectiveness of our humanitarian efforts. In traveling the world, I have seen the recipients of your generosity. In 1998 I visited the areas of Central America which had been ravaged by Hurricane Mitch. Here the distribution of food and clothing was quickly organized, and the cleaning and rebuilding of devastated homes and shattered lives was a miracle to behold.

There is not time to go on recounting the reach of these great and significant programs. In extending help we have not asked whether those affected belong to the Church, for we know that each of earth's children is a child of God worthy of help in time of need. We have done what we have done largely with the left hand not knowing what the right hand is doing. We seek no commendation or thank-yous. It is compensation enough that when we help one of the least of these, our Father's children, we have done it unto Him and His Beloved Son (see Matthew 25:40).

We shall go on in this work. There will always be a need. Hunger and want and catastrophes will ever be with us. And there will always be those whose hearts have been touched by the light of the gospel who will be willing to serve and work and lift the needy of the earth.

As a correlated effort, we have established the Perpetual Education Fund. It has come about through your generous contributions. It is now operating in 23 countries. Loans are extended to worthy young men and women for education. Otherwise they would be trapped in the stagnated poverty their parents and fore-bears have known for generations. Some 10,000 and more are now being assisted, and experience to this date indicates that with such training they are now earning three to four times what was previously possible.

The Spirit of the Lord guides this work. This welfare activity is secular activity, expressing itself in terms of rice and beans, of blankets and tents, of clothing and medicine, of employment and education for better employment. But this so-called secular work is but an outward expression of an inward spirit—the Spirit of the Lord, of whom it was said, He "went about doing good" (Acts 10:38).

May heaven prosper this great program, and may heaven's blessing rest upon all who serve therein, I humbly pray, in the sacred name of Jesus Christ, amen.

# SUNDAY MORNING SESSION

## APRIL 4, 2004

M AY I FIRST SAY TO ALL the Church, and to others, thank you for your great kindness to Sister Hinckley and me. You have been and are so gracious and generous. We are touched by all you do for us. If all the world were treated as we are treated, what a different world it would be. We would care for one another in the Spirit of the Master, who reached out to comfort and heal.

Now, my brothers and sisters, President Packer has spoken to you as a grandfather. I should like to pick up a thread from the tapestry he has woven. I too am now an old man, older even than he, if you can imagine that. I have been around for a long time, I have traveled far, and I have seen much of this world. In hours of quiet reflection, I wonder why there is so much of trouble and suffering almost everywhere. Our times are fraught with peril. We hear frequently quoted the words of Paul to Timothy: "This know also, that in the last days perilous times shall come" (2 Timothy 3:1). He then goes on to describe the conditions that will prevail. I think it is plainly evident that these latter days are indeed perilous times that fit the conditions that Paul described (see 2 Timothy 3:2–7).

But peril is not a new condition for the human family. Revelation tells us that "there was war in heaven: Michael and his angels fought against the dragon; and the dragon fought and his angels,

"And prevailed not; neither was their place found any more in heaven.

"And the great dragon was cast out, that old serpent, called the Devil, and Satan, which deceiveth the whole world: he was cast out into the earth, and his angels were cast out with him" (Revelation 12:7–9).

What a perilous time that must have been. The Almighty Himself was pitted against the son of the morning. We were there while that was going on. That must have been a desperately difficult struggle, with a grand, triumphal victory.

Concerning those desperate times, the Lord spoke to Job out of the whirlwind and said: "Where wast thou when I laid the foundations of the earth? . . . When the morning stars sang together, and all the sons of God shouted for joy?" (Job 38:4, 7).

Why were we then happy? I think it was because good had triumphed over evil and the whole human family was on the Lord's side. We had turned our backs on the adversary and aligned ourselves with the forces of God, and those forces were victorious.

But having made that decision, why should we have to make it again and again after our birth into mortality? I cannot understand why so many have betrayed in life the decision they once made when the great war occurred in heaven. But it is evident that the contest between good and evil, which began with that war, has never ended. It has gone on and on and on to the present.

I think our Father must weep because so many of His children through the ages have exercised the agency He gave them and have chosen to walk the road of evil rather than good.

Evil was manifest early in this world when Cain slew Abel. It increased until in the days of Noah, "God saw that the wickedness of man was great in the earth, and that every imagination of the thoughts of his heart was only evil continually.

"And it repented the Lord that he had made man on the earth, and it grieved him at his heart" (Genesis 6:5–6).

He commanded Noah to build an ark "wherein few, that is, eight souls" would be saved (1 Peter 3:20).

The earth was cleansed. The floods receded. Righteousness was again established. But it was not long until the family of humanity, so very many of them, returned to the old ways of disobedience. The inhabitants of the cities of the plain, Sodom and Gomorrah, are examples of the depravity to which men sank. And "God [utterly] destroyed the cities of the plain" in a summary and final desolation (Genesis 19:29).

Isaiah thundered:

"Your iniquities have separated between you and your God, and your sins have hid his face from you, that he will not hear.

"For your hands are defiled with blood, and your fingers with iniquity; your lips have spoken lies, your tongue hath muttered perverseness" (Isaiah 59:2–3).

It was so with the other prophets of the Old Testament. The burden of their message was a denunciation of wickedness.

And the peril of those times was not peculiar to the Old World. The Book of Mormon documents that in the Western Hemisphere the armies of the Jaredites fought to the death. The Nephites and the Lamanites also fought until thousands had died and Moroni was forced to wander alone for the safety of his own life (see Moroni 1:3). His great and final plea, directed toward those of our day, was a call to righteousness: "And again I would exhort you that ye would come unto Christ, and lay hold upon every good gift, and touch not the evil gift, nor the unclean thing" (Moroni 10:30).

When the Savior walked the earth, He "went about doing good" (Acts 10:38), but He also denounced the hypocrisy of the scribes and Pharisees, speaking of them as "whited sepulchres" (see Matthew 23:27). He lashed out at the money changers in the temple, saying, "My house is the house of prayer: but ye have made it a den of thieves" (Luke 19:46). This too was a time of great peril.

Palestine was part of the Roman Empire, which, in its governance, was ironfisted, oppressive, and clouded over with evil.

Paul's letters cried out for strength among the followers of Christ, lest they fall into the ways of the wicked one. But a spirit of apostasy ultimately prevailed.

Ignorance and evil enveloped the world, resulting in what is known as the Dark Ages. Isaiah predicted, "Darkness shall cover the earth, and gross darkness the people" (Isaiah 60:2). For centuries, disease was rampant and poverty reigned. The Black Death killed some 50 million people during the 14th century. Was not this a season of terrible peril? I wonder how humanity survived.

But somehow, in that long season of darkness, a candle was lighted. The age of Renaissance brought with it a flowering of learning, art, and science. There came a movement of bold and courageous men and women who looked heavenward in acknowledgment of God and His divine Son. We speak of it as the Reformation.

And then, after many generations had walked the earth—so many of them in conflict, hatred, darkness, and evil—there arrived the great, new day of the Restoration. This glorious gospel was ushered in with the appearance of the Father and the Son to the boy Joseph. The dawn of the dispensation of the fulness of times rose upon the world. All of the good, the beautiful, the divine of all previous dispensations was restored in this most remarkable season.

But there was also evil. And one manifestation of that evil was persecution. There was hatred. There were drivings and forced marches in the time of winter.

It was as Charles Dickens described in the opening lines of his *A Tale of Two Cities:* "It was the best of times, it was the worst of times, . . . it was the season of Light, it was the season of Darkness, it was the spring of hope, it was the winter of despair."

Notwithstanding the great evil of these times, what a glorious season it has been and now is. A new day has come in the work of the Almighty. That work has grown and strengthened and moved across the earth. It has now touched for good the lives of millions, and this is only the beginning.

This great dawning has also resulted in a tremendous outpouring of secular knowledge upon the world. Think of the increased longevity of life. Think of the wonders of modern medicine. I stand amazed. Think of the flowering of education. Think of the miraculous advances in travel and communication. Man's ingenuity knows no end when the God of heaven inspires and pours out light and knowledge.

There is still so much of conflict in the world. There is terrible poverty, disease, and hatred. Man is still brutal in his inhumanity to man. Yet there is this glorious dawn. The "Sun of righteousness" has come "with healing in his wings" (Malachi 4:2). God and His Beloved Son have revealed Themselves. We know Them. We worship Them "in spirit and in truth" (John 4:24). We love Them. We honor Them and seek to do Their will.

The keys of the everlasting priesthood have turned the locks of the prisons of the past.

> *The morning breaks, the shadows flee;*
> *Lo, Zion's standard is unfurled!*
> *The dawning of a brighter day, . . .*
> *Majestic rises on the world.*
> > *["The Morning Breaks,"*
> > Hymns, *no. 1]*

Perilous times? Yes. These are perilous times. But the human race has lived in peril from the time before the earth was created. Somehow, through all of the darkness, there has been a faint but beautiful light. And now with added luster it shines upon the world. It carries with it God's plan of happiness for His children. It carries with it the great and unfathomable wonders of the Atonement of the Redeemer.

How grateful we are to the God of heaven for His beneficent

care of His children in providing for them, through all the perils of eternity, the opportunity of salvation and the blessing of exaltation in His kingdom, if only they will live in righteousness.

And, my brothers and sisters, this places upon each of us a grand and consuming responsibility. President Wilford Woodruff said in 1894:

"The Almighty is with this people. We shall have all the revelations that we will need, if we will do our duty and obey the commandments of God. . . . While I . . . live I want to do my duty. I want the Latter-day Saints to do their duty. Here is the Holy Priesthood. . . . Their responsibility is great and mighty. The eyes of God and all the holy prophets are watching us. This is the great dispensation that has been spoken of ever since the world began. We are gathered together . . . by the power and commandment of God. We are doing the work of God. . . . Let us fill our mission" (in James R. Clark, comp., *Messages of the First Presidency of The Church of Jesus Christ of Latter-day Saints,* 6 vols. [1965–75], 3:258).

This is our great and demanding challenge, my brothers and sisters. This is the choice we must constantly make, just as generations before us have had to choose. We must ask ourselves:

> *Who's on the Lord's side? Who?*
> *Now is the time to show.*
> *We ask it fearlessly:*
> *Who's on the Lord's side? Who?*
> *["Who's on the Lord's Side?"*
> Hymns, *no. 260]*

Do we really comprehend, do we understand the tremendous significance of that which we have? This is the summation of the generations of man, the concluding chapter in the entire panorama of the human experience.

But this does not put us in a position of superiority. Rather, it should humble us. It places upon us an unending responsibility to reach out with concern for all others in the Spirit of the Master, who taught, "Thou shalt love thy neighbour as thyself" (Matthew 19:19). We must cast out self-righteousness and rise above petty self-interest.

We must do all that is required in moving forward the work of the Lord in building His kingdom in the earth. We can never compromise the doctrine which has come through revelation, but we can live and work with others, respecting their beliefs and admiring their virtues, joining hands in opposition to the sophistries, the quarrels, the hatred—those perils which have been with man from the beginning.

Without surrendering any element of our doctrine, we can be neighborly, we can be helpful, we can be kind and generous.

We of this generation are the end harvest of all that has gone before. It is not enough to simply be known as a member of this Church. A solemn obligation rests upon us. Let us face it and work at it.

We must live as true followers of the Christ, with charity toward all, returning good for evil, teaching by example the ways of the Lord, and accomplishing the vast service He has outlined for us.

May we live worthy of the glorious endowment of light and understanding and eternal truth which has come to us through all the perils of the past. Somehow, among all who have walked the earth, we have been brought forth in this unique and remarkable season. Be grateful, and above all be faithful. This is my humble prayer, as I bear witness of the truth of this work, in the sacred name of Jesus Christ, amen.

# SUNDAY AFTERNOON SESSION

APRIL 4, 2004

$M$Y BROTHERS AND SISTERS, it's about over. As we conclude this historic conference, the words of Rudyard Kipling's immortal "Recessional" come to mind:

> *The tumult and the shouting dies;*
> *The captains and the kings depart—*
> *Still stands Thine ancient Sacrifice,*
> *An humble and a contrite heart.*
> *Lord God of Hosts, be with us yet,*
> *Lest we forget—lest we forget!*
> *[In James Dalton Morrison, ed.,*
> Masterpieces of Religious Verse
> *(1948), 512; see also "God of Our Fathers,*
> *Known of Old,"* Hymns, *no. 80]*

As we return to our homes, may we carry with us the spirit of this great convocation. May what we have heard and experienced remain with us as a residual of love and peace, an attitude of repentance, and a resolve to stand a little taller in the radiant sunlight of the gospel.

May our testimonies of the great foundation principles of this work, which have been burnished more brightly, shine forth from our lives and our actions. May a spirit of love, of peace, of appreciation for one another increase in our homes. May we be prospered in our labors and become more generous in our sharings. May we reach out to those about us in friendship and respect. May our prayers become expressions of thanks to the Giver of all good and of love for Him who is our Redeemer.

Now, my brothers and sisters, I reluctantly desire a personal indulgence for a moment. Some of you have noticed the absence of Sister Hinckley. For the first time in 46 years, since I became a General Authority, she has not attended general conference. Earlier this year we were in Africa to dedicate the Accra Ghana Temple. On leaving there we flew to Sal, a barren island in the Atlantic, where we met with members of a local branch. We then flew to St. Thomas, an island in the Caribbean. There we met with a few others of our members. We were on our way home when she collapsed with weariness. She's had a difficult time ever since. She's now 92, a little younger than I am. I guess the clock is winding down, and we do not know how to rewind it.

It is a somber time for me. We've been married for 67 years this month. She is the mother of our five gifted and able children, the grandmother of 25 grandchildren and a growing number of great-grandchildren. We've walked together side by side through all of these years, coequals and companions through storm and sunshine. She has spoken far and wide in testimony of this work, imparting love, encouragement, and faith wherever she's gone. Women have written letters of appreciation from all over the world. We continue to hope and pray for her and express from the depths of our hearts our appreciation for all who have attended her and looked after her and for your great faith and prayers in her behalf.

Now, as we go to our homes, I feel to say:

> *God be with you till we meet again;*
> *By his counsels guide, uphold you. . . .*
> *When life's perils thick confound you,*
> *Put his arms unfailing round you. . . .*

*Keep love's banner floating o'er you;*
*Smite death's threat'ning wave before you.*
*God be with you till we meet again.*
      *["God Be with You Till We*
      *Meet Again,"* Hymns, *no. 152]*

Every man, woman, and child, boy and girl, should leave this conference a better individual than he or she was when it began two days ago. I leave my blessing and my love with each of you, in the sacred name of Jesus Christ, amen.

# 174TH SEMIANNUAL GENERAL CONFERENCE

# SATURDAY MORNING SESSION

OCTOBER 2, 2004

As we open this great conference, we note the absence of Elders David B. Haight and Neal A. Maxwell of the Quorum of the Twelve Apostles. Each of them served long and very effectively. We mourn their passing. We greatly miss them. We extend our love to their dear ones. We are confident that they are carrying on this great work on the other side of the veil.

We recognize that in the natural course of events there are recurring vacancies which make necessary filling these as they are created. After fasting and prayer, we have called Elder Dieter Friedrich Uchtdorf and Elder David Allan Bednar to fill these vacancies in the Quorum of the Twelve Apostles. We present their names to you this morning. You may not know them, but you will soon get acquainted with them. Those of you who feel you can sustain them in this sacred calling will please signify by the uplifted hand. Any who may be opposed?

Their names will be included in the sustaining of all of the authorities later in the conference. Now we ask these Brethren to take their places on the stand with members of the Twelve. They will speak to us Sunday morning, and you will get to know them better.

Now in opening the conference, I wish to comment briefly on

the condition of the Church. It continues to grow. It is touching the lives of more and more people every year. It is spreading far and wide over the earth.

To accommodate this growth we must, of necessity, continue to build houses of worship. We now have, at some stage, 451 meetinghouses of various sizes under construction in many parts of the earth. This tremendous building program is phenomenal. I know of nothing to equal it. Our structures are beautiful. They add to the ambience of any community in which they stand. They are well maintained. We have had long experience in constructing houses of worship, and out of that vast experience we are producing better buildings than have ever previously been constructed in the Church. They combine beauty with great utility. If they look much the same, it is because that is intended. By following tried and tested patterns we save millions of dollars while meeting the needs of our people.

We continue to build temples. We recently broke ground for a new temple in Sacramento, California, the seventh in that state, where we have the second largest membership of any state in the United States.

The temples in the Salt Lake City area are extremely busy and at times are overloaded. For this reason, we have determined to build a new temple in the Salt Lake Valley. The location of the site will be announced shortly. It may appear that we are unduly favoring this area. But temple attendance is such that we must accommodate those who wish to come. And if the present growth trends continue, we shall probably need yet another.

We are also pleased to announce that we will construct another temple in Idaho, where we have the third largest membership in the United States. Plans are going forward for one in Rexburg. Now we are also planning to build another in the city of Twin Falls. This temple will serve thousands of our members who live between Idaho Falls and Boise.

Temples are now under construction in Aba, Nigeria; Helsinki, Finland; Newport Beach and Sacramento, California; and San Antonio, Texas. We are replacing the temple which was destroyed by fire in Samoa. When those which have thus far been announced are dedicated, we shall have 130 working temples. Others will be constructed as the Church continues to grow.

We are now working on a major undertaking in Salt Lake City. It is imperative that we preserve the environment around Temple Square. This makes necessary a very large construction project. Tithing funds will not be used for this construction. The income from Church businesses, rents on the property, and other such sources make this possible.

We must do extensive work on the Salt Lake Tabernacle to make it seismically safe. This marvelous structure has been used for 137 years this month. The time has come when we must do something to preserve it. It is one of the unique architectural masterpieces in the entire world and a building of immense historical interest. Its historical qualities will be carefully preserved, while its utility, comfort, and safety will be increased. We are grateful that we have this Conference Center, where we can meet for such gatherings as this. I now ask myself, "What would we do without it?"

I am pleased to report that the Perpetual Education Fund continues to grow, as does the number of those who are the beneficiaries of this wonderful undertaking.

We are strengthening our missionary program. We are striving to bring a greater measure of spirituality into the work of our vast body of missionaries.

Our educational program continues to grow, extending its influence wherever the Church is established.

The Book of Mormon was recently included as one of the 20 most influential books ever published in America. We are now joining hands with a commercial publisher to enlarge the distribution of this sacred volume, this second witness of the Lord Jesus Christ.

And so, brothers and sisters, I might continue. Suffice it to say that I believe the Church is in better condition than it has been at any time in its entire history. I have been around now for nearly 95 years of that history, and I have seen much of it firsthand. I am satisfied that there is greater faith, there is a broader measure of service, and there is a more general measure of integrity among our youth. There is greater vitality in all aspects of the work than we have ever seen before. Let us glory in this wonderful season of the work of the Lord. Let us not be proud or arrogant. Let us be humbly grateful. And let us, each one, resolve within himself or herself that we will add to the luster of this magnificent work of the Almighty, that it may shine across the earth as a beacon of strength and goodness for all the world to look upon, is my humble prayer, in the name of Jesus Christ, amen.

# PRIESTHOOD SESSION

## OCTOBER 2, 2004

$M$Y DEAR BRETHREN, it is good to be with you in this very large priesthood meeting. I suppose this is the largest such gathering of priesthood ever assembled. What a contrast with the occasion described by Wilford Woodruff when all of the priesthood in all the world assembled in one room in Kirtland, Ohio, to receive instruction from the Prophet Joseph.

We have heard excellent counsel tonight, and I commend it to you.

As I offer concluding remarks I rather reluctantly speak to a theme that I have dealt with before. I do it in the spirit of the words of Alma, who said, "This is my glory, that perhaps I may be an instrument in the hands of God to bring some soul to repentance" (Alma 29:9). It is in that spirit that I speak to you tonight. What I have to say is not new. I have spoken on it before. The September issues of the *Ensign* and *Liahona* magazines carry a talk I gave some years ago on the same subject. Brother Oaks has touched on it tonight.

While the matter of which I speak was a problem then, it is a much more serious problem now. It grows increasingly worse. It is like a raging storm, destroying individuals and families, utterly ruining what was once wholesome and beautiful. I speak of pornography in all of its manifestations. I do so because of letters that come to me from broken-hearted wives. I should like to read portions of one received only a few days ago. I do so with the consent of the writer. I have deleted anything that might lead to disclosure of the parties concerned. I have exercised limited editorial liberty in the interest of clarity and flow of language. I quote now:

> Dear President Hinckley,
>
> My husband of 35 years died recently. . . . He had visited with our good bishop as quickly as he could after his most recent surgery. Then he came to me on that same evening to tell me he had been addicted to pornography. He needed me to forgive him [before he died]. He further said that he had grown tired of living a double life. [He had served in many important] Church callings while knowing [at the same time] that he was in the grips of this "other master."
>
> I was stunned, hurt, felt betrayed and violated. I could not promise him forgiveness at that moment but pleaded for time. . . . I was able to review my married life [and see how] pornography had . . . put a stranglehold on our marriage from early on. We had only been married a couple of months when he brought home a [pornographic] magazine. I locked him out of the car because I was so hurt and angry. . . .
>
> For many years in our marriage . . . he was most cruel in many of his demands. I was never good enough for him. . . . I felt incredibly beaten down at that time to a point of deep depression. . . . I know now that I was being compared to the latest "porn queen." . . .
>
> We went to counseling one time and . . . my husband proceeded to rip me apart with his criticism and disdain of me. . . .
>
> I could not even get into the car with him after that but walked around the town . . . for hours, contemplating suicide. [I thought,] "Why go on if this is all that my 'eternal companion' feels for me?"
>
> I did go on, but zipped a protective shield around myself.

I existed for other reasons than my husband and found joy in my children, in projects and accomplishments that I could do totally on my own. . . .

After his "deathbed confession" and [after taking time] to search through my life, I [said] to him, "Don't you know what you have done?" . . . I told him that I had brought a pure heart into our marriage, kept it pure during that marriage, and intended to keep it pure ever after. Why could he not do the same for me? All I ever wanted was to feel cherished and treated with the smallest of pleasantries . . . instead of being treated like some kind of chattel. . . .

I am now left to grieve not only for his being gone but also for a relationship that could have been [beautiful, but was not]. . . .

Please warn the brethren (and sisters). Pornography is not some titillating feast for the eyes that gives a momentary rush of excitement. [Rather] it has the effect of damaging hearts and souls to their very depths, strangling the life out of relationships that should be sacred, hurting to the very core those you should love the most.

And she signs the letter.

What a pathetic and tragic story. I have omitted some of the detail but have read enough that you can sense her depth of feeling. And what of her husband? He has died a painful death from cancer, his final words a confession of a life laced with sin.

And sin it is. It is devilish. It is totally inconsistent with the spirit of the gospel, with personal testimony of the things of God, and with the life of one who has been ordained to the holy priesthood.

This is not the only letter I have received. There have been enough that I am convinced this is a very serious problem even among us. It arises from many sources and expresses itself in a variety of ways. Now it is compounded by the Internet. That Internet is available not only to adults but also to young people.

I recently read that pornography has become a $57 billion

industry worldwide. Twelve billion of this is derived in the United States by evil and "conspiring men" (see D&C 89:4) who seek riches at the expense of the gullible. It is reported that it produces more revenue in the United States than the "combined revenues of all professional football, baseball and basketball franchises or the combined revenues of ABC, CBS, and NBC" ("Internet Pornography Statistics: 2003," Internet, http://www.healthy-mind.com/s-port-stats.html).

It robs the workplace of the time and talents of employees. "20% of men admit accessing pornography at work. 13% of women [do so]. . . . 10% of adults admit having internet sexual addiction" ("Internet Pornography Statistics: 2003"). That is their admission, but actually the number may be much higher.

The National Coalition for the Protection of Children and Families states that "approximately 40 million people in the United States are sexually involved with the Internet. . . .

"One in five children ages 10–17 [has] received a sexual solicitation over the Internet. . . .

"Three million of the visitors to adult websites in September 2000 were age 17 or younger. . . .

"Sex is the number 1 topic searched on the Internet" ("Current Statistics," Internet, http://www.nationalcoalition.org/resourcesservices/stat.html).

I might go on, but you too know enough of the seriousness of the problem. Suffice it to say that all who are involved become victims. Children are exploited, and their lives are severely damaged. The minds of youth become warped with false concepts. Continued exposure leads to addiction that is almost impossible to break. Men, so very many, find they cannot leave it alone. Their energies and their interests are consumed in their dead-end pursuit of this raw and sleazy fare.

The excuse is given that it is hard to avoid, that it is right at our fingertips and there is no escape.

Suppose a storm is raging and the winds howl and the snow swirls about you. You find yourself unable to stop it. But you can dress properly and seek shelter, and the storm will have no effect upon you. Likewise, even though the Internet is saturated with sleazy material, you do not have to watch it. You can retreat to the shelter of the gospel and its teaching of cleanliness and virtue and purity of life.

I know that I am speaking directly and plainly. I do so because the Internet has made pornography more widely accessible, adding to what is available on DVDs and videos, on television and magazine stands. It leads to fantasies that are destructive of self-respect. It leads to illicit relationships, often to disease, and to abusive criminal activity.

Brethren, we can do better than this. When the Savior taught the multitude, He said, "Blessed are the pure in heart: for they shall see God" (Matthew 5:8). Could anyone wish for a greater blessing than this? The high road of decency, of self-discipline, of wholesome living is the road for men, both young and old, who hold the priesthood of God. To the young men I put this question: Can you imagine John the Baptist, who restored the priesthood which you hold, being engaged in any such practice as this? To you men: Can you imagine Peter, James, and John, Apostles of our Lord, engaging in such? No, of course not.

Now brethren, the time has come for any one of us who is so involved to pull himself out of the mire, to stand above this evil thing, to "look to God and live" (Alma 37:47). We do not have to view salacious magazines. We do not have to read books laden with smut. We do not have to watch television that is beneath wholesome standards. We do not have to rent movies that depict that which is filthy. We do not have to sit at the computer and play with pornographic material found on the Internet.

I repeat, we can do better than this. We must do better than this. We are men of the priesthood. This is a most sacred and marvelous gift, worth more than all the dross of the world. But it will be amen to the effectiveness of that priesthood for anyone who engages in the practice of seeking out pornographic material.

If there be any within the sound of my voice who are doing so, then may you plead with the Lord out of the depths of your soul that He will remove from you the addiction which enslaves you. And may you have the courage to seek the loving guidance of your bishop and, if necessary, the counsel of caring professionals.

Let any who may be in the grip of this vise get upon their knees in the privacy of their closet and plead with the Lord for help to free them from this evil monster. Otherwise this vicious stain will continue through life and even into eternity. Jacob, the brother of Nephi, taught, "And it shall come to pass that when all men shall have passed from this first death unto life, insomuch as they have become immortal, . . . they who are righteous shall be righteous still, and they who are filthy shall be filthy still" (2 Nephi 9:15–16).

President Joseph F. Smith, in his vision of the Savior's visit among the spirits of the dead, saw that "unto the wicked he did not go, and among the ungodly and the unrepentant who had defiled themselves while in the flesh, his voice was not raised" (D&C 138:20).

Now, my brethren, I do not wish to be negative. I am by nature optimistic. But in such matters as this I am a realist. If we are involved in such behavior, now is the time to change. Let this be our hour of resolution. Let us turn about to a better way. Said the Lord:

"Let virtue garnish thy thoughts unceasingly; then shall thy confidence wax strong in the presence of God; and the doctrine of the priesthood shall distil upon thy soul as the dews from heaven.

"The Holy Ghost shall be thy constant companion, and thy

scepter an unchanging scepter of righteousness and truth; and thy dominion shall be an everlasting dominion, and without compulsory means it shall flow unto thee forever and ever" (D&C 121:45–46).

How could any man wish for more? These supernal blessings are promised to those who walk in virtue before the Lord and before all men.

How wonderful are the ways of our Lord. How glorious His promises. When tempted we can substitute for thoughts of evil thoughts of Him and His teachings. He has said:

"And if your eye be single to my glory, your whole bodies shall be filled with light, and there shall be no darkness in you; and that body which is filled with light comprehendeth all things.

"Therefore, sanctify yourselves that your minds become single to God, and the days will come that you shall see him; for he will unveil his face unto you" (D&C 88:67–68).

To you deacons and teachers and priests who are with us tonight, you wonderful young men who have to do with the sacrament, the Lord has said, "Be ye clean that bear the vessels of the Lord" (D&C 133:5).

To all of the priesthood, the statement of revelation is clear and unequivocal: "The rights of the priesthood are inseparably connected with the powers of heaven, and . . . the powers of heaven cannot be controlled nor handled only upon the principles of righteousness" (D&C 121:36).

Now I know, my brethren, that most of you are not afflicted with this evil. I ask your pardon for taking your time in dwelling on it. But if you are a stake president or a bishop, a district or branch president, you may very well have to assist those who are affected. May the Lord grant you wisdom, guidance, inspiration, and love for those who so need it.

And to all of you, young or old, who are not involved, I congratulate you and leave my blessing with you. How beautiful is the life that is patterned after the teachings of the gospel of Him who was without sin. Such a man walks with unblemished brow in the sunlight of virtue and strength.

May heaven's blessings attend you, my dear brethren. May all of us reach out to any who need help, I pray, in the sacred name of Jesus Christ, amen.

# SUNDAY MORNING SESSION

OCTOBER 3, 2004

$M$Y BRETHREN AND SISTERS, at the outset, if you will bear with me, I wish to exercise a personal privilege. Six months ago, at the close of our conference, I stated that my beloved companion of 67 years was seriously ill. She passed away two days later. It was April 6, a significant day to all of us of this Church. I wish to thank publicly the dedicated doctors and wonderful nurses who attended her during her final illness. My children and I were at her bedside as she slipped peacefully into eternity. As I held her hand and saw mortal life drain from her fingers, I confess I was overcome.

Before I married her, she had been the girl of my dreams, to use the words of a song then popular. She was my dear companion for more than two-thirds of a century, my equal before the Lord, really my superior. And now in my old age, she has again become the girl of my dreams.

Immediately following her passing there was a tremendous outpouring of love from across the world. Great quantities of beautiful floral offerings were sent. Large contributions were made in her name to the Perpetual Education Fund and her academic chair at Brigham Young University. There were literally hundreds of letters. We have boxes filled with them from many we know and from very many we do not know. They all express admiration for her and sympathy and love for us whom she left behind.

We regret that we have been unable to respond individually to these many expressions. So I now take this occasion to thank you every one for your great kindness toward us. Thank you so very, very much, and please excuse our failure to reply. The task was beyond our capacity, but your expressions have shed an aura of comfort in our time of grief.

I am grateful to be able to say that in our long life together I cannot remember a serious quarrel—small differences occasionally, yes, but nothing of a serious nature. I believe our marriage has been as idyllic as anyone's could possibly be.

I recognize that many of you are similarly blessed, and I compliment you most warmly, for when all is said and done there is no association richer than the companionship of husband and wife, and nothing more portentous for good or evil than the unending consequences of marriage. I see those consequences constantly. I see both beauty and tragedy. And so I have chosen to say a few words today on the women in our lives.

I begin with the Creation of the world. We read in the book of Genesis and in the book of Moses of that great, singular, and remarkable undertaking. The Almighty was the architect of that creation. Under His direction it was executed by His Beloved Son, the Great Jehovah, who was assisted by Michael, the archangel.

There came first the forming of heaven and earth, to be followed by the separation of the light from the darkness. The waters were removed from the land. Then came vegetation, followed by the animals. There followed the crowning creation of man. Genesis records that "God saw every thing that he had made, and, behold, it was very good" (Genesis 1:31). But the process was not complete.

"For Adam there was not found an help meet for him.

"And the Lord God caused a deep sleep to fall upon Adam, and he slept: and he took one of his ribs, and closed up the flesh instead thereof;

"And the rib, which the Lord God had taken from man, made he a woman, and brought her unto the man.

"And Adam said, This is now bone of my bones, and flesh of my flesh: she shall be called Woman" (Genesis 2:20–23).

And so Eve became God's final creation, the grand summation of all of the marvelous work that had gone before.

Notwithstanding this preeminence given the creation of woman, she has so frequently through the ages been relegated to a secondary position. She has been put down. She has been denigrated. She has been enslaved. She has been abused. And yet some few of the greatest characters of scripture have been women of integrity, accomplishment, and faith.

We have Esther, Naomi, and Ruth of the Old Testament. We have Sariah of the Book of Mormon. We have Mary, the very mother of the Redeemer of the world. We have her as the chosen of God, described by Nephi as "a virgin, most beautiful and fair above all other virgins" (1 Nephi 11:15). She it was who carried the child Jesus into Egypt to save His life from the wrath of Herod. She it was who nurtured Him in His boyhood and young manhood. She stood before Him when His pain-wracked body hung upon the cross on Calvary's hill. In His suffering He said to her, "Woman, behold thy son!" And to His disciple in a plea that he care for her, He said, "Behold thy mother!" (John 19:26–27).

Crossing through His life we have Mary and Martha, and Mary of Magdala. She it was who came to the tomb that first Easter morning. And to her, a woman, He first appeared as the resurrected Lord. Why is it that even though Jesus placed woman in a position of preeminence, so many men who profess His name fail to do so?

In His grand design, when God first created man, He created a duality of the sexes. The ennobling expression of that duality is found in marriage. One individual is complementary to the other.

As Paul stated, "Neither is the man without the woman, neither the woman without the man, in the Lord" (1 Corinthians 11:11). There is no other arrangement that meets the divine purposes of the Almighty. Man and woman are His creations. Their duality is His design. Their complementary relationships and functions are fundamental to His purposes. One is incomplete without the other.

I recognize that we have many wonderful women among us who do not have the opportunity of marriage. But they too make such a tremendous contribution. They serve the Church faithfully and ably. They teach in the organizations. They stand as officers.

I witnessed a very interesting thing the other day. The General Authorities were in a meeting, and the presidency of the Relief Society were there with us. These able women stood in our council room and shared with us principles of welfare and of helping those who are in distress. Our stature as officers of this Church was not diminished by what they did. Our capacities to serve were increased.

There are some men who, in a spirit of arrogance, think they are superior to women. They do not seem to realize that they would not exist but for the mother who gave them birth. When they assert their superiority, they demean her. It has been said, "Man can not degrade woman without himself falling into degradation; he can not elevate her without at the same time elevating himself" (Alexander Walker, in *Elbert Hubbard's Scrap Book* [1923], 204).

How very true that is. We see the bitter fruit of that degradation all about us. Divorce is one of its results. This evil runs rampant through our society. It is the outcome of disrespect for one's marriage partner. It manifests itself in neglect, in criticism, in abuse, in abandonment. We in the Church are not immune from it.

Jesus declared, "What therefore God hath joined together, let not man put asunder" (Matthew 19:6). The word *man* is used in the generic sense, but the fact is that it is predominantly men who bring about the conditions that lead to divorce.

After dealing with hundreds of divorce situations through the years, I am satisfied that the application of a single practice would do more than all else to solve this grievous problem. If every husband and every wife would constantly do whatever might be possible to ensure the comfort and happiness of his or her companion, there would be very little, if any, divorce. Argument would never be heard. Accusations would never be leveled. Angry explosions would not occur. Rather, love and concern would replace abuse and meanness.

There was a popular song we sang many years ago, the lyrics of which said:

> *I want to be happy,*
> *But I won't be happy*
> *Till I make you happy, too.*
> *[Irving Caesar, "I Want*
> *to Be Happy" (1924)]*

How true this is.

Every woman is a daughter of God. You cannot offend her without offending Him. I plead with the men of this Church to look for and nurture the divinity that lies within their companions. To the degree that happens, there will be harmony, peace, enrichment of family life, nurturing love.

Well did President McKay remind us that "no other success [in life] can compensate for failure in the home" (David O. McKay, quoting J. E. McCulloch, *Home: The Savior of Civilization* [1924], 42; in Conference Report, Apr. 1935, 116).

Likewise, the truth of which President Lee reminded us: "The [greatest] work you will ever do will be within the walls of your own home" (Harold B. Lee, "Maintain Your Place as a Woman," *Ensign*, Feb. 1972, 51).

The cure for most marital troubles does not lie in divorce. It lies in repentance and forgiveness, in expressions of kindness and concern. It is to be found in application of the Golden Rule.

It is a scene of great beauty when a young man and a young woman join hands at the altar in a covenant before God that they will honor and love one another. Then how dismal the picture when a few months later, or a few years later, there are offensive remarks, mean and cutting words, raised voices, bitter accusations.

It need not be, my dear brothers and sisters. We can rise above these mean and beggarly elements in our lives (see Galatians 4:9). We can look for and recognize the divine nature in one another, which comes to us as children of our Father in Heaven. We can live together in the God-given pattern of marriage in accomplishing that of which we are capable if we will exercise discipline of self and refrain from trying to discipline our companion.

The women in our lives are creatures endowed with particular qualities, divine qualities, which cause them to reach out in kindness and with love to those about them. We can encourage that outreach if we will give them opportunity to give expression to the talents and impulses that lie within them. In our old age my beloved companion said to me quietly one evening, "You have always given me wings to fly, and I have loved you for it."

I once knew a man who has since passed on but who insisted on making all of the decisions for his wife and children. They could not buy a pair of shoes without him. They could not take a piano lesson. They could not serve in the Church without his consent. I have since witnessed the outcome of that attitude, and that outcome is not good.

My father never hesitated to compliment my mother. We children knew that he loved her because of the way he treated her. He deferred to her. And I shall ever be profoundly grateful for his example. Many of you have been blessed likewise.

Now, I might go on, but it is not necessary. I wish only to give emphasis to the great, salient truth that we are all children of God, both sons and daughters, brothers and sisters.

As a father, do I love my daughters less than I love my sons? No. If I am guilty of any imbalance, it is in favor of my girls. I have said that when a man gets old, he had better have daughters about him. They are so kind and good and thoughtful. I think I can say that my sons are able and wise. My daughters are clever and kind. And "my cup runneth over" (Psalm 23:5) because of this.

Women are such a necessary part of the plan of happiness which our Heavenly Father has outlined for us. That plan cannot operate without them.

Brethren, there is too much of unhappiness in the world. There is too much of misery and heartache and heartbreak. There are too many tears shed by grieving wives and daughters. There is too much negligence and abuse and unkindness.

God has given us the priesthood, and that priesthood cannot be exercised, "only by persuasion, by long-suffering, by gentleness and meekness, and by love unfeigned; by kindness, and pure knowledge, which shall greatly enlarge the soul without hypocrisy, and without guile" (D&C 121:41–42).

How thankful I am, how thankful we all must be, for the women in our lives. God bless them. May His great love distill upon them and crown them with luster and beauty, grace and faith. And may His Spirit distill upon us as men and lead us ever to hold them in respect, in gratitude, giving encouragement, strength, nurture, and love, which is the very essence of the gospel of our Redeemer and Lord. For this I humbly pray, in the sacred name of Jesus Christ, amen.

# SUNDAY AFTERNOON SESSION

OCTOBER 3, 2004

W E HAVE EXPERIENCED another great conference. What remarkable meetings these are. What a great purpose they serve. We gather together in a spirit of worship and with a desire to learn. We renew our relationships as members of this large family of Latter-day Saints who live in many lands, who speak a variety of languages, who come out of difficult cultures, who even look different. And we recognize that we are all one, each a son or daughter of our Father in Heaven.

In a few minutes this great Conference Center in Salt Lake City will be emptied. The lights will be dimmed and the doors locked. It will be so with thousands of other halls across this broad world. We shall return to our homes greatly enriched, I hope. Our faith will have been strengthened, our resolve fortified. Where we have felt defeated and beaten, I hope that a new courage has come into our lives. Where we have been wayward and indifferent, I hope that a spirit of repentance has taken hold of us. Where we have been unkind or mean and selfish, I hope that we have determined that we will change. All who walk in faith will have had that faith strengthened.

Today is Monday in the Far East. Tomorrow is Monday in the Western Hemisphere and in Europe. It is a time that we have designated as family home evening. On that occasion I hope that fathers and mothers will gather their children about them and talk of some of the things they have heard in this conference. I would wish they might even write down some of these things, reflect on them, and remember them.

Now as we conclude I wish to remind you of another matter. I would hope that we might go to the house of the Lord a little more frequently. As I indicated at the opening session, we have done all that we know how to do to bring temples closer to our people. There are still many who have to travel long distances. I hope they will continue to make that effort until such time as a temple is justified in their midst.

Most of our temples could be much busier than they are. In this noisy, bustling, competitive world, what a privilege it is to have a sacred house where we may experience the sanctifying influence of the Spirit of the Lord. The element of selfishness crowds in upon us constantly. We need to overcome it, and there is no better way than to go to the house of the Lord and there serve in a vicarious relationship in behalf of those who are beyond the veil of death. What a remarkable thing this is. In most cases we do not know those for whom we work. We expect no thanks. We have no assurance that they will accept that which we offer. But we go, and in that process we attain to a state that comes of no other effort. We literally become saviors on Mount Zion. What does this mean? Just as our Redeemer gave His life as a vicarious sacrifice for all men, and in so doing became our Savior, even so we, in a small measure, when we engage in proxy work in the temple, become as saviors to those on the other side who have no means of advancing unless something is done in their behalf by those on earth.

And so, my brothers and sisters, I encourage you to take greater advantage of this blessed privilege. It will refine your natures. It will peel off the selfish shell in which most of us live. It will literally bring a sanctifying element into our lives and make us better men and better women.

Every temple, large or small, has its beautiful celestial room. This room was created to represent the celestial kingdom. When the Mesa Arizona Temple was extensively renovated some years ago and was opened for public tours, one visitor described the celestial room as God's living room. So it well might be. It is our privilege, unique and exclusive, while dressed in white, to sit at the conclusion of our ordinance work in the beautiful celestial room and ponder, meditate, and silently pray.

Here we can reflect on the great goodness of the Lord to us. Here we can reflect on the great plan of happiness which our Father has outlined for His children. And so I urge you, my brothers and sisters, to do it while you have strength to do it. I know that when you get old, it becomes extremely difficult to get up and down. But what a great blessing it is.

Now, my brothers and sisters, I express to you again my love. May heaven smile upon you. This work is true. Never doubt it. God, our Eternal Father, lives. Jesus is our Redeemer, our Lord, the Son of the living God. Joseph was a prophet, the Book of Mormon is of divine origin, and this is God's holy work in the earth. I leave you my witness, my love, my blessing as we separate to go to our homes. May God be with you till we meet again is my humble prayer, in the sacred name of Jesus Christ, amen.

# SECTION 2

# MEMBER
# MEETINGS

# LAIE, HAWAII,
# REGIONAL CONFERENCE*

JANUARY 23, 2000

MY BELOVED BRETHREN AND SISTERS, aloha. It's wonderful to say aloha. I learned the meaning of that way back in 1960, 40 years ago, when I was blessed to supervise the work in Hawaii and Asia.

Well, it's nice to be here. What a wonderful place to be, on a beautiful, magnificent morning in Hawaii. As I awoke this morning and looked out the hotel window at the breakers hitting the shore, I said to myself, "Surely, this is paradise." This is a great and beautiful place which we call Hawaii—a special place, a wonderful place of love and faith and friendship and goodness and honesty and truth. I'm glad to be back here, so grateful for this opportunity to participate with you in this great regional conference, when all the Saints of Oahu gather together to refresh our testimonies of the work of the Lord. I'm grateful to see so many friends here—people I've known over the years, people whom I appreciate so very, very much.

The Lord bless you. Bless you for your goodness. Bless you for your faith. Bless you for your testimony. Bless you for your kindness, your goodness, the fact that you bow before Him in prayer. What a wonderful thing that is, to actually pray to the Lord. That practice is declining in our nation. But you people who are assembled in this conference this morning get on your knees in

*delivered extemporaneously

269

recognition of the fact that you don't have all the answers, and you pray to the God of heaven to express your gratitude and invoke His blessings upon your life. What a wonderful thing it is.

I thank you for the fact that you pay your tithes and offerings. I don't need to thank you; you get thanks enough in the very process of that practice, for you know, as I know, that when you pay your honest tithes and offerings, the windows of heaven are opened and blessings are showered down upon you. That which you give is never missed; it becomes not a sacrifice but an investment under the wondrous powers of the Almighty to bless you.

Thank you for your prayers. You pray for us, and I want to tell you that we appreciate it and that we pray for you, that you will remain faithful and true and grow in number in this beautiful part of the earth.

The reason we came here is to dedicate a temple—that's the reason I came. Brother Packer came to attend this conference, but he's also going to attend the temple dedication. We're here to dedicate another sacred house of the Lord on the Big Island, in Kona. You've had this magnificent temple here in Laie for all these many years, since 1919. And now there will be another one.

I want to offer you people a challenge, that with a temple in Kona—which will draw many of the Saints, all of the Saints practically, from the Big Island, and I suppose from Molokai, Maui, Lanai, and a few other islands—you will not let the work in this Laie Temple diminish because of the growth in the other temple district, but that you will redouble your efforts and your faithfulness in going to the temple here and keep this temple as busy or busier than it has been.

Now, if each of you will make that resolution within your heart, it will happen, and the Lord will bless you, and you will be happier. I make a promise to you that every time you come to the temple you will be a better man or woman when you leave than you were when you came. That's a promise. I believe it with all my heart.

The Lord bless you in this great area. I know that you've come from the other side of the mountain, but Laie is still a part of you because of the house of the Lord here, because of the university here, because of the Polynesian Cultural Center, because of Laie. There is a place in your hearts for this spot of earth that somehow carries with it a feeling of faithfulness before the Lord.

Joseph F. Smith bought this ground as a place of refuge, as it were, at that time for our people. I hope, regardless of what happens, with the changing fortunes of our lives, this will always remain a special and wonderful place, as I believe it will be, entertaining the great and marvelous work of the Almighty through the temple work. The vicarious service to the dead is the most unselfish service of any that I know of in this life, where no one comes with any expectation of thanks for the work which he or she does.

I am grateful for the great educational programs which are centered here, which bespeak the philosophy of this Church before all the world, and for the great undertaking of the PCC [Polynesian Cultural Center], which was constructed to tell others, to explain to others of the great worldwide interest of this Church, simply illustrated in the cultures of the Polynesians. We have centered here something that's unique in all the earth. I pray that we may preserve it and keep it beautiful and clean and brilliant—great expressions of the faith of our people.

Well, now, my dear brothers and sisters, I think I'm going to say something about a simple little statement: "Keep the faith." I see men and women who serve in the Church with valiance, who love the Lord apparently and seek to do His work. Then they're released from service, and somehow some of them—not many, I'm grateful to say—drift away and fail to keep the faith. I'd like to try to impress upon you this morning, with all the capacity that I have, the importance of keeping the faith.

President J. Reuben Clark said to me one time, "Never assume that as you grow old the power of the adversary will disappear from

271

your life. You will know that power for as long as you live, and particularly if you strive to live in faithfulness." Keep the faith.

I've been thinking today of Sister Toma. I don't know how many of you have ever heard of Sister Toma. I knew her 40 years ago. I first became acquainted with her on Okinawa. She had grown up there. She had married there. The missionaries came to her family's door and touched their lives briefly. Then came the war, and Okinawa became a literal hellhole on earth. A fireball of warfare raked that island up and down. A few people hid in caves, ate whatever they could find—the leaves, flowers, even insects and bugs—to stay alive. She was there. She had married. She had three little children. Her husband fell sick and couldn't do a thing. There she stood, alone with these three little children and a sick husband. She said to God, "Take me. I cannot stand it anymore." The answer came back, "Do not forsake your husband and your children." She said it gave her the strength to carry on.

Finally the war came to an end. They moved to Naha, bought a little house, bought a little business, and began to make it profitable; then he sickened and died. He was the first branch president in Naha, Okinawa.

I remember so very, very vividly the occasion in 1962 when we went to their home and he was on a mat on the floor, seriously ill. We got down on our knees and administered to him and pleaded with the Lord to spare his life. It didn't happen. He died. But he didn't die until after we had established a place to build a meetinghouse there. I'd asked him to find a suitable place, and the next time we went, he said, "I've found a place."

We went there, and I said, "It won't do. This is not a good enough place for a chapel. This is a backyard."

And he said, "Where would you like it to be?"

We walked around Naha and found a place, and I said, "This is where it ought to be."

He said, "You'll never get that ground. This is the burial place of a Nahan king." Well, I said we ought to try to get it.

He worked with us, and somehow, in the providence of the Lord, we got that site. He was the branch president at the time.

In any event, Brother Toma died, and Sister Toma was left alone. The business partner pulled out and left her in a terrible situation of debt. She sold the home which they had and bought a very small, tiny, little home. She worked from 5:00 in the morning until 11:00 at night, day after day after day. She kept the faith through all that, with all of that, wondering why in the world the God of heaven would have taken her husband when she had a family of young children. She kept the faith and struggled to rear her children. Those nights when she would come home and say, "Tonight we will sing hymns," the children knew then that there would be no food that night for them. Somehow, somehow they survived.

One son, Rick, came to this school here, to this campus, and then went on to Provo. The others did the same. They prospered. They actually began to become leaders in their industry. They wrote to their mother and told her to sell her home and come to live with them. Eventually, they bought her a beautiful home in Tokyo, and she lived out her days working in the Tokyo Temple and was a faithful temple worker there. She died three or four years ago. The motto of her life was this: "Morning will come. Morning will come." That was an expression of her faith, and morning came into her life.

I never can go to Okinawa that I do not think of Misao Toma, a woman who kept the faith notwithstanding the adversities of her life, though bitter and terrible, who finally blossomed into a bright and brilliant and comfortable and wonderful old age because of the faithfulness of her life, which she inculcated in the lives of her children, every one of them. Keep the faith, my brothers and sisters.

We were in Ohio not long ago, dedicating a new temple, and

our daughter Kathy was with us. I try to take one of my girls with us to take care of their mother. She took care of them when they were small, and they take care of her now that she's small.

I had been a year or two ago up in Ontario, Canada, and, through the graciousness of a member of the stake presidency, had discovered the burial place of my great-grandfather, which was unknown to us. He had joined the Church in the very early years of the Church. While the Saints were in Kirtland, missionaries went from Kirtland up into Ontario. His was one of those early baptisms. He was a young man, married with small children, when a small-pox epidemic raged through that part of the country and took his life. He was there buried in a place which we found.

When we were in Ohio, Kathy and her mother were seated on the front row of the celestial room, and her daughter was there also, with some of our great-grandchildren. I looked down at her and at her daughter and at her daughter's children—my daughter, my granddaughter, my great-granddaughter—and then there came into my mind this great-grandfather of mine. I thought of my great-grandfather who first joined the Church; and my grandfather, who was valiant in the Church; and my father, who was very active in the Church. I recognized something that I had never thought of before. I was right in the middle between three generations who had gone before me in the Church and three generations who were coming after me in the Church.

I said to myself, "Don't you ever be found a weak link in the chain of your generations." Now, my brothers and sisters, don't you ever be found a weak link in the chain of your generations. That's my message to you this day.

You are a part of the great processes of God under which men and women have gone before you. All that you have of body and mind will be transmitted through you to the generations yet to come, and it is so important, so everlastingly important, my brothers and sisters, that you become not a weak link in that chain of your generations. Keep the faith. Be faithful. Walk with integrity. In storm and sunshine, be faithful. In richness or in poverty, be faithful. In youth or old age, be faithful. Keep the faith.

This is the work of the Almighty. Don't you ever forget it. God has spoken from the heavens in declaration of the truth of this, His work. And there is no voice greater than His voice. His Son has spoken to man upon the earth and declared His identity, His reality, His great and divine place in the plan of His Father, as the Redeemer and the Savior of the world. And these truths will last as long as the earth lasts. Keep faith in these great and sacred truths, my brethren and sisters. Come what may, keep the faith. Think of Sister Toma and the great adversity through which she passed. Keep the faith, my brothers and sisters.

How tragic it is, how very, very tragic, when we see occasionally, once in a great while, a returned missionary who slips back into old and careless ways. That's a tragedy that we ought to work with all our might to avoid. Think of the tragedy that comes when a man begins to get a little learning and knowledge, as he supposes, and in an act that leads to apostasy, kicks over the faith of his fathers. What a tragedy that is.

What a beautiful and magnificent thing it is to see humble and sweet and good people who keep the faith through thick and thin, through adversity and prosperity. Keep the faith.

I remember coming here to Hawaii on one occasion and we were invited to stay with an elderly woman. She had been on one of the outer islands and had there been very faithful and very true. She lost her husband and became a widow. Finally, she moved to Oahu.

We were invited to stay in her home. I went into the home of that woman, and while she was getting dinner, I looked around. There was a library there—great books, good books, wonderful books, books of literature, books of great things, books about exploration, and shining above all were the sacred scriptures and companion volumes. I said to myself, "What a miracle this is.

Here's a little woman who's come out of the bush, as it were, who's lost her husband, who's now in her old age, living in the beauty of such things as this and remaining faithful and true in the Church."

Well, my brothers and sisters, that's my wish for you today. Keep the faith. How magnificently God has blessed you. How richly blessed you are, when all is said and done. You are so richly blessed to have lived here in this land of peace and beauty, a place that speaks of love, leis, and all of the other things that we call "the Aloha spirit."

God bless you. May His peace be with you. Teach your children the ways of the Lord, and lead them that they may keep the faith. Isaiah said, "And all thy children shall be taught of the Lord; and great shall be the peace of thy children" (Isaiah 54:13). Have you ever seen children without peace, children addicted to drugs, children addicted to crime? There is no peace in their lives. There's only misery, trouble, failure, dismay, and death. The way of peace is the way of the Lord. Bring up your children in the ways of truth and righteousness.

I'd like to say parenthetically, you don't have to beat them to do that. Be kind to them. Speak with a spirit of love. Pray with them while they're very, very young. Read to them, and you won't ever have to worry about beating them. They may make a mistake or two, but when they do, may there be forgiveness in your hearts.

Well, God bless you. I don't know whether I'll ever come here again. I'm getting to be very old, pretty soon 90 years of age. I can't believe it.

From Kona we're going to fly to Tarawa on Monday. We'll meet with our people there at the airport in the Gilbert Islands, the very place where so many gave their lives in one terrible battle in the last World War.

And then we'll go on to Cairns, Australia, which is way up north where nobody ever goes to see the people. And then we'll go to Jakarta, where we have a meeting with the president of

Indonesia, the fourth largest nation in the world, who has become very friendly with us and has invited us to stay at his palace. We're not staying there; we're going to stay in a hotel so we don't give up our agency. In any event, we're going to have a nice visit with him, a man whom we've grown to love and appreciate.

Then we'll go to Singapore and hold a meeting with our people there, people from Penang and Kuala Lumpur. Then we'll go to Guam and hold a meeting there and come back home and hope we're still going because we've got another temple dedication next month.

Thank you, my beloved brothers and sisters. Thank you for who you are, for the goodness of your lives. Keep the faith. Never throw away the faith. You cannot afford to. Keep the faith. Hold out till the end, and God will bless you and crown your days with sweetness and peace and love. For this I humbly pray, as I speak my own love for you, my brothers and sisters of many races, all gathered in this favored place. I invoke the blessings of heaven upon you and the peace of the Lord to be in your hearts and in your homes, in the name of Jesus Christ, amen.

# SINGAPORE MEMBER MEETING*

JANUARY 30, 2000

$M$Y BELOVED BROTHERS AND SISTERS, how happy I am to be here in this great city of Singapore. This is one of the great cities of the world. It is a tremendous place. Ever since the British came here so long, long ago and established the refueling station, an entrepôt station, for the reprovisioning of ships that traversed the Strait of Malacca, this has been a very important place in all the world.

While on a mission in England 67 years ago, on Christmas Day in the year 1933, I sat in the living room of a little family in Lancashire, England, and heard the King of England call the British family of nations home. One of those places that he called home, as he circled the globe, was Singapore. It was a part of that great empire, until finally the empire was largely dissolved and Singapore and other colonies broke away and established themselves as independent entities. Since then they have grown in majesty and might and wonder before the whole world.

I count one of my great peculiar blessings, my brothers and sisters, the tremendous experiences I had in this part of the world 40 years ago or so. Beginning in 1960, I was given responsibility for the work in Asia. I traveled up and down through this whole part of the earth—from Japan and Korea on the north, then on down through Taiwan, Hong Kong, the Philippines, Thailand, Malaysia;

*delivered extemporaneously

278

on down to Singapore and Jakarta and over into India—until I knew this part of the world like the back of my hand.

I came here first about 35 to 37 years ago. The president of the mission in Hong Kong, President Jay Quealy, and I came to Singapore. We wanted to see how this place looked. We had no work here then. We thought there might be a few members. We came here and stayed in the old Raffles Hotel, named for Sir Stamford Raffles of long ago. We searched around and talked with the American embassy and the British embassy and other people and found, out of the millions who lived here, four members of the Church: a soldier and his wife from England who were stationed here, a chartered accountant here from England, and one other whose vocation I do not remember.

We had a little meeting in our hotel room. We talked together of the gospel; we shared our experiences; we talked of one another. I later met that soldier and his wife again in England, where they remained faithful and did very well. We had a marvelous time in that little group of only four people, Brother Quealy, and myself.

Who would ever have dreamed that this theater would be largely filled tonight with Latter-day Saints who live in this great community and those who have come down from Malaysia to this meeting? My brothers and sisters, you are an answer to prayer. You are an answer to my prayers. I have prayed over this part of the world. I have wept over this part of the world. I have talked with the Lord over this part of the world. I believe that the Lord has heard and answered my prayers. I don't take full responsibility for that. Many, many people have worked to make all of this come to pass, but I repeat, it was my peculiar responsibility back in 1960 to have received an assignment to Asia.

The world was divided up into various territories. President Henry D. Moyle [of the First Presidency], who was doing it, said to me, "I've got somebody for every place in the world except the Orient," and by that he meant Japan, which was large, and Hong

Kong. He said, "I don't know who to send there. Nobody wants to go." I said, "I'll go." I'd never been here before, but I came, and the things I've seen, the experiences I've had, the miracles I've witnessed are absolutely wonderful, my brothers and sisters.

As I listened tonight to Brother Tan, President Woo, and President Collins, I said, "What hath God wrought in touching the hearts and minds and lives of these wonderful people in this great and unique area of the earth!" Well, I've seen it. It is a miracle to behold.

You are men and women of faith. Every man and woman here this night could stand and bear testimony that he or she has a witness of the living God. Every man and woman in this hall tonight could stand and bear witness that he or she has a testimony of the living Christ. Every man in this hall could stand and bear testimony that the gospel has been restored. Every one of you say your prayers—you get on your knees; you talk to the Lord; you give thanks; you ask Him to bless you in your various undertakings. What a marvelous and wonderful thing that is. You live the gospel. You accept responsibility in the Church, and the Lord is blessing you. As I look into your faces, I say, "What handsome and beautiful people these people are."

We were in Jakarta the other day, and there were 1,800 people in a meeting of this kind. It was difficult to believe. I remember going to Jakarta when we had nobody there. Well, marvelous miracles have come to pass.

Now, my brothers and sisters, as surely as you know the gospel is true, as certainly as you include God in your daily prayers, it is your responsibility and obligation to stand on your feet and live the life of a Latter-day Saint. That is not an easy thing to do in a society of this kind. It is very difficult and demanding, but it will bring to you magnificent and wonderful blessings.

The things of the past have been wonderful, but the things of the future will be greater. Numbers will be added to the Church here. We now have a fairly reasonable population, but that will double and triple. I hope that every one of you will feel a responsibility to share the gospel, as opportunity comes to you, with those who are not of this faith.

We recognize the good that every other church in the world does. We have no quarrel with other churches. We do not argue, we do not debate or anything of the kind. We simply say to people not of our faith, "You bring with you all the truth that you have and let us see if we can add to it." That is the mission and the message of this Church, and you are the fruit of that. It is wonderful.

As we came in here, we met two young men. I said, "Are you going on missions?" One young man said, "I just sent my papers in." The other man said, "I'm getting my papers ready to send in." I said to myself, "It's for real. It's happening. Things are working as they should work."

It should be the ambition, the desire, the hoped-for experience of every young man in this Church to go into the world as a teacher of the eternal gospel, as a missionary of The Church of Jesus Christ of Latter-day Saints. I don't know where you'll go. Some of you may even be sent here or to other parts of Asia. It will prove to be a tremendous and wonderful experience for you. You will live close to the Lord. You will pray as you never prayed before. You'll teach, and you'll do great good that will bless your life as long as you live. There is no question in my mind concerning that.

So, to all of these little boys who are here tonight, I want to urge you to save and prepare and think of and dream of and pray for the experience of a mission in The Church of Jesus Christ of Latter-day Saints.

I said to one of the brethren tonight, "How much does it cost you to go to Hong Kong to go to the temple?" He said, "Oh, between 500 and 800 Singaporean dollars." That's a lot of money, isn't it? Bless you for what you have done. The Lord bless you for the fact that you have made that sacrifice and taken advantage of that great and marvelous opportunity of going to the temple in Hong Kong.

I want to throw out to you the challenge of promoting the growth of the Church in this area to a point where someday we can have a Singapore Temple of The Church of Jesus Christ of Latter-day Saints. You live among those for whom a great work needs to be done in the house of the Lord, a great vicarious work. If it gets done, you're going to have to do it. I believe with all my heart that within this great city somewhere we could locate a temple. I don't know how the design will be; land is terribly expensive. But we built a temple on very expensive land in Hong Kong, and you're familiar with that. We could do the same here.

Hurry along. Bring people into the Church. Bring them in with love. Bring them in with kindness. Bring them in with the example of your lives. So live the gospel that they will see in you something of wonder and beauty and be encouraged to inquire, study the gospel, and join the Church and thus build the membership here so that the time could come in the not-too-distant future when we might have a sacred house of the Lord in this part of the earth.

You are here where you speak English. That's quite an advantage for a man like me, to talk with people who speak English without an interpreter. I'm glad the English established their language here. I heard Margaret Thatcher say on two occasions that the great gift of the English people to America was two-fold: the English Bible and the English law. The same thing can be said for Singapore, where they brought the English Bible and the English law. I'd like to add one other: the English language.

Now, brothers and sisters, how nice to look into your faces. You people from Singapore, you from other parts of the earth, the United States particularly, how good to see you here. Thank you for what you are doing here. Thank you for the great missionary service which you are carrying forward.

President George Bush, the former and the father, visited us at one time, and he said to me, "How do you get established in a particular place?"—such a place as Singapore. I said, "Well, what usually happens is that some man who is an engineer or banker or lawyer or something of that kind with a special skill is sent there by his company. He's lonely. He finally gets his wife and children there. They are all lonely. They pray for others to come. They write letters and say, 'Please send some missionaries.' Before long, we've got a dozen people, then 100 people, then 500 people, and then 1,000 people, then 5,000 people. That is the way this gospel is carried over the earth in the many, many lands and among many people."

Thanks be to you missionaries who are here. You are devoted and able young men. How the Lord loves you for a great work which you are doing.

We lost four missionaries yesterday in the United States in an automobile accident. Four of them were killed—a terrible tragedy. The whole Church will mourn the loss of those wonderful young men. Everybody in this Church loves the missionaries. There never will be a time in your life when you have people praying for you the way they pray for you now. In homes all across the world, families get on their knees and pray for the missionaries who are out in the field, out across the world doing the Lord's work. Thank you for all you do.

I just want to say from the bottom of my heart that you people are loved by the Lord, as much as any people on the face of this earth. You people are as worthy of the blessings of the gospel as are the Saints who live in Salt Lake City. You people are loved by the Lord as much as are the Saints in Salt Lake City. You belong to a great family, 11 million strong, scattered over the earth, speaking a great variety of languages, doing things in a variety of ways, but we are all one family with a knowledge of the living God; with a knowledge of a living Christ; with a testimony of a great prophet who opened this dispensation of the gospel; with a conviction concerning the Book of Mormon, another testament which has come forth in this dispensation for the blessing of the sons and daughters of God—another testament of Jesus Christ.

To think, my brothers and sisters, that in this Church every worthy man may hold the priesthood of God. Every worthy man may "speak in the name of God the Lord, even the Savior of the world" (D&C 1:20). Every man may serve in the governance of the Church. Every man may place his hands upon the heads of his wife and children and bless them. What a marvelous thing it is. What a great thing we have to offer the world.

We have a great lay priesthood who do all of this work. I look at Brother Jackson, who was in Jakarta with us day before yesterday; he's a doctor, running around to the American embassies to see who has the flu, but he serves as a bishop—as the head of a flock, the father of a Church family, a helper to the people, a defender of the people, one who loves and cherishes his flock and sees to it that things go forward in the right way. So it is with all of you bishops and branch presidents who serve here.

God bless you. I love you. I want you to know that. You are my people. You've been my people for a very, very long time. I love the people of Asia, whether they be Japanese or Chinese, whether they be Korean or Filipinos, Taiwanese or Thailanders, Malaysians or those of Singapore, Indonesia, or India or any of these great areas of the earth where live so very many millions of our Father's children.

I love you. I wish I could throw my arms around every one of you and tell you that.

May the Lord bless you. I leave a blessing with you, an apostolic blessing, speaking in the name of the Lord and in the authority of His priesthood, that as you live in righteousness, keeping the commandments of God, the windows of heaven will be opened and blessings will come down upon you. You will have food on your tables and clothing on your backs and shelter over your heads. May this be your blessing is my humble prayer, as I leave my witness of the truth of this, the everlasting gospel of the Lord Jesus Christ. God be with you till we meet again.

We'll never forget you. We'll remember you. Somehow, I hope maybe we'll have the opportunity of coming back to see you again.

The Lord bless you, my dear, dear, dear friends, I humbly pray in the name of Him whom we all love and serve, even the Savior and Redeemer of the world, who gave His life for each of us in a great and marvelous act of atonement, even Jesus Christ, amen.

# GUAM MEMBER MEETING*

## JANUARY 31, 2000

$A$LOHA. SO GOOD TO BE with you, my beloved brethren and sisters. I'm grateful to see so many of you here. This is a marvelous sight. When you realize that there's another hall that's filled with people where this service is being transmitted and that it goes from here to Saipan, it says a very great deal about the spread of the work in this part of the world.

I came to Guam many years ago, about 35 years ago. I had asked President McKay if some member of the First Presidency couldn't come to Asia. There had never been a man go to Asia who was a member of the First Presidency back in those years when I had responsibility for the work in Asia. President McKay said, "You talk with Brother Hugh B. Brown and see if he will go with you." And so I talked with Brother Brown, and he consented to go.

We flew to Honolulu first and then to Guam. Here we met with a little group of people, maybe 15 people, in a room while the plane was being refueled. The plane stopped for about an hour, and the time was about six o'clock in the morning. The Saints, who were not lazy, got up and came to that little meeting. Now to look at this gathering tonight is an inspiration, my dear friends.

How grateful I am to be with you. I'm thankful for the effort that you made to be here. I'm thankful for the growth of the work

*delivered extemporaneously

across the world, for the marvelous manner in which the Lord is prospering His cause in the earth. It is tremendous and wonderful.

I look at these older couples here who are here as missionaries and those who are with the Church education program and with the family history program. I'm glad to see that you had the courage and the faith to leave home and all the soft life that you enjoyed there to come here to this part of the world and do that which the Lord would have you do. You'll remember this as long as you live. This will stand out as a high point in your lives. You'll never forget it. You'll tell your children and your grandchildren and your great-grandchildren about it. You'll write it in your journal, and it will go down to the generations that follow you. Thank you for your great service. I say that in behalf of the entire Church. We're indebted to you for the great and good work which you do.

I want to say to those service people who are here in the service of the United States, thanks for your faithfulness in coming here and remaining true to the Church and doing what you ought to do to move forward the work of the Lord. And to everyone else who is here, these wonderful people who come into the Church, what a strength you are. We've had a wonderful time. It's been very tiring, but it's been wonderful.

We started in Hawaii and had a regional conference there with 15,000 members of the Church. Then we went over to Kona on the Big Island and dedicated a new temple there. Then we flew to Tarawa, a little spot of earth out in the middle of the broad Pacific, where we met with about 1,500 people—good people, very poor people, somewhat primitive in the way they live, but with wonderful hearts and a great love for the Church and this work which is moving forward.

From Tarawa we went to Australia—Cairns, up north where few people ever go—and met with the great Saints there. From there we flew to Jakarta and had a meeting of this kind at which

1,800 were present. It was marvelous to be with those people in that great city of Jakarta.

From there we went to Bali. I don't know why we went to Bali. Somebody wanted us to see the monkeys. Anyhow, we met there at the airport with five little beautiful people, the only members of the Church on that island of Bali. We had a wonderful visit with them and foresaw the promise of the Lord. Those five will become many through the years that follow as this work grows in that part of the earth.

Then to Singapore, that magnificent and beautiful city down at the base of the Malaysian Peninsula—there we had another congregation of about 1,500 people who were there from Singapore and from the cities of Malaysia.

Now we're here on this beautiful island of Guam. I'm so glad to be here to shake your hands, look into your faces, have leis placed upon our necks as a token of love and appreciation, and feel of your great kindness. Tomorrow morning we'll fly to Honolulu, then on home, and we'll start over on some other work of some kind for as long as we can keep going.

We're getting old. I'm in my 90th year. I'll soon be 90 years of age. As I've said before, I feel like the last leaf on the tree with a heavy wind blowing. But we're going to keep it up for as long as we possibly can.

Now, my beloved, dear friends, I wish to say a few words about the gospel and our place in it and our responsibility concerning it. I pray for the guidance of the Spirit, the direction of the Lord, in that which I say.

Wherever I go and meet with groups of this kind, one question comes in my mind: "What does the Lord expect of us as Latter-day Saints?" My brothers and sisters, I think He expects us to be Latter-day Saints in the truest meaning of that word. He expects us to take upon us His holy name and to act in His cause and to live as He would have His sons and daughters live.

What does He expect of us? He expects that we will be good people, clean and decent, and rise above the sins of the world and stand tall and strong and live the gospel in its fulness. He expects us to conduct ourselves in such a way as to bring honor and respect to this, His great cause and kingdom. He expects us to live the gospel as those who have taken upon themselves a great and solemn and wonderful covenant. That's what He expects of us.

He expects we will be good neighbors, kind to others, to those not of our faith; that we will treat them with generosity and love and respect; that when they have troubles, we will reach out to assist them and lift them and help and bless them.

Jesus was asked, "Which is the great commandment in the law?" And He said, "Thou shalt love the Lord thy God with all thy heart, [might, mind, and soul]. This is the first and great commandment. And the second is like unto it, Thou shalt love thy neighbour as thyself" (see Matthew 22:36–39). Now, that is not easy to do, but we must work at it and work at it constantly. We cannot be a little group that hugs one another only, gets together and lives in a clannish kind of way. We must reach out to assist others, and their respect and appreciation for this Church will grow as we do so. The God of heaven expects us to be helpful to others, to be good neighbors, to be friends to all within our reach.

He expects us to be good parents—fathers and mothers, husbands and wives. He expects husbands to treat their wives with deference and respect. He expects wives to treat their husbands with kindness and helpfulness. He expects us to be good parents to our children.

We have the great concept that every one of us is a child of God. We sing about it. We teach it. We believe it, but sometimes we don't act as if we did. We were in a meeting of this kind the other night somewhere—I don't remember where, and it's just as well. I saw a young mother grab two little boys, one by each arm, and lift them up and carry them out into the hall. And I said to myself, "She's not dealing with monkeys; she's dealing with boys." To see her grab those two little boys and then see them dangling and kicking and crying while she was doing it—let us look to our children with love. They are our Father's children, and ours is a custodial relationship to them for their lives.

I want to tell you that there's no need to beat your children. There is a tendency with a lot of people to lick their children. You don't need to do that. President Joseph F. Smith taught that very strongly. We need to rear them in love and appreciation and respect.

I'm grateful to be able to say that I had a father who never laid a hand upon his children but had some wonderful, magic way under which he would talk with us when we did that which was not right and made us feel ashamed of what we had done and resolve within our hearts to be different.

Rear your children in the nurture and admonition of the Lord. Isaiah said, "And all thy children shall be taught of the Lord; and great shall be the peace of thy children" (Isaiah 54:13). Do you want your children to have peace? Peace comes of righteousness. Peace comes of doing the right thing. You don't find peace where there are drugs, where there are gangs, where there's anything of the kind.

Rear your children in such a way that they will love you all the days of their lives. I think of my wife and her daughter here tonight. When our children were young, their mother took care of them. Now she's much older, and they take care of her.

Develop within yourselves a spirit of accepting whatever call comes to you in the Church. I don't care what it is. If you will accept every call that comes to you within the Church, you will grow in a remarkable and marvelous and wonderful way. With responsibility comes growth, and the Lord will magnify you and make you equal to every responsibility which is given you. My beloved brothers and sisters, and you older couples who are here tonight, you are an example of that, and you're happy. You look happy. You're doing the kind of work that will make you happy, and you'll be blessed of the Lord. Accept every responsibility.

I remember talking when I was a stake president with a young man to make him president of the elders quorum. He said, "You're talking to the wrong man." I said, "I'm talking to the right man." He went on to tell me of his background. He'd been an orphan boy. He'd grown up down in Alabama. The only thing he'd ever learned to do was to make straw brooms. Then he went into the army and was stationed at Kearns, out southwest of Salt Lake, and there he learned to know the Church and was baptized. When he was released from the service, he came back to live there.

He thought he was of no value. We made him the president of an elders quorum that contained university professors and businessmen. But this little fellow from Alabama had the wonderful capacity of knowing how to talk with people. He just talked with them in simple ways and brought them into the Church and gave marvelous leadership to that quorum. That will happen with any of us who will make the effort and do that which is expected of us.

Live the Word of Wisdom. I don't have to talk with you about that. You know that's true. You know that every blessing promised of the Lord comes to those who live that sacred law. What a marvelous and wonderful thing we're witnessing in the world. Finally, after all these years, science, medicine, governments have reached the conclusion that we've known ever since the Prophet received the revelation, which we call the Word of Wisdom, concerning tobacco—that it is not good for man.

Live the Word of Wisdom, and live it rigidly. You don't need any tea. You don't need any coffee. We've all understood that we can live without those things. You certainly don't need liquor, and you don't need to smoke cigarettes. Every one of you is smart enough to know that. Live the Word of Wisdom.

Pay your tithing. Put the Lord to the test. See if He will not open the windows of heaven and shower down a blessing upon you "that there shall not be room enough to receive it" (see Malachi 3:10). He will bless you. I don't mean to infer that He'll make you rich and wealthy. I do mean to say, without any hesitation whatever, that He will bless you and bring joy into your lives and blessings that are as real as anything on this earth. Those who live the law of tithing are given a great and sacred promise. That is not my promise; that's the promise of the God of heaven. He has the power to keep His word, and it's my testimony to you, my brothers and sisters, that He keeps His word.

Live worthy to hold a temple recommend. There is nothing more precious than a temple recommend, when all is said and done. Now, all of you can't get to the temple all of the time. Hawaii is a long way from here, and it's expensive to go there. But whether you can go there or not, qualify for a temple recommend and keep a recommend in your pocket. It will be a reminder to you of what is expected of you as a Latter-day Saint.

Cultivate a testimony of the Restoration of the gospel. You know this work is true as well as I do. You know that the God of heaven has spoken as well as I do. You know that the Lord Jesus Christ communicated with the Prophet Joseph as one man speaks to another. You know that as well as I do. But you have to cultivate, you have to nourish, you have to feed your testimony of these things by reading the scriptures and by being active and faithful in the Church.

If you don't have a testimony, go to work to get one. The Lord told us how to do it. He said that he that doeth the will of the Father "shall know of the doctrine, whether it be of God, or whether I speak of myself" (John 7:17). That's as true as anything on earth. It's just that simple. It's a law of God that carries with it a marvelous and remarkable promise.

Cultivate a testimony of the Lord. Learn to know and love the Lord Jesus Christ. Read the scriptures. Read the New Testament. Read 3 Nephi. Read the Doctrine and Covenants. Learn to know the Lord Jesus Christ. This proclamation which Brother Packer referred to, which you all have with you ["The Living Christ: The Testimony of the Apostles"]—I wish you'd all take it home with you tonight and read it before you go to bed. Ponder what is said in it. This is the testimony and the witness of 15 Apostles speaking out of the authority of the holy apostleship concerning the Savior and Redeemer of mankind, the Lord Jesus Christ (see *Ensign*, Apr. 2000, 2–3).

Finally, come to know our Father in Heaven. Say your prayers. Get on your knees and pray to the God of heaven, and He will hear and answer your prayers. I know that. I've experienced that. You've experienced it. We pray for you; I want you to know that. You pray for us, and I want to thank you for your prayers. It's those prayers that keep us going.

God bless you, my dear friends. May the peace of heaven be with you. May you walk in righteousness as Latter-day Saints. It's so good that you've come to Guam. You'll never have that opportunity again, likely, to have left home and come here, so many of you. And you who are natives to this part of the earth, what a choice and wonderful and beautiful place this is. Enjoy it, and thank the Lord for it, and improve it by the goodness of your lives. How we love you. I mean that with all my heart.

I've had the good fortune, my brothers and sisters, of working with many people like you. For eight years I had responsibility for the work in Asia. In fact, I have been up and down this part of the world, from northern Japan to southern India, all over along the highways and in the byways of Asia, with people of your kind whom I have learned to love and respect and admire. You're just as able, you're just as faithful, you're just as good as any people on the face of the whole earth. The God of heaven loves you and respects you and blesses you. I know that, and you know that.

Well, we must leave. We've been here long enough. Thanks for coming, again I say. The Lord bless you, you haoles, you pakehas who will go home someday soon, including the mission president and his wife. Oh, how grateful you ought to be. You'll go home with sweet memories of this experience.

For those who are natives to this land, may the Lord bless you. May you live to see the work strengthen and grow in this part of the earth, that whereas we have a thousand, we will someday have ten thousand in this part of God's kingdom. I leave you my blessing and my love. In the authority of the holy apostleship, my beloved brothers and sisters, I call down the blessings of heaven in your behalf, that as you live in righteousness and walk in the ways of the Lord, He will bless you and protect you and preserve you. May you find great happiness as you live the gospel from day to day. May you serve the Lord in righteousness and have cause to get on your knees and thank Him for the blessings of each day is my humble prayer, in the name of Jesus Christ, amen.

# Provo, Utah, Seminar for New Mission Presidents*

## June 23, 2000

N ow, I should not confess this—I do not have a prepared talk. I have not had time. But I think I would like to speak out of my heart on one or two things.

I know you have received instruction from A to Z; every facet and feature of missionary work has been dealt with at great length and sometimes three or four times over. I had a lot to do with that years ago, but I am not going to do it today. I assume you've heard enough of how to have many, many baptisms and how to keep them active in the Church. You have learned all of that technique, and you are ready to go out and be disappointed. It is going to be a surprise to you when you hit the field, I am sure. It is to all of us, but nonetheless I congratulate you most warmly and thank you in behalf of all of the Church for the fact that you are going, that you responded readily to these missionary calls that have been extended to you, that you have committed yourselves and committed to the Lord that you will do the very best of which you are capable. That I know will come to pass.

I have just finished a long tour with Brother Holland. It was on that tour that he learned to speak so well, because he had many opportunities to practice. We were in Thailand, a country with which I was familiar.

*delivered extemporaneously

Back in 1960, when the world was divided up among the Brethren, I was given the responsibility for the Far East—Hawaii and the Far East. I remember so very, very vividly the heartache and the heartbreak of some of those days that were so discouraging and at times fruitless and at times so very, very difficult. And now to go back there and see what has happened brings into my mind the thought that you never can foretell the consequences of your work as a missionary in this Church. You don't know what will come of it. You may be turned down. You may have the door slammed in your face. You may have all of these things that happen so frequently and think that you have accomplished absolutely nothing. But miracles come out of these very, very small beginnings.

The first time I went to Thailand, in 1966, we met with the minister of education, who also had responsibility for religious work in Thailand. Marion Hanks was with me. We went to his office and told him what we had in mind, what we would like to do, and he said, "We don't need you." We tried to pursue it a little further, and he said, "This country is 95 percent non-Christian. We already have 10 churches to take care of the other 5 percent, and there is no need for adding another." He was very curt and almost mean. In any event, we were turned down. We did not know quite what to do.

We went to Lumpini Park in Bangkok, that great city of 10 million people, and offered a dedicatory prayer on the work in the nation of Thailand. We began to make application for visas, and our missionaries were granted visas for three months. The understanding was that they would have to leave the country every three months and have their visas renewed. It was a very expensive and costly and difficult and discouraging practice that interfered greatly with the work.

Well, that continued over the years. Then we had two missionaries who did a very unfortunate thing. They climbed on a Buddha and had their photographs taken, and the man who ran the film developing shop reported them to the government. They were arrested, and terrible troubles followed. We had very great difficulty. They were going to jail them and do other things but finally consented to their leaving the country. That brought about further restrictions upon our work, but we kept at it. We kept at it. The Book of Mormon was translated by a wonderful little woman, whom we met the other day, still alive and still going.

The other day we went to Thailand by invitation—not to look up the education minister and be insulted, but to partake of the courtesy and the kindness of the officials of Thailand.

The mayor of Bangkok, under the providence of the Lord, is a friend. He was kind of an unruly boy at the university over there. His father was a Rotarian. When Richard Evans traveled around the world in his capacity as president of Rotary, this man met him. The man said, "I have a son who is letting his hair grow and is tampering with drugs. Isn't there a university in the United States to which I can send him where he won't be exposed to those things?" Brother Evans said, "Try BYU." So he came to BYU and stayed in Provo for seven years. His eldest child was born there. He got a master's degree and then a doctorate in microbiology. He went back. His father was in politics. His father became the vice-premier of Thailand, and the son ran for mayor and was elected. Between the two they were able to secure, through their government, authorization under which we are allowed 150 missionaries who don't have to renew their visas every three months. They can go forward with their work.

Now, to me, that is an absolute miracle. That is the unseen consequence, my brothers and sisters, of that which was begun in 1966 and has come to pass in a miraculous way. We have about 40 couples and single elderly women who are there teaching English in the schools, and the people love them. At a great banquet in the Hyatt Hotel in Bangkok, they put on a big dinner for us and for the teachers, honoring them and thanking them for their service. It is almost impossible to believe, but it is a fact, an actual fact.

We dedicated a building down in Fukuoka, Japan, the southern end of Japan. I remember going down there about 1961 and trying to get a little branch established and the great difficulties which we had. Now there are stakes of Zion, and there is a beautiful new dedicated house of the Lord in which those people will worship Him in spirit and in truth.

You see in Korea the marvelous thing that has come to pass. When we first went to Korea in 1960, we had nothing—a few members, a little handful of members that came of the efforts of Dr. Ho Jih Kim, who had come to the United States and studied at Cornell and was baptized there. He translated the Book of Mormon there. He went back to his native land and worked there under the direction of the mission headquarters in Japan. He got a little nucleus started, but it was very small when he died.

I have seen the struggles there from the days of the great poverty in that nation and the difficulties of the people. I remember holding a meeting in a high school gymnasium with a big stove in the middle with a stovepipe that ran over to the wall. In the middle of my talk, the stovepipe fell down, and that closed the meeting effectively, with the stove burning and the pipe gone. But now stakes of Zion, missions, and a beautiful temple are there. It is magnificent.

I never go to the Philippines that I do not go to the American military cemetery, where in 1961 we prayed over the land and opened it for the preaching of the gospel. It was again discouraging. We took four missionaries from Hong Kong and rented a little house and got them settled in it and left them all alone in that great nation. There was only one native member of the Church in all of that great nation that we were able to find. Now, I do not know— we must have 500,000 or 600,000 in that nation. The largest indoor gathering that I have ever participated in was a meeting that we held in the great Araneta Coliseum, where we had 30,000 people indoors.

You cannot foretell the consequences of the great work which comes to pass out of the feeble beginnings of missionary work. You are going to get discouraged in this service. I have no doubt of it. I hope you do. It will humble you down a bit. There will be no arrogance in the face of discouragement. But look ahead, my dear brethren and sisters, look ahead to the years down the line and see the flowering of your effort. Because as surely as the sun rises in the morning, this work will come into flower in the missions where you serve.

I think of the man who probably was the most successful missionary ever in the history of this Church. It was not Wilford Woodruff, great as his work was with the United Brethren, where he baptized about 1,800 with tremendous consequences. I think the greatest work ever done by any man serving a mission for this Church was done by Dan Jones in Wales.

Dan Jones was born in Wales. When he was 17, he went to sea and finally came to America after traveling about the world. He got part ownership of a little vessel that came up the Mississippi from New Orleans to St. Louis. That vessel got in a wreck and was destroyed. He got a wealthy backer somehow, and they built the *Maid of Iowa,* a 60-ton vessel which would carry 300 people. He found himself transporting some Mormons from England up the Mississippi.

At the time there was serious persecution against the Church. He read the anti-Mormon writings that were issued by the *Warsaw Signal* and other publishers. He said, "It can't be as bad as they say it is." He investigated the Church and was baptized on a cold winter day in the Mississippi River.

On a subsequent trip he met Joseph Smith, and they became friends. Dan Jones was one of those who went to Carthage Jail with the Prophet. On the 26th of June, 1844, he was imprisoned with the Prophet. And when all of the others had gone to sleep, the Prophet said, "Are you willing to die for this cause?" And he said, "I think death would be little enough for a cause such as this." Joseph said to him, "You will yet go to your native land of Wales and preach the gospel."

The Prophet sent him out of the jail to get the help of a lawyer for the next day, Mr. Browning, and Dan could not get back in. He escaped with his life. Seven months after the Prophet was martyred, Dan was called to Wales, and he was a fiery, feisty preacher.

He had a great system of doing missionary work. He would write to a town somewhere in Wales to the mayor and the chief of police and say in effect, "I'll be there on July 15 to convert the whole city. Get ready for me." When he would come, the mayor and the chief of police would all be there at the railroad station to meet him. He preached the gospel as few people have ever preached it, I think. He was a roller-coaster preacher. When he left to come home off that mission, he—with his associates, but I think largely attributable to him—had baptized 3,600 people who came into the Church. He brought many of them to Zion. He went down to Manti, where he was elected mayor, and lived there for a few years. He did farming, which he did not like as an old sailor.

An interesting sidelight of that is that one of these Welsh people he took with him was the grandfather of President Ralph Pulman, who presided over a stake in Wales and later over the Vancouver mission and later over the Cardston Temple. His grandfather is buried in the Manti cemetery. But the grandfather became disaffected over something, and his son left the Church and went back to Wales. The grandson was never brought up in the Church. But after his father died, missionaries knocked on Ralph Pulman's door, and he responded to the message. He had in his veins, I believe, what we used to call the believing blood, which his grandfather had had when Dan Jones preached to him.

Dan was called back to Wales and baptized another 2,000

people, making 5,600 altogether in the course of his mission. Now, he had some associate missionaries, but he was their president, and he was their fiery preacher.

When the papers wouldn't publish what he wanted them to, he made a deal with his brother, who was a Methodist minister. His brother had a printing press. His brother printed tracts and other literature for him on weekdays and denounced him from his own pulpit on Sundays. They got along. Dan finally bought a press of his own and published a magazine, a little history, and other things. He would challenge everybody. He was just a confrontational worker.

The consequences of that work—there are thousands and thousands of people who live in this state today and all over the West who are the descendants of those converts from Wales who came into this Church as a result of Dan Jones's preaching. He wore himself out. He died at the age of 51 of tuberculosis—a worn-out man. But the great and significant thing to me is the tremendous consequences of that effort.

Brothers and sisters, you can never foretell the consequences of the service of a missionary. In Fukuoka the other day, Brother Matsuda told us the story of when he was a missionary under Kan Watanabe—those names don't mean anything to you, but they mean a lot to me. Kan, the mission president, said to his missionaries, "I don't know how to do missionary work. I just want to ask one thing of you. Just try a little harder. Just make that little extra touch of effort."

Brother Matsuda said, "We were out tracting. We had been tracting all day. We did not get an invitation in all day long, and evening came. We were tired and worn out. My companion said to me, 'Let's go home.' I said, 'Let's try one more door.'" They knocked on a door, and they were turned down. They decided to try one more. They were turned down. They said, "Well, let's give it one more try." They did, and a man and his family invited them in and came into the Church. That man has served as a bishop, and his children have been on missions. That is the unforeseen consequence of missionary effort.

Well, brothers and sisters, I repeat, it is all over the world. I don't care where you go—up and down the nations of South America. Brother Faust could tell you of Brazil and the beginnings of the work there under Brother Melvin J. Ballard, who dedicated South America in 1925 in Buenos Aires. The work did nothing for a long time, and finally it became alive. Brazil is now filled with converts, great congregations. We are building three new temples in Brazil to try to accommodate the need there. What a marvelous and wonderful flowering of the tough and difficult early beginnings of the work in that part of the world.

Where you are now going it is pretty well settled. Very few of you will have member districts to look after. Some of you may, but not very many. For the most part, you will have stakes wherever the work is organized. You will live in nice, comfortable homes. You will drive nice, comfortable, air-conditioned cars. You will be nice, comfortable, air-conditioned people, enjoying the companionship of nice, comfortable, air-conditioned missionaries. In any event, you are headed for a great and marvelous and wonderful experience, the end of which no one can foretell or even guess at, my brothers and sisters.

I have had the opportunity of traveling across this world, and I think I have been almost everywhere now, from the small islands of the Pacific where we have a handful of members who are struggling along, to the great cities where we have large congregations of people.

In the early days of the Church, the brethren asked the Prophet what they could do which would be of the greatest worth. The Prophet through revelation gave the response of the Lord:

"And now, behold, I say unto you, that the thing which will be of the most worth unto you will be to declare repentance unto this people, that you may bring souls unto me, that you may rest with them in the kingdom of my Father" (D&C 15:6; see also D&C 16:6).

I like that language—that the thing which will be of the most worth unto you will be to do missionary work. The thing of most worth is not the buildings we have. It is not this great building or the other buildings in this area. It is not the BYU campus. It is not the welfare program. It is not the educational program of the Church. It is not any of these things. The thing which is of most worth, as the Lord has repeatedly declared in revelation, is the teaching of the gospel of Christ to those who know not its saving message.

You are not going out into a sidebar activity. You are going out to do that which the Lord has said is the most important activity of all of the many activities of His work. God bless you.

We send you with love and our prayers and our respect and our confidence, charging you to love your missionaries and work with them. Take care of them. Do not give up on them. Work with them. Love them. Love them into activity. Love them into righteousness. Love them into obedience. Be a father to them. Be as a mother to them. Be kind to them. They will never forget you. They will remember you all the days of their lives. They will name their children after you. They will send you wedding invitations, more than you want to receive.

Well, I simply leave you my testimony of this great work and emphasize the fact that when all is said is done, nothing we do, and we do a great many things—so many things it has become staggering almost, the extent of our activities—but nothing, I repeat, according to the Lord's frequently repeated statement, is of as great a worth as is the declaration of the message of the gospel to those who know not its saving truths.

I leave you my testimony of the truth of this work. I leave you my love and my blessing and say, God be with you till we meet again. May you know the companionship of the Holy Spirit as you have never before known it in all of your lives. May you have listening ears attuned to that Spirit and a quality of obedience that will cause you to follow the promptings which you receive. Then you will be happy. In three years from now, when it is time to go home, you will shed more tears when you leave your field of labor than you are shedding today to go to your field of labor. For this I pray, humbly and gratefully, in the name of Jesus Christ, amen.

# Brigham Young University, Rededication of Harold B. Lee Library

NOVEMBER 15, 2000

PRESIDENT BATEMAN, IT IS A GREAT pleasure and a great honor to be with you today. This is a historic occasion. I think if I were a student here and another student asked me where I was going, instead of saying, "I am going to the library to study," I think I'd just say, "I'm going underground." What a very interesting building that has been constructed here, with many, many advantages and many interesting and wonderful features. I think this is one of the great and historic days in the history of this university.

I very much appreciate what has been said here. I feel so deeply grateful for this marvelous new addition to the Harold B. Lee Library and that it carries, as Brother Monson says, the name of this very good and able and delightful man. I am grateful for the faith that has made possible this construction project, the gifts and donations of wonderful and generous and kind and gracious and thoughtful people.

Of all the wonderful buildings we have on this campus, none, I believe, is as important as the library. A library is the very heart and substance of a university. Without access to vast quantities of information, neither faculty nor students can do an adequate job. It is the fountain of research. It is the source of information both old and new. It is a place for the ever-present challenge to dig for knowledge beyond that which is given in the classroom.

I have visited some of the great libraries of the world. As a young man, I once did some work in the library of the British Museum. What a marvelous and awesome place it is. What an environment in which to study. I have been a guest at the great Vatican Library in Rome. There I have seen the beautiful illuminated codices that go back through centuries of time to the period when books were first made. I constantly stand in awe as I reflect on the human quest for knowledge and understanding of man and his universe.

Libraries become the depositories of all of the knowledge that has gone before us. Men have come and gone, generations of them. Fortunately, we still have preserved the thoughts, the words, the writings of the great intellects who have laid, stone upon stone, the very bulwark of our civilization.

How marvelous a thing is a book. Here sheets of paper, filled with writings and illustrations, are bound together with a protective cover on either side. A book can be held in one's hand. It can be opened and leafed through. It can be read, studied, pondered, even speculated upon. Books represent the accumulated workings of the human mind, the endless treasure of man's thoughts as he has contemplated himself and the phenomena with which he is surrounded. How grateful I am for books and for those who have tenderly watched over and guarded them through the centuries. And now in modern times there have been added the remarkable resources that come of the computer and its associated tools. With the touch of a button, one can reach back through the knowledge treasuries of the past and across the wide expanse of the earth to glean a fact here and a fact there. It is, really, a miracle.

These libraries are precious temples of learning. Here students through the generations will come and search, will discover and study great writings of the past which will lead to marvelous findings to bless the future.

Much of this is a divine pursuit in the seeking of eternal truth. It can lead only to greater understanding and greater appreciation for the work of the Almighty that goes forth among His children.

Needless to say, we are profoundly grateful for this library, for this tremendous new facility on this great and beautiful campus—a place to which students may come and grow under the beneficent influence of the Holy Spirit. All of us are indebted to those good and generous and kind men and women who have contributed so much to make this great facility possible. May it be loved and respected and appreciated, I humbly pray, in the name of Jesus Christ, amen.

# Satellite Broadcast, Church Educational System Fireside for Young Adults

## September 9, 2001

MY DEAR YOUNG FRIENDS, we are gathered tonight in this great Conference Center and in numerous Church halls elsewhere. There must be hundreds of thousands of you. It is a stimulating experience and a tremendous challenge to be with you. It is a wonderful opportunity to speak with you.

I may repeat tonight some things I have said before. But I am not going to give you the six B's that I gave your younger brothers and sisters a year ago, which have since been memorized by many and even set to music. Maybe I will get out a book someday on these, because I believe the youth of the whole nation could profit from their observance. The difficulty I have in doing such things was expressed by Madame Curie long ago. She said: "So little time. So much to do." And that is your problem also—"So little time. So much to do."

I am told that you are 18 to 30 years of age. Oh, to be 18 or 25 or 30 again! You can do anything when you are that age. I am 3 times 30, plus 1. But I have not lost my interest in you, your problems, or your great opportunities.

The world is full of naysayers who think that people your age have lost their way. I disagree. Let me say that I am very proud of you. I think you are the finest generation this Church has ever produced. Because of you, I have no fear concerning the future. You are ambitious. You are trustworthy. You are loyal to the Church and its principles. You have great confidence in one another. You work together with love and appreciation and respect one for another. You are faithful, and you are true. You love the Lord, and you pray.

Do you have problems? Of course you do. You have many problems. Many of you worry about what to do with your lives, how you will earn a living. Many of you worry about marriage, about having a good companion who will love you and whom you will love. You look forward to the time when you will have children and hope within yourselves that you will be good fathers and mothers. You face problems that at times seem insurmountable. You try to find a way out but only become frustrated. You pray about these matters. But you don't seem to get the answers you seek.

You live in a world of loose moral standards. You have been taught one thing by your parents and the Church, and you see another thing often practiced by those who seem to succeed and do well. Most of you have held to high standards. Possibly some few of you have slipped. To you I would like to say that I assure you that even if this is the case, you have not lost everything. With sincere repentance on your part, the Lord will forgive and those about you will forgive. I hope that you will somehow come to forgive yourselves and put your trust and faith in the Lord, who will be kind and gracious to you.

Already you have paid a terrible price for your mistakes. They have haunted you day and night. They seem never to leave you. Confess them, if that is necessary, and then get them behind you. Parents and bishops stand ready to help. Your bishops have been ordained and set apart and promised wisdom beyond their own in working with you and assisting you. Isaiah said:

"Though your sins be as scarlet, they shall be as white as snow; though they be red like crimson, they shall be as wool.

"If ye be willing and obedient, ye shall eat the good of the land" (Isaiah 1:18–19).

Most of you are in school. Most of you are attending universities which are not Church universities. While doing so, you attend institute. Permit me to say that there is no way that all of you could be accommodated at BYU—Provo, BYU—Idaho, BYU—Hawaii, or the LDS Business College. I wish that this might be possible, but it cannot be. Please do not feel left out. Grasp the opportunity of the moment wherever you may be. Love the school of your choice. Make it your dear mother, your alma mater. Take from it the very best it has to offer. And hold on to the institute program. Gather with your peers in these far-flung facilities. Listen to good and able teachers. Participate in the social programs. Studies have shown that you are as likely to marry in the temple if you do this as if you were at one of the Church-owned schools. I pray that you will be blessed of the Lord, that you will receive a good education, that you will find wonderful companionship, that you will look upon these days as among the most fruitful of your entire lives.

I do not downgrade the Church schools. They are tremendous institutions. I wish we could build and maintain many more. But we cannot. They are terribly expensive. I am so glad that we have them, and I compliment those of you who are attending these institutions. I myself did not attend BYU. I attended the University of Utah and received there my baccalaureate degree. I have no regrets. As chairman of the BYU board of trustees, I am grateful for our Church institutions, but I am also grateful that there are opportunities elsewhere, many of them, and that the institute program represents a very serious attempt on the part of the Church Board of Education to see that our students have opportunities for religious training and Church association wherever they may be.

And so God bless you, my dear young friends, wherever you are. You are doing that which the Lord would have you do. Said

He, "Seek ye out of the best books words of wisdom; seek learning, even by study and also by faith" (D&C 88:118).

You are engaged in an intense gathering of knowledge, the accumulated wisdom of all of the ages of man. As members of this Church, ours must be a ceaseless quest for truth. That truth must include both spiritual and religious truth as well as secular.

Joseph F. Smith, who served 17 years as President of the Church, declared: "We believe in all truth, no matter to what subject it may refer. No sect or religious denomination in the world possesses a single principle of truth that we do not accept or that we will reject. We are willing to receive all truth, from whatever source it may come; for truth . . . will endure. No man's faith, no man's religion, no religious organization in all the world, can ever rise above the truth" (*Gospel Doctrine*, 5th ed. [1939], 1).

But you must distinguish between truth and sophistry. There can be a vast difference between the two, and unless we are careful we may find that we are believing in the sophistry of man rather than the truth of God.

I read the newspapers. I read those who write syndicated columns. I occasionally listen to the commentators on television and radio. These writers are brilliant. They are men and women of incisive language, scintillating in expression. They are masters of the written word. But for the most part their attitude is negative. Regardless of whom they write about or speak about, they seem to look for his or her failings and weaknesses. They are constantly criticizing, seldom praising. This spirit is not limited to the columnists and the commentators. Read the letters to the editor. Some of them are filled with venom, written by people who seem to find no good in the world or in their associates.

Criticism, fault-finding, evil speaking—these are of the spirit of the day. To hear tell, there is nowhere a man of integrity holding public office; all businessmen are crooks; the utilities are out to rob you. Even on campus there is heard so much the snide remark, the sarcastic jibe, the cutting down of associates—these, too often, are the essence of our conversation. In our homes, wives weep and children finally give up under the barrage of criticism leveled by abusive husbands and fathers. Criticism is the forerunner of divorce, the cultivator of rebellion, sometimes the catalyst that leads to failure. In the Church, it sows the seed of inactivity and finally apostasy.

I come to you tonight with a plea that we stop seeking out the storms and enjoy more fully the sunlight. I am suggesting that as we go through life we try to "accentuate the positive." I am asking that we look a little deeper for the good, that we still our voices of insult and sarcasm, that we more generously compliment virtue and effort.

I am not asking that all criticism be silenced. Growth comes of correction. Strength comes of repentance. Wise is the man or woman who can acknowledge mistakes pointed out by others and change his or her course. What I am suggesting is that you turn from the negativism that so permeates our modern society and look for the remarkable good among those with whom you associate, that we speak of one another's virtues more than we speak of one another's faults, that optimism replace pessimism, that our faith exceed our fears. When I was a young man and was prone to speak critically, my wise father would say, "Cynics do not contribute. Skeptics do not create. Doubters do not achieve."

We are experiencing a serious economic downturn. You read of thousands of layoffs. This may be a difficult season for you. You worry much about your personal affairs. You worry about money. You worry about marriage. You worry about the future. There may be some lean days ahead for some of you. There may be troubles. None of us can avoid them all. Do not despair. Do not give up. Look for the sunlight through the clouds. Opportunities will eventually open to you.

I finished the University of Utah in 1932. It was the very

bottom of the most serious depression of modern times. The unemployment rate in Utah was then more than 30 percent. There was much of cynicism. It was a time when men stood in soup lines and some committed suicide in despair. But somehow we managed to eat and keep going. Opportunities gradually opened, first here and then there. In 1982 I spoke at the 50th anniversary of my graduating class. I met there men and women who had become prominent in many undertakings. They had begun almost in poverty, but they kept climbing upwards. They had become leaders. They had looked for the positive in life, praying with faith and working with diligence.

No matter the circumstances, I encourage you to go forward with faith and prayer, calling on the Lord. You may not receive any direct revelation. But you will discover, as the years pass, that there has been a subtle guiding of your footsteps in paths of progress and great purpose.

The growth of the Church gives us reason to be upbeat. In 1968 I received the assignment to supervise the work in all of South America. I traveled back and forth over that great continent many times. The work was weak everywhere. There were perhaps a half dozen stakes in all of that part of the world. Now, in the nation of Brazil alone there are 188 stakes. In Mexico there are 197 stakes. It is difficult to believe, but it is a fact.

We shall likely see from now until the 2002 Olympics are behind us a great deal of writing concerning the Church. Much of it is likely to be negative. Journalists may mock that which to us is sacred. They may belittle that which we call divine. They may accuse us of being opposed to intellectualism. They will in large measure overlook the glory and the wonder of this work.

But I want to tell you that what they write will not injure us. We may be offended by it, but the work will go forward. With their negative attitudes they will overlook the wonder of the spark that was kindled in Palmyra, which is now lighting fires of faith across the earth, in many lands and in many languages. They will have great difficulty understanding us because the Spirit of God is something that is foreign to them. With their humanistic outlook they will fail to realize that spiritual promptings, with recognition of the influence of the Holy Ghost, are as potent and real a thing as any other manifestation in this life.

George Santayana said:

> *O world, thou choosest not the better part!*
> *It is not wisdom to be only wise,*
> *And on the inward vision close the eyes;*
> *But it is wisdom to believe the heart.*
> *[In Charles L. Wallis, ed.,* The
> Treasure Chest *(1965), 93]*

Looking to our history, our critics may see little of divinity in the great work of the Prophet Joseph and those associated with him. Were our forebears human? Of course they were. They doubtless made some mistakes. Some of them acknowledged making mistakes. But the mistakes were minor when compared with the marvelous work which they accomplished. To highlight the mistakes and gloss over the greater good is to draw a caricature. Caricatures are amusing, but they are often ugly and dishonest. A man may have a wart on his cheek and still have a face of beauty and strength, but if the wart is emphasized unduly in relation to his other features, the portrait is lacking in integrity.

These early leaders made no pretense at being perfect. They recognized that there was only one perfect man who ever walked the earth. The Lord has used imperfect people in the process of building His perfect society. If some of them occasionally stumbled or if their characters were slightly flawed in one way or another, the wonder is the greater that they accomplished so much.

I wish to say a few words on intellectualism—that quality which some say we deny in our work. A so-called scholar recently expressed the view that the Church is an enemy of intellectualism.

This strikes particularly at you people in your present circumstances. If he meant by intellectualism that branch of philosophy which teaches "the doctrine that knowledge is wholly or chiefly derived from pure reason" and "that reason is the final principle of reality," then, yes, we are opposed to so narrow an interpretation as applicable to religion. (See *The Random House Dictionary of the English Language,* 2nd ed. [1987], "intellectualism," 990.)

Such an interpretation excludes the power of the Holy Spirit in speaking to and through man. Of course we believe in the cultivation of the mind. The emphasis in the classes you are taking in your various courses demands the cultivation of the mind and the use of its powers. But the intellect is not the only source of knowledge. There is a promise, given under the inspiration of the Almighty, set forth in these beautiful words: "God shall give unto you knowledge by his Holy Spirit, yea, by the unspeakable gift of the Holy Ghost" (D&C 121:26).

The humanists who criticize us, the so-called intellectuals who demean us speak only from ignorance of this manifestation. They have not heard the voice of the Spirit. They have not heard it because they have not sought after it and prepared themselves to be worthy of it. Then, supposing that knowledge comes only of reasoning and of the workings of the mind, they deny that which comes by the power of the Holy Ghost.

The things of God are understood by the Spirit of God. That Spirit is real. To those who have experienced its workings, the knowledge so gained is as real as that received through the operation of the five senses. I testify of this. I am confident that each of you can testify of it. I urge you to continue throughout your lives to cultivate a heart in tune with the Spirit. If you do so, your lives will be enriched. You will feel a kinship with God, our Eternal Father. You will taste the sweetness of joy that can be had in no other way.

Do not be trapped by the sophistry of the world, which for the most part is negative and which seldom, if ever, bears good fruit. Do not be ensnared by those clever ones whose self-appointed mission it is to demean that which is sacred, to emphasize human weakness, and to undermine faith rather than inspire strength. "Look to God and live" (Alma 37:47).

Well did Jacob say long ago:

"O that cunning plan of the evil one! O the vainness, and the frailties, and the foolishness of men! When they are learned they think they are wise, and they hearken not unto the counsel of God, for they set it aside, supposing they know of themselves, wherefore, their wisdom is foolishness and it profiteth them not. And they shall perish.

"But to be learned is good if they hearken unto the counsels of God" (2 Nephi 9:28–29).

As you walk your various paths, walk with faith. Speak affirmatively and cultivate an attitude of confidence. You have the capacity to do so. Your strength will give strength to others. Do not partake of the spirit so rife in our times. Rather look for good and build upon it. There is so much of the strong and the decent and the beautiful to build upon. You are partakers of the gospel of Jesus Christ. The gospel means "good news." The message of the Lord is one of hope and salvation. The voice of the Lord is a voice of glad tidings. The work of the Lord is a work of glorious accomplishment.

I am not suggesting that you simply put on rose-colored glasses to make the world about you look better. I ask, rather, that you look above and beyond the negative, the cynical, the critical, the doubtful, to the positive and the affirmative.

Some years ago I clipped an article on Commander William Robert Anderson, the man who first took a submarine under the North Pole from the waters of the Pacific to the waters of the Atlantic. It was an untried and dangerous mission. In his wallet he carried a tattered card with these words: "I believe I am always divinely guided, I believe I will always take the right road, I believe

316

God will always make a way where there is no way" (in Christopher S. Wren, "If It's 3-to-1 against Anderson: Can a Congressman Afford a Conscience?" *Look*, April 20, 1971, 48).

In a dark and troubled hour, Jesus said, "Let not your heart be troubled, neither let it be afraid" (John 14:27).

On one occasion the ruler of the synagogue came to Jesus pleading for help for his dying daughter. While he yet spoke to the Master, those of the ruler's house came and said, "Thy daughter is dead: why troublest thou the Master any further?" (Mark 5:35).

"As soon as Jesus heard the word that was spoken, he saith unto the ruler of the synagogue, Be not afraid, only believe" (Mark 5:36).

I commend those tremendous words to you. Be not afraid, only believe.

Believe in God, our Eternal Father, He who is greatest of all, who stands ever ready to help us and who has the power to do so. Believe in Jesus Christ, the Savior and the Redeemer of mankind, the worker of miracles, the greatest who ever walked the earth, the Intercessor with our Father. Believe in the power of the Holy Ghost to lead, to inspire, to comfort, to protect. Believe in the Prophet Joseph as an instrument in the hands of the Almighty in ushering in this, the dispensation of the fulness of times.

Believe in the sacred word of God, the Holy Bible, with its treasury of inspiration and sacred truth, in the Book of Mormon as a testimony of the living Christ. Believe in the Church as the organization which the God of heaven established for the blessing of His sons and daughters of all generations of time.

Believe in yourselves as sons and daughters of God, men and women with unlimited potential to do good in the world. Believe in personal virtue. There is no substitute for it anywhere under the heavens. Believe in your power to discipline yourselves against the evils which could destroy you. Believe in one another as the greatest generation ever yet to live upon the earth.

I leave you my testimony of the truth of this work. I know it is true. I know that it is the work of the Almighty. I bear witness of Him who is our Father and our God, of Him who is our Lord and our Redeemer. I bear witness of the divine calling of the Prophet Joseph and of those who have succeeded him in this high and holy office.

I pray the blessings of the Lord upon you, my beloved brothers and sisters. How much I love you. I love you with all my heart. I pray for you. I plead with the Lord to bless you with joy in your lives, with the strength to be virtuous, with the will to do what is right, with capacity to learn things both secular and spiritual, with answers to your prayers as you walk in righteousness, and I do it all in the sacred name of our Redeemer, even the Lord Jesus Christ, amen.

# Washington, Utah, Buena Vista Stake Conference*

## January 20, 2002

W<small>ELL, MY BROTHERS AND SISTERS</small>, it is nice to be with you. It is wonderful to look into your faces and see your faith, optimism, love for the Lord, and appreciation and respect one for another. It is good to see you in church on Sunday morning, all cleaned up and in your best clothes to come and worship the Lord. Thank you for being here. Thank you for your faith. Thank you for what you do.

I look at this beautiful building and have in my heart a great appreciation and love for the Saints across the world who pay their tithes and offerings and make it possible for the Church to carry forward this great program of building houses of worship and temples to the Most High. What a wonderful thing is going on. We are grateful to you for all the good that you do and pray that you may pass an inheritance to your children, that they will be even more faithful than you are, that the Church will grow better through the years and stronger and do greater good across the world.

This is a tremendous year in the history of the Church. We will be exposed to the world as we have never been before. In three weeks the Olympics will come to Salt Lake City. It won't be our celebration. We are trying to be very careful about that. We don't want to make this the "Mormon Olympics." The Olympics are for

*delivered extemporaneously

Salt Lake City, but we will be benefited and blessed as men and women by the thousands and tens of thousands come and see us at our best. I hope we'll be at our best and we'll be hospitable, friendly, gracious, and kind to all who come. I hope that great blessings will come to the Church as a result of it.

Brigham Young, at a time when our people were hungry and cold and poor and miserable, when gold had been discovered in California and so many of them wanted to go there, stood in their midst and told them to stay here. He said, among other things, "This will become the great highway of the nations. Kings and emperors . . . will visit us here." He told how the ungodly would be envious of our homes and possessions. (See James S. Brown, *Life of a Pioneer: Being the Autobiography of James S. Brown* [1900], 122.) I think we are seeing that. I suppose we will have the president of the United States with us. I know that we will have heads of states of Europe with us, and we will be blessed and benefited.

It has been my privilege and opportunity to be interviewed by media men and women from across the world already. They are interested in us. They are interested in a lot of things that really don't matter, but they are also interested in some of the basic and fundamental and good things.

Yesterday, or the day before, we were interviewed by the correspondent of *Time* magazine. It was amazing to me that he didn't ask about the Mountain Meadows Massacre and he didn't ask about polygamy. He talked about the growth of the Church—how it was possible, what we were doing, and so on. It is tremendously significant. We'll have barbs, of course we will, but by and large, I think, we will be praised and our virtues seen in a way that has never happened before.

Later on this year, we'll have other significant things. We'll dedicate more temples: one in Snowflake, Arizona; one in Mexico—that will make twelve in Mexico; one in Texas—that will make three or four for Texas; and the Nauvoo Temple on the 27th of June, the anniversary of the death of the Prophet Joseph Smith.

John Taylor's watch showed that the Prophet was killed at about 5:21 P.M. At 5:21 P.M. on that Thursday, the 27th of June, we will be dedicating the temple in Nauvoo. And you people may gather in this hall and be a part of that dedication. The service will be repeated again on Sunday, so that if you can't be here on Thursday afternoon, you can be here on Sunday.

I offer a challenge to every one of you—every one of you eight years of age and older—to prepare yourselves now. Be worthy to come to this stake center and hear and participate in the dedication of the temple in Nauvoo. It will be a beautiful and magnificent building, and those will be sacred services and, I believe, inspirational services, as we bring to closure the reconstruction of that magnificent house of the Lord, the original of which was built by the Prophet Joseph, left by our Saints, destroyed, and now rebuilt. I may say, it will be a better building than the original. Because of code requirements, it will be a little different. On the outside, it will look very much the same, except the angel is going to be standing tall instead of lying down. The Church is on the move now; that will be expressive of that.

Get yourselves ready to participate in those services. They will be wonderful. You can join in the great Hosanna Shout. You can sing the powerful hymns of Zion as that building is dedicated. I'm sure you will enjoy it. I don't advise you to go to Nauvoo. I don't know where we are going to put all the people.

Now I think I'd just like to turn to the first section of the Doctrine and Covenants, where the Lord sets forth in revelation the great purposes of bringing to pass His work in this dispensation. He says:

"That every man might speak in the name of God the Lord, even the Savior of the world; [Think of that!]

"That faith also might increase in the earth;

"That mine everlasting covenant might be established;

"That the fulness of my gospel might be proclaimed by the weak and the simple unto the ends of the world, and before kings and rulers . . . that they might come to understanding" (D&C 1:20–24).

Just a word or two about each of those.

1. "That every man might speak in the name of God the Lord, even the Savior of the world." And I'd like to add to that, "and speak in testimony of God the Lord, even the Savior of the world."

People ask me—these television reporters, radio reporters, magazine reporters, newspaper reporters—"What is different about your Church?" I say, among other things, we believe that the priesthood is not reserved for a few trained and schooled men, but rather that every man might have the opportunity, if he will live worthy of it, of holding the priesthood of God and speaking in His holy name and in the name of His Beloved Son.

Brethren, you are the beneficiaries of that great blessing. This is one of the distinguishing features of this, the Church of God in these days—that not just this man and this man and this man and this man trained in a seminary may serve as a minister, but that every man might speak in His holy name and act in His authority as one who holds His priesthood.

Brethren, do you know what you have? Do you know the strength of this priesthood? Do you appreciate what it gives to you? Are you worthy of it? Are you living the kind of life that makes you worthy to hold the priesthood of the Almighty, to speak in the name of Christ and exercise that priesthood? There is nothing like it on all the face of the earth. It is God's holy power, bestowed upon man to act in His name in behalf of His sons and daughters.

Live worthy of it. Stand taller. Be cleaner. Be a little kinder, a little gentler, a little better to your wives, to your children. No man, I believe, can exercise the priesthood in righteousness who does not treat his wife with respect and concern and love, and his children likewise. Every man who holds the priesthood of God in this Church ought to be a better man by reason of that fact. Live worthy, my brethren, live worthy of the great and marvelous gift which God has brought to pass to bless you with as His sons, recognized by Him. Don't stoop to anything mean or cheap or evil of any kind. Stay away from pornography. Stay away from all of that kind of evil. Live above it, and be men of God, as His sons blessed with a gift precious and great and marvelous which has come through those ordained by the Savior when He was upon the world.

2. "That faith also might increase in the earth." I guess I do not need to dwell on that one. I haven't time. But you see it everywhere—the faith that grows in the hearts of Latter-day Saints. This woman who has just spoken is a convert to this Church and is learning about the faith that is growing in her heart. You see it everywhere. How grateful I am for the faith of the Latter-day Saints. The Lord bless you for the faith which you cultivate in your lives.

3. "That mine everlasting covenant might be established." That covenant was made by Jehovah with Abraham: "I will be your God, and you will be my people." That covenant has been fortified and strengthened and enlarged in those things which we enter into in the temple. Live worthy of it.

4. "That the fulness of my gospel might be proclaimed by the weak and the simple unto the ends of the world, and before kings and rulers . . . that they might come to understanding."

Every one of you can be a missionary. Every one of you can befriend somebody, lead him to the Church, stay with him, help him, be a friend to him as he grows in faith and faithfulness as a member of this Church. You don't have to go across the world, really, when all is said and done. You can do it right here. What a significant and wonderful thing that is. This is a great harvest field of the Church, my brethren and sisters. I believe that. There is nothing that will bring you greater satisfaction than to be responsible for someone being led to this Church, standing with him or her, befriending him or her, watching him or her grow in faith and faithfulness. Miraculous is the conversion process of this Church.

I received a letter last week. I'd like to read it to you.

My wife, Cheryle, and I were married in 1968 in the Church of God. We never set foot in the church after that for the next 32 years. Then, a series of inexplicable events took place in the months preceding December 2000 that led to Cheryle and I attending church for the first time since being married. It was Christmas Eve, and we went to The Church of Jesus Christ of Latter-day Saints in Stockton, Missouri. We met a number of kind and wonderful people and learned of many things that day. One lady, Shirley Goodman, greeted Cheryle with a hug. How wonderful that was.

The following Sunday, New Year's Eve, Cheryle and I returned for a second time. During the Sunday School class following sacrament, as I sat there pondering all the new information I was absorbing, asking myself, "Could all of this be true?" the teacher asked me to read Moroni 10:4. As I read this passage, I had the most astonishing, warm feeling penetrate me to my soul. I knew, right then and there, what I always wanted to know about the truthfulness of the existence of God, why we are here, and our purpose for life. I have never felt such gladness as my prayer was answered!

After church I asked my friend [who had been the instrument in their coming], "How do I become a member?" He arranged a series of discussions with two missionaries for Cheryle and me. Three weeks later, January 21, 2001, Cheryle and I were baptized, and the following week we were confirmed into The Church of Jesus Christ of Latter-day Saints. What a glorious day!

A couple months later, I was ordained into the Melchizedek Priesthood and received a calling as second counselor to the elders quorum president. Now Cheryle is the second counselor to the Relief Society president. A year has passed, and in a few weeks, Cheryle and I will be going to the St. Louis Temple to receive our endowments and be sealed for eternity. We can hardly wait!

Isn't that a marvelous letter? That is the process that is going on across the world. Wouldn't you like to be a part of it? Wouldn't you? Really, you can be. The Lord will bless you if you will ask for His blessings. He will open opportunities for you. It can be your privilege to introduce someone to the Church in a quiet, inoffensive, friendly way. Not with great pressure or anything of the kind, but inoffensive. Then, stay with it. Every convert needs a friend. He needs a responsibility. And he needs teaching with the good word of God. All of us can do that. It is within our capacity to do that. You don't have to be a genius. You have to be credible and have the desire.

God bless you, my brothers and sisters. What a pleasure it is to be with you. I'm so glad you came this evening. I love the Latter-day Saints. I love this Church. I'm proud of our people. I'm proud of what is happening. I thank the Lord for the outpouring of His blessings upon the Latter-day Saints. I pray that God will bless you, that He will open the windows of heaven and shower down a blessing upon you that there will not be room enough to receive it, that as you see your children grow in faith and faithfulness you will know that He has blessed you in a magnificent and wonderful way.

I have a testimony—real, burning, and vital—of the truth of this work. I know that God, our Eternal Father, lives and that Jesus is the Christ, my Savior and my Redeemer. It is He who stands at the head of this Church. All I desire is that I go forward with this work as He would have it go forward. And for this I humbly pray, as I leave with you my love and my blessing, in the name of Jesus Christ, amen.

# BOSTON, MASSACHUSETTS, MISSIONARY MEETING*

## MARCH 22, 2002

How NICE TO BE WITH YOU, how very nice. You look a little expectant; I do not know how to satisfy that, but I have you smiling at least. You must learn to smile. You must look happier, you missionaries. You look so somber. Smile, smile. Every one of you, smile. That's it. You look better. You just look happier. You look more welcome, really, when you smile.

You have a tremendous responsibility, tremendous. Everything concerning the growth of this Church rests on your narrow shoulders, my brothers and sisters. This work is important, and you are a very, very important part of it.

Do not ever downgrade what you are doing. Do not ever do anything which would downgrade your efforts. You are only going to be here for 18 months or two years, whatever the case may be. It will pass, as President Packer says, "ever so fast." It will be gone almost before you know it, and you will never have another opportunity like this as long as you live—when you are young and you are single and you are devoted to a single thing and nothing else. You do not have to worry about earning a living. You do not have to worry about going to school. You do not have to worry about the boys or the girls. You just have to worry about yourself and your companion.

*delivered extemporaneously

What a glorious and wonderful season this is, really. It is tremendous. This is the great opportunity of your life. It will not come again. If you glorify it, if you magnify it, it will remain with you and bless your days throughout your life. If you stumble along and just endure the time, you will regret it the rest of your life. This is your great season of opportunity. May the Lord bless you, and may that consciousness, that realization, come into your hearts that says every morning when you get up, "This is another day of opportunity. We might meet someone today. We just might meet someone who will become a member of this Church and do great good and be the beginning of generations of Latter-day Saints." What a glorious opportunity.

And you sisters, you are only here for 18 months. Smile through it and work your heads off. There will never be another opportunity like this. You did not come to get a husband. You elders did not come to get a wife. You came to serve the Lord and not yourselves. Please, please, please use it for the greatest possible advantage that you can.

To these wonderful older couples I would like to say a word of appreciation. What a wonderful thing to have you here doing this good work in this favored part of the earth—this cold old New England, this place of the beginnings of our nation. What an opportunity to come back here and serve the Lord at a time when you thought you were just going to spend your time teaching your grandchildren. Instead of that, you have left them at home, and you have come back here, and you are happy. I hope you are. If you are not, something is wrong with you.

It is good to be with the missionaries again. It used to be that we would spend a lot of time with the missionaries. For 44 years I have been meeting with your kind all over this earth. What a wonderful, wonderful time we have had with them. What a glorious thing to look into your faces and envision the lengthened shadow of that which you do. Someone once said that every great institution is the lengthened shadow of a great man, and you are today casting that shadow. This shadow is represented in your work, and out of that humble little convert that you may have may come generations of wonderful people—your lengthened shadow.

While we have been riding with President Hutchins today, I asked him how he came into the Church. He was born here in Massachusetts, in Walpole. He and his wife both come from Walpole, wherever in the world Walpole is—I have no idea. But anyhow, that is where he was born. His wife developed an interest in knowing something about the Church because of a relative who was a member. She thought she would like to have the missionaries come and teach them. Her husband said okay, so the missionaries came. She listened, and he resented it—I guess that is the right word—he did not like them. He gave them a difficult time. Finally, when they were through with the series of lessons, he invited them not to come back.

Then, later on, a long string-bean of a boy from California came and asked if he could not come and talk with them. So he and his companion came.

This young man had a nice way about him, and he taught Brother Hutchins to pray. He taught him to address our Heavenly Father, give Him thanks, and ask for His blessings, closing in the name of Jesus Christ.

It touched Brother Hutchins's heart. Gradually, over a period of time, he reached a point where he studied again and was baptized in the Church. Now, I do not suppose that this lean missionary from California may have thought he had done a great thing. But he did something. He baptized a man and a woman and their children into this Church.

They were befriended by the people in his branch. Three couples were very kind to them. The men played tennis with him. The women entertained them, and they were friendly at all times. They embraced them and made them feel warm and at home.

The branch president gave him a job immediately. That job was to be Scoutmaster to four little Scouts. He had never been a Scoutmaster before; he did not know anything about it. He said, "What are you supposed to do?" And the branch president said, "You are supposed to take them hiking." So he took them hiking and led them along.

Well, he grew in the Church. He has always had a responsibility from that day forward. He had three children. But he decided he needed to improve his life, and he went out to the BYU and spent four years getting a degree there. He came back here. He has now been, for about 30 years, the chief of police in a little town around here. I do not know where it is, and I do not know the name of it. But anyhow, you better be good to him because he is the chief of police. He has been a bishop and other things. Today he is the stake president, having served for nine years.

I said to him today when we went to look at the temple, "I hold you responsible for this temple." I came here a long time ago with Neal Maxwell, and I told the brethren in the preliminary meeting on Saturday of the struggle to get a temple in this area. I thought we could build a temple in Hartford, Connecticut, that would serve both the New York area and the Boston area and up into New England. We searched and we searched and looked for site after site after site and never had a feeling of peace concerning where it should be. I came here to Boston, and I told the stake presidents in that meeting of the struggle that I had been through in trying to find a place to put a temple. President Hutchins raised his hand. He said, "We have just the place. I think we own it. Maybe we do, maybe we don't. Maybe we sold it long ago." I said, "I would like to see it."

I left the meeting in the hands of Brother Maxwell, and President Hutchins and I went out to where the temple now stands. I got hold of Bishop Bennett and looked at it. I said, "Do we own it?" He said, "We don't know. We tried to sell it off once.

I don't know whether we sold it or not." Anyhow, I said, "The first thing I'll do when I get home Monday will be to see whether we still own this temple site."

When I got home, I immediately had the real estate department check the titles and found that we still owned it. We have been through a lot of heartache, a lot of trouble and lawsuits and difficulty, but the fact of the matter is that the temple stands on that site, and it was suggested by this man who sits in the back of the hall here, a convert to the Church, because of a missionary who labored in this mission.

He is eternally grateful to the missionary who taught him. He said, "I know where that man is. We have kept in touch with him all these years. There is a great sense of gratitude in my heart for what he brought to us." President Hutchins now has children. He is going to have grandchildren. They are going to have children. A great chain of generations of Latter-day Saints has been established through that one baptism.

You never can foretell the consequences of that which you do, my brothers and sisters. And the man or the woman or the boy or the girl on whom you call today, with whom you speak, with whom you may leave a Book of Mormon, who even may turn you down, may later become interested and come into this Church.

I remember hearing a story from a mission president of a missionary who had left a copy of the Book of Mormon with a family, and they put it on a bookshelf and never looked at it. It just sat there and sat there; finally they sold the home. They were cleaning out all of their books and there was the Book of Mormon. They said they were going to throw it out, but for some unknown reason, they just put it back on the shelf and left it there. The family that bought their home saw it and never looked at it.

Then the father in that family broke his leg in an industrial accident. He just had to sit there and lie there for two or three weeks because of the seriousness of this compound fracture. He said to his wife one day, "Get me that book off the bookshelf, that Book of Mormon. Let's see what it is. We have never even looked at it." So she brought it down, and he began to read it. It took hold of him. The Spirit touched his heart, and eventually he came into the Church. Strange are the ways of the Lord in touching the hearts of people. You never can tell the consequences, my brothers and sisters, of that which you do.

My son, who today is a mission president, told the story of tracting out a family in Germany many years ago. They would have nothing to do with it. He bore his testimony. About two or three years later, missionaries again knocked on that door, and because of the testimony of the earlier missionaries, they listened to the missionaries who came. Out of that family in Germany has come a bishop, a stake president, and others who are faithful and true and wonderful in this Church. You never can tell the consequences of that which you do, my brothers and sisters.

I phoned a widow last week who had lost her husband. They lived down in a little town in southern Utah, a little one-horse town—one horse and two automobiles. I would like to tell you the story of that man. He grew up down in that sparse, dusty country. Anybody here from Escalante? Nobody has the honor to be here from Escalante? Does anybody know where Escalante is? Do you know where Beryl is? Anybody know where Beryl is? Well, they lived in Beryl. This is the story of Brother Normand Laub, if you ever met him.

This boy grew up in that part of southern Utah—he and his brother. The war came along, and they decided to join the service. They told the recruiting officer that they wanted to stay together as brothers throughout all of their time in the service. They were put in a tough outfit. They traveled through the battles of the Pacific. Both of them were on the initial landing barges that came into Leyte Gulf and landed there when the American forces came back to the Philippines. They came in under terrible fire, and they were climbing up a hill when a Japanese shell hit his brother, pierced his spine. This other boy, of whom I speak, held his dying brother in his arms and wept. There came into his heart a great bitterness, an intense hatred for those who had killed his brother and so many others. He vowed that he would fight with great viciousness if it meant that.

Well, he came up through that jungle area of the Philippines, on up to Manila, and was a sergeant in the first group of the American forces that entered the University of Santo Tomas, the university grounds where there were imprisoned many of the civilians of Manila whom the Japanese had imprisoned. They were gradually starving to death. They freed those people in Santo Tomas. They have been looked upon almost as angels ever since.

In any event, Brother Laub passed through the war. He came home, lonely and embittered. He was called on a mission—I think it was to the Central States—and something happened to him. He became acquainted with the Savior. He read the New Testament. He read the Book of Mormon. He prayed. He brought those elements into his life. A great spirit of love filled him. The hatred of the past disappeared. He became a changed man. He came home after honorably filling a mission and married a girl from that area. He got 80 acres of sage-covered ground, cleared it and planted it, and became a very successful grower of alfalfa.

He cubed that alfalfa, and there was a big market for it in Japan. He shipped it to Japan. Subsequently, the head man of the company that bought it in Japan invited him to come to Japan. They had established a relationship, and he decided he would go. And so he and his wife went. They were treated royally, beyond anything they could have imagined from those who had been his former enemies.

While he was in Japan, he decided to go back down to the Philippines. He did so—went down to Manila, and from there down into the jungle where his brother had been killed. While

332

there they were met by a few of the native people who were very friendly. He struck up a correspondence with a woman; they wrote back and forth. He said, "I'm going to send you a book that will change your life if you will read it and pray about it." So he sent the Book of Mormon.

This family read it and were converted to its truth; they were touched in their hearts. They went up to Tacloban, the nearest branch, 40 miles away through the jungle, and became acquainted with the Church. Eventually they joined the Church. They established a little branch down in Jaro, on the Leyte Gulf. Brother Laub went back to her again 10 years later and found this branch. He listened to the people and felt of their spirit.

I was curious when Brother Laub died as to whether that branch was still functioning. And so my secretary sent an e-mail to the Area President, and we had a reply that indicated that this little branch has 165 members, that they have about 30 Melchizedek Priesthood holders—95 percent of whom are active. There have been 14 missionaries go out from that branch, including 5 who are out today.

Now, that is the fruit of the kind of work in which you are engaged, my brothers and sisters. How wonderful it is. How beautiful it is. Of course you get cuffed around. Of course it is hard. It is bitter cold; it is terrible. I wore the heaviest coat I have to come here today. I know it is cold. It is miserable. This Massachusetts climate is terrible. But anyhow, you are here, and you are going to be here. You won't be through until you have been released, so make the best of it. Work your heads off.

In a surprising way the Lord will honor you for all that you do. You may not have a single baptism while you are here, or you may have 10 baptisms. Whatever the case might be, the Lord will bless you, and you will look back upon these days with gratitude and appreciation for as long as you live. You will tell your children, your grandchildren, and your great-grandchildren, if you live long enough, about those wonderful days that you spent in Massachusetts as a missionary of The Church of Jesus Christ of Latter-day Saints.

Now, this is not the most fruitful area in the world. You had 310 baptisms last year in this mission, right, President? That is about 1.7 per missionary. The missionaries right in Salt Lake City baptize many more people. But this is where you are called and where you are serving.

Now, I looked at the record very carefully, and I said to myself, "These missionaries brought 310 people into the Church last year. They worked so hard, they prayed so much, and there was a harvest of 310." Then I looked at the retention records and did a little calculation. I figured by the end of another year, two-thirds of those people will not be active, will drop away. I said to myself, "What a tragedy. After all of your work, after your fasting, your prayers, your labors in sunshine and in shadow, in heat and cold, two-thirds of those who are baptized will become inactive." I think I am about right in that calculation.

Something is wrong. The wards have let you down. The stakes have let you down. The members of the Church have let you down. You to a degree have let yourselves down, and I am so deeply concerned about this matter of retention of those whom you baptize. It is a great tragedy in my mind to have that kind of thing happening.

We are changing the emphasis of this work a little. We are discontinuing the stake mission as such and putting the local missionaries directly under the responsibility of the bishop to get the wards working with you, to see if we cannot strengthen this process, to have happen what happened with President Hutchins. When he was baptized, there were families in that branch that put their arms around the Hutchins family to make them feel at home and warm and comfortable, to answer their questions, to befriend them, to take them to tennis matches, to have them to dinner, and so on. There is not enough of that going on in this Church.

I want to read to you about something that happened in Brazil, Brother Zwick's country. This is a quote, and it is a little long, but I do not want any of you to go to sleep. I want you to listen to every word of it. It is important.

Brother Paulo Henrique Itinose was called as bishop of the Santana Ward, Araçatuba Brazil Stake, on May 6, 2001. It was an unusual call, as he had just completed the previous month nine years of service as president of the stake [he went from being stake president to bishop]. Reflecting on the time of his call, he commented, "I had participated for many years in [member-missionary coordinating council] meetings, in training meetings with the Area Presidency, and in stake councils searching for a way to improve the retention of new converts. In all our time and effort with this subject, we have seen little improvement. We have a serious and concerning problem."

Bishop Itinose began by analyzing the several hundred membership records in his ward, one by one, studying those members that were active and those that were not. He discovered something that strongly affected him: while those who were baptized with at least one other member of the family made up fewer than 40 percent of his total membership, they constituted 92 percent of those active in the ward. With this information in hand, he became determined to work with the missionaries in focusing the ward missionary effort on teaching families. Bishop Itinose added, "I realized that to teach families, especially parents, we as ward members would have to get more involved."

Along with the president of the stake and the president of the mission, a plan was created.

Couples were called as stake missionaries, where prior to this mostly youth had been called. Investigators would quickly be introduced to members at ward activities, and personal attention by ward members would help the investigators integrate into the ward socially, complementing the spiritual conversion. That is important.

When youth were interested in learning about the Church, missionaries would work to teach them with their parents, and ward auxiliary leaders would share with the parents the programs of the Church. Couples would be used to help bring the parents along with the youth. Ward members would be encouraged to provide more referrals, especially focusing on families. The ward mission leader [and that is what we are going to have all over the Church] would coordinate all activities with the missionaries, and the bishop and the ward council would stay closely involved. Communication throughout the week would be very important—not only on Sunday, [but] throughout the week. If children were anxious to be baptized and parents were not yet ready, missionaries would be patient. Children and youth would help bring their parents with them. Baptism would be a natural choice of their new-found home in the Church.

While the mission president, President Zollinger, was very positive about the energy of the ward, not all missionaries were immediately convinced. Elder Michael Enslow, one of the missionaries laboring in the ward, explained, "We are taught to find the elect. Most of those who are baptized are baptized in two to three weeks. My fear was that if youth were required to wait for their parents, those ready for baptism would lose the feelings they had."

Bishop Itinose explained his own experience of being baptized alone in his family as a 15-year-old. He had seen many others baptized who no longer were active. He hoped that by focusing on families and by ward members being actively involved, more strength could be generated in the investigators. He believed the desires in the youth would spark an interest in the parents.

It took a few discussions full of honesty and emotion for the missionaries and the ward members to come to a unified vision. Elder Enslow explains, "After that meeting with the bishop, I started to work differently. I started to focus more on the family and on teaching the parents. And by doing this, it changed my motives and goals. Instead of worrying about baptisms, I started worrying about the person growing a personal testimony. I started worrying more about the whole family's needs. Baptism became a means rather than an end, with our true goal becoming conversion."

Together the members of the ward and the missionaries went to work. Members introduced more friends to the missionaries. As soon as missionaries were able to teach in a home, members accompanied them. When youth desired to learn about the Church, ward members joined the missionaries in asking the whole family to be taught. Ward auxiliary leaders demonstrated to parents the strengths of the programs of the Church. The bishop took a personal interest in those being taught.

It has now been nearly a year that Bishop Itinose has led the ward. Thirty-two people have been baptized. Eighteen were baptized as part of a family, fourteen alone. The bishop explains about those who were baptized without other family members, "Even when parents are not interested in the Church themselves, we spend a lot of time with them explaining the many programs of the Church. For the most part they become very supportive, encouraging their children to stay firm as the youth face challenges in the months ahead. The parents become our strong ally."

Isn't that a great story? Doesn't that say something that is wonderful and significant? There is nothing like family. A little boy or a little girl is precious, of course, but they have parents. If you can get the parents involved, it may take a little longer, it may take a little more effort, but the end result will be more lasting, more permanent. The chances of saving the whole family are far greater when that is the case. And even if the parents do not come in, if they listen they will be prone to encourage their children to be faithful and active and remain so. And then they may come in later.

Now, that is my message to you tonight.

Brothers and sisters, be careful. Be wise. Do not get involved in anything which could compromise this great and marvelous opportunity which you have. You are missionaries. You are working as servants of the Lord. He is the only paymaster you have, and His pay is very generous, and it is everlasting. Don't ever forget it. God bless you, my dear companions, in this great work. How we love you.

A woman who does a little housekeeping came to our home this morning just as I was preparing to leave. She had only one thing to say when she came in. She said, "Our son's papers have just been sent in to go on a mission." Her smile was broad and radiant and hopeful and wonderful. She was excited. She does not know where he is going. It might be to Denver; it might be to Denmark. Nobody knows yet. Wherever he goes, it will be the best mission in the world for him. His going will bless that home in a marvelous and wonderful way. Those parents will pray as they have never prayed before. Their thoughts night and day will be on that missionary son. They will await his letters very anxiously. They will want to know what he is doing and how he is getting along. They will look forward to the day when with honor he will return, an honorably released missionary of The Church of Jesus Christ of Latter-day Saints, a young man who has gone out to serve the Lord, to serve his Father in Heaven in the Father's great work of bringing to pass the immortality and eternal life of man.

God bless you, my dear associates in this great work, is my humble prayer in behalf of every one of you. How I love you, I repeat. In the name of Jesus Christ, amen.

# BRIGHAM YOUNG UNIVERSITY—IDAHO COMMENCEMENT EXERCISES

APRIL 27, 2002

PRESIDENT BEDNAR HAS SAID THAT this will be the shortest commencement ever. I am grateful for the opportunity to live through that experience. Commencement exercises are usually interminably long.

Thank you very much for the honor you have accorded me. I cannot tell you how grateful I am. Thank you so very much.

As we have been reminded, this is the first commencement for BYU—Idaho, and it is a special privilege to be the first recipient of an honorary doctorate from this institution.

May I take just a moment to tell you about the change that has occurred at this school. As chairman of the Church Board of Education, I have long been troubled over the fact that we are educating an ever-diminishing percentage of the young people of the Church. While reflecting on this fact, the thought came—and I am confident it was inspiration—that we could increase the number touched by our higher education program if Ricks were to become a four-year school offering baccalaureate degrees. There would be fewer transfer students, and this would make it possible for BYU in Provo to accept more students.

This would be a drastic move for Ricks, but it would be worth the effort. Hopefully, without giving any offense to the Ricks family and their illustrious forebear for whom the college was named, we could rename it BYU—Idaho, as we previously had changed the name of the Church College of Hawaii to BYU—Hawaii.

I felt strongly that if we were to do this, it should be done while President Bednar presided over the school. We recognized that he has a unique capacity. He is not shackled by academic tradition. He has an understanding of how computer learning can be used in such a situation.

He has succeeded brilliantly. It has been a complex undertaking, and I do not know of anyone else who could have accomplished this. I commend him and thank him for his remarkable work. I likewise commend and thank the faculty, who have been so cooperative, who have been so enthusiastic, and who have been willing to give up certain prerogatives in order to accomplish this.

We determined that we would have to give up intercollegiate athletics. They are so costly. I recognize that many of you students feel this has been a terrible sacrifice, that it is almost impossible to conceive of a four-year institution that does not have an exciting program of intercollegiate sports. But I assure you that this is not unique.

For instance, I suppose all of you have heard of Emory University in Georgia. It is an outstanding institution, widely renowned. The president of that university recently wrote: "Emory University is not known as an athletic powerhouse. It has no football program. It has no stadium. It is without a basketball arena to hold thousands of spectators. Students are not attracted here by athletic scholarships. Nor, on an Emory team, are they ever to achieve national fame in a bowl game or a nationally televised Final Four in basketball" (William M. Chace, "Athletics and Academic Values Don't Have to Compete at a Research University," *Emory Edge*, Feb. 2002).

Emory University essentially carries forward the same kind of program that you do. And there are others who do likewise.

So much for that. And now to get into a commencement address.

I am always impressed with two hymns which we sing in the Church. The first was written by one of our own, Evan Stephens. It reads:

> *Shall the youth of Zion falter*
> *In defending truth and right?*
> *While the enemy assaileth,*
> *Shall we shrink or shun the fight? No!*
> *True to the faith that our parents have cherished,*
> *True to the truth for which martyrs have perished,*
> *To God's command,*
> *Soul, heart, and hand,*
> *Faithful and true we will ever stand.*
> *["True to the Faith," Hymns, no. 254]*

That is a wonderful declaration. All of us ought to sing it occasionally. We ought to sing it with conviction and power and determination.

The other was written by Frederick W. Faber, who lived long ago. It also concludes with a stirring statement:

> *Faith of our fathers, holy faith,*
> *We will be true to thee till death!*
> *["Faith of Our Fathers," Hymns, no. 84]*

That too is a great declaration. To everyone who sings it, to everyone who utters those words, it is a statement, a resolution, of determination: "Faith of our fathers, holy faith, we will be true to thee till death!"

If there is anything that the people of this sad old world need, it is to stand and make such a declaration. How we need faith! How we need the strength that comes of it. How we need the will to exercise it. How we need the determination to practice it. Keep the faith. This is my message to you this morning.

What a wonderful generation you are. You are young and bright and forward looking. You are men and women of integrity, of high hopes, of ambition. Never before in the history of this Church has there been a better generation than you, notwithstanding all of the seductive voices that constantly invite you to abandon the faith of your fathers and indulge in that which is faithless and empty.

I think of the 14-year-old boy Joseph reading in the family Bible those challenging words of James:

"If any of you lack wisdom, let him ask of God, that giveth to all men liberally, and upbraideth not; and it shall be given him.

"But let him ask in faith, nothing wavering. For he that wavereth is like a wave of the sea driven with the wind and tossed" (James 1:5–6).

With that promise before him, he said:

"Never did any passage of scripture come with more power to the heart of man than this did at this time to mine. . . . I reflected on it again and again, knowing that if any person needed wisdom from God, I did; for how to act I did not know, and unless I could get more wisdom than I then had, I would never know. . . .

" . . . I at length came to the determination to 'ask of God,' concluding that if he gave wisdom to them that lacked wisdom, and would give liberally, and not upbraid, I might venture" (Joseph Smith—History 1:12–13).

Think of the consequences of that act of faith. On that spring day, after centuries of time, the curtains were parted, and there appeared before him God the Eternal Father and the risen Lord. From that grand event has come all that this Church is today. You are here because of it. You would not be here if Joseph had not gone in prayer in simple faith.

Someone—I think it was Emerson—has said that every great

342

institution is the lengthened shadow of a great man (see Ralph Waldo Emerson, "Self-Reliance," in Charles W. Eliot, comp., *Harvard Classics,* 50 vols. [1909–10], 5:68). I would add that it is the lengthened shadow of a man who acted in faith.

And so my challenge to you this morning is that throughout your lives you cultivate and act with faith—faith in yourselves; faith in your associates; faith in the Church; faith in God, your Eternal Father.

*Keep faith with yourselves.*

Channing Pollock, a great playwright in his day, once said, "We begin with a banner inscribed 'Excelsior' and gradually the dust of battle obliterates everything but the second syllable" (*Guide Posts in Chaos* [1942], 206). Think of that. So many players in the game of life get to first base. Some reach second. A handful make third. But how few there are who get home and score.

I once read these challenging words in a national magazine:

"Above all, let's cut out the rotten excuse that we are only human. That we are entitled to some daily quota of error or indifference. Only human? What an incredible denial of the human potential. Only human? This is the ultimate insult.

"Remember that man's greatness does not lie in perfection, but in striving for it."

My beloved young friends, keep faith with the best that is in you. Shakespeare said, "This above all: to thine own self be true, and it must follow, as the night the day, thou canst not then be false to any man" (*Hamlet,* act 1, scene 3).

You did not come into the world to fail. You came into the world to succeed. You have accomplished much so far. It is only the beginning. As you move forward on the trail of life, keep the banner of faith in self ever before you. You may not be a genius. You may not be exceptionally smart. But you can be good, and you can try. And you will be amazed at what might happen when in faith you take a step forward.

343

Never lose faith in yourself. Never lose faith in your capacity to do good and worthwhile things. You cannot be arrogant. You cannot be conceited. You can be quiet and humble and forward looking and full of hope—the hope that blossoms into faith.

*Keep faith with your associates.*

You will never be alone. In this world we work together to accomplish things. We marry and have companions. We have children. We have associates in the Church. We work with others in our daily pursuits.

Never lose faith in your opportunity to lift those who are in need, to give strength to those who are weak, to give encouragement to those who falter by the way.

You will have about you, throughout your lives, those who stumble and fall. You can lift them. Said Paul to the Romans, "We then that are strong ought to bear the infirmities of the weak." And then he added these significant words: "And not to please ourselves" (Romans 15:1). We have an obligation to assist one another, to build one another. Declared Jesus to Peter:

"Simon, . . . Satan hath desired to have you, that he may sift you as wheat:

"But I have prayed for thee, that thy faith fail not: and when thou art converted, strengthen thy brethren" (Luke 22:31–32).

The Lord has admonished us through revelation, "Wherefore, be faithful; stand in the office which I have appointed unto you; succor the weak, lift up the hands which hang down, and strengthen the feeble knees" (D&C 81:5).

Keep faith with your associates. You can help them, and they can help you. The Almighty has designed that we work together, that we assist one another, that we bless one another in our association.

In a complex and difficult operation, the chief surgeon usually gets the credit. But in the operating room he must have faith in those about him if he is to be successful. His assistant doctors, the anesthesiologist, the skilled nurses who work with him—they are a team. He could never do it alone. Keep faith with your associates.

*Keep faith with the Church.*

This Church is the way of truth and life and salvation. I care not what course you may pursue in your future lives. I care not to what heights you may aspire. You will do better if you remain true to the faith of your forebears. Last Saturday I set apart the presidency of the new Lubbock Texas Temple. The president is a retired cardiologist, a good doctor who has saved the lives of many people. He has been a man of great skill and great learning and great service. The first counselor has been a dean in a large university, a man of learning and a man of capacity who has done very well. The second counselor is a government employee and a man who has won the esteem of his associates and given great and distinguished public service. To me it is wonderful that while climbing upward in their various professions they have remained faithful and true Latter-day Saints. And now, to crown their lives of service comes a great and sacred opportunity to preside over a new temple, a house of the Lord, where they will administer ordinances in the authority of the holy priesthood, whose power will reach beyond the veil of death.

Be true to this Church. Keep faith with this glorious work which the God of heaven has restored to the earth in this, the wondrous dispensation of the fulness of times. It is the Church of God the Eternal Father. It is the Church of the Lord Jesus Christ, whose name it bears. It is true, and I testify of that. It is wonderful, and I bear witness of that. Those who have gone before you have paid a terrible price for that which you have today. They have looked to you and hoped and prayed that you would be ever true to the cause which was so precious to them.

*Keep faith with God, our Eternal Father, and the risen Lord Jesus Christ.*

I have seen in my lifetime those who started out walking in the sunlight of faith. But gradually, through arrogance and conceit, through pride and a desire for the honors of men, they have turned their backs on God and forsaken Him. They have literally traded their birthright for a mess of pottage. They have thrown away that which was most precious and substituted a hollow shell. Like the prodigal son who wasted his inheritance "with riotous living" until he would fain eat husks with the hogs, they have sought satisfaction in the husks of life (see Luke 15:12–16). Their lives have become empty, unfulfilled. They have forsaken their God, who gave them life, and their Redeemer, who bought them with His blood.

Declared Jehovah to ancient Israel: "I am the Lord thy God, which have brought thee out of the land of Egypt, out of the house of bondage. Thou shalt have no other gods before me" (Exodus 20:2–3).

Keep that humility which will cause you to get on your knees in prayer, in acknowledgment of His power and goodness. He will not fail you. He will hear your prayers. He will answer your prayers. In the stillness of the night, you will hear the whisperings of His Spirit to direct you in your times of distress and need. Those times will come to you as they do to all. Keep faith with God, and He will never let you down. He will never turn His back upon you. To you He has said, "Be still and know that I am God" (D&C 101:16). And His Beloved Son has declared, "I am the way, the truth, and the life" (John 14:6). There is none other to bless you as your Father in Heaven and His divine Son will bless you.

> *Faith of our fathers, holy faith,*
> *We will be true to thee till death!*

I lay upon you this charge and invoke the blessings of heaven upon you as you leave this institution to go forward in other pursuits. May you walk with faith, with sure and certain faith, and may heaven smile upon you is my humble prayer, in the name of Jesus Christ, amen.

# PORT OF SPAIN, TRINIDAD, MEMBER MEETING*

MAY 20, 2002

How good you look, you wonderful people. I am so delighted to see you. It's wonderful to be with you.

We have been down in South America. We have been in Brazil dedicating a new temple. We have been in Asunción, Paraguay, dedicating a new temple. Somewhere on that long journey between Paraguay and Salt Lake City, we had to stop so the crew could rest overnight. I said, "Let's stop someplace where we can meet with the Saints where we have not been before." We have been in many of the places as we have traveled to and from South America, but we have never been to Trinidad. We decided that we would stop here—and I am so delighted that we have done so—to look at your faces, my dear brothers and sisters, and tell you how much we appreciate you, how much we love you, and how much we want to see you happy and successful and doing wonderful things. It is good that we can gather together in this hall this evening.

We are honored with the presence tonight of Mrs. Donna Carter, who is the minister of religion here. Thank you for coming to be with us. Thank you ever so much.

Now, I want to congratulate these boys and girls. You sang beautifully, and we are going to listen to you again. We are very

*delivered extemporaneously

347

glad of that. We are grateful to the woman who has led you and taught you these songs.

I want to say a word of appreciation to the missionaries—these wonderful young men and women who give of their time so freely to this work. We have 60,000 of them now out across the world. You are part of a great gathering of young men, for the most part, who are unselfishly giving of your time and your talents and your abilities to come out and bless the people and help them and teach them the gospel of Jesus Christ.

And to these older couples who are here—and older brethren and sisters—I want to say thank you for being here. You have come and sacrificed. You were comfortable at home, and when a call came to you to come to Trinidad, you came. You did not know what you were coming to. But I want to tell you that as long as you live, there will remain in your hearts a great love and appreciation for the people of this beautiful island nation. Thank you for being here.

And President and Sister Van Noy, who preside here—they have been here for two years now. They have spent a good part of their lives in Africa and other places as representatives of various American universities, and now they are here to serve the Lord for these three years. They had to make a sacrifice, and I want to thank them for what they have done.

We are just here to tell you that we love you. We so appreciate you good people who are members of this Church. We pray for you. We love you. We try to help you. We will never forget you and this visit here. You will always remain in our memories.

On the way down, we stopped at Jamaica and had a similar meeting of the Saints in that land. This Church has now grown to be a very large organization, with congregations in 160 nations, with 11 million-plus members. We are part of a great family whose objective it is to love and appreciate and respect and build one another and to reach out in building other people. We have tried to do that.

The Church carries on a great humanitarian effort. We have extended aid to people of many nations who are not of our faith when trouble and distress, when floods and hurricanes and things of that kind have hit them. That is part of the gospel of Jesus Christ—to help those who are in distress and need. That we try to do, and we do it in a very effective and wonderful way, in many cases working with other churches to do so.

Now, I want to read to you a short statement which I will use as a text for what I say tonight. This is a statement that the prophet Alma gave to his son Helaman, who was going out to do missionary service. They were talking about the people, and Alma said these words to Helaman:

"Teach [the people] an everlasting hatred against sin and iniquity.

"[Teach] them repentance, and faith on the Lord Jesus Christ; teach them to humble themselves and to be meek and lowly in heart; teach them to withstand every temptation of the devil, with their faith on the Lord Jesus Christ.

"Teach them to never be weary of good works, but to be meek and lowly in heart; for such shall find rest to their souls" (Alma 37:32–34).

That, my brothers and sisters, really sums up the great responsibility which we have to teach people to shun sin and iniquity. Teach them to reach out in service to others. Teach them to walk in meekness and lowliness of heart, going about doing good.

Now, considering my age and the fact that I do not know how long I will live, I do not suppose that I will ever visit Trinidad again. There are too many other places in the world I would like to go. I have never been to Mongolia. We have members of the Church there. I would like to go to Mongolia. I have never been to Vladivostok. I would like to go to Vladivostok. I would like to go to areas in Russia that I have never visited. I have been to Moscow and some of those places, but I have never been to large areas of Russia. I would like to go there while I am still alive.

Tonight I am here with a message of what I would like to see happen while I yet live. I would like to see all of us work together to keep the Church growing and strengthening, to spread this work across the world. Everyone we teach, every man, woman, or child who joins this Church is improved in his or her life by the doctrine which we teach. A better man, a better woman results from faithful observance of the gospel principles. And every time we teach someone and baptize someone, we do that individual a great favor.

We are not out to injure other churches. We are not out to hurt other churches. We do not argue with other churches. We do not debate with other churches. We simply say to those who may be of other faiths or of no faith, "You bring with you such truth as you have and let us see if we can add to it." Now that, in essence, is the nature of our missionary work. "You bring with you all that is good and let us see if we can add to that good." And that is the spirit in which we work.

I am satisfied that there are so very, very many people in this area who do not belong to any church, who are not active in any church. You know some of them. Reach out to them, help them, lift them, encourage them in every way you can. Refer them to the missionaries, who will teach them, and in so doing they will teach them to shun sin and iniquity, as Alma speaks of it in this scripture.

Now, secondly, when they come into the Church, put your arms around them. Make them feel at home. Let them know that they are among friends. That is so very, very important.

I know a man in Liverpool, England. He was walking along the streets, and he was drunk. Two missionaries walked up to him and began to talk with him. In his drunkenness he said, "I have lost my son. My only son died the other day, and I am trying to drown my sorrow in liquor."

The missionaries said, "Can we come and teach you sometime when you are sober?"

And he said, "Yes." And so they arranged an appointment and went to see him. They brought with them a member of the Church who was about his age, who could be a friend to him. They taught him, and he joined the Church and remained active.

He came to Salt Lake City and went to general conference. He went to the temple in Preston, England. Today that man serves as president of the Sunday School in the Liverpool stake of Zion.

Now, that is the way it works. He had a friend who worked with missionaries in teaching him, and that friend walked with him in the different and sometimes difficult ways of this Church so that he could understand and have no difficulty in accepting it.

My brothers and sisters, I place upon you a responsibility to put your arms around others, welcome them, make them feel at home, answer their questions, and give them encouragement when they come into the Church. In so doing, you will bless their lives many times over.

I would like us as members of this Church, wherever we may be, all across the world, to work harder at strengthening the youth of the Church against the sin and iniquity which they constantly face. It is in America. It is in Canada. It is in Mexico. It is in Central America. It is in South America. It is in Trinidad. It is everywhere— sin and iniquity.

You do not have to be involved in that. You must say to yourself, "I simply will not do it. I do not believe in it, and I will not do it." And I believe that if you do that, you can protect yourself against sorrow and trouble. Pornography now is such a terrible thing. It is so inviting; it is made so by those who seek to make money out of it. We cannot touch it without destroying ourselves. We cannot touch drugs without destroying ourselves. We cannot become involved in sexual misbehavior without bringing sorrow and regret into our lives.

To all of these little boys and girls here, I want to say to you, keep yourselves straight and clean and good and decent. Shun evil. Do not use the name of the Lord in vain. Do not do any of those things. You are better than that. You do not need to do it. And I plead with you that you will not do it. You will please your fathers and your mothers if you shun those things. It can be done; I have no doubt of that.

Next, I would like to see greater love in our homes. There is too much difficulty between husbands and wives, too much meanness, too much cutting one another down, too much of the kind of behavior that does not become a Latter-day Saint. You parents who are fathers and mothers of children, treasure your children. Look to them with love. Lead them. You do not have to beat them; you simply have to lead them with love. They will follow after you if you do that. And I make you a promise that if you do so, the time will come when you will feel so grateful that you have done so that you will get on your knees and thank the Lord for the precious children that have come to you and grown up under your direction.

Sister Hinckley and I have 5 children, all married; 25 grandchildren; 32 great-grandchildren, and they are still coming. We have not reached the end yet. We are proud of every one of them. We have our eldest daughter with us. She has been very active in the Church—been Relief Society president and Young Women president and has served in many capacities. She lost her husband a year or so ago. He died very suddenly of a heart attack. She is now a widow.* But she has 5 children of her own and 14 grandchildren, who bring her comfort and association and on whom she can shower her love and her blessings.

Now, you men here, I want to say to you, be good to your wife. The time will come when you will regret it if you are not. She is your companion. Under the plan of the Lord, the man does not walk ahead of the woman. The woman does not walk ahead of the

* *President Hinckley's daughter has since remarried.*

352

man. They walk side by side in the great responsibility of being husband and wife, and father and mother.

I make a great plea, as strong as I know how to make it, to you men: Treasure your wife, look after her, and bless her. If you ever get to heaven, you will get there in company with your wife. You will not go there alone and progress on the way to immortality and eternal life. The family, under the concept which we teach, is eternal in nature.

Now, you do not have a temple here, and you cannot get to a temple very easily. I suppose the closest one is in Caracas, Venezuela—some of you may be able to get there. In those holy houses you may be joined together as husband and wife under the authority of the holy priesthood for time and for all eternity. And God will bless your union if you make the effort.

We ought to be paying our tithes and offerings. Now, you say, "I cannot afford to pay any tithing." Well, maybe you can; maybe you cannot. I believe you can.

A bishop in Provo presiding over a ward at BYU reported to his stake president that he has 107 couples in his ward. And every one of those couples came to tithing settlement, and every one was a full-tithe payer. And they said to their bishop, "We cannot afford not to pay tithing. We are living so skimpily. Our income is low. Our expenses are high. If anybody in this world needs the help of the Lord, we need it. And we believe that the way to get that help is to make the contribution of our tithing each month from the meager resources which we have."

Now, the Church can get along without your tithing, but I do not believe that you can get along without paying it. The Lord has made marvelous promises, speaking through the prophet Malachi in the Old Testament. He promised that if people would pay their tithes and their offerings, He would open the windows of heaven and shower down upon them a blessing that there would not be room enough to receive it. (See Malachi 3:10.)

Now, my brothers and sisters, I do not make that promise. The Lord made that promise. I think He is capable of fulfilling that promise. It is my testimony to you tonight that He keeps His promises. I have seen it so often in my own life and in the lives of my associates.

Finally, be friendly to those not of our Church. We live in a world of many religious denominations. We are all part of the human family. We are all sons and daughters of God. Many of us, most of us in these lands, are believers in the Lord Jesus Christ. We are Christians. We need to turn the other cheek, to give the second coat, to go the extra mile, to lift those in trouble and distress, of whatever faith they may be.

We need to build one another within the Church more than we are now doing. My brothers and sisters, let us live together as sons and daughters of God, as believers with faith in the Lord Jesus Christ, building and strengthening one another, and building and strengthening those about us. If we will do so, God will bless us. We will be a happy people. We will be a growing people. We will be a people who will get on our knees and thank the Lord for His blessings upon us. I could wish for you no greater thing than this.

Now, go forward. Go forward in the faith. Be loyal to the Church. Be loyal one to another. Be true to the faith. Be stalwart in doing that which is expected of you.

Respond to every call in the Church. Your branch president, your district president, your mission president may ask you to fulfill an assignment or a calling. You may say, "I do not have time." But I want to promise you that if you will do what you are asked to do, you will be able to do it, you will grow as you do it, and you will enjoy doing it. And when the task is done, you will be grateful for the service which you have given.

Thank you, my dear friends, for being the good people you are. Thank you for the love which you carry in your hearts. Thank you for the testimonies which you have of this work. Thank you for observing the Word of Wisdom. Thank you for paying tithing, those of you who do, and for the resolution of those who do not that you will do so. Thank you for getting on your knees and praying to the God of heaven each morning and each evening.

In the name of the Lord Jesus Christ, I want to testify that I know that God, our Eternal Father, lives, that He hears and answers our prayers. I know that. I have had my prayers answered too many times to ever doubt that.

I know that Jesus Christ lives, the Son of the living God, who gave His life as an atonement for the sins of all of us. He made it possible for all men to be resurrected as a free gift from the Lord Himself, and He has opened the way under which, if we walk in obedience, we may go on to exaltation and eternal life in the world to come. I know that.

I know that the Book of Mormon is true. There is nothing evil in this book. There is so much of good. It is a companion to the Holy Bible. It does not supplant the Holy Bible; it testifies of the Holy Bible. It is another witness for the Lord Jesus Christ. I know that the priesthood is upon the earth, that these men who are here with me hold that priesthood. The men in this congregation hold that priesthood and exercise it in righteousness. I know that. I know that these blessings are with us.

I have seen in my lifetime the miracle, the absolute miracle, of the growth of this work as it has touched the lives of people all over the earth. I have met with them in many lands under many circumstances—all across the United States and Canada, up and down Mexico, in all the nations of Central America, in all the nations of South America, in the islands of the sea—such places as Samoa and Tahiti, Jamaica and Trinidad, and other island nations. I have met with them all up and down Africa. I have met with them all over Europe. We are all one great family of those who walk in faith before the Lord.

I commend you. I love you. I pray heaven's blessings upon you.

I thank you for being here tonight. I thank the Lord for the opportunity of being with you and say as we leave you, God be with you till we meet again. May we never forget the sweet feeling we had as we met together this evening, I humbly pray in the name of Jesus Christ, amen.

# KIEV, UKRAINE, MEMBER MEETING*

SEPTEMBER 9, 2002

GOOD EVENING. HOW WONDERFUL to look into your faces, you wonderful, good people. I am so grateful for this opportunity to see you and to be with you. And I am grateful for the effort which you have made to be here. I pray for the direction of the Holy Spirit that I may say something that will be helpful to you.

I am glad to be back here in this wonderful land, back here in Ukraine. I came here 21 years ago. At that time, there was not a member of the Church in all of this nation. I went to Russia—to Moscow, to St. Petersburg, then known as Leningrad. I went to Riga in Latvia. There was not a single member of the Church in all of this part of the world. And now to look at you tonight, you wonderful people who have embraced the gospel and made it a part of your lives—how thankful I feel for you. How I pray that the Lord will bless you, that He will prosper you, that you will be happy, that you will add to your numbers, that the Church will grow here.

Who would ever have thought that this beautiful hall would have so many Latter-day Saints in it? I want to express my thanks, my appreciation to those who have made it possible for us to meet here in these lovely circumstances.

Now, I am getting to be an old man. I am 92 years of age. I do

*delivered extemporaneously

357

not know how much time I have left, but while I still have the capacity to speak, I want to give you my witness that this is the Church of Jesus Christ in these latter days; that God has spoken again; that He has introduced His Beloved Son, the Lord Jesus Christ; and that the priesthood has been restored, with all the keys thereof, for a blessing in this great and wonderful age in which we live.

I am grateful to be here with my dear wife. I am going to ask her to stand up here with me for a minute. Come over here, dear.

We are both old. She will be 91 pretty soon. We have been married for 65 years. We are not as strong as we once were. We wobble around, but we have had a good life, haven't we?

*Sister Hinckley:* Very good.

*President Hinckley:* Well, thank you very much.

*Sister Hinckley:* I love you.

*President Hinckley:* We brought our daughter to take care of her mother, and we brought my cane to take care of me.

Now, my dear friends, I want to talk with you briefly about a matter. Can you turn to 1 Peter 2:9? Let's read it:

"But ye are a chosen generation."

I believe that with all my heart. What a wonderful time it is to be alive, with all the blessings of science that have prolonged our lives, with all of the opportunities that we have—and on top of all of that, this wonderful restored gospel. We are a chosen generation. I hope, my brothers and sisters, that you will remember that.

This is the greatest age in the history of the world when you and I have come to earth and partake of all the blessings that are available to us and, in a particular way, the blessings of the gospel of Jesus Christ. How much this Church means to us. How wonderful it is.

"A royal priesthood."

This is the day which Peter foresaw when there should be a

358

royal priesthood upon the earth, available to all men who would accept the gospel.

My dear brethren, do you realize what you have when you have the priesthood of God? You can serve in the governance of this Church. You can hold office. You can administer its affairs. More important even perhaps than that, the priesthood carries with it the power and authority to lay hands upon the heads of your family and bless them. Do you know of any group in the world where a father has the right and the privilege and the opportunity to lay his hands upon the head of his wife and his children and bless them in the name of the Lord? What a priceless privilege that is. And I want to say to the fathers here, live worthy of this great blessing. Yours is the right to exercise that priesthood, but only if you live worthy of it. We cannot exercise it unless we live worthy of it. Please, dear brethren, keep your lives in order. Be true and faithful in every respect.

I was disturbed to hear that two-thirds of the men in Russia die of alcohol-related problems. I was disturbed to hear that two-thirds of the marriages in Russia end in divorce. That is what is wrong with this modern world. The Lord has blessed us that no such thing need happen to us. He has given us the Word of Wisdom, which should prompt every Latter-day Saint to refrain from those things which will destroy his life and ruin his happiness.

Now, associated with this royal priesthood are the great blessings of the temple. On Saturday we rededicated the temple in Freiberg, Germany. After 17 years of use, the building has been completely renovated and enlarged. And in that holy house, the powers of the royal priesthood are exercised so that that which is sealed on earth becomes sealed in heaven and the blessings of eternal family life are assured and preserved through this life and throughout all eternity. Can there be a greater blessing than that?

Yesterday we dedicated a new temple in The Hague in the Netherlands. It is a beautiful structure, and after all of these many years, the Saints in the Netherlands and Belgium and France will have the opportunities of that holy house and the exercise of the priesthood therein.

I see many young men here tonight, members of the Church. I hope, my dear young brethren, that you will marry in the Church, that you will marry these wonderful young women who have embraced the gospel, and that the privilege of temple marriage may be yours. There is no substitute for it. There is nothing under the heavens to compare with it—the exercise of the royal priesthood, binding in the heavens that which is bound upon the earth.

"An holy nation."

I do not think that refers to a political nation. I think it refers to the family of God, to members of the Church. You are a part of that great membership, a great family 11 million strong scattered through 160 nations as followers of the Lord Jesus Christ. This is indeed an holy nation, this great and glorious Church.

Finally: "A peculiar people."

We are a peculiar people. We are different. We do not smoke. We do not drink. We pay our tithing. We cultivate a strong family life. The Church is directed by lay leaders and not professional ministers. All of this makes of us a peculiar people, and isn't that wonderful? What a great compliment that is—to be recognized as a peculiar people.

Well, there it is, my brothers and sisters, as Peter foresaw. "A chosen generation, a royal priesthood, an holy nation, a peculiar people; that ye should shew forth the praises of him who hath called you out of darkness into his marvellous light" (1 Peter 2:9).

The Lord has called you out of darkness into His glorious light. And we show our love and appreciation by doing what He would have us do.

My dear brothers and sisters of this great nation of Ukraine, the Church is young here. You are pioneers in this part of the world. The Church had its pioneers in early days, and you are now pioneers in this time. And the work will grow stronger; I have not the slight-est doubt of that. You will be looked back to with appreciation and gratitude.

I pray the Lord will bless you. Oh, how I hope He will bless you. Many of you have serious economic problems. It is hard to make the money pass around and do what you need to have done. I believe with all my heart that you need the blessings of the Lord. You pray for those blessings, and He has set forth a law under which He will bless you, and that is the law of tithing.

You say you cannot afford to pay it. You cannot afford not to pay it, my brothers and sisters. You have made a covenant with the Lord, and He has said that He would open the windows of heaven and shower down a blessing upon you (see Malachi 3:10). That is not my promise. That is the Lord's promise, and the Lord has the power to fulfill His promises.

I remember a Chinese man and woman in Taiwan. They were baptized, joined the Church. The next Sunday the wife said, "We must pay our tithing."

The man said, "We can't pay our tithing. We can't pay our tithing and buy rice."

She said, "But we were baptized, and with that came a promise to be obedient."

Well, they talked together. Finally, she prevailed. They picked up the money that they had saved for tithing and took it to the branch president. Then they returned home, and he said to her, "Now what are you going to do? How can we buy food?"

She said, "I don't know, but the Lord has made a promise."

The next day he went to work again. His boss called him in. He said to him, "I have been watching you. You are a good worker. I am going to increase your pay." He handed him an envelope, and when he opened it, it was exactly the amount of the tithing he had paid.

Now, I know that is difficult for very many of you. But I plead with you to take the Lord at His word and exercise faith and do that which is expected. Let Him fulfill His promise, which I testify He will do.

Now, my brothers and sisters, in conclusion, I want to tell you how much I love you. This is the first time I have seen you. I am so glad that I have come. At my age I ought to stay home, but I have come to see you and to thank you for all the good that you do, for the goodness of your lives, for your love for the Lord, for the service which you give, for the responsibilities which you carry in the various branches.

Thank you for all you do. I promise you that it will not be a sacrifice. It is never a sacrifice when you get back more than you give. It becomes an investment, and that is what is happening as you serve. You grow in capacity and strength. You become a better man or a better woman. You become a better neighbor. You become a better friend. You become a better citizen of the nation in which you live. And this nation of Ukraine is stronger because of your faithfulness in this Church.

Please know that we pray for you. We know that you pray for us, and we are deeply grateful to you. But please be assured that we also pray for you, that the God of heaven will smile with favor upon you and bless you with the righteous desires of your hearts.

You look so wonderful to me. You look so bright and so happy. I just wish that I could come down and put my arms around every one of you and say, "Thank you, and the Lord bless you." I am sorry I cannot do that; we would be here all night. But please know that that is how I feel.

And I want you to remember that you were in Kiev and came to a meeting and heard President Hinckley say that this is the Church of God. God lives; of that I testify. And what a wonderful thing it is to know that. I hope that every man and woman in this congregation tonight knows that—and that Jesus is the Christ, the Redeemer of the world. What a wonderful thing it is to know that.

Most people of the earth do not know that. You do. If you do not, you can come to know it.

I know that Joseph Smith was truly a prophet of God, that the Book of Mormon is true, that the priesthood is upon the earth, and this is the work of God. Please, please accept my testimony, which I add to your testimonies.

God bless you, my dear friends. I may never see you again. There will be a sweet and enduring memory of this great congregation, many of whom have come long distances to be here. May the Lord bless you, I humbly pray as your fellow servant, in the name of Jesus Christ, amen.

# PHILADELPHIA, PENNSYLVANIA, MISSIONARY MEETING*

OCTOBER 25, 2002

How NICE TO BE WITH YOU. What a wonderful privilege it is to be with you, you bright and able and consecrated young men and women and you dear older couples who sweeten the whole thing, who are doing such a wonderful work here. Thank you for your presence. How grateful we are to you; how really grateful we are for your tremendous service. You are the lifeblood of the Church. You are the thing that makes the work grow. You are the thing that makes it vital and strong and uplifting, spreads it across the world. We are so deeply grateful to you. We expect so very, very much of you, and the wonderful thing is that you produce. You do. You give it your best.

I have said many times, when I have looked at an audience like this, that you are not very much to look at but you are all the Lord has. That is the way with all of us. We are not exceptional people. We are very ordinary people, but we have an extraordinary assignment and a tremendous calling and a wonderful opportunity. God bless you, my dear associates, in this great and wonderful work.

Now, I have listened very intently to what has been said here, what Brother Condie said and what Brother Ballard has said. All he has been trying to tell you to do is to equip yourselves better to do the work which lies ahead of you, my brothers and sisters. He wants

*delivered extemporaneously

you to lift your heads out of the book—instead of just quoting from rote, to speak by the power and the inspiration of the Holy Spirit and in so doing to speak into the hearts of the people. In this city of brotherly love, where people are so mean and unfriendly and have dogs that bark at you and all of those things, you just have to rely on the Spirit of the Lord, and you won't have that Spirit unless you ask for it and work for it. I believe that with all my heart.

The Lord has said this with reference to what Elder Ballard has just been saying:

"And ye shall go forth in the power of my Spirit."

Do you have that? Are you going forward in the power of the Spirit of the Lord, or are you just getting up in the morning and going through the ritual of the thing?

"And ye shall go forth in the power of my Spirit, preaching my gospel, two by two, in my name" (D&C 42:6).

Don't you ever forget that your responsibility is to speak in the name of the Lord, my brethren and sisters. You are His representatives. The mantle of His power rests upon you. You young men, you young women, you carry something that is almost beyond you, and yet it isn't beyond you because that power and authority has been bestowed upon you. Don't you ever forget. And in your missionary service you are going forth in the name of the Lord, "lifting up your voices as with the sound of a trump, declaring my word like unto angels of God" (D&C 42:6). I don't suppose you ever regard yourself as an angel, but that is what you are really, when all is said and done—like unto angels of God.

I was holding a meeting of this kind once with President Henry D. Moyle in Chicago. We had two missions there and a great crowd of people in that hall, and we went on all day. When we separated for a break, I went out and walked around in the lobby, and a fine stylish-looking woman said, "Who in the world is this group in there, all dressed in black suits?" And I said, "They are Mormon missionaries." She said, "They look like angels dressed in black."

Well, that is what you are. You are angels dressed in black, speaking with the power of the Almighty.

"And ye shall go forth baptizing with water, saying: Repent ye, repent ye, for the kingdom of heaven is at hand. . . .

"Again I say unto you, that it shall not be given to any one to go forth to preach my gospel, or to build up my church, except he be ordained by some one who has authority" (D&C 42:7, 11).

You have been ordained, and you have authority to preach the gospel.

"And the Spirit shall be given unto you by the prayer of faith; and if ye receive not the Spirit ye shall not teach" (D&C 42:14).

Well, my brethren and sisters, my associates in this work, except ye have the Spirit ye shall not teach. We have some lessons, yes. We have gone to extremes in making them rigid. We have to free up a little. You have to recite less and testify more.

Now, you have to pray for this. I know that you pray; of course you pray. You pray every morning. You pray every night. And I hope you pray during the day. But when you pray, do you really ask the Lord, as His servants, to speak through you, to let His power rest upon you and let the Holy Ghost bear witness to the people as you testify to them? Do you really pray that way? Have you really learned to plead with the Lord as if your very life depended upon it? It is necessary because your very life does depend on it, my brethren and sisters—your life as a missionary of the gospel of Jesus Christ.

There is a great statement made in the 109th section of the Doctrine and Covenants concerning you who are here today. Said the Prophet, and this came by revelation:

"And we ask thee, Holy Father, that thy servants may go forth from this house armed with thy power, and that thy name may be upon them, and thy glory be round about them, and thine angels have charge over them;

"And from this place they may bear exceedingly great and

glorious tidings, in truth, unto the ends of the earth, that they may know that this is thy work, and that thou hast put forth thy hand, to fulfil that which thou hast spoken by the mouths of the prophets, concerning the last days" (D&C 109:22–23).

That was the plea of the Prophet Joseph Smith, speaking under revelation concerning you, my brothers and sisters.

Now, you are young, but you have this very heavy burden, serving as ambassadors of the Lord Jesus Christ. When I was in the mission home 69 years ago, President David O. McKay spoke to us, and I have never forgotten what he said. He said, "You young men and women go forth as ambassadors of the Lord Jesus Christ." Think what that means.

We had call on us the other day the ambassador to the United States from the European Union, a wonderful and remarkable man. He represents the European Union of 15 nations of Europe who are now bonded, united together, in their great economic undertakings. He is their spokesman. He has authority, plenary powers, to speak in their behalf. He was a very impressive man, and I looked at him and I thought of you—60,000 of you across the world teaching this gospel with plenary powers. Do you know what *plenary* means? Full. Complete. This ambassador has full powers to speak in behalf of those he represented. You are granted plenary powers to speak in behalf of the Lord Jesus Christ. Think of what that means!

You can't afford to be lazy. You can't afford not to get up in the morning. You cannot afford not to study the prophets of old. You cannot afford not to be acquainted with them and their great work. You cannot afford not to get along with your companion. You cannot afford to be thinking all the time of the girl you left at home. She is home. You are here. She has her work to do, and you have your work to do, and it is pretty important, and you only have two years in which to do it—you young ladies, a year and a half; you old people, as long as you can take it.

Now, I think I would like to do something I did a long time ago. I used to do it a lot before I grew so old. I would like to turn to the book of Timothy and read you a few things and speak of them for a moment.

Timothy was the young companion of probably the greatest missionary who ever walked the earth, and that was Paul. And Paul wrote two letters to Timothy, a young man, a young missionary. I picture him in a dark suit with a red tie and a wrinkled collar, thinking of the girl at home. This is what Paul said to Timothy:

"Let no man despise thy youth."

All except you older couples are young. People look at you, and they say, "You don't know anything about the gospel; you are just a youth."

"Let no man despise thy youth; but be thou an example of the believers, in word, in conversation, in charity, in spirit, in faith, in purity" (1 Timothy 4:12).

If you will do that, they will overlook your youth, and you will be magnified and appear before them as young men of great and uncommon wisdom, my dear brethren.

Be an example in word, in what you say; in conversation, in your discussions together; in charity, your spirit of love toward them; in spirit, with the Holy Ghost resting upon you; in faith that bridges from you to them; and in purity, as young men of purity and virtue and strength and cleanliness.

"Neglect not the gift that is in thee, which was given thee by prophecy, with the laying on of the hands of the presbytery" (1 Timothy 4:14).

I want to say to you that you are called by prophecy. I believe that. I have seen that. I have had to do with this missionary work over a very, very, very long period of time, and there is no doubt in my mind that you were called by the spirit of prophecy, "with the laying on of the hands of the presbytery." Who are the presbytery?

The presbytery are the elders, the elders of the Church—the stake president, in most cases, who set you apart.

Now then, said Paul to Timothy: "Take heed unto thyself"—listen to this—"and unto the doctrine; continue in them: for in doing this thou shalt both save thyself, and them that hear thee" (1 Timothy 4:16). What a wonderful direction Paul gave to young Timothy.

He went on to say this: "For God hath not given us the spirit of fear; but of power, and of love, and of a sound mind" (2 Timothy 1:7). God hath not given us the spirit of fear, but of power—the power of the message; and of love—love for the people, love for what we have to offer; a sound mind—the simple, understandable principles of the restored gospel of Jesus Christ.

"Be not thou therefore ashamed of the testimony of our Lord" (2 Timothy 1:8). Never, my brothers and sisters, be thou ashamed of the testimony of our Lord. I like that statement even more than I like Paul's statement that he is "not ashamed of the gospel of [Jesus] Christ: for it is the power of God unto salvation" (Romans 1:16). Here is a great charge, a mandate that is laid upon us: "For God hath not given us the spirit of fear; but of power, and of love, and of a sound mind. Be not thou therefore ashamed of the testimony of our Lord."

"Study to shew thyself approved unto God, a workman that needeth not to be ashamed, rightly dividing the word of truth" (2 Timothy 2:15).

In this, you young men and you young women, "flee also youthful lusts" (2 Timothy 2:22). You didn't come to Philadelphia to find a wife. You didn't come to Philadelphia to find a husband. You came to Philadelphia as a missionary of The Church of Jesus Christ of Latter-day Saints, to give your full time and your full interests for the period for which you were called to the service of the Lord. There will be time enough when you go home to find a wife. This is not that time. Flee youthful lusts.

Finally, Paul, this old grizzled veteran, said to Timothy, "I charge thee therefore before God, and the Lord Jesus Christ, . . . preach the word; be instant in season, out of season; reprove, rebuke, exhort with all longsuffering and doctrine" (2 Timothy 4:1–2).

And then in conclusion he gives that last and marvelous testimony:

"For I am now ready to be offered [to give his life], and the time of my departure is at hand.

"I have fought a good fight, I have finished my course, I have kept the faith:

"Henceforth there is laid up for me a crown of righteousness, which the Lord, the righteous judge, shall give me at that day: and not to me only, but unto all them also that love his appearing" (2 Timothy 4:6–8).

We had a missionary killed a couple of nights ago in an automobile accident—a terrible misfortune, a tragedy, a terrible tragedy. Be careful. I want to say to you, be very, very, very careful. He was a good missionary, an able missionary, and he has gone the way which Paul describes here, having fought a good fight and finished his course, having kept the faith. I don't know when our time will come. None of us do. But I hope we can say that, each of us.

Now, you have met here today to be strengthened, to be uplifted, to be encouraged, to be helped, to make of yourselves a better missionary. I hope that every one of you, when you leave here today, will say to yourself, "I am going to try a little harder. I am going to give a little more to it. I am not going to worry about sending those e-mails home every 36 hours. Once a week I will write to my folks, yes, but I am not going to worry about home." You have a father and mother to look after home; you don't need to. You are here to represent the Lord. "I am going to work a little harder and then try a little harder. Maybe I can't memorize the lessons. Maybe I don't have it in my head to memorize the lessons."

Well, do your best. It will be important that you do so, but do it in such a way that you can be flexible. If you feel inspired to give lesson number 3 or 4 or 5 or 6, don't regret it.

I commend to you that which you have heard this day. I express my great love for you. I just love the missionaries. I looked at a picture the other day that someone took in London 69 years ago, and there I was, dark hair, a two-button suit, sharp and bright and happy with my associates—just wonderfully happy. And I said to myself, "What a great day that was. What a marvelous season that was in your life, and everything that you have done since then that has been of any worth to you has come out of that experience which you had back in those days." And I felt like falling to my knees and thanking the Lord for His blessings.

Now, I make you a promise. If you will give it the very best you have, you will never get over it. I told this ambassador the other day that the nations of Europe will never have better friends in the United States than the young men and young women who have served as representatives of this Church in those nations. They did not go as tourists. They went as messengers of peace into the homes of the people, where they learned to know them and love them and appreciate them and respect them. And they will never lose their love for them.

I make a promise to you that you will never lose your love for the wonderful people of the areas in which you serve. May God bless you, my dear friends, brothers and sisters, co-workers in this great undertaking, is my humble prayer as I leave with you my witness and testimony of the truth, the absolute truth of this great and singular thing, different from all other things on the face of the earth—the Church and kingdom of God, even The Church of Jesus Christ of Latter-day Saints. Of this I testify as I leave my love with you, in the name of our Redeemer, Jesus Christ, amen.

# PLEASANT GROVE, UTAH, REGIONAL CONFERENCE— LEADERSHIP TRAINING SESSION*

## JANUARY 18, 2003

Brethren, it is wonderful to be with you, to look into your faces. You are the men that make things go in this part of the Church, and we are grateful to you.

I want first to express my great appreciation for the tremendous service which you give. You bishops and members of bishoprics, you members of high councils, you members of stake presidencies, you members of quorum presidencies—what a great work you are doing. It is wonderful! Thank you so very much for your dedicated service. Really, you are not perfect, but you are working in that direction, doing the best you know how, and I thank you.

I apologize for taking you from your homes two Saturdays in a row. Last week you were listening to us [during the Worldwide Leadership Training Meeting on January 11]; now you are listening again. I just say thank you so very much.

I want to express my great appreciation to each of you for your part in the forward movement that the Church is experiencing. The Church was never in better shape than it is today. I want to say that. The Church was never stronger than it is today. The Church was never larger than it is today. I think the Church was never more effective in the lives of its people than it is today.

I have a great and profound feeling of gratitude for the wonderful

*delivered extemporaneously

372

things that are happening—great and good things—thanks to you leaders. You are where the rubber hits the road. You are the men who work directly with the people, who listen to their problems, who counsel them, who direct them in their work. And you are doing a great job.

Now, with all of that, we are not perfect. We all have a long way to go. We recognize that and realize it. I am satisfied that all of us want to do a little better. I do not think we rise in the morning and get on our knees without asking the Lord to give us strength and capacity to do that which is expected of us. And I believe with all my heart that when we retire at night, with very few exceptions, we get on our knees and pray the Lord will help us and give us the power and capacity and the strength and the time to do that which is expected of us.

We know you carry a very heavy load. We know that. The First Presidency and the Twelve have spent a lot of time in the last few months going over the entire program of the Church, every facet of it, to see if there is not something that we could cut out to lighten the load, particularly on the bishops. And after all this talk, about the only thing we have come up with is to extend the time of a temple recommend from one year to two. That will save you a couple of hours, but it will not make a big material difference. But it will be helpful.

Now, if you know of any program in this Church that we ought to do away with, let us know, will you? And we will see if it is possible.

We have each of the heads of the organizations come in and visit with us, the Presidency, and they make their case. Believe me, when you get through, you think they are the most important people in the world and theirs is the most important program. And I am sure that is the experience that you have.

Well, we are doing a lot of things. Maybe not all of it is necessary, but it is all designed to help, to lift, to encourage, to instruct, to strengthen our people—young, middle-aged, and old. And I believe, on balance, that we are moving in, really, a wonderful way.

My secretary is here with me. Every week we sit down together for quite a period of time and work on what we call cancellation of sealing cases. These are requests which come in from people all across the Church to have their temple sealings cancelled. There was a time in a young couple's life when they knelt at the altar and, in the presence of God, looked into one another's eyes and joined hands and pledged their love and their loyalty one to another for time and for all eternity. And then time passed. And some of them began to think—the men, particularly—that they were so handsome and bright and able that they were deserving of a little more than they had. They began to get into forbidden paths. Now comes a heartbroken wife, a woman with children in so many cases, who says, "My husband has abandoned me. He has left me, committed adultery. There was no love on his part. I would like a cancellation of my sealing so that I am free to marry another man and be sealed to him."

These are very difficult decisions to make. These things are not light and small things. These are very serious things that occur to people who have made the most solemn kind of a covenant in the house of the Lord in the presence of God and out of whose lives has gone the light of love and appreciation and respect and decency. And in its place has come meanness and slamming around and terrible behavior, much of it too gross to describe here.

Brethren, teach our people. Teach them the gravity of the covenants which they make in the house of the Lord. Teach them the meaning of loyalty one to another. Teach them the meaning of respect one for another. Teach them the meaning of responsibility toward one another as they stand before the Lord as husband and wife and parents of children. My dear brethren, teach them with faith and example. Try to keep them from the work of the adversary, who is so powerful and effective these days and who is bringing so much of sorrow and difficulty.

They look at pornography on the Internet and become all ensnared in the kind of thing that eventually destroys them. Literally, it destroys them; they are never the same again. They cannot be the same. So my great plea today in this matter is to teach them with kindness and with love and respect. I hope you can do that without prying too deeply into their personal affairs, but do it in such a way, inspired of the Lord, to lift them out of that situation of temptation into which more and more and more of them are falling and becoming entrapped. I hope that you will do that.

Brethren, are we careful? We are overworked. We leave early in the morning. We go to work. We spend all day there. We come home at night tired and, in so many cases, irritable. We have to watch it, brethren. We really do.

Now, to each of you, if you are guilty in any way of any kind of hypocritical behavior, plead with the Lord. Get on your knees and plead with the Lord to give you strength to curb your temper and go in the house with a smile on your face and a kiss on your lips, if you please, and with love in your heart to those to whom you are married and to the children of that marriage.

Of course they are noisy. I have reached an age when I have a lot of great-grandchildren, and I cannot understand how energetic they are. They come to visit us, and we have to put everything four feet above the floor to keep them from breaking it or tearing it apart.

Let us not live a life, brethren, that would bring regret. I want to say to you that when you get as old as I am—if you make it—it is not going to matter very much how much money you made, what kind of a house you lived in, what kind of a car you drove, the size of your bank account, any of those things. What is going to matter is that dear woman who has walked with you side by side as your companion through all of the years of life, those children and grandchildren and great-grandchildren, their faithfulness, and their looking to you and speaking of you with respect and love and deference and kindness.

God bless you, brethren. May His blessings rest upon you in your homes. That is the thing that will really count—your homes. The only thing you will take with you, when all is said and done, is your family relationships. You are not going to take a dollar, not five cents, not even a Pleasant Grove nickel.

Brethren, the only thing you are taking with you is your family relationships. That is all—no money, no cars, no real estate, no stock options, nothing of that kind.

God bless us to be good fathers, while we can be, and good husbands to our good wives, I humbly pray.

Now, just one or two other things.

I worry about our young people. We have wonderful young people. You have them in your stake by the hundreds—faithful, diligent, wonderful young people who go to seminary and learn the things of the gospel and try to do the right thing.

We have never had a better generation of youth than we have in the Church today. I am satisfied of that. They are better schooled. They are better trained. They know the scriptures better. They are just wonderful young people, but unfortunately too many are falling through the cracks. They are being enticed by these evil things. They are watching video tapes. They are playing the Internet. They get involved in some of this trashy stuff—trashy entertainment, sleazy entertainment that is brought into this part of the country.

Get close to them, please. You bishoprics, get close to your deacons. Reach down and learn to know those boys.

I grew up in a ward in which there were five deacons quorums—1,500 people in that ward and five deacons quorums. The bishop served for 24 years, and he knew all our names. He never saw us that he did not call us by our first name. And we appreciated it, and I think we tried to become decent, faithful kids and grow into decent, faithful Latter-day Saints.

Reach down and be close to these young people. You may have to neglect some of the old wood, which is pretty much lost anyway. But reach down to this coming generation, and love them and reach out to them and help them and give them encouragement. Their fathers and their mothers may not be active in so many cases.

I interviewed all the missionaries once in Argentina. I found that 50 percent of them—50 percent of them—came out of homes where the parents were either nonmembers or totally inactive. But somebody had worked with those boys and girls until they had gone on missions. And that is our job and our responsibility. If the fathers cannot do it, we will have to if we want to save them.

And, likewise, see that the girls receive the kind of attention that they need, because the performance of the girls, which used to be above the boys, has come down now, until generally across the Church they are about the same—and not as good as they ought to be.

I want to make one more plea, and that is that we look after those who come into the Church as converts. I am satisfied we do not need to lose those who come into the Church as converts to the Church. But the fact of the matter is we do lose them. We lose them in such large numbers, and it is absolutely inexcusable, in my judgment. That is strong talk, but I believe it with all my heart, and I think it is the most serious problem we face in the entire Church—the loss of those who come in as converts. They need someone very, very close to them, to walk with them, to help them, to answer their questions, to give them assurance and strength as they wobble along as new members of this Church. My brethren, please, please, if you cannot do it yourselves—and I do not believe you can—there is someone else in your ward who can do it. You have a ward mission leader, and you have a lot of other people who can become friends, if they are asked to, with these new members and assist them until they develop the strength to become solid and substantial members of the Church.

You have a lot of sleepy elders. Please see that one or two are assigned to walk beside those new converts—and likewise with the women, and likewise with the young men and young women—to help them, to keep them in the way of the Church. God will bless you as you do so.

You are in the area of the world where the Church is strong, where faith is strong, where the performance is wonderful, and where the work moves forward as it does not quite anywhere else in all the world, with the exception of maybe a ward here or a ward there. But you have to watch it, or we will begin to slip here, because the influences here are the same influences which extend across the world. The power of Satan is made manifest everywhere, and it is in our midst. There are plenty of people who just love to point to us and say, "They teach one thing, but this is the way they are." Now, there is not much substance to that, but that is what they like to do.

God bless you, my dear brethren, you fathers, your wives, your children, and all with which you have to do.

Be honest with your employer. Do not take undue advantage. You have an obligation to him. You work for him. He compensates you for your time and your skills. You must perform.

You have an obligation in your Church responsibility. You have an obligation in your families. You must have family home evening. You must spend some time with your children. And you have an obligation to yourself. You must balance those four obligations as leaders in the Church. If you are not doing it, I urge you to sit down quietly and have a moment of introspection together and try to prioritize your time in such a way that you can cover those four bases adequately.

God bless you. I leave you my witness and testimony of the truth of this work. It is true. There is no substitute for it. There is none. It is God's work. He has restored it in this dispensation. Men and women by the thousands have died for it. A terrible price has been paid for it. It is so important. It is the little stone cut out of the mountain without hands which must roll forth to fill the earth. And you are there to see that it happens.

May the Lord bless you. We love you. How much we love you and appreciate you. Thank you, everyone, for being so kind and generous and thoughtful toward me. I want you to know that I very much appreciate it. I do not know how much longer I am good for, but I will wobble along for as long as I can and enjoy the company of such good and faithful men as you.

I bear my witness and leave my blessing and express my love in the name of Jesus Christ, amen.

# SATELLITE BROADCAST, 125TH ANNIVERSARY OF THE PRIMARY

## FEBRUARY 8, 2003

$M$Y DEAR YOUNG FRIENDS, my beloved boys and girls, I am so grateful to be with you when you celebrate Primary's 125th birthday.

I think there never was before a meeting such as this of boys and girls. I speak to you from the great Conference Center here in Salt Lake City. It is filled with children, their parents, and their teachers—21,000 of them. And in thousands of other halls all across the world you have gathered to celebrate this great occasion. My words will be translated into many languages. We live in various countries, and we salute different flags. But we have one great thing in common: we are all members of The Church of Jesus Christ of Latter-day Saints. And your coming together in these many different places is a sign of the wonderful growth which this Church has experienced since it was first established.

There was not always a Primary in the Church. During the first 48 years of its history, boys and girls did not have their own organization. Then a very dear woman whose name was Aurelia Spencer Rogers thought that the little boys ought to have their own organization where they could be "trained to make better men."

Her suggestion was taken to the President of the Church, who at that time was John Taylor. He thought that if an organization would be good for little boys, it would also be good for little girls because they would make the singing sound better. And so, way back 125 years ago, the first Primary met, with 224 boys and girls "to be taught obedience, faith in God, prayer, punctuality, and good manners" (in Daniel H. Ludlow, ed., *Encyclopedia of Mormonism*, 5 vols. [1992], 3:1146).

From that small beginning, Primary has grown until it is a part of the Church all across the world. Today there are almost a million of you children in Primary.

This is good, because boys and girls ought to have their organization, just as young men and young women and the older folks of the Church have their teaching organizations.

The three women who have spoken to you [the Primary general presidency] direct the work of the Primary all over the world. Among them they have 23 children, so they know what you are interested in.

How fortunate you are, my dear young friends, to have wonderful teachers. They love you very much, and they are very anxious to meet with you each week and instruct you in the ways of the Lord.

Brother Artel Ricks tells an interesting story of an inspired Primary teacher. Artel was a little boy five or six years old. One night his family sat around the dinner table and talked about tithing. They told him "that tithing is one-tenth of all we earn and that it is paid to the Lord by those who love Him."

He loved the Lord, and so he wanted to give the Lord his tithing. He went and got his savings and took one-tenth of his small savings. He says:

> I . . . went to the only room in the house with a lock on the door—the bathroom—and there knelt by the bathtub. Holding the three or four coins in my upturned hands, I asked the Lord to accept them. [I was certain He would appear and take them from me.] I pleaded with the Lord for some time,

381

but [nothing happened. Why would He not accept my tithing?] As I rose from my knees, I felt so unworthy that I could not tell anyone what had happened. . . .

A few days later at Primary, the teacher said she felt impressed to talk about something that was not in the lesson. I sat amazed as she then taught us how to pay tithing [to the bishop, the Lord's servant]. But what I learned was far more important than how to pay tithing. I learned that the Lord had heard and answered my prayer, that He loved me, and that I was important to Him. In later years I came to appreciate still another lesson my Primary teacher had taught me that day—to teach as prompted by the Spirit.

So tender was the memory of that occasion that for more than thirty years I could not share it. Even today, after sixty years, I still find it difficult to tell about it without tears coming to my eyes. The pity is that a wonderful Primary teacher never knew that through her, the Lord spoke to a small boy. ["Coins for the Lord," *Ensign,* Dec. 1990, 47]

I went to Primary when I was a small boy. In those days we met on Tuesday afternoon after school. It seems to me we were always tired and hungry in the late afternoon after school. But our teachers were so very kind and good to us. They frequently brought us a cookie to eat, but more important, they taught us rich and wonderful lessons.

Here we learned about Jesus and His great love for us. We learned about God, our Eternal Father, to whom we could go in prayer. We learned about the boy Joseph, who went into the woods to pray and whose prayer was answered with a visit of our Heavenly Father and His Son, Jesus Christ. Here we learned about the history of the Church, about the very courageous and faithful men and women and boys and girls who worked so hard to make it strong. Here we learned about being kind to one another and helpful in all circumstances. We learned that it is very important to assist with things to do around the home. We learned to behave in an orderly manner.

Primary is now held on Sunday. In many ways this is a better time. We are not tired out from being in school all day. I know that you think that Primary is long, but our teachers are well prepared, and we not only have good lessons but also activities.

Here we sing together those wonderful Primary songs. One that we sang when I was young went like this:

*Father, let thy light divine*
*Shine on us, we pray.*
*Touch our eyes that we may see;*
*Teach us to obey.*
*Ours the sacred mission is*
*To bear thy message far.*
*The light of faith is in our hearts,*
*Truth our guiding star.*
   [*"The Light Divine,"* Hymns,
   *no. 305*]

The words of that beautiful song were written by Matilda W. Cahoon, who was my day schoolteacher when I was a boy.

You now have this beautiful *Children's Songbook,* filled with many kinds of music written just for you. Some of these songs have been sung today. We have all joined in singing that wonderful song which was written for you Primary children but which has come to be sung by the entire Church. It is such a beautiful song. And it speaks of such a great and wonderful truth.

*I am a child of God,*
*And he has sent me here,*
*Has given me an earthly home*
*With parents kind and dear.*
*Lead me, guide me, walk beside me,*
*Help me find the way.*
*Teach me all that I must do*
*To live with him someday.*
   [*"I Am a Child of God,"*
   Hymns, *no. 301*]

What a wonderful song that is. And what a great truth it teaches. You have an earthly father. He is your mother's dear companion. I hope you love him and that you are obedient to him. But you have another father. That is your Father in Heaven. He is the Father of your spirit, just as your earthly father is the father of your body. And it is just as important to love and to obey your Father in Heaven as it is to love and obey your earthly father.

We speak with our earthly father. He is our dear friend, our protector, the one who usually supplies our food and clothing and home. But we also speak to our Father in Heaven. We do this with prayer. I hope that every night and every morning you get on your knees and speak with your Father in Heaven. I hope that in the morning you will express thanks for the night's rest, for warmth and comfort and the love you feel in your home. I hope that you will ask Him to watch over you and bless and guide you throughout the day. I hope that you will pray for your father and mother and brothers and sisters and that you will remember all who are sick and in need. I hope you will remember the missionaries of the Church as you pray.

In the evening before you go to sleep, I hope you will again get on your knees and thank Him for the blessings of the day. Thank Him again for your parents and for your teachers. Ask Him to bless you with good sleep and to bless all others, particularly those who are in need and who do not have enough food or a good place to sleep.

It is not asking too much, is it, to take a few minutes of each day to speak with your Father in Heaven when you know that you are a child of God?

If you really know that you are a child of God, you will also know that He expects much of you, His child. He will expect you to follow His teachings and the teachings of His dear Son, Jesus. He will expect you to be generous and kind to others. He will be offended if you swear or use foul language. He will be offended if you are dishonest in any way, if you should cheat or steal in the slightest. He will be happy if you remember the less fortunate in your prayers to Him. He will watch over you and guide you and protect you. He will bless you in your schoolwork and in your Primary. He will bless you in your home, and you will be a better boy or girl, obedient to your parents, quarreling less with your brothers and sisters, helping about the home.

And thus you will grow to be a strong young man or woman in this Church. You will also be a better member of the community.

Every man or woman who ever walked the earth, even the Lord Jesus, was once a boy or girl like you. They grew according to the pattern they followed. If that pattern was good, then they became good men and women.

Never forget, my dear young friends, that you really are a child of God who has inherited something of His divine nature—one whom He loves and desires to help and bless. I pray that our Heavenly Father will bless you. May He smile with favor upon you. May you walk in His paths and follow His teachings. May you never speak the evil language that boys and girls are inclined to speak at school. May you ever be prayerful unto Him, praying always in the name of His Beloved Son, the Lord Jesus Christ. May each of us resolve to always follow Him in faith. May life be kind to you, for you are indeed a child of God, worthy and deserving of His love and blessing.

Never forget that you are a member of The Church of Jesus Christ of Latter-day Saints. I pray that the Lord will bless you, and I give you my love in the sacred name of Jesus Christ, amen.

# SATELLITE BROADCAST, WORLDWIDE LEADERSHIP TRAINING MEETING

## JUNE 21, 2003

WHILE THE BRETHREN HAVE BEEN speaking, I have been thinking of you, my dear associates in this great work. In my mind's eye I have seen you across the world—in all the nations of Europe and to the east across Russia and to her neighbors; in Mexico, Central America, and in all the lands of South America; in Asia, in Japan, Korea, Taiwan, Hong Kong, the Philippines, Thailand, Malaysia, India, and on down to Singapore and Indonesia; in Australia and New Zealand and the isles of the Pacific; in Africa with all of its many nations; across Canada and the United States.

I think of the miracle of it all. I think first of the miracle of the growth of the Church. The little stone which was cut out of the mountain without hands is rolling forth to fill the earth (see Daniel 2:34–35). I think also of the miracle of speaking to you in these circumstances. We are men of different nations and different languages, but we are all servants of the living God, leaders in His Church and kingdom. It is a glorious miracle that we are thus able to join together. It is important that we do so. The Lord has provided the way.

We have some 350 or 400 new stake presidents every year. We have some 4,500 new bishops each year. Other officers are constantly rotating. New leaders must be trained, and some of the mature leaders may be inclined to say, "I have heard it all before."

Well, repetition is a law of learning. No matter how long we have served, we need constant refreshing and exposure to new ideas and different faces, all designed to bring about a strengthening of the work.

As I have been listening with you, a question has arisen in my mind as I believe it has in each of yours. That question is, "How can I find the time to do it all?" Let me say that there is never enough time to do it all. There is so much more than any of us can singlehandedly give attention to.

I think I know something of this. I have been where many of you are today. There is only one way you can get it done. That is to follow the direction which the Lord gave Joseph Smith. To him He said, "Organize yourselves; prepare every needful thing" (D&C 88:119).

Each of us has a fourfold responsibility. First, we have a responsibility to our families. Second, we have a responsibility to our employers. Third, we have a responsibility to the Lord's work. Fourth, we have a responsibility to ourselves.

First, it is imperative that you not neglect your families. Nothing you have is more precious. Your wives and your children are deserving of the attention of their husbands and fathers. When all is said and done, it is this family relationship which we will take with us into the life beyond. To paraphrase the words of scripture, "What shall it profit a man though he serve the Church faithfully and lose his own family?" (see Mark 8:36).

Together with them, determine how much time you will spend with them and when. And then stick to it. Try not to let anything interfere. Consider it sacred. Consider it binding. Consider it an earned time of enjoyment. Keep Monday night sacred for family home evening. Have an evening alone with your wife. Arrange some vacation time with the entire family.

Two, to your business or your employer you have an obligation. Be honest with your employer. Do not do Church work on his time. Be loyal to him. He compensates you and expects results from you. You need employment to care for your family. Without it you cannot be an effective Church worker.

Three, to the Lord and His work. Budget your time to take care of your Church responsibilities. Recognize first that every officer has many helpers, as we have been reminded today. The stake president has two able counselors. The presidency has a high council of dedicated and able men. They have clerks as they need them. Every bishop has counselors. They are there to lift the burdens of his office from his shoulders. He has a ward council, together with others to whom he may and must delegate responsibility. He has the members of his ward, and the more he can delegate to them, the lighter will be his burden and the stronger will grow their faith.

Every priesthood quorum president has counselors, as well as the membership of the quorum. It is so with the Relief Society. No bishop can expect to fill the shoes of his Relief Society president in ministering to the needs of the members of his ward.

Four, every Church leader has an obligation to himself. He must get needed rest and exercise. He needs a little recreation. He must have time to study. Every Church officer needs to read the scriptures. He needs time to ponder and meditate and think by himself. Wherever possible he needs to go with his wife to the temple as opportunity permits.

These four obligations rest upon each of us. With thoughtful consideration and careful planning, we can so budget our time as to accommodate them. We cannot, brethren, we must not neglect any one of them. The Lord does not expect us to be supermen. But if we will place ourselves in His hands, if we will plead with Him in prayer, He will inspire us and help us. He will magnify us and make us equal to the responsibility.

He has said, "Be thou humble; and the Lord thy God shall lead thee by the hand, and give thee answer to thy prayers" (D&C 112:10). He has further said, "God shall give unto you knowledge by his Holy Spirit, yea, by the unspeakable gift of the Holy Ghost" (D&C 121:26).

The challenge that faces every good leader is the challenge of learning to delegate. Every stake president, every bishop, every quorum president must pass responsibility to others so that he will have the time to do that which he alone must do. Brethren, if you are constantly complaining that you have too much to do, then you do have too much to do. You need to get rid of some of it because a disgruntled leader becomes a poor leader.

I asked a friend who had been made a bishop how he was getting along. He said, "I am having the time of my life. I watch others work, and they tell me how happy they are. I have the best job in the Church."

Now, of course, this man had an immense amount of work to do. There were many responsibilities which he could not give to others. But the frustration was gone. The worry was gone. He had the capacity to make assignments and to make those to whom assignments were given feel that everything depended on the way they performed. As a matter of fact, it did.

Brethren, I want to plead with you that you be happy in your work. Wear a smile on your face, and have a song in your heart as you serve the Lord.

I am an old man now. I simply do not have the energy to do what I once did. But I will not permit myself to be unhappy in doing what I can.

The demands are great. I feel a constant, unrelenting concern for what is being accomplished in the Church. I want to do better; I want to improve things. But I know that I cannot do it alone. I have two wonderful counselors, able and dedicated men. I have the Council of the Twelve. There is no better body of men on the face of the earth. I have the Seventy and the Bishopric. And I have all of you working together as one great family to assist our Father in bringing to pass His incomparable work concerning the immortality and eternal life of His children. I have the great blessing of prayer. And so does each of you. I have the opportunity to get on my knees and ask the Lord to show me the way and give me the strength and the will and the wisdom to accomplish that which He would have done.

There is no other work in all the world so fraught with happiness as is this work. That happiness is peculiar. It comes of serving others. It is real. It is unique. It is wonderful.

In conclusion, let me tell you of an experience recounted by L. Robert Webb when he served as a bishop. Bishop Webb said:

> I learned from my counselors at one point that an elderly sister had declined a calling in the ward. Sensing that something was [wrong], I made an appointment to go to her home to speak with her. When I got there, she and her husband were both present.
>
> After a little polite conversation I said that I understood that she had not felt comfortable in accepting a ward calling and asked what I could do to help. Both of them stared at the floor a long, long time before she answered. At last she spoke to explain that 50 years earlier, before they had been married, they had been intimate with one another and had been too ashamed to clear this up with the bishop before being married in the temple. For all of these years they had lived under the guilty burden of this transgression while paying generous tithes and offerings, . . . rearing a family in the faith, and sending children on missions.
>
> Though they were faithful, they were not whole. They were kept from the peace and contentment that should have been theirs in golden years by clouds of self-doubt and the tarnished memory of unresolved transgression. Outwardly they seemed secure and serene. Inwardly they were carrying a kind of damage and hurt that intruded on their spiritual confidence.

Together they had suffered this awful alienation from the Lord for a [very] long time.

I do not know *why* their ordeal lasted a lifetime. I only know *when* it ended as the Lord lifted them from their lonely lamentations. As I tearfully listened to their story, I prayed earnestly to know what I might do to relieve them. When they finished speaking I felt impressed to say simply: "It is over. You have suffered long enough. I am sure the Lord has forgiven you. Repentance consists of forsaking [the] sin and confessing. You forsook that guilty act long, long ago. Tonight you also confessed. Now you are free. I feel certain that the Lord has forgotten your transgression and is eager to dispel your guilt with redeeming grace."

After kneeling in prayer together we three stood encircled in one another's arms as they sobbed out the last of their pent-up suffering and anguish.

"Oh, Bishop, is it really over?" they asked.

I assured them that it was.

The loving kindness and the grace of the Savior poured into their lives in sweet forgiving. He reached past the things that separated them from him and embraced them in sweet communion. ["Vast and Intimate: The Atonement in the Heavens and in the Heart," *Brigham Young University 1998–99 Speeches* (1999), 78–79]

Yours, my dear brethren across the world, is the privilege of standing in the shadow of the Redeemer of the world as we carry forward this work. Ours is the opportunity to speak of the beauty of the atoning blood of the Lord Jesus Christ in behalf of His sons and daughters. Could there be a greater privilege than this?

Rejoice in the privilege which is yours. Your opportunity will not last forever. Too soon there will be only the memory of the great experience you are now having.

None of us will accomplish all we might wish to. But let us do the best we can. I am satisfied that the Redeemer will then say, "Well done, thou good and faithful servant" (Matthew 25:21).

God bless you, my beloved brethren. I leave with you my love for you. Each of you has a warm place in my heart. I leave my blessing upon you as my fellow servants in this great cause and kingdom. I do it all in the sacred name of the Lord Jesus Christ, amen.

# Accra, Ghana, Member Meeting[*]

## January 10, 2004

$M$Y BELOVED BROTHERS AND SISTERS, what a great blessing and what a great opportunity it is to meet with you on this solemn and wonderful occasion. We are here to dedicate the new temple of the Lord, this magnificent structure which we have built as a house unto the Most High God where His purposes might be accomplished.

This magnificent temple, which stands in your midst, is a witness and testimony to all the world that we believe in the immortality of the human soul. We know that just as we live here, we shall also live when we pass through the veil and that we shall go on as a part of the eternal purposes of our Lord in living and doing great and good things. We know that through the Atonement of Jesus Christ all men shall have the opportunity of the resurrection. If we obey the laws of God, we may go on to greater glory than anything we have ever dreamed of.

I am glad to be here. I feel so humble to be here for the dedication of this temple. We are grateful for this meeting where we have all assembled together. We are grateful for the social which we will have later in the day. We are grateful for the presence of every one of you. We are grateful to have these tribal leaders here among us. They honor us with their presence here today. Thank you for coming.

[*]*delivered extemporaneously*

It has been my pleasure to meet with you, as on previous occasions. I met with President Rawlings some six years ago; I had a very interesting meeting with him. And President Kufuor has been to Salt Lake City, where we met him, and we will also have a meeting with him tomorrow afternoon.

This is a great nation, this nation of Ghana. It is a nation where there has been peace and constitutional government for a long time. This nation stands as an example to all of the nations of Africa for its stability and good government. Pray that it may continue. Pray that peace may continue in the land and righteousness in the hearts of the people.

Now, I see many young men and women in this congregation today. You are members of The Church of Jesus Christ of Latter-day Saints. You are sons and daughters of God. We sing the song "I Am a Child of God." Do we realize what that means? That we have divinity within us and that it is our obligation to stand a little taller, be a little more godly, living up to the great inheritance which we have.

To you young men and you young women, I want to throw out a challenge today to make something of your lives. Do not drift along the way so many people are trying to do these days. Do not get involved in evil things, which only lead to sorrow, destruction, illness, and even death.

Rise to a higher level. Get all of the education that you possibly can. The Lord has instructed His people that we are to seek after learning. To you young men and you young women I want to throw out that challenge to gain all the education that you possibly can, because that will unlock the door of opportunity for each of you.

Now, to everyone who is here, I just want to say that if you will do four things, my brothers and sisters, your place in the Church will be secure. You will grow in faith. You will grow in prosperity. You will grow in your relationship with your Heavenly Father.

1. Attend your meetings. You must meet together if you are to grow in faith. It is your obligation to build and strengthen one another. And we grow in strength in the gospel as we meet together and share our testimonies and study the word of the Lord together. It is so very important.

Sister Hinckley likes to tell the story of one time when we arrived in Greece. We had no native Greek members there at the time, but there were a few American service people there. A woman said, "Are we going to have a meeting?"

Sister Hinckley said, "We are very tired. We are just traveling through."

And the woman said, "Can't we possibly have a meeting? I am so anxious for a meeting."

And so we held a meeting, a little group of us. We sang together. We prayed together. We bore our testimonies one to another.

She rejoiced and said, "What a glorious and wonderful thing it is to meet together."

So I want to urge every one of you to attend your meetings. It is so very, very important to attend your meetings.

Today while I was in the temple president's apartment, I read a story in the *Ensign* about a woman who had been excommunicated from the Church because of the manner of her life. Finally, with the urging of her mother, she began to come back. Then she finally reached a point where she met with the Saints, and she said, "As I sat in that meeting, I wept as I again heard the word of the Lord spoken." (See Susan L. MacDonald, "Could I Come Back?" *Ensign*, Dec. 2003, 13–15.)

Do not neglect to attend your meetings. You may have to walk a long way. You may have difficulty getting there. But it will be important that you be there. That is why we build meetinghouses. We are building meetinghouses all over the world, 400 of them every year, in order that our Saints can meet together. So, number one, attend your meetings.

2. Read the scriptures. Read the word of the Lord. The Savior said, "Search the scriptures; for in them ye think ye have eternal life: and they are they which testify of me" (John 5:39). If you want a testimony of the Lord Jesus Christ, read about His life in the New Testament and in the Book of Mormon, and your faith and your witness and your testimony and your love for Him will grow.

3. Pay your tithing. I believe in it with all my heart. I believe that the Lord does not bless people unless they are willing to show their obedience to His commandments.

The Church has built these beautiful facilities here. These facilities have come out of the tithes of people all over the world. You are a part of that great family, nearly 12 million strong now. You do not pay your tithing to make the Church rich. The Church can get along without your tithing, but I believe with all my heart that you cannot get along without paying your tithing to the Lord.

Now, I do not make any promise concerning the payment of tithing. I do not need to, because the Lord has. He has said, "I will . . . open you the windows of heaven, and pour you out a blessing, that there shall not be room enough to receive it" (Malachi 3:10). Now, that does not mean that you are going to get a fancy automobile; it does not mean that you are going to get a lot of those things. But it does mean that He will keep His word. It is He who has made the promise, and it is my testimony that He has the capacity to fulfill that promise and that He will do so.

4. Say your prayers. Get on your knees every morning and every night, and pray to the Lord. Pray with your families. It makes such a difference to pray to the Lord, expressing your thanks and invoking His blessings upon you. I have a testimony of prayer. I know that prayers are heard and answered.

Now, I make you this promise: If you will do just these four things—which are so easy to do, so simple to do, but which are expressions of faith—you will grow in strength and power and capacity as members of The Church of Jesus Christ of Latter-day Saints. I believe with all my heart that you will prosper.

Says King Benjamin in the Book of Mormon, "And behold, all that he requires of you is to keep his commandments; and he has promised you that if ye would keep his commandments ye should prosper in the land; and he never doth vary from that which he hath said; therefore, if ye do keep his commandments he doth bless you and prosper you" (Mosiah 2:22).

Attend your meetings, read your scriptures, pay your tithing, say your prayers, and you will be solid and faithful and strong in the Church.

Now, I have been noticing these beautiful cut flowers. Aren't they beautiful? Did you know they aren't good for long? They have no root. They cannot grow. They cannot increase. They have no soil in which to sink their roots. They are just the blossoms, and tomorrow they will wither and die, and you will throw them away. You want a flower that may not be as fancy, but if it has root in the beautiful earth of the gospel, then it will grow and multiply and blossom and reproduce its own kind, bearing seed. Just keep that in mind, will you, every one of you. See that in your lives there is root reaching into the good earth of the restored gospel of Jesus Christ.

My brothers and sisters, I give you my testimony. I know that God lives. I know that I am a child of God. I know that you are children of God. He is our Eternal Father. He hears our prayers. He may be approached in prayer. We may speak with Him as one man speaks with another. I know that Jesus is the Christ, the Redeemer of the world, the living Son of the living God, resurrected and eternal, my Savior and my King. I know that this volume [the Book of Mormon] is a second testimony, along with the Bible, of the truth of what I have just said, these two going hand in hand. The Bible is the testament of the Old World; the Book of

Mormon is the testament of the New World. They bear witness of the same thing.

I know that this is the Church and kingdom of God, and I know that if we will live the gospel, we will be happy and a blessed people.

I love you. I want you to know that. You are my brothers and my sisters. Thank you for all the good you do. May heaven smile upon you is my humble prayer in the sacred name of the Lord Jesus Christ, amen.

# ST. THOMAS, VIRGIN ISLANDS, MEMBER MEETING*

## JANUARY 12, 2004

$G$OOD EVENING, MY DEAR brothers and sisters. We have had a wonderful meeting so far, with this great choir, these children who have sung for us, the speakers we have had, and the prayer by President Hodge. Thank you for your prayer, President. I again say thank you for being here.

We have had a very, very, very interesting experience. I will tell you about it. We went to St. Kitts first. There we had a meeting with a little group of Saints, way out on another of these islands in this vast sea. It was just wonderful to be with those good, kind, gracious people.

Then we went to Accra, Ghana, to dedicate the temple there. We have built a new temple in Accra. It is a beautiful house of the Lord. Twenty-six years ago the first missionaries came to Ghana. There did not seem to be much prospect for growth. There were a few people there who were interested, but today we have 25,000 people in Ghana. So, after long efforts and much struggle to get a building permit, we have constructed a beautiful temple and a beautiful stake center and other facilities there, so that the Saints in that part of West Africa can have everything that every member of the Church can have anywhere in the world. The people in Salt

*delivered extemporaneously

Lake City cannot have more of the gospel than the Saints in Accra, Ghana, can have.

We are not at that point here, but I believe with all my heart that if we all join together, we could begin to reap a harvest here that would result in a large congregation and a beautiful part of the Church here in this part of the world.

On our way here today we stopped at Sal, off the west coast of Africa, where we had a little group of 50 or 60 people at the airport and had a meeting at noon today with them. What a great and precious joy it was to meet with those Saints.

The work rolls on all across the earth. When the Church was organized, the Lord gave a revelation. This was not the first revelation given, but it is the first one in the Doctrine and Covenants, and it talks about you—you know it? It talks about you.

"Hearken, O ye people of my church, saith the voice of him who dwells on high, and whose eyes are upon all men; yea, verily I say: Hearken ye people from afar"—that is where you are; you are afar—"and ye that are upon the islands of the sea, listen together" (D&C 1:1).

This great revelation of the gospel was to those upon the islands of the sea. Do you ever think of that, and what a wonderful thing that was? I had the privilege of opening the work in the Philippine Islands, and I used to read this to them. They are upon the isles of the sea. We have wonderful Latter-day Saints upon the isles of the sea all across the world: Samoa, Tahiti, Tonga, all of those places, as well as these places in the Caribbean and the Atlantic.

May the Lord bless you in your great desire to serve Him and do what is right. I want to read you a statement from Brigham Young, because I believe it with all my heart. Now, if you have any doubt about any principle of the gospel, I do not care what it is, any principle of the gospel, you think of this statement. Said he:

"Every principle God has revealed carries its own convictions of its truth to the human mind." Did you get that? "Every principle

God has revealed carries its own convictions of its truth to the human mind, and there is no calling of God to man on earth but what brings with it the evidences of its authenticity" (*Discourses of Brigham Young*, sel. John A. Widtsoe [1954], 65).

If you have a question about a doctrine or a principle of the gospel, what do you do? You put it to the test. You try it out. You see about it. If you worry about the Word of Wisdom, if you like your tea, if you like your coffee, and they tell you you should not drink tea or coffee, what do you do? You do not drink it. You put it aside. You give the test. You will soon discover that you can get along without it and that you are better off without it.

If you have any trouble believing that God lives, then pray, walk in His ways, read about His commandments, and there will come into your heart a conviction of the truth that He does live. He has said that "if any man will do his will, he shall know of the doctrine, whether it be of God, or whether I speak of myself" (John 7:17). Jesus said that concerning His Father.

If you want to have a testimony of the God of heaven, read the scriptures. The Lord said, "Search the scriptures; for in them ye think ye have eternal life: and they are they which testify of me" (John 5:39). Now, if you have any questions about that, you read the scriptures, you pray, and you come to know without any question that the God of heaven lives.

If you have any doubt about the reality of the Lord Jesus Christ, you study the gospel. You read the New Testament. You read the Book of Mormon, which testifies of the Savior. It is the testament of the New World, borne hand in hand with the testament of the Old World. And there will come into your heart, as sure as daylight comes in the morning, a knowledge that Jesus Christ is the Son of God.

Do you have any doubt about the law of tithing? Are you reluctant to pay your tithing? Are you unwilling to trust the Lord? Are you unwilling to accept Him at His word? He has said, "Bring ye all the tithes into the storehouse, that there may be meat in mine house, and prove me now herewith, saith the Lord of hosts" (Malachi 3:10). He will open the windows of heaven and shower down a blessing upon you which there will not be room enough to receive. That is the test. You apply the law, you practice the law, and then a knowledge of the truth of the law comes into your heart.

It is the same with everything in the Church. Family home evening—do you worry about whether you should have it? I hope not. If you do, try it. There will come into your hearts out of that experience a conviction of the truth of the principle.

I can remember when I was a small boy, five years old, President Joseph F. Smith announced to all the Church that they should gather their families together in family home evening. My father said, "The President of the Church has asked that we do it, and we are going to do it."

So we all gathered in family home evening. It was funny. He said, "We'll sing a song." Well, we were not singers. We were not like this chorus. We just tried to sing and laughed at one another. So we did with a lot of other things. But out of that experience there gradually came something that was wonderful—a practice that helped us, that drew us together as a family, that strengthened us, and there grew in our hearts a conviction of the value of family home evening. I have practiced that in my home. My daughter has practiced that in her home. She now has a son and daughters who practice it in their homes. And that is the way it goes.

If you want to build faith in your children, apply the principles of the gospel and let them have come into their hearts a knowledge and a conviction of the truth of this great latter-day work.

If you wonder whether the Book of Mormon is true, read it. The test is in the book itself. Read it, pray about it, and there will come into your hearts a testimony of the truth of this work, a fulfillment of the word of Moroni (see Moroni 10:3–5).

Let me tell you a story about the Book of Mormon. I heard a

man who was a banker in California tell this story. He said his secretary smoked, constantly smoked. She was addicted to smoking. She could not set it aside. She said to him one day, "How can I stop smoking?"

He reached down in his desk and took out a copy of the Book of Mormon and handed it to her. He said, "Now, you read this."

She said, "All right, I'll read it."

She came back a couple of days later and said, "I've read 200 pages, and I didn't see the word *smoking* anywhere. I didn't see the word *tobacco* anywhere. I saw nothing that referred to it."

He said, "Keep reading."

So she came back another couple of days later and said, "I've read 200 more pages—no mention of smoking, no mention of nicotine, no mention of anything associated with tobacco."

He said, "Keep reading."

She came back three or four days later. She said, "I've read the entire book. I didn't see tobacco anywhere; I didn't see smoking anywhere. But," she said, "there has come into my heart as a result of reading that book some influence, some power, that has taken from me the desire to smoke, and it is wonderful."

I sat down for dinner at the table of that man in California with that woman present, who at that time had become the president of the Relief Society as a result of that experience.

Now, my brothers and sisters, that is the way this gospel works. You accept the principle, and then you make the test. There will come into your hearts a knowledge of the truth. I do not hesitate to promise you that for one minute.

You are way off on these islands, apart from the main body of the Church. You must be strong. You must have a little more strength than we have where the Church is strong. You must stand up for your faith, work at it, live it, and enjoy it. It is so very important. Your eternal blessings hinge on this. And the Lord will bless you as you do so. I know that to be so. I have been with little groups like this all over this broad earth, and I know it works. I have been with Latter-day Saints everywhere, on every continent, and on the isles of the sea, including St. Thomas, and I want to tell you that it works.

I give you my testimony that God, our Eternal Father, lives. Isn't it a marvelous thing. This chorus sang "I Am a Child of God." Do you ever stop to think of the meaning of that—that you are a child of God; that there is something of divinity within you, something of the divine nature; that you are a son or daughter of God, who is the great Governor of the universe but who will listen to your prayers and hear you when you speak to Him. What a wonderful thing that is to think of and to reflect on. It is tremendous.

I pray that God will bless you, every one of you, in your homes. Live together in love and appreciation and respect.

You men, respect your wives. Treat them with kindness and courtesy, and try to be helpful to them. You do not have to be mean or anything of the kind.

You wives, support your husbands. They need it. They need your help and your support, and they are deserving of it as they plod their difficult way. Support them and help them and encourage them every way you can.

And your children—do not look upon them as noisy little brats. That is what they may be, but they are children of God. You are their earthly parents. Be as their heavenly parents and look upon them as God's children as well as your children. You do not have to beat your children to get them to be obedient. I believe that with all my heart. I never remember my father laying a hand on any of his children. I cannot even imagine it. If we did something wrong—and we certainly did enough things wrong—he would sit down with us and quietly reason with us until we felt ashamed of what we had done and made a resolution never to do it again. You do not have to beat your children. Treat them with kindness, and bring them up in love. You know, when you get old they will be the treasures of your lives. They will be the things that really count, when all is said and done.

I cannot take much more time; you have been here long enough. I want to tell you that we love you. We do. We pray for you. We know that you pray for us, and we thank you for your prayers. They sustain us and keep us going. Thank you so very, very much.

I leave my love and my blessing with you and my testimony of this gospel and pray that heaven may smile upon you, in the sacred name of the Lord Jesus Christ, amen.

# Satellite Broadcast, 175th Anniversary of the Restoration of the Priesthood

MAY 16, 2004

My DEAR, DEAR BRETHREN, I greet you most warmly as we commemorate together the 175th anniversary of the restoration of the priesthood, both the Aaronic and the Melchizedek.

What a marvelous and wonderful thing it was that after centuries of an absence of divine authority on the earth, the glorious day of restoration came. And think of the manner in which it came: it came directly from the heavens under the hands of those who held it when the Savior walked the earth. At that time, He was immersed in the waters of Jordan by John who was called the Baptist and who held the Levitical Priesthood. It was this same John, who later was beheaded to satisfy the hateful whims of a wicked woman, who appeared to Joseph Smith and Oliver Cowdery on the 15th of May 1829. His visit is evidence of life after death and the reality of the resurrection.

While Joseph was translating the Book of Mormon and Oliver was acting as scribe, they came across a passage concerning baptism. They had not been baptized. Something was missing. As recorded in the New Testament, Jesus said to Nicodemus, "Except a man be born of water and of the Spirit, he cannot enter into the kingdom of God" (John 3:5). It is necessary to receive baptism by immersion

406

in water by one holding the proper authority. What were they to do?

They left the work of translation and found a quiet and private place. Here they called on the Lord in fervent prayer, and, as Oliver described it, "On a sudden, as from the midst of eternity, the voice of the Redeemer spake peace to us, while the vail was parted and the angel of God came down clothed with glory. . . . We received under his hand the holy priesthood" (*Latter-day Saints' Messenger and Advocate,* Oct. 1834, 15–16; see also Joseph Smith—History, footnote on pages 58–59).

The official documentation of this event is set forth as section 13 in the Doctrine and Covenants. I memorized these words when I was ordained a deacon more than 80 years ago. I remember them still. As John placed his hands upon the heads of Joseph and Oliver, he said, "Upon you my fellow servants, in the name of Messiah I confer the Priesthood of Aaron, which holds the keys of the ministering of angels, and of the gospel of repentance, and of baptism by immersion for the remission of sins" (D&C 13:1).

The unique brotherhood of this priesthood is established by the opening words spoken by John: "Upon you my fellow servants." He spoke as a servant of the Lord. Likewise, each of us is a servant of the same Lord, bound together as brethren, as fellow servants— more than 300,000 Aaronic Priesthood holders working unitedly to advance the kingdom of God in the earth.

This priesthood, said John, "holds the keys of the ministering of angels." Think of that which you have, my dear brethren.

When Wilford Woodruff went on his first mission in 1834, he was ordained to the office of a priest. When he became an elderly man, he looked back to those days, and of them he said: "I went out as a Priest, and my companion as an Elder, and we traveled thousands of miles, and had many things manifested to us. I desire to impress upon you the fact that it does not make any difference whether a man is a Priest or an Apostle, if he magnifies his calling.

A Priest holds the keys of the ministering of angels. Never in my life, as an Apostle, as a Seventy, or as an Elder, have I ever had more of the protection of the Lord than while holding the office of a Priest" ("Discourse by Wilford Woodruff," *Millennial Star,* Oct. 5, 1891, 629).

If we are to enjoy the protection of ministering angels, we must live worthy of their companionship. You who have been ordained to the Aaronic Priesthood have something magnificent to live up to.

On this 175th anniversary, it may be appropriate to speak plainly concerning matters which could make you unworthy of this wonderful blessing. You live in a world where there is terrible evil. You are constantly confronted by those who use filthy language and indulge in filthy ways. Let the world do what it will. But you must never forget that you have something which the world does not have.

To begin with, you must not, under any circumstances, violate the Word of Wisdom, which came of revelation. For you, there must never be any drinking of alcoholic beverages, and that includes beer. Its consumption will only bring you trouble. Shun it. Stay away from it.

You must not partake of illicit drugs. There must be no experimentation with these vicious things, for they will rob you of self-mastery and self-discipline. If tempted, you must run from them. Do not touch them. Your peers may attempt to persuade you to try them. Even at the risk of losing friends, you must decline.

You must not watch pornography. It too can destroy you. It is totally wrong for any of you to watch such degrading material. Pornography is an evil thing. It leads to evil thoughts and evil behavior. It may be tempting. It was designed to be tempting. It was designed as a trap for you. It becomes addictive. You must not, you cannot run the risk of being pulled in by its seductive appeal.

I mention another practice which is becoming popular. I speak of tattooing one's body. If you have even considered such an idea, please pause and think. Before you go one step further, ask the Lord about it. He has said concerning your body:

"Know ye not that ye are the temple of God, and that the Spirit of God dwelleth in you?

"If any man defile the temple of God, him shall God destroy; for the temple of God is holy, which temple ye are" (1 Corinthians 3:16–17).

How can any boy who blesses the sacrament or passes the sacrament even think of having tattoos put upon his body?

Nor how could you, as one holding the priesthood and as one who is eligible to receive the ministering of angels, indulge in immorality of any kind? Never forget that every girl is a daughter of God. There is something divine within her. She is deserving of respect.

Have fun together, yes. Sing and dance, hike and skate, and enjoy the companionship of wonderful young women who are members of the Church and keep its standards. But draw the line where familiarity comes in. Some girls of weak will and weak ways will lower the bar of behavior. Any such act should make you retreat and avoid what could become a disaster.

I know that my language is plain. I speak bluntly. But I say these things because I love you and because I want you to be eligible at all times for the guiding, protecting ministering of angels. These angels may be unseen. But that does not diminish their presence or their power. If you are ever tempted to go beyond the limits of propriety, quickly call to mind that you are entitled to the ministering of angels.

This wonderful priesthood also holds the keys of the gospel of repentance. In the first place, this may apply to your own selves. If any of you have done anything which would decrease your stature as a holder of the priesthood, then repent and ask the Lord for forgiveness. Ask forgiveness of any whom you have offended. The

Lord has promised that He will forgive and that He will no longer remember the sin. Great is His mercy and infinite His willingness and power to forgive. In fact, He gave His very life as an atonement for the sins of all mankind. But it is so much better that you live in such a way as to have nothing of substance of which to repent.

This precious gift which you have been given, the Aaronic Priesthood, also holds the keys of baptism for the remission of sins. It is your obligation, and also your great opportunity, to serve as a missionary for this Church, if you live worthy of such service. You may become a witness of the truth to the people of the world, leading them to the waters of baptism. This is the gateway to membership in the Church. It is an expression of humility and repentance before the Lord. It carries with it a covenant between God and man. It is an act under which one's sins are remitted and there is birth into a new and better life.

This is all part of this remarkable priesthood which you hold. There is no adequate substitute for it under all the heavens. It is unique and marvelous. And it is yours. Young men, on this significant anniversary gathering, I plead with you, I ask you to live worthy of the tremendous thing which you have. You do not need to be prudes. You do not need to be self-righteous. You cannot be arrogant in any way. But you can be humble, living decently and cleanly, as you serve the Lord as one holding the priesthood after the order of Aaron.

If you so live, then you will become eligible to receive the higher priesthood, of which I now speak briefly.

Could anything be greater or more desirable than to hold the Priesthood after the Order of the Son of God? These words are so sacred that we do not ordinarily use them. Rather, we call this the Melchizedek Priesthood, after the high priest who was king of Salem—that is, Jerusalem.

The greatest of all high priests was Jesus Himself. Paul bears witness of this as he reminds us that "we have a great high priest, that is passed into the heavens, Jesus the Son of God" (Hebrews 4:14). As the Firstborn of the Father, He possessed all of the keys and authority of the eternal priesthood, which is "without beginning of days or end of years" (Alma 13:7).

Jesus bestowed this divine authority upon His chosen Apostles, saying, "I will give unto thee the keys of the kingdom of heaven: and whatsoever thou shalt bind on earth shall be bound in heaven: and whatsoever thou shalt loose on earth shall be loosed in heaven" (Matthew 16:19).

My brethren, I invite you to contemplate for a moment the wonder of this. No king, no president, no head of state, no man of business or secular activity of any kind has such authority by reason of his office. And yet it was given to these humble men who walked with Jesus as His Apostles.

Three of these Apostles—Peter, James, and John—appeared to Joseph and Oliver somewhere "in the wilderness" along the Susquehanna River (see D&C 128:20). They placed their hands upon their heads and conferred upon them this holy authority. We do not have the date, but evidence points to the fact that likely it was late May or sometime in June of the same year, 1829.

I can trace my priesthood in a direct line to this event. It goes as follows: I was ordained by David O. McKay; who was ordained by Joseph F. Smith; who was ordained by Brigham Young; who was ordained by the Three Witnesses; who were ordained by Joseph Smith Jr. and Oliver Cowdery; who were ordained by Peter, James, and John; who were ordained by the Lord Jesus Christ.

It has similarly come to you. Each of you brethren who hold this priesthood has also received it in a direct line from the bestowal made by Peter, James, and John. Its origin is not shrouded in the foggy mists of history.

Endless are its powers, endless its authority. It is by this authority that we are empowered to lay hands upon the heads of those who have been baptized and bestow upon them the priceless gift of the Holy Ghost. It is by this same authority that we are empowered to bless the sick, to anoint them with oil, and to seal that anointing and call down the powers of heaven in their behalf. It is by this same authority that we are empowered to lay our hands upon the heads of our wives and children and give them special blessings in times of need. It is by this same authority that we are empowered to govern in the affairs of the Church and kingdom of God.

But this authority can only be exercised in righteousness. The Lord has said "that the rights of the priesthood are inseparably connected with the powers of heaven, and that the powers of heaven cannot be controlled nor handled only upon the principles of righteousness.

"That they may be conferred upon us, it is true; but when we undertake to cover our sins, or to gratify our pride, our vain ambition, or to exercise control or dominion or compulsion upon the souls of the children of men, in any degree of unrighteousness, behold, the heavens withdraw themselves; the Spirit of the Lord is grieved; and when it is withdrawn, Amen to the priesthood or the authority of that man.

"No power or influence can or ought to be maintained by virtue of the priesthood, only by persuasion, by long-suffering, by gentleness and meekness, and by love unfeigned" (D&C 121:36–37, 41).

Now, my brethren, I wish to say to each of you, as I have already said to the holders of the Aaronic Priesthood, that the Lord expects that we will keep our lives in order, that we will live the gospel in every aspect, that we will shun evil and not partake of the mean and beggarly elements of life (see Galatians 4:9). I remind you, as I have reminded them, that we must not partake of the filth that seems to be washing over society as a great flood. I warn you particularly against pornography, with its titillating, inviting ways. It is so easy to experience. It is so difficult to get rid of once it has been tasted. Stay away from it, brethren, please. Rise above these sordid elements.

One further word: As husbands, as fathers, any kind of domestic abuse is entirely incompatible with the priesthood. Control your anger. Lower your voices. Speak with love and appreciation and respect.

May heaven's blessings rest upon you, the 1,300,000 living men who have been ordained to the Melchizedek Priesthood. May you be upheld and sustained by the power of the Holy Spirit. May you walk with your face in the sunlight and your resolution immovable. To you is extended this great and marvelous promise:

> I, the Lord, am merciful and gracious unto those who fear me, and delight to honor those who serve me in righteousness and in truth unto the end.
>
> Great shall be their reward and eternal shall be their glory.
>
> And to them will I reveal all mysteries, yea, all the hidden mysteries of my kingdom from days of old, and for ages to come, will I make known unto them the good pleasure of my will concerning all things pertaining to my kingdom.
>
> Yea, even the wonders of eternity shall they know, and things to come will I show them, even the things of many generations.
>
> And their wisdom shall be great, and their understanding reach to heaven; and before them the wisdom of the wise shall perish, and the understanding of the prudent shall come to naught. [D&C 76:5–9]

May this great, divine promise be fulfilled in your lives is my humble prayer, as I bear witness of the truth of these things, in the sacred name of the Lord Jesus Christ, amen.

# MADRID, SPAIN, MEMBER MEETING*

### MAY 29, 2004

THE COUNT HAS JUST COME IN. There are 7,935 participating in this conference this morning from Spain and Portugal. I think this is the largest gathering of Latter-day Saints ever held in these two countries. How grateful I feel to be with you, my beloved brethren and sisters.

How nice it is to be back in Madrid again—this great, marvelous, and wonderful city. I first came here in 1955. My wife and I came together. There were no members of the Church that we knew of anywhere in Spain or Portugal. Now to see this marvelous gathering of Latter-day Saints—people who carry in their hearts a love for the Lord, who like to live in righteousness, who like to live together as families, who love their children and love one another, who seek to be good neighbors and good citizens of the nation— how grateful I feel to you.

This is the first long trip I have made since my beloved wife passed away. She passed away on the 6th of April. She was just tired. She was 92 years of age, and I miss her. But my memories are sweet and wonderful. I have a perfect faith that while we are temporarily separated, we shall be reunited and again enjoy one another's association.

We had a marvelous funeral service in the Salt Lake Tabernacle

*delivered extemporaneously

with very many people present. Among those who came was the Catholic bishop, Bishop Niederauer of the Salt Lake Catholic diocese. We are good friends. We have a different theology. We don't agree on everything in doctrine, but we are not disagreeable. We love and appreciate and respect one another. That is the way it should be.

Yesterday we visited the Prado Museum. I was impressed with something I saw there. I saw the representation by the great artists of the world of the Godhead: the Father, the Son, and the Holy Ghost—three individuals. I thought of our wonderful declaration of faith: "We believe in God, the Eternal Father, and in His Son, Jesus Christ, and in the Holy Ghost" (Articles of Faith 1:1)—three distinct beings who are united in blessing all mankind.

God stands as the Father of us all. He is the great Governor of the universe, and yet He is my Father. I am a child of God. What a wonderful concept that is, that I am a child of God, that I have something of divinity within me that has come from God Himself, that He is my Eternal Father, and that we are His sons and daughters. And, therefore, we are brothers and sisters and ought to live together as brothers and sisters.

That is the doctrine which comes out of the Fatherhood of God and the brotherhood of man. "We believe in God, the Eternal Father, and in His Son, Jesus Christ, and in the Holy Ghost."

We live in a world of conflict and trouble, of hatred and meanness. I had pointed out to me this morning the place where the terrible bombing of the trains took place in Madrid. I said to myself, "There could be no such thing, there would be no such thing, if all men believed in God the Eternal Father and that we are all brothers and sisters."

My dear and beloved friends, how marvelous it is that we can belong to a Church whose foundation lies in this great and significant doctrine that God is our Father, that Jesus Christ is our Savior, and that the Holy Ghost is our companion. Think of it. Reflect on it. Pray about it. Live up to that great part of divinity that is within you.

I'd like to go to another article of faith: "We believe that men will be punished for their own sins, and not for Adam's transgression" (Articles of Faith 1:2).

Each of us is accountable to God. We have a responsibility to Him, and we will be judged according to our behavior. We cannot excuse ourselves by saying that we are here because of Adam's transgression. We are on our own. We must be responsible, and we must see that our behavior is such that we can look to God with a clear conscience and a sense of accountability.

"We believe the Bible to be the word of God . . . ; we also believe the Book of Mormon to be the word of God" (Articles of Faith 1:8).

What a marvelous thing it is that to the testimony of this great book, the Bible, the scripture of the Old World, we add the testimony of the New World, the Book of Mormon, and that they can go hand in hand, testifying that Jesus is the Christ, the Son of the living God.

I cannot understand why the world does not accept the Book of Mormon. The scripture says that in the mouths of two or more witnesses shall all things be established (see Matthew 18:16; 2 Corinthians 13:1). Here is one witness. Here is the other witness. The Bible is the stick of Judah. The Book of Mormon is the stick of Joseph. They have become one in the hands of God. (See Ezekiel 37:16–17.) They stand as a witness, in this time of the world, of the living reality of Jesus Christ, our Redeemer.

"We believe all that God has revealed, all that He does now reveal, and we believe that He will yet reveal many great and important things pertaining to the Kingdom of God" (Articles of Faith 1:9).

How wonderful it is that we believe in modern revelation. I cannot get over the feeling that if revelation was needed anciently, when life was simple, that revelation is also needed today, when life is complex. There never was a time in the history of the earth when men needed revelation more than they need it now.

I want to testify to you, my brothers and sisters, that the book of revelation is not closed. God directs this day and time and speaks as certainly today as He did in the days of Abraham and Isaac and Jacob.

"We claim the privilege of worshiping Almighty God according to the dictates of our own conscience, and allow all men the same privilege, let them worship how, where, or what they may" (Articles of Faith 1:11).

How very important that is—that while we believe in worshipping God according to our doctrine, we do not become arrogant or self-righteous or prideful but that we extend to others the privilege of worshipping according to their desires. Much of the trouble in the world comes from conflict between religions. I am happy to be able to say that I can sit down with my Catholic friends and talk with them, that I can sit down with my Protestant friends and talk with them. I would stand in their defense, as this Church has done and will continue to do, in defending them in this world. I am so grateful for what Brother Mendoza said concerning freedom of religion, freedom of worship, and its great importance as a factor in bringing peace in the world.

Finally, "We believe in being honest, true, chaste, benevolent, virtuous, and in doing good to all men; . . . We believe all things, we hope all things, we have endured many things, and hope to be able to endure all things. If there is anything virtuous, lovely, or of good report or praiseworthy, we seek after these things" (Articles of Faith 1:13).

I wish every Latter-day Saint would read that thirteenth article of faith every day and put it in practice. We believe in being honest, men and women of integrity, whose word is good. We believe in being true—true to the best that is within us, true to the faith,

417

true to the Church, loyal to one another, virtuous, moral, clean before the Lord, living in righteousness above the sins of the world, keeping ourselves clean and decent and good.

Be loyal to one another as husbands and wives. Be loyal to one another as parents and children. "If there is anything virtuous, lovely, or of good report or praiseworthy, we seek after these things."

Now, my brothers and sisters, we are about to leave you. We fly home in an hour or so. I don't know whether I will ever get back or not. I do not know. I am an old man. I don't know how much longer I am good for, but I shall never forget you. I have had an experience here that has been absolutely marvelous.

As I looked into the faces of the priesthood yesterday, I saw strong men. It has been so wonderful. And now, as I look into your faces, you beautiful men and women with your beautiful children, I feel so grateful.

I leave you my witness of the truth of this work. This is God's holy work, restored in this, the last dispensation, the dispensation of the fulness of times, for the blessing of His children. God be with you till we meet again somewhere, sometime, is my humble prayer, which I ask in the sacred name of Jesus Christ, amen.

# Manhattan, New York, Member Meeting[*]

## June 12, 2004

I AM SO HAPPY TO BE HERE with you. What a great opportunity this is, what a tremendous blessing. I pray that the Lord will guide me in that which I say.

When I approached this Radio City Music Hall tonight, I looked up at the marquee, and it said in great letters where all of New York could see it, "Youth Jubilee, Church of Jesus Christ of Latter-day Saints." I said to myself, "What a remarkable and wonderful thing that is, that there should be on the marquee of this great institution the name of the Church where all who pass this way—hundreds of thousands, even millions—might see it."

Now, we are here for a great purpose. We are here to dedicate the house of the Lord. I came here two years ago—a little more than two years ago. I am going to read from my journal, if I may. I never disclosed this to anybody before, but I think I would like to do it.

We were up in New Hampshire. This is March 23, 2002:

> Brother Zwick and I left the Manchester chapel at noon and flew to White Plains, New York. We were taken to the Church property in Harrison. We had land there which we bought as a site for a temple. For six years we have been trying

*delivered extemporaneously

to get permission to build a temple but thus far have failed in our attempts. The neighbors simply do not want us.

We visited the new Inman chapel, where we have constructed a new building. It is an excellent building. I was very much impressed with it. We have two wards meeting here, each presided over by a young and able bishop. We then drove to the Harlem chapel, where we have a building that is small but suitable for the present purposes. We also own a little lawn space adjoining. This could become the site for a new building when we need it.

We then went down to visit a new property we acquired on 87th Street. This building will have to come down and a new chapel will be built.

We then went down to a property we had purchased that runs between 14th Street and 15th Street. It is comprised on 14th Street of three old brownstone buildings, each about 20 feet wide, making the total frontage of 60 feet. The property fronting on 15th Street will become a chapel and will serve our needs for some years to come.

We then went to our Lincoln Center property. I went all through this very carefully with the thought that the upper portion might be converted to a beautiful and serviceable temple. The more I saw of it the better I felt about it. We would do here what we have done in Hong Kong. We would create a multipurpose facility. The chapel on the fifth floor and the space on the sixth floor would be converted to a temple. We would have a separate entrance, and only those with recommends would be permitted to take the elevators to the fifth floor.

We may be able to put a tower on the building with the figure of Moroni on top. The entire building would be devoted to Church purposes, and I am inclined to think that we could get a permit to do this.

I have prayed about this, and I feel enthusiastic. There would be no parking for anyone here, but people would come from all over the New York City area by subway. There is a subway station right here.

There is no better neighborhood in New York of which I am aware. This would serve a marvelous purpose.

My diary entry for Sunday, March 24, 2002, the next day:

We gathered at our Lincoln Center building. Here we had an hour-and-a-half meeting.

In the course of my remarks, I indicated that I had come to New York to see what could be done about getting a temple in this area. For six years we have struggled along thus far without making any substantial headway. I am determined to see that we can accomplish this. I feel satisfied that the Lord desires that His people in this area should have easy access to a temple.

I told them that I felt confident that within two years we could dedicate a temple which would be available to them. I did not tell them of what I had in mind, but it was clearly in my mind as I spoke. I urged them to get ready to go to the temple.

And on that Sunday morning, I said this:

One of the reasons I have come here—the only reason I have come here—was to see what we could do to move along a temple in this area. We have a beautiful temple in Boston. We have a beautiful temple in Washington, D.C. Each city is a long distance from New York. We have all of you people who want to have the privilege and the opportunity of going to the house of the Lord. We have had so much trouble. We bought the site in Harrison, and we have had it for about six years. We have had hearings and hearings and hearings. We must do something. I cannot foretell what will happen, but I can only give you this promise—that somehow, whether it is there or some other place, I am going to see that we get a temple built in this New York area while I am still alive.

I might interpolate to say that I am still alive, though barely so. I said then:

I am an old man; I am nearly 92. But I am going to say that within two years we will have a temple here for dedication. Please do not hold me to the exact date, but I feel so strongly that you are deserving of a house of the Lord, that you are deserving of a temple to which you may go and do your work and receive the blessings that are to be found there and only there. That is why I am here in New York—not to talk to you this morning, but for a greater purpose. Now, I want to say to you, in view of what I have just said, that you get yourselves ready. Get yourselves ready to be worthy to go to the house of the Lord. Many of you are worthy, and you make a great sacrifice to go long distances. But go. Get a temple recommend in your pocket, in your purse, so that you may go to the house of the Lord.

Well, I have come back to fulfill that promise. I am sorry that I am late. I said that I would be back in two years. I meant roughly two years. We are here now in June. And the miracle has occurred. That marvelous thing has come to pass, and the house of the Lord has been built within the shell of that great building which we have on Broadway and Columbus.

I would like to take you back now a few years to Hong Kong.

I went to Hong Kong about six or eight years ago with the idea that we needed a temple in the great realm of China, where there are millions upon millions of people, and in Hong Kong, where we had a very sizeable membership, and which would serve all of Southeast Asia. Hong Kong seemed to be the place to put it.

I went with our building supervisor, and we looked all over Hong Kong. Real estate in Hong Kong costs like it does in New York City—you pay $10 million for a piece of land the size of a postage stamp.

We looked all over that colony—it was then a colony. We

looked everywhere. We could not find a suitable site. We were staying at the Marriott Hotel in Hong Kong, just as we are now staying at the Marriott Hotel in New York. We went back to our hotel room after that very long and difficult day. I could not sleep. I prayed very earnestly, asking the Lord to bless us, to let us know what should be done.

In the middle of the night I awoke. There was on my mind an impression of something that could be done. We owned a very choice piece of property in Kowloon. We had been there for years. It was the location of the mission home.

I got up and took a piece of paper and sketched out a structure with a temple on the top, the baptistry down underground—to follow the instruction found in the Doctrine and Covenants that the baptistry should be beneath "where the living are wont to assemble" (see D&C 128:13). We could put also in that building a chapel and a temple president's residence. I just drew it out in rough form.

I said to my associate the next morning when we had breakfast, "I would like to show you something." I told him of this experience. That resulted in the construction of the Hong Kong Temple.

The temple which we have built here in New York is patterned after that same edifice that we have in Hong Kong and which has worked so beautifully and so successfully and is such a choice and excellent piece.

I want you to know, my brothers and sisters, that I believe that the inspiration of the Lord lies behind what has happened here, which we will bring to a conclusion, as it were, tomorrow when this sacred house of the Lord is dedicated. There you will have in this great metropolitan community a sacred house to which you may go and do your temple work.

It is interesting to me that I decided when I became the President of the Church that I would make every effort of which I was capable to see that we had temples of the Lord wherever they

423

might be needed, that our people would not have to travel halfway across a continent in order to get to a temple. We now have temples in most of the great cities of the world: New York now, Los Angeles, Chicago, Washington, London, Frankfurt, Mexico City, São Paulo, Tokyo, Hong Kong, Manila—all of these great metropolitan areas. We have them also in more remote areas.

Sister Hinckley is not with me today. I am sorry. We dedicated a temple in Accra, Ghana, in January. In coming home from that trip on the plane, she suffered from something. She just seemed to faint from lack of energy and great weariness. She never recovered from it and passed away on the 6th of April. I know that she would have liked to be here on this occasion.

We were here some years ago and held a regional conference in this same hall [Radio City Music Hall]. I remember she stood up here at this pulpit. She was a small woman, and she sort of kicked up her heel at the back and said, "Who would ever dream that a little girl from Nephi, Utah, would ever dance on the stage of Radio City Music Hall?"

Now, let me add just another word on the temple. I am so grateful that this has been accomplished. It is now available to you. Anybody who knows how to ride the subway can get there and will be able to do his or her work.

To you young people who are here tonight, yours will be the great and marvelous and wonderful privilege of going to that holy house and there be baptized for the dead. What a glorious and wonderful experience that will be. Think of it! You will be able to go into that temple and stand as proxy in behalf of some individual long since dead who has been held up in his eternal progress because he has not been baptized. And you, little you, you young boy or you young girl can go there and serve in that capacity. Be worthy of it, my dear friends. Please be worthy. Take advantage of that great and wonderful and marvelous opportunity.

Now, while we are talking of things of eternity, I would like to say further that this is a very sober time in the history of our nation. Buried yesterday was President Ronald Reagan. I do not care whether you are a Democrat or a Republican, but he was a man who left his mark upon the world. He was a good friend of this Church. I visited with him on two or three occasions. President Spencer W. Kimball visited with him. President Ezra Taft Benson visited with him. President Thomas S. Monson visited with him.

When he came to Salt Lake, I read to him from the Book of Mormon the statements found therein that this is a choice land, choice above all other lands, and that its freedom would remain so long as the people worshipped the God of the land, who is Jesus Christ (see Ether 2:12). I read those words to Ronald Reagan and then presented to him a copy of the book where those words are found.

I counted him as a friend. I have tonight in my shirt these cufflinks which he gave me, which have on their face the seal of the president of the United States of America and on the reverse side the name of Ronald Reagan.

I should also like to say while we are talking of these sacred things that our nation is engaged in a terrible and great conflict. I hope that there is not a day that passes that you and I, every one of us, does not get on our knees and pray for this land of which we are a part and those who preside here, that they may be guided and blessed to do that which the Lord would have done.

Now, so much for that.

I think I would like to talk to you young people for a minute, so many of whom are here in the music hall in front of me. You are a tremendous generation. How fortunate you ought to feel that you are a part of this great season in the history of the world. No generation that ever lived has been so richly blessed as has been this generation. God has poured out knowledge and light and understanding in this time of the world's history unequaled in any other season of the earth. I do not know why you and I were spared to come forth at this time, but somehow in the great providence of the Lord it has come to pass.

With all the wonderful blessings we have of medicine, hygiene, public infrastructure to take care of our needs, education—every marvelous opportunity that has come to us, and on top of all of that you and I are the partakers of the gospel of Jesus Christ.

We have a tremendous responsibility. I do not hesitate to say that. So much depends on us. If not me, who? If not now, when? It is our job here and now to do our best to make a difference. I would like to leave that thought with you tonight.

You say to yourself, you write it down, you keep it in your journal—keep before you this statement: "I will make a difference because of the gospel of Jesus Christ." I wish that everyone out in the other halls to which this service is being transmitted would look at himself or herself and resolve that "I will make a difference because of the gospel of Jesus Christ."

You can make a difference with your associates. Brother Robert D. Hales, who grew up here, has told of his boyhood experiences, as have Brother L. Tom Perry and Brother Henry B. Eyring. They made a difference. They worked with others, but their light shone forth in such a way that nobody detracted from it. They stood out among their associates. I have confidence that because of their manner of living and the things for which they stood so resolutely, the lives of others were blessed for good.

You fathers, make a difference. Make a difference as a father. Make a difference as a husband. Treat your wife with kindness and love and respect, and treat your children, who are sons and daughters of God, with love and honor and respect.

You wives, be helpful to your husbands. Give them encouragement. You are the one who can best give it to them.

You boys and girls, be obedient to your parents. Nobody loves you more than do your fathers and your mothers. Be what you ought to be. Listen to them. If you do, the Lord will bless you and help you.

In your business associations, make a difference because of the gospel of Jesus Christ. You never need to be ashamed of being a Latter-day Saint. You can walk with pride but not with arrogance. You do not have to be arrogant; you do not have to be self-righteous. You just have to reflect in your lives, in a quiet and certain way, the meaning of the gospel of which you are a part. Now, that kind of difference will have an effect upon people.

I want to say one thing further. I have desired to put a little more fun in your lives. What you have done tonight, my young friends, here in the music hall has been a wonderfully significant thing. I have watched you dance and listened to your music, and I have had only one sorrow, and that is for those who must have gone to such tremendous effort to make you do it the right way. What tremendous effort has gone into this.

I said to the Brethren one day, "Let us make the gospel and the Church fun for the young people of the Church. Bring in some fun for the young." This I would like to leave with you. You can be serious, and you must be serious. You can study the scriptures, and you must study the scriptures. You can go to seminary and institute; you must go to seminary and institute. But you can have a little fun along with it. And what a tremendous job you have done tonight.

I have seen things of this kind now in Ghana; in São Paulo, Brazil; in Anchorage, Alaska; and now in New York. And every one of them has been inspirational and wonderful and beautiful.

Well, my brothers and sisters, the time is about gone. I did not know whether I would make it this long because I run on batteries these days. I have a pacemaker. I look through glasses. I have batteries in my ears. I have a cane at my side. But I am going to make it at least to my 94th birthday, which is next week.

Well, I repeat, what a tremendous joy it is to be with you. How grateful I am for all who have worked with you and all who work in the Church here. The Church is growing here in a wonderful way. We are trying to meet your needs, to see that you have everything that we can offer anybody anywhere in the world. I believe that we are accomplishing that. We want you to have good facilities, and we are grateful that you now have this temple. God bless you.

Do I know this is the work of the Lord? I certainly do. I have been around a long time. I have seen a lot of things. I have seen very much of this world. I have been everywhere, I think. I have spoken on every continent and borne testimony of this work on every continent.

I think I have been almost everywhere, wherever our people are found—and many places where they are not. The more I have traveled and seen people, those in the Church and those out of the Church, the more grateful I feel for this wonderful gospel. There is no substitute for it.

There are many, many, many wonderful people in many churches in many parts of the earth, but the Lord indicated that this is the true and living Church, with which He is well pleased (see D&C 1:30). Those are His words and not mine. I believe in them as coming from Him. That certainly should not make me arrogant; it should make me very humble and teachable and kind and generous and gracious. That is what I want to be.

God bless you. I testify to you that He lives. He is our Heavenly Father, the great Governor of the universe, but He is my Father and your Father. He will listen to me, and He will listen to you. He will hear our prayers, and He will answer them—not always as we wish, but the time will come when we will see that He has answered in wisdom.

Jesus is the Christ, the Redeemer of the world. He is the Author of our salvation, the God of this earth in many respects, the great sacrificial Lamb who left His royal courts on high and came to be born among a people who crucified Him. Out of that great act of atonement, He has opened the door of the resurrection for every man who walked the earth and the door of exaltation for everyone who will walk in obedience to His commandments.

The conversation which took place in the grove in this great state of New York was as personal and as real as is my conversation with you this night. I bear testimony of that. The priesthood is here. The Book of Mormon is here as another witness, going hand in hand with the Bible, of the divinity of the Lord.

May we walk in faith and faithfulness and in obedience, with love and honor and respect and integrity, is my humble prayer, as I leave my blessing with you, in the sacred name of Jesus Christ, amen.

# Satellite Broadcast, Conferences of Stakes and Districts in Venezuela and Surrounding Areas

## September 12, 2004

My BELOVED BRETHREN AND SISTERS, what a great privilege it is to speak with you. I greet you in the name of the Lord. While we are at this moment separated by thousands of miles, our hearts are united as one. We pray for you, as we know that you pray for us. We are all sons and daughters of God, brothers and sisters in a very real sense.

I am not a stranger to Venezuela. I developed a love for your nation and its people when I first came there 35 years ago. My journal for April 27, 1969, says that I flew from Bogotá to Caracas, arriving Sunday evening. There were a handful of members. The few Saints met in small rented facilities. I noted that Venezuela's economy was the strongest of any nation in South America.

I have been there many times since, most recently only last February 23, when I was in Maracaibo briefly.

Today you have 4 missions, 22 stakes, 10 districts, 155 wards, and 95 branches, with a total membership of more than 120,000. You have excellent buildings all across the land and, capping all, a beautiful temple in Caracas.

We of this Church have been not only mindful of our own people, but we have also reached out to others, regardless of membership. We have tried to be helpful in times of distress. Our records show that we have contributed more than two and a half million dollars in humanitarian aid to the people of Venezuela.

Just as we have experienced growth in Venezuela, we have done so all across the world. What a wonderful thing this is. But it also brings problems. There are only three of the First Presidency and twelve of the Apostles. There was a time when we could go personally throughout the world and attend stake conferences. That no longer is possible, and so we are trying an experiment today. By means of satellite transmission, we are speaking to all of you as if we were in your individual meetinghouses.

To every member of the Church, wherever you may be, I wish to say, be good people. Be good citizens of your communities. Be faithful and true. Be true to the wonderful Church of which you are a part. Every one of you is important. Every one of you is a member in a great fellowship of Latter-day Saints. Every one of you is a son or daughter of our Heavenly Father. Put your confidence in the Lord. Let these words found in Proverbs be your constant guide:

"Trust in the Lord with all thine heart; and lean not unto thine own understanding.

"In all thy ways acknowledge him, and he shall direct thy paths" (Proverbs 3:5–6).

We live in complex times. We so much need the Lord to direct our paths. There are not easy solutions to the problems with which we deal. We are faced with sickness, with economic problems, with worry and concern over many matters.

When I was a small boy living on a farm, my brother and I slept out of doors in the summertime. Night after night we would look up into the heavens and find the constellation of stars that includes the North Star. This is the polar star. You do not see it in the Southern Hemisphere. But since time immemorial, sailors crossing the great seas of the Northern Hemisphere have navigated by this star because it is immovable. It is fixed and invariable. It is constant.

Whether we look at it at 10:00 at night or 2:00 in the morning, it is in the same place. Regardless of conditions, it is a great, dependable constant in a changing sky.

From looking at that star I learned a great lesson which has remained with me throughout my life. I learned that there are fixed and constant points by which we may guide our lives. I should like to talk with you about some of these.

The first is that God is our Eternal Father. He is the great God of the universe. There is none to excel Him. He is over all, and yet He is our Father. We can pray to Him with assurance that He will hear. Alma declared, "Look to God and live" (Alma 37:47). He is our never-failing source of strength. He is our dearest friend with whom we may speak in prayer. The marvel to me is that He hears and answers prayers. I believe that. I know that. I have had too many experiences to ever deny this.

Alma taught his son Helaman in these words: "Counsel with the Lord in all thy doings, and he will direct thee for good; yea, when thou liest down at night lie down unto the Lord, that he may watch over you in your sleep; and when thou risest in the morning let thy heart be full of thanks unto God; and if ye do these things, ye shall be lifted up at the last day" (Alma 37:37).

Speak with Him in the sacred name of Jesus Christ. It is Jesus who is the great Mediator between man and God. And it is in His name that we address our Father in Heaven.

The next great constant in our lives is the Atonement of the Lord Jesus Christ. This is the greatest event in human history. There is nothing to compare with it. It is the most fundamental part of our Father's plan of happiness for His children. Without it, mortal life would be a dead-end existence with neither hope nor future. The gift of our divine Redeemer brings an entire new dimension to life.

> *He marked the path and led the way,*
> *And ev'ry point defines*

*To light and life and endless day*
*Where God's full presence shines.*
*["How Great the Wisdom and*
*the Love," Hymns, no. 195]*

Because of our Savior's sacrifice, instead of dismal oblivion, death becomes only a passage to a more glorious realm. The resurrection becomes a reality for all. Eternal life becomes available to those who walk in obedience.

We do not fully understand why there is so much suffering in the world. It is a fact that even the righteous suffer. I think often of my own grandfather. When the Saints were driven from Nauvoo, he went as a young man into northern Missouri. There he fell in love with a beautiful girl, and they were married. In 1850 they set out for Zion in the mountains of the West. They began their journey of a thousand miles with great hopes and expectations. They had traveled only a relatively short distance when the terrible disease of cholera struck their camp. His beautiful young wife and his half-brother were both stricken and died. He dug a grave and buried them together. Then he lifted in his arms his 11-month-old baby daughter and brought her on the three-month-long and tedious journey to the valley of the Great Salt Lake.

As I have read that chronicle, I have thought of what a terrible tragedy that was. I have thought of the haunting loneliness and utter despair he must have felt. I think there came a refinement into his life because of that experience. He lived to become a great leader, a builder, and the president of a large stake of Zion when there were only 25 stakes in all the Church in all the world. He bequeathed an inheritance of faith to his large posterity, among whom I am one.

Possibly out of our suffering the Almighty will bring a refinement to our souls, whether it be in this life or in eternity.

Another great, eternal, and constant truth on which we may rely is that God has restored His Church and kingdom in this last and final dispensation. If all else were to fail, the truth would remain that He has spoken again, that He and His Beloved Son have parted the curtains to restore the keys, powers, and authority of all previous dispensations.

The Book of Mormon is here as a second witness of the divinity of our Lord. For 175 years now it has been before the world for all to see and read. It has come as a voice from the dust speaking words of testimony concerning the reality and the majesty of our Lord. It has brought comfort and assurance and conviction to millions who have read and prayed concerning it. Many of you are among this number.

The priesthood is upon the earth, brought back by those who held it anciently, and made available to men of this generation, all who would live worthy of it. This precious priesthood brings heavenly blessings. Even boys who are ordained to the lesser priesthood are promised the ministering of angels. Have you ever thought of what a marvelous and wonderful thing that is?

Every father in this Church who has received the Melchizedek Priesthood has the opportunity and privilege of blessing his wife and of blessing his children. He, in effect, becomes a patriarch to his own family. In addition, every worthy member may receive another blessing, a patriarchal blessing given by an ordained patriarch acting in the authority of this holy priesthood.

This priesthood gives the men of this Church the authority to govern in the affairs of the Church. We are not dependent upon those who are trained in seminaries. The Lord takes common men and bestows upon us great responsibility and the power to accomplish that which is expected of us. I witness miracles all across this Church throughout the world. I see many men who have been very ordinary who are called to serve in bishoprics, in stake presidencies, as mission presidents, and in many other capacities. They literally blossom into able and strong leaders. What a wonderful thing— even a miraculous thing—it is to see them as they serve.

Another great verity, as constant as the polar star, is the bestowal of eternal blessings available in the house of the Lord under the authority of this divine priesthood, as the Brethren have pointed out to you today. You Saints of Venezuela have in Caracas a beautiful temple. I know that it is a very long distance from where many of you live. But I hope that once in a while you can make that long journey and go to the house of the Lord. That house stands for all to see as a living witness of the fact that the people of this Church believe in the immortality of the human soul. In these sacred temples, blessings are bestowed that can be had in no other place and that can be received only by those who are worthy to receive them.

Many of you, I know, have serious personal problems with which you constantly wrestle. For many, the times look dark and extremely discouraging. But the Lord has not left you alone. We have a hymn that we sing in our meetings:

> *When upon life's billows you are tempest-tossed,*
> *When you are discouraged, thinking all is lost,*
> *Count your many blessings; name them one by one,*
> *And it will surprise you what the Lord has done.*
> *["Count Your Blessings," Hymns,*
> *no. 241]*

In times of darkness, try to get to the house of the Lord and there shut out the world. Receive His holy ordinances, and extend these to your forebears. At the conclusion of a session in the temple, sit quietly in the celestial room and ponder the blessings you have received in your own behalf or that you have extended to those who have gone beyond. Your heart will swell with gratitude, and thoughts of the eternal verities of the Lord's great plan of happiness will infuse your soul.

To ancient Israel the Lord said:

If ye walk in my statutes, and keep my commandments, and do them;

Then I will give you rain in due season, and the land shall yield her increase, and the trees of the field shall yield their fruit.

And your threshing shall reach unto the vintage, and the vintage shall reach unto the sowing time: and ye shall eat your bread to the full, and dwell in your land safely.

And I will give peace in the land, and ye shall lie down, and none shall make you afraid: and I will rid evil beasts out of the land, neither shall the sword go through your land. . . .

For I will have respect unto you, and make you fruitful, and multiply you, and establish my covenant with you. . . .

And I will set my tabernacle among you: and my soul shall not abhor you.

And I will walk among you, and will be your God, and ye shall be my people. [Leviticus 26:3–6, 9, 11–12]

God bless you, my dearly beloved friends. You are of my people, and I am of your people. We are one great family, now 12 million strong, scattered through 160 nations of the world. But we are all individuals, each with our own problems, our strengths, our weaknesses, our hopes, and our aspirations.

Pray to the Lord, and then live worthy of an answer to your prayers. Reach out in love one to another. Help each other.

Husbands, love and cherish and treat with great kindness and respect your wives and your children. You have no greater possession in all the world than these.

Wives, love and encourage your husbands, and nurture your children in truth and righteousness.

May heaven smile upon you, my beloved brothers and sisters. May there be peace and goodness in the land. I bear witness of the truth of this work, and I leave my blessing with you in the sacred name of our Lord Jesus Christ, amen.

# Ogden, Utah, Regional Conference[*]

## September 19, 2004

M Y DEAR BROTHERS AND SISTERS, I really should not be here. I am only a substitute. President Faust was to have been here. He has not been feeling very well. I volunteered to come in his place. I know you wish he were here; so do I.

I ought to be home preparing for conference. I have six talks to give altogether. I need your prayers. I need your help. I am going to leave just as quickly as I can to go back home and get to work on something for conference.

I would like to just take a bit of a theme if I might:

"Trust in the Lord with all thine heart; and lean not unto thine own understanding.

"In all thy ways acknowledge him, and he shall direct thy paths" (Proverbs 3:5–6).

We live in very complex times. We deal with serious problems—all of us. There is not any question in my mind that in this congregation today there are those who are deeply concerned about various matters—they wonder about them, what to do about them, and how can they handle this and handle that.

"Trust in the Lord with all thine heart; and lean not unto thine own understanding.

"In all thy ways acknowledge him, and he shall direct thy paths."

I think I would like to share with you a few experiences I have had in the last two or three days in pondering in faith these teachings found in Proverbs.

The other day there came to my office a young woman from Brazil—a wonderful young woman, a beautiful young woman, a very able young woman. She is a surgeon. She had saved the life of one of our missionaries in a medical procedure. It had led her to an interest in the Church, and she joined the Church and has become a very strong, powerful advocate of the Church.

She had come up here to intern for a few days with a very accomplished surgeon. That surgeon took care of my wife when she was ill, and he came with this young woman to this meeting.

That stirred within me many memories and sentimental experiences as he, a good and faithful member of the Church, embraced me with tears in his eyes. It brought back, of course, a thousand memories of my own beloved companion—the girl that I knew for so long; the girl of my dreams, as it were; and the girl who became my wife for 67 years and who now again has become the girl of my dreams, whom I miss so very, very much.

I thought of the great importance of marriage, of a problem with which I deal constantly, and that is the failure on the part of so many of our people in their marriage relationships—people who go to the house of the Lord, people who profess their love one for another, people who kneel at the altar and join hands and enter into solemn covenant one with another, and then they get careless. Something comes into their lives, and they drift apart. There is abuse. There is name-calling. There is bitterness. There is sadness. There is heartbreak. There is disappointment. There is failure.

Oh, my brothers and sisters, I want to plead with you, all of you, to look to one another and see the good and the virtue and the strength in your companion and cultivate and nurture that love which properly belongs there. Look not elsewhere, but look to one another in faith, confidence, appreciation, respect, and love one for another—and fathers and mothers toward children, and children toward their parents.

We live in an age when there are so many separations of children from their parents. Parents do not know how to rear their children. I read in the *Wall Street Journal* the other day that some parents in New York decided that they would have drinking in their own home with their children and all of their children's friends. What a misbegotten concept that is. What a tragic thing it leads to.

My brothers and sisters, I plead with you again this morning to cultivate the Spirit in your homes and still your voices and focus your thoughts on those things which will lead to happiness and peace and quality in your lives.

Lay aside the evils of the world. Stay away from pornography in all its elements. It is a terrible, cankering, and wicked thing which is going on in which men sit down at computers and partake of this evil, in which young people also partake. Lift your thoughts higher. Trust in the Lord, and lean not to your own understanding or your own information.

Rise to the divinity within you. We have just sung a great song, "I Am a Child of God." Think of that. If ever you are in some misbegotten way, you start singing the words of that song and recognize that there is within you an essence of divinity. You are a son or daughter of God, and what a marvelous and wonderful and beautiful thing that is. You cannot afford to stoop to any of these mean and beggarly elements that we find all around us in our society today, my brothers and sisters.

I want to talk about rearing children just a little. In doing so, I repeat an experience I have shared before. I was out at my daughter's home yesterday. It is the home in which we reared our children. When we were young, we built that home, my wife and I, and began the great adventure of family life. That old lot on which I built that home had been a garbage dump, really, for the neighbors next door. It was a tough thing to make it green and beautiful and delightful.

In any event, the first tree I planted on that lot was a honey locust tree. I planted it at the corner of the house where the wind blows out of the canyon. I dug a hole one spring day, put the root in, put dirt back, poured water on it, and left it to grow. I paid no attention to it.

Ten years later I looked out the window one winter day when all the leaves were off of the trees, and there was that tree leaning way to the west. It had grown all out of shape. It was an ugly tree. It had not grown as I had hoped it would grow.

I went out through the snow and leaned against it to try to push it up. It just sort of mockingly seemed to say to me, "You cannot move me. You cannot begin to move me. You have neglected me too long." So I went out to my toolshed and got a block and tackle. I put one end on the tree and the other end to a secure post and pulled. The tree shook a little, but nothing happened.

Finally, I got my pruning saw. I cut off that great limb that was leaning to the left, leaving only one little spike up straight. After I had made that terrible cut, I looked at that open wound, from which the sap was coming. I could have wept as I looked at that wounded tree. It has now grown straight and tall and strong and good, but, oh, the ordeal that it suffered. When that tree was young I could have tied it in place with a simple piece of string, and that is all it would have taken to have held it in place and caused it to grow straight and tall.

So it is with children, my dear parents. A little string gently handled can lead to an erect, wise, and great character—a little piece of string gently handled, not with harshness, not with meanness, not with abuse, but with kindness and love and forethought and faith and expectation and prayer, my brothers and sisters.

Somebody made mention of the walnut tree from which was

built the pulpit in the new Conference Center. That walnut tree I planted long ago in a place where it could grow straight and tall. The result is that when it grew old and died, it was still a great piece of wood from which was cut the lumber which became the pulpit of the great Conference Center that we have in Salt Lake.

"Trust in the Lord with all thine heart; and lean not unto thine own understanding.

"In all thy ways acknowledge him, and he shall direct thy paths."

Trust in the Lord in other matters. I had a very interesting experience only yesterday morning. Many years ago I was deeply offended. I had taken from me, by legal but unethical means, a very substantial asset to satisfy the selfish whims of a man who wanted it. It pained me at the time. It disturbed me and caused me great concern and great worry. But I decided that I would not let that canker my soul. I would not let that stand in the way of my attitude and my feelings. I got on my knees and prayed to the Lord for the heart to forgive and forget. That is what happened. It passed completely from my mind years ago.

Yesterday a group of men came to see me. They were the successors of the man who had offended me. They had had on their minds all of these years, 25 years, some sense of the wrong that had been done. They came to apologize and to see what they could do to make up for that loss. I loved them for it. I said, "I do not care what you do. I do not care if you do anything more than what you have done. You have done enough, really, to make me feel well. I leave the rest to you. I am over it. I put it behind me. I cut it out of my thinking, and I left it upon the shoulders of the man who had offended me."

I have thought since then of the way so many go through life carrying grudges. We say we forgive, but we cannot forget. The Lord has said, "I will forgive thy sins and remember them no more against thee" (see D&C 58:42). Brothers and sisters, I plead with you, if you have in you any element of grudge against anybody, an unforgiving attitude, get rid of it. It will destroy you. It will poison you. It will affect your lives. It will affect your children. Get rid of the cankering elements that come of bitter memories.

The Lord said, "Though your sins be as scarlet, they shall be as white as snow; though they be red like crimson, they shall be as wool" (Isaiah 1:18). Be willing to forgive. I was reading in some magazine just the other evening the story of a girl in the East who lived a very dissolute life; who had been in prison, convicted for her crimes; and who now had found the Church and found the love and fellowship and forgiveness for which she had longed.

Rise to the divinity within you, my brothers and sisters. "I am a child of God." Never forget your divine birthright. Live worthy of it. Walk in faith and faithfulness before the Lord, and He will bless you and magnify you and make you strong and able to meet the qualifications needed in your lives.

We have heard great sermons today on the Son of God, of His tremendous outreach for us, His love for us, His willingness to reach down and lift us, build us, strengthen us, and help us in our weakness. Let us take to our homes this day a remembrance of the things we have heard, and let us dwell upon them, discuss them in our family home evenings, and talk about them—see what we can do to improve our lives. The Lord will bless us as we do so.

I want to express my love and gratitude and appreciation to you wonderful people, you Latter-day Saints, you members of The Church of Jesus Christ of Latter-day Saints.

Thank you for all you do. Thank you for the desires of your hearts, your great wish to do the right thing. Thank you for your faith. You send your boys on missions and your daughters on missions. You make great sacrifices to bring them up in the Church, to build in their hearts faith, strength, virtue, kindness, and love. Thank you for your efforts.

Thank you for the spirit of forgiveness that you carry in your hearts. Thank you for the payment of your tithes and offerings. Thank you for your desire to see the work succeed. Thank you for the fact that you get on your knees and pray to the Lord. He will hear your prayers and will answer them with blessings upon your heads. I make that promise without hesitation and without concern.

I leave you my witness and my testimony of the divinity of this work. God, our Eternal Father, lives. I know that. He hears and answers prayers, as has been testified here this day. I could not deny it, for I have prayed; I have had prayers answered—not always in the way that I would wish they might be answered, but I have seen the answer to my prayers, and I cannot deny it.

Jesus is the Christ. He is the Son of the living God, the great Prince that left His Father's throne and came to earth, born under the most humble of circumstances in a vassal nation. He walked the roads of Palestine. He healed the sick and caused the blind to see. He raised the dead and went about teaching good. He gave His life on Calvary's cross for each of us in a great atoning sacrifice— something beyond our comprehension but which has brought to us a gift which could come in no other way, and that is the absolute assurance of the resurrection and the absolute reality of the opportunity of eternal life if we will live the gospel which He taught.

The Father and the Son appeared to the boy Joseph. There can be no doubt in my mind concerning that. I think of the events in the history of this Church—the First Vision, followed by the coming forth of the Book of Mormon, which was recently described as one of the 20 most influential books in this nation. I see the effect that this book has had on people, the millions of lives that it has touched. I think of the restoration of the priesthood, the organization of the Church, and the growth of this Church from that small body that was organized at the Peter Whitmer farm to its present stature, now 12 million strong scattered over the earth in 170 nations.

Last Sunday we spoke to all the Saints in Venezuela in one

meeting, originating in Salt Lake City, by means of satellite. We spoke to 23,265 people in Venezuela. I can recall the time when I first went there years ago when we had maybe 75 members of the Church in all of that great nation—and to see what is there now. We saw it grow. This is the little stone which was cut out of the mountain without hands and is rolling forth to fill the whole earth. It will continue to do so and expand and grow.

We will pass on, and there will be others who will take our place, but the work will remain and grow in strength and power and majesty and fill the whole earth. Of this I testify, my brothers and sisters, as I express my love and leave my blessing with you in the sacred name of Jesus Christ, amen.

# FIRST PRESIDENCY
# CHRISTMAS DEVOTIONAL

## DECEMBER 5, 2004

MY BELOVED BROTHERS AND SISTERS, it is:

> *Christmas in lands of the fir tree and pine.*
> *Christmas in lands of the palm tree and vine*
> *Christmas where snow peaks stand solemn and white*
> *Christmas where corn fields lie sunny and bright. . . .*
> *Everywhere, everywhere, Christmas tonight.*
> *For the Christ child who comes is the Master of all,*
> *No palace too great, no cottage too small.*
> > *[Phillips Brooks, "Everywhere,*
> > *Everywhere, Christmas Tonight"]*

These words of Phillips Brooks describe us as we gather together in this great celebration of the birth of our Lord.

Our Conference Center here in Salt Lake City is filled with people, and our image, as we speak, travels by way of the satellite, the Internet, and through television across the earth to lands of winter and lands of summer, to "lands of the fir tree and pine," and "the palm tree and vine." We are all together as one great family to sing and speak of the joys of Christmas. What a wonderful and glorious season this is. As the spirit of Christmas enters our hearts, we feel a little kinder, a little more generous, a little more happy, and more like the kind of people we ought to be at all times.

Our thoughts turn to those less fortunate. Our prayers are offered in behalf of those who are sick, of those who are hungry and cold, of those who are without friends, and of those who are on the battlefields where the nations are at war.

God be thanked for the gift of His glorious Son, the only perfect man ever to walk the earth. There is none to excel Him. There is none to compare with Him. He is the great example for all of us, our revered teacher and, most importantly, our Redeemer, through whose atoning sacrifice we are assured the blessings of immortal life.

As the bells of the choir are heard, we adapt the words of Tennyson's "Ring Out, Wild Bells":

> *Ring out false pride in place and blood,*
> *The civic slander and the spite;*
> *Ring in the love of truth and right,*
> *Ring in the common love of good.*
> *Ring out old shapes of foul disease;*
> *Ring out the narrowing lust of gold;*
> *Ring out the thousand wars of old,*
> *Ring in the thousand years of peace.*
> *Ring in the valiant man and free,*
> *The larger heart, the kindlier hand;*
> *Ring out the darkness of the land,*
> *Ring in the Christ that is to be.*
> *[The Complete Poetical*
> *Works of Tennyson, ed.*
> *W. J. Rolfe (1898), 190]*

We open the scripture and read these marvelous and beautiful words concerning the birth of our Lord. They are taken from the vision of Nephi.

And it came to pass that I saw the heavens open; and an angel came down and stood before me; and he said unto me: Nephi, what beholdest thou?

And I said unto him: A virgin, most beautiful and fair above all other virgins.

And he said unto me: Knowest thou the condescension of God?

And I said unto him: I know that he loveth his children; nevertheless, I do not know the meaning of all things.

And he said unto me: Behold, the virgin whom thou seest is the mother of the Son of God, after the manner of the flesh.

And it came to pass that I beheld that she was carried away in the Spirit; and after she had been carried away in the Spirit for the space of a time the angel spake unto me, saying: Look!

And I looked and beheld the virgin again, bearing a child in her arms.

And the angel said unto me: Behold the Lamb of God, yea, even the Son of the Eternal Father! [1 Nephi 11:14–21]

There is nothing in sacred literature more descriptive and beautiful concerning the birth of the Lord. Nephi continues:

And after he had said these words, he said unto me: Look! And I looked, and I beheld the Son of God going forth among the children of men; and I saw many fall down at his feet and worship him. . . .

And I beheld that he went forth ministering unto the people, in power and great glory; and the multitudes were gathered together to hear him. . . .

. . . And I beheld multitudes of people who were sick, and who were afflicted with all manner of diseases, and with devils and unclean spirits; and the angel spake and showed all these things unto me. And they were healed by the power of the Lamb of God; and the devils and the unclean spirits were cast out. [1 Nephi 11:24, 28, 31]

Nephi envisioned not only the matchless beauty of His life, but

447

also the hatred that led to His Crucifixion on Calvary's hill. His vision paralleled that of the prophet Isaiah, who said, "He was wounded for our transgressions, he was bruised for our iniquities: the chastisement of our peace was upon him; and with his stripes we are healed" (Isaiah 53:5).

Let us never forget as we celebrate Christmas with song and story, with gifts and mundane baubles, the greater message that Jesus Christ, the Firstborn of the Father, came into the world "that the world through him might be saved" (John 3:17).

Let us remember always that through His infinite Atonement salvation will come to all, and the opportunity for exaltation will be afforded those who walk in obedience to His commandments.

How magnificent, how glorious His ways and His teachings. Peace was His message. As Isaiah declared, "How beautiful upon the mountains are the feet of him that bringeth good tidings, that publisheth peace; that bringeth good tidings of good, that publisheth salvation; that saith unto Zion, Thy God reigneth!" (Isaiah 52:7).

The Savior's comforting words ring in our minds: "Peace I leave with you, my peace I give unto you: not as the world giveth, give I unto you" (John 14:27).

Following His Resurrection He walked among men both in the Old World and in the New. He ministered to them, He taught them, He showed them His wounded hands and feet and side. And then, "while they beheld, he was taken up; and a cloud received him out of their sight.

"And while they looked stedfastly toward heaven as he went up, behold, two men stood by them in white apparel;

"Which also said, Ye men of Galilee, why stand ye gazing up into heaven? this same Jesus, which is taken up from you into heaven, shall so come in like manner as ye have seen him go into heaven" (Acts 1:9–11).

He has come again to usher in a dispensation. And He will

come yet again in clouds of glory to usher in a millennium and reign as King of Kings and Lord of Lords.

Now at this season of the year we honor also His great testator, the Prophet Joseph Smith. We recognize the 199th year of his birth with honor, love, respect, and faith. It was he who declared concerning the risen Lord:

"And now, after the many testimonies which have been given of him, this is the testimony, last of all, which we give of him: That he lives!

"For we saw him, even on the right hand of God; and we heard the voice bearing record that he is the Only Begotten of the Father—

"That by him, and through him, and of him, the worlds are and were created, and the inhabitants thereof are begotten sons and daughters unto God" (D&C 76:22–24).

And to this testimony we add our testimony at this glorious Christmas season. He lives, resplendent, magnificent, the wondrous Lord Immanuel. He lives, the Eternal Son of the Ever-Living Father. He lives, the Great Creator, the Jehovah of the Old Testament, the Savior of the New, the Wondrous Light in a dark and troubled world. He lives to bless us, to teach us, to heal us, to touch our troubled hearts, to give substance to our greatest dreams, to assure the immortality of our souls.

To each of you, wherever you may be, as His servant and witness, I invoke the blessings of heaven upon you. May each of you at this glad season have bread on your tables, clothing on your backs, a roof over your heads, and, most of all, a conviction in your hearts of Him who is the Son of God, the Only Begotten in the flesh, who loves us and in whose name we meet and act, even the sacred name of Jesus Christ, amen.

# BRIGHAM YOUNG UNIVERSITY—HAWAII COMMENCEMENT EXERCISES

## DECEMBER 11, 2004

**M**Y DEAR FRIENDS, both young and old—you who are graduates, and you who are here to honor the graduates—I salute you on this very important day.

Today I wish to speak to you as an old friend. I realize that I am old, now well into my 95th year. I have some difficulty with my feet. But I have concluded that if a man has to have something go wrong, it is better that it be with his feet than with his head.

Seventy-one years ago last June I left for a mission in the British Isles. Few missionaries were sent then because of the terrible Depression. There was very little money, and a mission was simply not the thing to do.

The day I was to leave, my wise father had his secretary type out a card with these great words from the 5th chapter and 36th verse of Mark in the New Testament: "Be not afraid, only believe."

You are acquainted with the circumstances under which the Lord spoke these words. The 12-year-old daughter of the ruler of the synagogue was dying. The ruler pleaded with the Lord in her behalf, but while he was so doing word came that she was gone. Those about him said it was too late. But the Lord said, "Be not afraid, only believe."

He went to the home of the ruler. He dismissed those who

450

were weeping and wailing. He entered the room where she lay, took her by the hand, and said, "Damsel, I say unto thee, arise" (Mark 5:41).

"And straightway the damsel arose, and walked. . . . And they were astonished with a great astonishment" (Mark 5:42).

There is great power in these simple words, "Be not afraid, only believe." There is the power of decision. There is the power of resolution. There is the power of effort. There is the power of faith. I have carried these words with me through all of these many years. They have been a guide to me in the momentous decisions that I have faced from time to time.

They have blessed me in making decisions concerning my work. They have blessed me in the most important decision of my life, the marriage to my beloved companion of 67 years. They have sustained me in the loneliness that I have experienced since her passing. They have sustained me in the very perplexing and difficult decisions I have had to make in the years of my ministry as an officer of this Church.

For instance, some years ago I felt very strongly we needed a much larger hall than the Tabernacle in which to convene our conferences and other gatherings. To do so would mean tearing down an existing building and constructing another at a cost of millions and millions of dollars. I wrestled with that decision. I prayed about it. I talked with my counselors and with the Quorum of the Twelve and the Presiding Bishopric. And I said to myself, "Be not afraid, only believe."

The wisdom of that decision is now beyond question. After 137 years, we must of necessity close the Tabernacle on Temple Square for a period and strengthen it in many ways while preserving its appearance, so that it may stand for many years yet to come. I ask myself, "What would we do without the new Conference Center? Where would we hold our meetings?"

Only last Sunday we gathered in that beautiful and magnificent hall for the First Presidency Christmas Devotional. Some 21,000 people filled it, and hopefully you were able to get the services here.

That same statement, "Be not afraid, only believe," has guided me in a hundred other decisions of great import.

If we are to move forward to accomplish that which the Lord expects of us, we must walk by faith. We can see only so far ahead, and our vision beyond this point must be a vision of faith.

And so, to you young men and women who are leaving this institution today to move out into a larger world, I say, as you do so, "Be not afraid, only believe."

1. Believe in yourself. Believe in your capacity to do great and good things. Believe that no mountain is so high that you cannot climb it. Believe that no storm is so great that you cannot weather it. You are not destined to be a scrub. You are a child of God, of infinite capacity.

Believe that you can do it—whatever it is that you set your heart on. Opportunities will unfold and open before you. The skies will clear when they have been dark with portent.

May the blessings of heaven rest upon you, my dear young friends, as you step into the future.

2. Believe in your companion. No one other factor will make such a difference in your life as the companion you marry. Choose wisely and deliberately and carefully. Eternity is a very long time, and you will wish to be married for eternity in the house of the Lord.

As I look back upon my life and think of the wonder of the companion who walked so long beside me, I cannot get over the tremendous influence that she had on me. She was the mother of my children. She gave them life. She nurtured them. She guided them through their formative years. She loved them and dreamed of them and prayed for them.

She was so wise and good. She just seemed to have present in her all of the good qualities of her most sterling forebears. All of these seemed to come together in that one little girl who bewitched me when I was young and in love.

Now a beautiful marker of enduring granite marks her final resting place, and engraved in that stone, beneath her name, are the words, "Beloved Eternal Companion."

And so she will be mine and I will be hers through all of the eternities to come.

My dear young friends, choose wisely, and then do all you can, throughout your entire lives, to magnify and strengthen your companion. Never put her down. Never belittle her. Never domineer her. The greatest compliment my wife ever paid me was when she said, "You gave me wings to fly, and how I have loved it."

Never be mean or cheap or niggardly with her. Be absolutely loyal. Never let your thoughts wander and never look in the direction of any other.

If you will do so, heaven will bless your marriage. Your children will grow in righteousness, and love will mark your days and nights.

3. Believe in your associates. "No man is an island," as John Donne observed long ago ("Meditation 17," *Devotions upon Emergent Occasions* [1624]). No man lives unto himself. We all live in a world where we must work together. Sometimes our associations are not the happiest. But we can improve the matter if we return good for evil at all times. There is so much of politicking, so much of petty meanness, so much of scheming and ruthless ambition among associates. It is difficult to learn to keep one's peace and in the midst of all such to walk the high road. The Lord will bless you as you do so.

4. Believe in the Church of which you are a member. This is God's holy work. He has brought it to pass in this, the last and final dispensation, the dispensation of the fulness of times. It is His cause and His work, and it is designed to assist Him in bringing to pass the "immortality and eternal life of man" (Moses 1:39).

The Church is perfect, but it is made up of imperfect individuals.

Never let the actions of another destroy your faith in this grand and marvelous work.

Accept every responsibility that you are given, and execute it with faith and diligence. The Lord will bless you. He will magnify you. Your life will be the richer, your experience the sweeter because of your service. This Church is not man's creation. It is man's opportunity afforded him by his Maker. It is eternal in its nature, in its doctrine, in its program.

> *True to the faith that our parents have cherished,*
> *True to the truth for which martyrs have perished,*
> *To God's command,*
> *Soul, heart, and hand,*
> *Faithful and true we will ever stand.*
> *["True to the Faith," Hymns, no. 254]*

5. Believe in the Prophet Joseph Smith. Read the Book of Mormon—again and again. Each reading will bring an enlarged understanding and a stronger knowledge of its divine origin. Read the revelations received by the Prophet. Ponder their meanings. Reflect on his accomplishments during the relatively short time that he lived.

As has been said many times, either this work is true or it is false. If it is false, we are all engaged in a terrible fraud. If it is true, it is the most important work on earth. There is no middle ground.

You young men and women who have completed your baccalaureate work, which was preceded by elementary school and high school, know how hard it has been for you to prepare term papers. Now think of Joseph Smith, the young man, largely without benefit of formal schooling, who produced this Book of Mormon of 531 pages, this book of Doctrine and Covenants and the Pearl of Great Price of 352 pages, and a voluminous history and other writings that have challenged some of the best minds of this and earlier generations.

I really believe that no one can objectively look at his accomplishments and deny the divinity of his calling.

6. Believe in prayer. No matter your capacity, no matter your ability, you need help beyond your own. That help will come if you will get on your knees and plead with the Lord in prayer for strength and direction and guidance. We all need the humility that leads to prayer. We all need the humility that comes of getting on our knees in silent pleading. Prayer is befitting whether in success or failure. If there is success, there should be expressions of gratitude. If there is failure, there should be pleas for help.

7. Finally, believe in God, your Eternal Father, and in His Beloved Son, your Redeemer. How majestic is our God, how wonderful His ways. And how reassuring, how comforting, and what a marvelous and wonderful blessing to know that we are His children, that He loves us, that He will listen to us, and that He will bless us.

The words of David's psalm remind us:

"When I consider thy heavens, the work of thy fingers, the moon and the stars, which thou hast ordained;

"What is man, that thou art mindful of him? and the son of man, that thou visitest him?

"For thou hast made him a little lower than the angels, and hast crowned him with glory and honour" (Psalm 8:3–5).

Believe in His immortal Son, the Lord Jesus Christ. Under His Father's direction, He was the Creator of the earth. He was Jehovah of the Old Testament. He was Jesus Christ, the Messiah of the New Testament. It was He who gave His life on Calvary's hill for each of us. Through His great atoning sacrifice, He has made possible the resurrection for all and eternal exaltation for those who will keep His commandments.

Approach the Father in the sacred name of Jesus Christ. There will come into your heart comfort, peace, and faith.

And so, my beloved brothers and sisters, you face the future. You leave here to step out into the world. "Be not afraid, only believe." For this I humbly pray in your behalf, in the holy name of Jesus Christ, amen.

# SECTION 3

---

# MESSAGES
# TO THE
# GENERAL
# PUBLIC

# Washington, D.C., Address
# to the National Press Club

## March 8, 2000

*President Hinckley is the first President of the Church to address the National Press Club. The audience included members of Congress, ambassadors and other diplomats, religious leaders, and journalists from around the world. A question-and-answer session followed the address; Jack Cushman, president of the National Press Club, read the questions, which were submitted by the audience.*

MY THANKS TO ALL WHO are here today. I am deeply honored by your presence. This is a very large gathering, and it is somewhat intimidating, particularly since I know who you are and what you do.

I have wondered about what to talk about here. I couldn't get any help from anybody. I asked several people and just got a blah response. I am not going to talk about my new book, unless it comes up in the questions. I am not going to talk about the election in California yesterday [on a proposition to ban same-sex marriage], unless it comes up. I've chosen rather to speak on the Church, giving you something of a sampling of its operations.

We now have more members overseas than we have in the United States and Canada, and the percentage overseas is growing, although we are growing significantly also in the United States and Canada. I believe that no other church which has risen from the soil of America has grown so large or spread so widely. It was not many years ago that we were largely a Utah church. Now our people are found everywhere across North America and beyond the seas around the world. We are now operating in more than 160 nations. Our worldwide membership is approaching 11 million.

Of these, approximately 4 million are women who belong to

what we call the Relief Society. I think it is the oldest women's organization in the world—and perhaps the largest. It has its own officers and board, and these officers also sit on other boards and committees of the Church. People wonder what we do for our women. I will tell you what we do: we get out of their way and look with wonder at what they are accomplishing.

I think I might capsulize what we are doing across the world by telling you of an experience I had. I was in Mexico City to speak to the graduating class of the school which we operate in that area. I was introduced to one of the graduates, a young woman. Her mother and her grandmother had come for the graduation exercises.

The grandmother had lived in the bush. She had never learned to read or write. She was totally illiterate. Her daughter had received a little schooling, not very much. She could read a newspaper headline or something of that kind. Now came this beautiful young woman. She was in the graduating class. I asked her, "What are you going to do now?"

She replied, "I have received a scholarship to the medical school of the national university."

That to me was a miracle—from the bush and total illiteracy to refinement and medical school in three generations. She spoke not only her native Spanish but English as well. She gave full credit to the Church and its programs for what had happened to her.

We all know that education unlocks the door of opportunity. And so we pour large resources into educating our youth. Brigham Young University in Provo, Utah, is our crown jewel. It is the largest church-sponsored private university in America, with an enrollment approaching 28,000. Its graduates are now found across the nation and even across the world. They serve on the faculties of nearly every large university in America. They are in business, the professions, and almost every honorable vocation. A substantial number are here in Washington, and some of those are here today.

We operate other schools. But we cannot accommodate all who might wish to attend these. And so we operate institutes of religion contiguous to the campuses of colleges and universities throughout the land. Here our youth are involved in religious studies and have a wonderful time socializing together, and this socialization frequently leads to marriage.

In the early days of the Church, when our people were gathering from the British Isles and Europe, our leaders set up what was known as the Perpetual Emigration Fund. The Church loaned money to those who did not have sufficient so that they might gather to Utah. As they were employed, they repaid the loan, and this became a revolving fund for so long as it was needed.

We face a new challenge today. In the underdeveloped countries we have young men and women, many of them of capacity but without opportunity to improve themselves. They cannot do so without help. We are now assisting some and are working on a plan to assist many more to acquire education in their own lands through a revolving Perpetual Education Fund, we might call it. We are providing a ladder by which they can climb out of the impoverishment that surrounds them to make something better of their lives, to occupy places of honor and respect in society, and to make a contribution of significance to the nation of which they are a part.

We are already engaged in microcredit undertakings, whereby small amounts are loaned to those for whom a hundred or two or three hundred dollars can spell an actual change in their future. When given such credit, these people become entrepreneurs, taking pride in what they are doing and lifting themselves out of the bondage that has shackled their forebears for generations. From a bread shop in Ghana to a woodworking business in Honduras, we are making it possible for people to learn skills they never dreamed of acquiring and to raise their standard of living to a level of which they previously had little hope.

As the Church moves out across the world and into the future, we face two very serious problems. The first is the training of local leadership. All of our local congregations are presided over by local men, volunteers who work at their regular vocations and carry on as they are called to serve in such capacities as bishops.

I have just been down in Mexico, and I am amazed at the quality of leaders who are being developed. These are men and women of strength and capacity. They are quick learners. They are devoted and faithful. They have become better husbands and fathers and wives and mothers under the family-strengthening programs of the Church. They are an asset to the society of which they are a part, as will be the generations who come after them. That is the beauty of this work. When you touch the life of a man of this generation, that influence is felt through generations yet to come.

The second problem we face is providing places of worship as we grow so rapidly in these areas. We are constructing nearly 400 new houses of worship each year. It is a huge task. It is a tremendous undertaking. But we must accomplish it, and we are doing so. Some of these houses are relatively small, and many of them are large. They are all attractive. They are well kept. They have beautiful landscaping. They are a credit to every community where they are found. And they become a wonderful example to the people.

Thirty years ago I had the responsibility for our work in South America. I recall the first time I went to Santiago, Chile. There were perhaps a hundred members of the Church in the entire nation. We had a little school of about 10 students who met in a tiny building that was little more than a shed. A short time ago I was back in Santiago and spoke to a congregation assembled in a large football stadium with 57,500 in attendance. I could scarcely believe what I saw.

They were well dressed, clean, and attractive. They did not smoke, not one of them. They did not drink, not one of them. They were there as families, for the most part—fathers and mothers and children. There is no generation gap among such people. There is love and honor and respect in the family circle. This is the result of Church teaching and Church family programs.

Every good citizen adds to the strength of a nation. With that assumption, I do not hesitate to say that the nation of Chile is better for our presence, and the same thing is happening in every other place where we are operating.

It is my philosophy that everyone who comes into this Church should immediately have a responsibility under which he can grow. The genius of our work is that we expect much of our people. They grow as they serve, and there are numerous opportunities to challenge them.

We do not have a professional priesthood. None of us who serve as officers of this Church was trained in a religious seminary. We may not have the polish of those who have been, but we bring to our service an enthusiasm for the work and a love for the people that are wonderful to witness and inspiring to experience.

We believe in the old adage that many hands make light work. We have a lay priesthood, and every worthy man is eligible to receive this priesthood. Each bishop of the Church has two counselors, devoted and able men, to assist him. None is a professional, but all are dedicated. Bishops serve for a period of about five years; then they are released, and others take their place. The result is a constant development of leadership and a renewing strength of direction. Those who are released as bishops go to other responsibilities. There is opportunity for everyone to serve according to his or her capacity.

Our tremendous missionary program builds leaders while men and women are still young. We now have nearly 60,000 missionaries serving throughout the world, every one on a volunteer basis. Most of them are young men, some are young women, and we have a few retired couples. They serve from 18 to 24 months.

I met two young women recently. They are both from

Mongolia, and I am pleased to see the Mongolian ambassador here today. They are missionaries of this Church serving in Salt Lake City. We send missionaries from Salt Lake and elsewhere in the States to Mongolia and other places, and some come here from such places and partake of the culture which we have here. They learn English. They see the Church at its strongest. They will return to their native lands greatly transformed from what they were when they came here.

As you know, the Winter Olympics are coming to Salt Lake City in 2002. I understand Mitt Romney was here the other day telling you about it. If requested, we shall have no trouble in offering capable translators and interpreters for the many languages that will be represented.

I can walk down the streets of Salt Lake City and meet people who speak a score or more of languages: Spanish, Portuguese, German, French, Italian, Danish, Dutch, Swedish, Norwegian, Finnish, Russian, Albanian, Czech, Slovak, Serbian, Japanese, Chinese—both Mandarin and Cantonese—Mongolian, Estonian, various dialects of the Philippines, and whatever else you wish to have. I think it is a tremendous phenomenon. All have learned these languages while serving as missionaries. And as they have learned the language of the land in which they have served, they have had companions in this service who are natives of those lands and who in turn have learned English from them. This cross-fertilization of languages and cultures is a tremendous thing. Misunderstanding grows out of ignorance and suspicion. As we learn to know those of various cultures, we come to appreciate them. The cause of peace is strengthened in a very real sense by this tremendous program.

We now have 333 missions across the world. Each becomes a bridge to better understanding among people, to greater appreciation for other cultures.

Now another thing. For a long time we have tried to take care of our own who find themselves in distress. We operate large farming projects, not only in the United States but in other nations as well, to insure against times of economic distress and catastrophes of one kind or another. In our Church welfare program we have dairies, bakeries, canneries, meat-packing plants, and other facilities, modern in every respect, to meet the needs of those in distress. We have bishops' storehouses that resemble supermarkets, but they have no cash registers. They are there to serve the poor.

We also are trying to reach out to those who find themselves in terrible trouble because of war, earthquake, flood, drought, and other disasters. Human suffering anywhere and among any people is a matter of urgent concern for us. We have our own Latter-day Saint Charities organization, and we have worked with other nongovernmental agencies in extending humanitarian aid. These include Catholic Relief Services, Mercy Corps International, the American Red Cross, the Red Crescent, the Salvation Army, Habitat for Humanity, and other groups across the world.

Today, this very day, as they have been during previous days, two helicopters have been flying rescue and mercy missions over the floodwaters of Mozambique and Zimbabwe. When governments in that part of the world said they could do no more, we rented two helicopters at great expense to fly rescue missions. Additionally, we have sent cash—together with food, clothing, and medicine—to these suffering people. Those helped are not our members. Our humanitarian efforts reach far beyond our own to bless the victims of war and natural disaster wherever they may be.

Last year alone we sent humanitarian aid to assist with 829 projects in 101 countries, giving $11 million-plus in cash and $44 million in material resources for a total $55 million-plus. I would like to suggest that this is no small effort. And the costs would have been much higher had it not been for the voluntary services of the very many who packed the goods in our warehouses in Salt Lake City and who unpacked them at the points of distribution.

We have dug wells in African villages, fed people, and supplied them with clothing and shelter. We have given aid in the Mexico fire of 1990, in the Bangladesh cyclone of 1991, in the China earthquake of 1991, in the Bosnia civil conflict of 1992, in Rwanda in 1994, in North Korea in 1996 to '98, in Central America in 1998, and in Kosovo in 1999, and today we are assisting substantially in Venezuela, Mozambique, and Zimbabwe.

Time will not permit me to speak of the many efforts we have made to assist those of this nation who find themselves in difficulty. Suffice it to say that we have been pleased to reach out to many Americans who have been victimized by flood, hurricane, and tornado.

One more item. Our family history archives in Salt Lake City are now the largest in the world. Satellite libraries are found in this land and others. They are open to everyone regardless of faith or religious affiliation. More than half of the people who use them are not of our faith. People everywhere desire to learn of their roots. Our family history Web site receives about eight million hits per day. I think we would have genealogical information on every man and woman in this hall. We invite you to visit our family history resources right here in the Washington area. They are found in the chapel near our temple in Kensington and in other locations. You will be made to feel welcome.

As you look into the microfilm reader, you may be surprised to find the names of your parents, of your grandparents, of your great-grandparents, and of your great-great-grandparents, those who have bequeathed to you all you are of body and mind. You will feel a special connection to those who have gone before you and an increased responsibility to those who will follow.

We are now completing in Salt Lake City a great new Conference Center. Brigham Young built the famed Tabernacle on Temple Square. It was a bold undertaking to construct so large a hall in that remote pioneer community. But now it has become inadequate for our needs. For the first time, our world conference in April will be held in a magnificent new hall which seats 21,000. I know of nothing to compare with it as a house of worship and a place for cultural presentations. It is beautiful, and it is magnificent, and from its pulpit our message will be carried by satellite around the earth.

Now, I have had time to touch on only a few of the very many things we are trying to do, but I hope that I have given some small indication of our activities as we move this work forward. Our desire everywhere is to make bad men good and good men better. Wherever we go, we go in the front door. Our representatives honor the laws of the nations to which they go and teach the people to be good citizens. We teach, we train, we build, we educate, we promote opportunity for growth and development. We give hope to those without hope, and there is nothing greater you can give a man or a woman than hope.

You ask how all of this has been accomplished. It takes money, you say. Where does it come from?

It comes from observance of the ancient law of the tithe. Just as Abraham paid tithes to Melchizedek, the great high priest of the Old Testament, so do our people contribute their tithes to the work of the Lord. They do so cheerfully with faith in the promise of Malachi that God will open the windows of heaven and shower down blessings upon them (see Malachi 3:10). We do not pass the plate. We do not play bingo. We pay our tithing and can testify to the goodness of the Lord.

This law is set forth in 35 words in our scriptures (see D&C 119:4). Compare that with the rules and regulations of the IRS.

We are a church, a church in whose name is the name of the Lord Jesus Christ. We bear witness of Him, and it is His example and His teachings we try to follow. We give love. We bring peace. We do not seek to tear down any other church. We recognize the good they do. We have worked with them on many undertakings.

We will continue to do so. We stand as the servants of the Lord. We acknowledge that we could not accomplish what we do without the help of the Almighty. We look to Him as our Father and our God and our ever-present helper as we seek to improve the world by changing the hearts of individuals.

Thank you very much, my dear friends. And now if you have questions, Mr. Cushman, we'll be glad to try to answer them.

*Jack Cushman:* Perhaps the most frequently asked question on all of these cards that I have is "What role is politics going to play for the Church and its members?" Can you comment a little bit on political activism among your members?

*President Hinckley:* Well, the Church as an institution does not involve itself in politics, nor does it permit the use of its buildings or facilities for political purposes. Now, we do become involved if there is a moral issue or something that comes on the legislative calendar which directly affects the Church. We tell our people who are citizens of this land and other lands that they as individuals have a civic responsibility to exercise the franchise that is theirs, so they become very active. But as a Church, as I have said, we do not become involved in tax matters or any other kinds of legislation unless there be a moral issue which we think is of great importance or something which may be directed to the Church—harmfully, as we view it—and then we would become involved. We do very little politicking. We look at Washington and smile. *[laughter]*

*Jack Cushman:* We welcome smiles in Washington.

A questioner says the Church actively supported Proposition 22, the ballot measure banning same-sex marriage, which California voters approved yesterday, and asks, "Does the Church take any credit for that result, and does this signal a more activist political posture?"

*President Hinckley:* I don't think it signals a more active political posture, but we were actively involved there. We were part of a coalition that very actively worked on that matter. We are not anti-gay. We are pro-family. I want to emphasize that. We are grateful for all who worked so diligently, and we are happy for the outcome of that vote, which was about 61 to 38 percent—by a very sizable margin. We are grateful because California is a bellwether state, and the fight there was very real. I'd like to add that the Church put no money into that as an institution. Members of the Church who spent or contributed money did so as individuals. They not only gave of their means, but they gave of their strength and their energy to win a great victory, I think, in terms of their attitude and position.

*Jack Cushman:* We will move beyond politics shortly, but we have a couple more.

*President Hinckley:* It doesn't scare me.

*Jack Cushman:* Someone asked, "Since George W. Bush's appearance at Bob Jones University really elevated this question of religion and politics this year, what is your opinion of his appearance there and the aftermath?"

*President Hinckley:* Oh, we haven't given it much thought. We have been persecuted a great deal during our history—terribly so. We've endured every kind of insult and difficulty. Fortunately, that has largely disappeared, and we are not going to fuss over that. I heard him the other night on the Larry King show, and I felt a little sorry for him. We'll stand as we have stood through all of these years and move forward with a smile on our face and a greeting in our hearts for anyone who speaks against us or for us.

*Jack Cushman:* "The Church is sending missionaries into the inner cities of the United States. What kind of racial sensitivity training, if any, are the missionaries given, especially regarding the history of the Church and African Americans?"

*President Hinckley:* Well, we do have some missionaries working among these people, and they bring out of these people some very strong leaders. It is an amazing and wonderful thing to see how people develop when they are given an opportunity and encouragement and direction. That's happening, and we have no problem with it. It is all a part of what we are doing. We are working in Africa, all up and down Africa, with tremendous results. We are grateful for good people wherever we find them, people with tremendous potential when they are given opportunity. We can only say we are happy to have them and do what we can to assist them.

*Jack Cushman:* When we stop talking about politics in Washington, we start talking about the Internet. A questioner asks, "Could you comment on the growth of the Internet and if you feel it has had a negative impact on the morality of society as a whole?"

*President Hinckley:* I don't know much about it. I'm an old man, unable to learn, evidently. My grandchildren could tell you all about it, but I'm not up to speed to the degree that they are. I don't know that the Internet has contributed greatly to immorality. We're already pretty well sunk down into a morass of that kind *[laughter],* but I regret anything which leads people to live below good standards, good values, virtue in their lives, and causes them to sink down into this lowly business where they make no contribution and do very little good and bring only harm to themselves. Now, as for the Internet, it is a great boon. As I say, we're getting eight million hits a day in our family history work.

*Jack Cushman:* An old man with a big Web page. *[laughter and applause]*

"Why is the Church growing so quickly? What purpose does it serve?"

*President Hinckley:* Well, it's growing because it has a commission to go in the world and teach the gospel to every nation, kindred, tongue, and people. We consider that a divine commission, and we are pursuing it very aggressively; and at the same time, while in that process, we think we are doing good. We think we are improving people's lives. We think that we are causing them to stand taller and straighter and be better people, and when all is said and done, I guess that is the purpose of any religion. We are trying to do our part and do it in a very aggressive but practical and hard-headed way, if you please, so that we build on a strong foundation for the future.

*Jack Cushman:* "How should members of the Church respond to efforts of some other religious groups to convert them to other beliefs and religions?"

*President Hinckley:* Well, I say this: We don't downgrade any religion. We recognize the good they all do. I say to those of other faiths, "You bring all the good that you have and let us see if we can add to it." Now, that's our attitude reduced to a very short statement, and it works.

*Jack Cushman:* A questioner asks, "How does one keep family ties strong when Church obligations keep one so busy?"

*President Hinckley:* We must have a member of the Church here in the audience. That could come only out of a member of the Church. I'm glad you are working hard. Keep it up, but do not neglect your families. That is number one. You're responsible for your own household. Those children are God's children, for whom you have a very serious and sacred responsibility. Do not neglect them. If you are too busy in your Church activities to take care of your family, then perhaps we had better find something else for you to do.

*Jack Cushman:* "When you watch television and see what is portrayed there and in films, do you feel that you're losing the crusade or the war?"

*President Hinckley:* No. I don't watch television very much. *[laughter]* No. I don't think we are losing the war; I think we are winning the war. I am an optimist. I believe the future looks good. We have a lot of problems to deal with, very serious problems. The American family is in trouble. I think no one could doubt that. We have many troublesome things: gangs, drugs, and everything else of that kind. But in spite of all that, there are so many good people in this land, so many people who want to do the right thing, that I'm totally optimistic about the future. I don't think we're going down to ruin and trouble. I think we're making a little headway, and we ought to be grateful for the opportunity and work a little harder at it.

*Jack Cushman:* "We hear a lot of talk from the presidential candidates, including the two front-runners now, about using faith-based organizations to do work that traditionally has been done by the government. Do you think this is going to let the government off the hook?"

*President Hinckley:* I don't think anybody is going to let the government off the hook the way things are going. I don't think the government is going to change much in that regard, but I want to say, we are doing what we can to take care of our own, and that is a tremendous effort. I think if you could look into the workings of our welfare program, you'd be amazed at what you see. We are trying to do our part to care for our own, and everyone that we take care of lightens the load of government, and we think that's a benefit to all the people of the nation.

*Jack Cushman:* "What is your position on prayer or meditation or moments of silence in public schools?"

*President Hinckley:* I believe in it, and I'll be glad to get through here so I can have a moment of meditation. *[laughter]* Well, all of us ought to pause once in a while and just stop and think of things. We are prone to talk too much and do too little. I think it is a wonderful thing to just indulge once in a while in moments of introspection and see what we are doing with our lives and what contribution we are making and where we could do a little better than we are now doing. I feel we would all benefit from that.

*Jack Cushman:* Do you think it is appropriate to have this as part of the daily instruction in a public school?

*President Hinckley:* In the public schools? I don't know that I want to comment on that. I think we may have taken a terrible step backwards some years ago, and I don't know whether we'll recover from it. You politicians know better than I do what the mood is to change the law, but regardless of that, we teach our people in their own private lives and in their own individual ways to pray, to get on their knees and talk with God and listen for His still, small voice and receive His inspiration and direction in their lives. We bear testimony of the fact that that yields great good. I don't hesitate to say that for a moment.

*Jack Cushman:* If you'll forgive the levity, somebody here really wants to know whether God has forgotten about BYU football. *[laughter]*

*President Hinckley:* That comes from an alumnus. I don't know. I hope not. I think we have got to bring about a turnaround, but they are working on it. They are working very hard on it. I hope that something good comes of it. I like to see a winner—I will say that.

*Jack Cushman:* "What do you consider to be the greatest challenge that the Church faces right now?"

*President Hinckley:* As I've said, training of leadership. Every local leader in Japan is Japanese. Every local leader in Hong Kong is Chinese. Every local leader in Sweden is Swedish, Norwegian, etc., etc. These are people who have to be trained in leadership. We carry forward a great program, and the product is wonderful to behold. I think we could even train you, Mr. Cushman. *[laughter]*

*Jack Cushman:* You're doing pretty well so far. *[applause]* They seem enthusiastic. *[laughter]*

"With more members of the Church outside the U.S. than in the U.S., does this present a need for greater decentralization of the administrative functioning of the Church?"

*President Hinckley:* We are doing that. We know we can't lick every postage stamp in Salt Lake City—of course we do. So we've established area offices across the world where we have three of what we call our General Authorities presiding over an area of the world. We now have such offices in Brazil, in Argentina, in Bolivia, in Chile, in Japan, in Hong Kong, in Manila, in South Africa, in West Africa, and so on. We are decentralizing in that respect. We have to.

*Jack Cushman:* A questioner asks whether you see a prospect for missionaries in China.

*President Hinckley:* Well, as I have said, we go in the front door. If we go to China doing missionary work, the Chinese government will know about it. They'll have to say when, and we'll respond. We have two or three branches of the Church in China which are composed of outsiders who are from the United States and other nations. We have one in Beijing. We have one in Shanghai. Of course, we have strong work in Hong Kong. We have strong work in Taiwan. But the Chinese government has its rules and regulations, and we believe in honoring, obeying, and sustaining the law, and that's where we stand at the moment.

*Jack Cushman:* Please tell us a little about your book *[Standing for Something]*, and how did you get a tough guy like Mike Wallace to write the introduction?

*President Hinckley:* Well, Mike is a good man. I've learned to know him, and I think very highly of him. I had an experience with him on *60 Minutes*. I didn't know what I was getting into, and my friends warned me against him, but he was kind to us. I've had a good relationship with him, and he consented to this letter, which was a good introduction. I guess that's what's selling the book. *[laughter]*

*Jack Cushman:* A questioner says, "Why did you write a book that is not about your Church? What are you trying to accomplish through this book?"

*President Hinckley:* To see if it could be done. We wanted to reach out further to other people. I talk of values in this book, virtues. I talk about America. I talk about a lot of these things that

I think are very, very important. I felt that the people of this nation—perhaps some of them—might be helped by it. It was with that in mind that I did so. Now, it isn't a book of theology, but it is a book of virtues and values, which are a part of theology. The teachings of the gospel bear fruit in the virtuous lives of the people. By dealing with those lives, I hope to accomplish some good in reaching out to people who may not be interested in our theology but would be interested in our position and stance on some of these values that are of everlasting benefit to this nation and people across the world.

*Jack Cushman:* Do you find when it comes to core values that basically all of the religions get it more or less right?

*President Hinckley:* Oh, I think they all do good. I believe that. I have many friends of other religions, and I'm satisfied they are very conscientious, good people who are trying to do good. I appreciate them for that. I think the world would be much poorer without religion, speaking generally.

*Jack Cushman:* "Do you find that the image of the Church is changing rapidly? slowly? Do you work at bringing about change in the way the Church is viewed by those outside the Church?"

*President Hinckley:* We're constantly trying to build understanding. As I indicated in my talk, ignorance leads to misunderstanding. When we don't know how other people act, what they believe, we view them with suspicion. When we get to know more about them, that suspicion turns to appreciation, and I think that's what we are trying to do and trying to accomplish. Now, compared with 100 years ago, 150 years ago, we live in a world that pretty well understands us and, I think, appreciates us. We are freed from that terrible persecution of the past. We are living in a new day, when the sunshine of goodwill pours in upon the Church and assists us in the spread of our work across the world.

*Jack Cushman:* And yet at times you hear, even from other

Christian faiths, that your Church is not a Christian church. How do you respond to that?

*President Hinckley:* I know. I can't understand it. I never can understand it. The very name of the Savior is in the name of the Church. I can't understand how they can possibly say that. The New Testament is a fundamental scripture for us. We have in addition to that the Book of Mormon, which becomes another witness for Jesus Christ. I can't understand why they take that position, but their position comes of the tradition of their fathers, I think. Our position comes from the Restoration of the gospel. So we have some differences. We don't worry much about that. We just go on with our work, talking positively, teaching positively, working affirmatively to make of the world a better place in which to live.

*Jack Cushman:* I find another political question crept into the deck here.

*President Hinckley:* I'll bet you put it there. *[laughter]*

*Jack Cushman:* It says, "Given the platform and positions taken by the Democratic Party, can you be a good Church member and a Democrat?" *[laughter]*

*President Hinckley:* Yes, I think so. I don't know why you couldn't. It depends on what you believe as a Democrat in terms of some things. There are some things we don't subscribe to. We've got lots of Democrats in the Church, lots of them, and they are good people. I don't worry about that too much. This is Washington; I'd better be careful of what I say, but we've got a Democratic presidency, and we've got another candidate now pretty well marked out. Look to the future.

*Jack Cushman:* This questioner says that Catholics are welcomed in Protestant church services, and vice versa. Do the Mormons invite other faiths into your Church services?

*President Hinckley:* Oh, sure. Of course we do. We invite anybody who would like to come. We welcome them, wish them to come, want them to come. We hope they will come. That's the whole thrust of our missionary effort. Yes, very much so. We don't shun them. We love them.

*Jack Cushman:* A number of people ask what the secret is to your staying so vigorous. I have to say it is on several of these cards. Are there health secrets that come from your religious practice? *[laughter]*

*President Hinckley:* Sure. We have what we call the Word of Wisdom, which is a religious principle with us which proscribes the use of alcohol and tobacco and such things and urges people to eat grains and such things as that. I have never smoked. I have never drunk. I have never done those things. Now, I don't know that that's the reason I'm going to be 90 on June 23, but the idea that I try to follow is to go to bed every night and be sure you get up in the morning. *[laughter]*

*Jack Cushman:* I'll try to remember that too. *[laughter]*

"What is your Church's teaching on divorce?"

*President Hinckley:* Well, we don't like it. We have divorce. We permit divorce. I very much regret that divorce is so rampant in the land. I think it is indicative of the breaking up of the family. I think it is a very sorrowful thing to witness that we have so much divorce, which comes of a disrespect on the part of men and women and a lack of appreciation and an unwillingness to give and take a little here and there. If every man would make his prime concern the comfort and well-being of his wife, and every wife would make her chief concern the comfort and well-being of her husband, we would have very little divorce in the land.

*Jack Cushman:* Perhaps it's another journalist in the audience; he wants you to think back to the time when you were considering Columbia University and the School of Journalism. What was it that made you decide that wasn't such a great idea?

*President Hinckley:* That's a long time ago. The fact is when I came home from my mission in England—I'd graduated from the University of Utah before I went—I stopped in New York on the way home to inquire at Columbia. I came home, and the leaders of the Church asked me to come and do some work there, and I ceded to their requests and have been there ever since. Can't get out of the rut. *[laughter]*

**Jack Cushman:** Neither can I.

Before I ask our last question, and thank you for coming here, I would like to give you a certificate of appreciation, which you can add to the many other certificates that adorn your wall. We really appreciate your taking your time.

The last question, believe it or not, came right from these very people. "With a voice of authority, do you think you could convince Senator [Orrin] Hatch here to stick around and sing a few songs for us?" *[laughter]*

**President Hinckley:** One of our major principles is the sanctity of free agency, and if he chooses to sing, I'll stay and listen, but if he leaves, I'll go out right behind him.

**Jack Cushman:** I'd like to thank you, President Hinckley, for coming today. I'd like to thank our audience for coming. I would ask you all, please, since we have such a crowd, would you please remain seated until Mr. Hinckley has left the ballroom. . . . We are adjourned, ladies and gentlemen. Thank you very much.

# Unitus Award
# Luncheon*

OCTOBER 10, 2000

*Unitus, a humanitarian organization founded by a group of Latter-day Saints, presented President Hinckley with its Humanitarian of the Millennium Award at a luncheon in the Joseph Smith Memorial Building in Salt Lake City. The award recognized President Hinckley's efforts to help the poor and those devastated by natural disasters.*

THANK YOU VERY, VERY MUCH. This is a very large group. You are doing a great work.

I have walked among the poor across the earth. I've been everywhere, I think, where the poor try to live out a troubled existence—Mexico; Central America; all through South America; Asia; among the very poor people of the Philippines, Cambodia, Vietnam, and all through that area; Burma; all up and down Africa, where there is so much of suffering, so much of deprivation, so much of trouble and sorrow; and Eastern Europe, where there is all kinds of sorrow and trouble today, where there is poverty because of mismanagement of government.

Well, my heart has ached—I don't know how to express it—as I have seen those people in the favelas of Brazil. All through South America you see those little paper shacks climbing up the hills of the major cities everywhere. There is so much of poverty, and with poverty goes ignorance, the lack of education. Without education, those people cannot be lifted. It is my firm conviction that education is the key which will unlock the door of opportunity for those people.

I'm so grateful for the microloans that you have been making and encouraging to be made. It has seemed almost impossible that

*delivered extemporaneously

a few dollars—$100, $50, $200—can spell the difference between walking in the mud throughout one's days and getting started with some entrepreneurship in some little business that will grow and lead to a decent living and the means with which to do what the Lord, I think, would like to have us do.

I cannot believe that our Father in Heaven enjoys seeing His sons and daughters walking in poverty. I think our Father in Heaven would be pleased if they all prospered and did well enough to live comfortably and decently and properly and have time in their lives to do some of the refining, good things of life.

When you serve the poor, you serve the Master. I have no doubt of that whatever.

"Thou shalt love the Lord thy God with all thy heart, and with all thy soul, and with all thy mind.

"This is the first and great commandment.

"And the second is like unto it, Thou shalt love thy neighbour as thyself" (Matthew 22:37–39).

Who are our neighbors? The people of the world are our neighbors. We no longer live in a little secluded area. We no longer consider ourselves isolated from the world. It is a marvelous thing that we do in sending out missionaries to the far ends of the earth, where they partake of the culture and the systems of the lands in which they live. It has such a tremendous and dramatic effect. They never get over their experiences. They want to be helpful, they want to be generous, and you are affording them an opportunity to be so.

I am so very deeply grateful and touched in my heart by what you are doing. The Lord will love us, I think, to the degree to which we lift and help those in distress. I believe that with all my heart, mind, and soul. The accumulation of means is not a bad endeavor when those means are used to bless the needy of the earth.

I want to congratulate every one of you who have been so

generous and worked so hard to bring about this program of help-fulness across the world. Poverty is everywhere. It is here in this land, and I have seen it here. It is in every other nation under the sun. The Savior said, "For ye have the poor always with you" (Matthew 26:11). We see that in so very, very many places. You are finding them and trying to change that and eradicate that great plague which sweeps over the earth.

I read just yesterday that AIDS has affected 18 million people in Africa, and it is anticipated that it will affect more than 30 million before they get any control of that terrible malady. That comes of ignorance, loss of understanding, and loss of helpfulness. It goes with the picture of being poor in so many, many cases.

Thanks to you, my dear friends. God bless you and give you success is my humble prayer, in the name of Jesus Christ, amen.

# Award Banquet, Sons of the American Revolution*

## November 17, 2000

*The National Society of the Sons of the American Revolution gave President Hinckley its Gold Good Citizenship Award in recognition of his service and acts of good citizenship. President Hinckley was asked to speak at a banquet during which the award was presented to him.*

I AM VERY GREATLY HONORED, my dear friends, by this wonderful award of recognition. You gave me a silver medal of this kind a few years ago. Now you are giving me the gold. You must be running out of candidates. Nonetheless, I count it a very distinct honor and don't quite know how to express the appreciation of my heart for this great recognition, which I shall treasure and look after.

I saw on the invitation to come here tonight that you were invited to wear your medals. I have a few of them, but I think of all that I have, this beautiful gold medal stands at the top. I am so deeply grateful to every one of you.

All of us are proud to be Americans. All of us are proud of the great inheritance and legacy which we have as citizens of this great nation, whose forebears were men and women of courage and tenacity and high ideals and great and marvelous accomplishments.

To me it is an absolute miracle that in spite of what we are going through today, this very day [disputed presidential election results], we have the assurance in our hearts that somehow we'll muddle through, that the United States of America will go on living and growing and being a great power in the earth. We have lawyers in abundance who are appearing before the courts on both sides. Words without end will be spoken in a persuasive way, and I

*delivered extemporaneously

don't know how it is going to come out, but I have total confidence. There isn't a bit of doubt in my mind that out of this trial through which we are going will come the onward rolling of this great and remarkable and most wonderful of all nations upon the face of the earth, this land of which you and I are a part and from whose early forebears there has come down this remarkable heritage.

I never get over what the Founding Fathers of this nation accomplished. I don't care where you go. I don't care what you read. I don't care what the history of other places is, I think it would have been well nigh impossible to have assembled together at one time the group of men who wrote the Declaration of Independence and the Constitution of the United States. In his inaugural declaration, Washington spoke out in behalf of America and said that the people of this land need to worship the God of the land, through whose genius this nation has come to be (see *The Inaugural Addresses of the Presidents of the United States, 1789–1985* [1985], 1–2). I believe that with all my heart. I'm grateful for America. I'm grateful for the things for which she stands.

The president of the United States has been in Vietnam today, and according to TV news, people there were disappointed that he didn't apologize for the war. I don't know how he could have apologized for the war. Fifty-eight thousand Americans gave their lives in that hot and sultry land. Insofar as I am concerned, there is no cause for an apology. I'm so glad that he has taken that position.

We can hold our heads high before the world, my dear friends. We don't have to apologize for America. We're not perfect. We make mistakes. We have problems. We spend an awful lot of time arguing with one another. We have Democrats and Republicans and all that goes with those things. But when all is said and done, as I have traveled over this earth the last couple of years—back and forth, up and down, including to Vietnam recently—I come home and feel like getting down on my knees on the ground and my lips touching the earth of this sweet and good and wonderful land, which has been watched over, as I believe, by the power of the Almighty, that there might be somewhere on earth a nation which would represent His ways, His words, His documents, His system of government.

Thank God for America. Let us so live that we may improve as the years pass, that it may grow ever stronger, that it may shine brighter before all the nations of the earth. For this I pray, and I thank you on this occasion for your great kindness to me. Thank you so very much. God bless our dear land.

# UTAH VALLEY STATE COLLEGE COMMENCEMENT EXERCISES

## APRIL 27, 2001

*President Hinckley was invited to be the keynote speaker at these commencement exercises, during which he and Sister Hinckley were both given honorary doctorate degrees.*

I SALUTE YOU ON THIS very important day. I particularly congratulate you graduates. It is tremendously significant what you have done. You have accomplished what you set out to do. That is a significant thing. In the process you have had a good time in your association with others, and you have learned much. Now ahead of you lies the great challenging season of your lives. Some of you will go on for further study, and I hope that will be good. Some of you will go to work, and that will be a challenge. Most of you will marry, and that will be an adventure.

You are doing today what I have not seen done before. You are honoring two old people.

In June I will celebrate my 91st birthday. Marge and I will commemorate our 64th wedding anniversary this coming Sunday. In all of these years we have experienced very much of what life has to offer—skimpy times and times of prosperity, the rearing of children and grandchildren and great-grandchildren, with all of the challenges incident thereto. There have been times of disappointment and times for celebration.

If you will permit me, I will speak from my generation to yours, with love. If I speak in a personal vein, please forgive me. Standing at this point in my life and looking back, I absolutely marvel at the things we have seen, the events we have experienced, the remarkable and wonderful opportunities we have known. We have tromped and traveled around this world. As I look about, it seems to me that we have been almost everywhere. We have walked on China's great wall; toured Vietnam during its season of intense conflict; seen firsthand the ravages of war; listened to bullets zing past our hotel window during a coup in Seoul, Korea; mourned with the survivors of a deadly shipwreck in the South Pacific; and searched for earthquake victims in Peru.

Such experiences have taken us across the seas south and west and east. The world's sights have been wonderful to behold. We have marveled at the symmetry of Fujiyama in Japan and stood in awe before the transcendent beauty of the great mountains of Switzerland, France, and Italy. We have seen the Taj Mahal by moonlight in India, the orchards of Russia in the bloom of spring, and the rice lands of China at harvest time. We have wandered the pampas of Argentina, looked up at the towering peaks of Bolivia, and walked in the great and beautiful cities of Europe. We have known the splendor of New Zealand, the wide expanse of Australia, the highlands of the Andes, the exotic fauna of the Amazon, and the peaks and plains of every nation in South America.

We love the sights and smells, the grand varieties of culture—with their costumes, customs, and music—eyes dark and light, hair black and blonde, and the incredible range of creativity in everything from architecture to food.

With all that we have seen, the most intriguing thing is the people. We have met them at all economic and social levels. We have been in the shantytowns of the world, among the poor and the distressed, those who will go to bed hungry this night, as they have done every other night of their lives. We have mingled with the affluent and the wealthy, men and women of government and industry, of education and business.

We have learned something through all of these years. We have learned that there is something precious and wonderful about human life wherever it is found, whatever its circumstances. There is born within us an upward reach that constantly struggles for improvement. We are possessed of an ambition to make the best of our circumstances, and most wonderful to behold is a universal spirit of unselfishness in behalf of those in trouble and distress.

A couple of years ago we went to Honduras and Nicaragua when Hurricane Mitch unceasingly, for days, dumped great rolling waves of water upon that area. We saw the mud as high as the tops of the windows in the homes. We witnessed people working together, with shovels and wheelbarrows, assisting one another to dig out the mud and make their homes again habitable. As the floods roared down the valleys, there was a marshaling of enterprise when the people did what they could together, and then they were magnanimously aided by those from other areas of the world, including a very significant contribution from this area.

I have seen parents and relatives struggle, skimp, go without, do whatever is necessary to put their sons and daughters through school, knowing that education is the key to opportunity. I have discovered that life is not a series of great heroic acts. Life, at its best, is a matter of consistent goodness and decency, doing without fanfare that which needed to be done when it needed to be done. I have observed that it is not the geniuses that make the difference in this world. In fact, many of them are in jail for trying to find shortcuts to wealth and opportunity. I have observed that the work of the world is done largely by men and women of ordinary talent who have worked in an extraordinary manner.

And so I say to you on this commencement day, speaking out of an experience of very many years, and with love and a concern in my heart—to you I say, as you go forth from this great institution, wherever life may take you, wherever you may find yourself in the years that lie ahead, regardless of your vocational pursuits, walk the road of simple virtues.

I could wish that all of you would become great and famous people. I would hope that out of this graduating class would come scientists who will dream great dreams and make tremendously significant discoveries. I could wish that out of this class would come powerful political leaders, full of wisdom and foresight to bless the people. I would hope that from your ranks would come leaders of business, education, the professions—every kind of activity that will lead to prosperity and public recognition. Commencement speakers like to talk of these things, to set forth lofty ideals and weave dreams of great accomplishment.

I hope for you the very best that life has to offer, but I hope even more for a few simple things—things that come of the heart, things that come of the spirit, things that come of the divine within each of us.

Is it too simple a thing to wish at commencement that all of you might live lives filled with kindness? We live in a harsh and mean world. It is spoken of as "the jungle." It is often so ruthless, so heartless, so mean and vicious. What a marvelous thing is a little human kindness. A touch of love can do absolute wonders.

I heard of a school teacher once who went into a rural community of the South. She had in her class a little girl who was a dismal failure. She failed at everything. The teacher studied her and reached a conclusion. She concluded there was something wrong with this girl's eyes. On a Saturday, at her own expense, she took the student to a nearby large city. She had her eyes tested. It was evident what her problem was. From her meager purse that teacher bought glasses for her student. She literally changed the course of that girl's life.

I don't want to embarrass Pamela Atkinson, but I think I could count instance after instance where she has reached out in great kindness to those who were in deep trouble and distress.

Be decent. Bring into your lives the miracle of the golden rule: "Therefore all things whatsoever ye would that men should do to you, do ye even so to them" (Matthew 7:12). Women weep in despair as inconsiderate husbands constantly find fault, seeing no good in anything their wives do. I have dealt very much with divorce and troubled marriages. I have come to one conclusion, and that is if we will make the comfort and well-being of our companion our greatest concern, happiness will follow. There are fathers and mothers who destroy their children with vicious criticism that only brings on discouragement and failure. There would be far fewer troubles in the world if there were just a little more common decency among people.

Be honest. It is such a simple thing and yet so very difficult for so very many people. Great is the man, regardless of his other accomplishments, who is known as one of integrity, on whose word all can depend. Said Shakespeare, "To thine own self be true, and it must follow, as the night the day, thou canst not then be false to any man" (*Hamlet,* act 1, scene 3).

Churchill once said that the first victim of war is truth. It seems, in so very many cases, that truth is also the first victim of business and many other activities.

My dear friends, these things are so simple that they scarcely seem worthy of mention. And yet they are the very fabric of life. When all is said and done, when you have lived your life and grown as old as I am, you will recognize that it is the simple virtues that count, that make the great differences in our lives. It is better to sleep at night with a clear conscience than to worry oneself sick while living a fraud.

And so I speak to you today as an old man, talking to you whose lives are ahead of you. I leave with you two verses of scripture, one from the Old Testament and one from the New. From Deuteronomy: "And now, Israel, what doth the Lord thy God require of thee, but to fear the Lord thy God, to walk in all his ways, and to love him, and to serve the Lord thy God with all thy heart and with all thy soul" (Deuteronomy 10:12). And from the book of James: "Pure religion and undefiled before God and the Father is this, To visit the fatherless and widows in their affliction, and to keep himself unspotted from the world" (James 1:27).

When all is said and done, our success in life will not be spelled out in the money we make, in the honors we attain, in the plaudits of men, but in those virtues which become the essence of that which is greatest within each of us.

Think upon that a little. Think of it in terms of what really counts in life, of what builds relationships between people, of what really moves the world forward in peace, and then act accordingly. Observe the simple and seemingly unimportant values, and then the larger virtues will take care of themselves.

Thank you, my dear young friends, and God bless you as you go forward with your lives.

# Rotary International Convention

AUGUST 31, 2001

*Rotary International, one of the world's oldest service organizations, held its annual convention in Salt Lake City in 2001. President Hinckley was invited to address the convention participants from the Tabernacle on Temple Square.*

WELCOME, DEAR FRIENDS, to this old and remarkable—and warm—building. It was constructed by our pioneer forebears as a house of worship and as a place of assembly for good people such as you and good causes such as Rotary International. Many of the great and gifted leaders of the world have spoken from this pulpit. It accommodated the general conferences of our Church for well over a century until we outgrew it.

As you have heard, we have now completed and are using the great new Conference Center built just to the north of us. It seats 21,000 and is the largest structure devoted to religious worship of which I know. But this dear old Tabernacle will continue for the foreseeable future to be the home of the Mormon Tabernacle Choir and the place in which we hold such assemblies as this.

It has been the home of this great choir through most of its history, and *Music and the Spoken Word* has been carried to the nation as a public service for more than 70 years—a remarkable phenomenon in itself. It is the oldest network broadcast on the air. How well I recall the voice of Richard L. Evans, who once served as your international president, as he provided narration for the choir in this historic hall.

I wish tonight to congratulate Rotary International on the

remarkable work it has done in combating the dread disease of polio. I can never forget going to the county hospital in this city to visit a young friend many years ago. He had been stricken with polio and lay helpless in a great iron lung as it wheezed in and out to cause his own lungs to contract and expand. He was totally dependent upon that machine. I stood there with his wife and their three children. He died a few days later.

Polio was once the summer dread of every mother. Now, largely through your efforts, it has been nearly eliminated from the earth. Scientists have produced the vaccine, but you have made it available in many areas of the world. What a tremendous undertaking, and what a great blessing to humankind. The entire world is indebted to you.

But the task is not yet done. There are still cases in remote areas. Now tonight I am pleased to announce that we, as a Church, stand ready to give another $100,000, provided Utah Rotarians will match that amount.

We wish to assist in your "race to the finish" and hope you will never rest until this dread disease is totally eradicated. When that happens, it will mark the completion of a great miracle and a wondrous gift to the human family.

Smallpox is now gone. Once it took whole communities. Measles has gone. Last Saturday I participated in the groundbreaking of a new cancer research hospital on the University of Utah campus in this city. I believe and have confidence that because of this great institution and others like it, the scourge of cancer will be removed from the earth.

I rejoice in the efforts of such men and women as you who have worked and are working so energetically to improve the lot of mankind.

I warmly congratulate President [Richard D.] King on his leadership of this great worldwide organization. I know him, and I know something of what he has accomplished. I likewise congratulate your president-elect, Bhichai Rattakul of Thailand. I became acquainted with this great and good man just over a year ago in his native land. His son, who was educated at Brigham Young University, a Church school, was then the mayor, or governor, of Bangkok. When we were there, they entertained us and our associates in an evening I will always remember with appreciation.

Rotary has always stood for the best in humanity. It has stood for service to others and for kinship across the world among all peoples. No one can adequately measure the consequences of your great efforts. Millions have been blessed. Illness has been avoided. Poverty has been weakened. Because of the vast outreach you have given and the great good you have done, there have been smiles on the faces of those who were downcast.

We know the meaning of this kind of service. We also have done much of this in our humanitarian efforts across the world, far beyond our own membership. President Rattakul could tell you of the teaching done by our people in his land. We have brought new light and understanding, food and sustenance, clothing and shelter, and medical supplies to thousands upon thousands across the earth.

We count you as our brethren and our sisters in a great effort to lift the burdens under which so many struggle, to give food to those in need, to bring health where there has been sickness.

God bless you, you of Rotary, who measure your efforts by Rotarian Herbert J. Taylor's standards. Of the things you think, say, or do, you ask:

1. Is it the truth?
2. Is it fair to all concerned?
3. Will it build goodwill and better friendships?
4. Will it be beneficial to all concerned?

Would that all societies and organizations could live by those measures.

May heaven prosper you in your great undertakings. May we

work together to build a better world where there is less of disease, less of suffering, more of self-reliance, more of integrity.

I hope that while you are in our city that you will have a good time, an unforgettable time; that you will be lifted and inspired by what you see; and that you will wish to return.

Thank you, my dear friends, and God bless you in your tremendous work.

# Fillmore, Utah, Sesquicentennial

SEPTEMBER 8, 2001

*This address was given extemporaneously at a ceremony to
commemorate the sesquicentennial of the founding of Fillmore by
Brigham Young in 1851. President Hinckley's grandfather
Ira N. Hinckley lived in Fillmore with his family in the late 1800s.
He served there as the second president of the Millard stake. The home they
lived in, no longer owned by the Hinckleys, is still in use today.*

T HANK YOU FOR INVITING us to be here, and thank you for your presence. It is so good to come to Fillmore again. I'm delighted and pleased.

When the mayor said something about the fact that you're still here, I was reminded of a sign—an old, weather-beaten sign—that hung by a nail on a fence down in Texas which read:

> Et out by jackrabbits,
> Drowned out by flud water,
> Burned out by drought,
> Sold out by sheriff,
> Still here.

You are still here. I came here this afternoon in 23 minutes, from takeoff at the Salt Lake airport to touchdown at the Fillmore airstrip. When you compare that with the miserable coming here of Brigham Young and Heber C. Kimball and others in 1851, you can't help having in your heart a great sense of appreciation. I came here in Jon Huntsman's plane. He has roots here. One side of his family came here in 1851, and another side in 1853. So we're back onto an area of his roots.

So far as I know, this is the only community in Utah that was established to accommodate the seat of territorial government. Permit me to review a little history with which you are already familiar.

Brigham Young's visit here in 1851 was to choose a site for the capital city of the territory. His party camped on Chalk Creek. The next morning he looked around and then planted his cane on the spot from which a survey of the future city was made. It is very interesting to me that at that time and a little later there was no settlement. So far as I know, and I may be wrong, no plow had ever broken the soil of the Pahvant Valley. But there was water for irrigation. And there was some indication of the fertility of the soil.

A new city was born that day. Four years earlier in the Salt Lake Valley, President Young had planted his cane to mark the site of a temple. Here he planted his cane to mark the site of a new territorial capital. A new county was also created, with the county and the city bearing the two names of the president of the United States, Millard Fillmore. I do not know of another place where this has occurred anywhere in the nation.

Those pioneer men were possessed of great dreams. A large capitol building was planned right over here, with four wings and a central dome. However, only one structure was built, and fortunately that still stands. The political leaders, who were also the Church leaders, decided it was too difficult to come so far, and Salt Lake City again became and has remained the capital city of Utah. But Fillmore was launched. The original company began to plan for housing that winter, and they reported that they found the soil so dry and hard that they could scarcely break the ground for their homes.

Now, as all of you know, and we've been reminded here, my grandfather, Ira Nathaniel Hinckley, was called by Brigham Young in 1867 to go to Cove Creek and build a fort as protection against the Indians. In a period of seven months, with little more than a plumb bob and a spirit level, a hammer, and a saw, he and his associates built the stone fort and the barn. I may say parenthetically that when the Hinckley family reacquired the fort to restore it for presentation to the Church, it took a great deal longer to do the work and cost many times what the original fort and barn had cost.

My father, Bryant S. Hinckley, was taken there as a baby and spent the first 10 years of his life there. It was an exciting place for a small boy. The stagecoach would come in from Fillmore, some 30 miles to the north, or from Beaver, about 20 miles to the south, horses and coach thundering up to the great front gate with the horses frothing at the mouth and the stage passengers anxious for refreshment.

One day he and his brother Ed got hold of the telegraph operator's pistol. It was supposedly not loaded. Ed pulled the trigger and shot Father in the leg. Grandfather sent for the doctor in Beaver, who eventually arrived at the fort. He took a darning needle and probed the wound while Grandfather held the pain-wracked child in his arms. The doctor could not remove the ball, notwithstanding all of the painful probing which he did. Father carried it to his grave at the age of 94. He used to pride himself on the fact that he was the only man ever shot at Cove Fort.

In 1877 Grandfather was called by Wilford Woodruff to serve as president of the Millard Stake of Zion, in which capacity he served until 1902, a period of 25 years. When Grandfather became stake president, there were five functioning wards and three more were added. They covered the membership of the Church in all of this large area.

For a quarter of a century, in all kinds of weather, summer and winter, Grandfather traveled up and down through all the settlements in this valley. He was reputed to have fine horses and an excellent carriage. In fact, in 1878 Jesse N. Smith came here and asked him to go to Arizona with him, where they designated the site of and laid out the city of Snowflake, where we are building a beautiful temple which will soon be dedicated. I do not know whether it was Grandfather's fine carriage and horses or his experience in creating settlements that prompted Jesse N. Smith to invite him to go on this expedition.

In those early days, I am told, he was a well-to-do man, but in complying with the wishes of the presiding Brethren, the stake established an academy—a Church school. He gave generously to this undertaking. It took a very substantial part of his fortune and a good deal of money from others. The attempt was made, but the academy evidently was not unduly successful. The one later established at Hinckley proved more so.

When my father was 85 years of age, I brought him and my children here to Fillmore, and then we went on down to Cove Fort and then on to southern Utah and Nevada. He had lived here in Fillmore from the time he was 10 until Grandfather took some of his children up to the Brigham Young Academy. Today we walked about the town, visiting the museum, noting where he lived as a boy, and walked around the old school where his teacher was his older sister Jean, who married Lafayette Holbrook, who was the clerk in this stake.

This whole area, in those days, was a primitive and difficult place. It was a rough place. It was a difficult place to live. There were the Indians; there were droughts; there were other factors which made it a very hard and difficult place to make a living.

In 1853, two years after the establishment here, the Gunnison Massacre occurred up where Hinckley now stands, where John W. Gunnison and his associates and 96 officers, making a survey of all of this area, were ambushed by the Indians and eight of them were killed.

With some education, Father left Fillmore to work for his brother-in-law, Lafe Holbrook, over in the place where silver had been discovered—Frisco, a little distance west of Fillmore. It was a tough and mean place. It partook of the spirit of all of these frontier settlements, but it was worse because it was a mining community. It sprang up like something out of a desert. Six thousand people eventually lived here. While it was at the height of its activity, there were 23 saloons in the town. As Father described life in Frisco, "On Christmas and holidays if they didn't kill a man before breakfast, it was unusual. And whenever you would hear a shot, everyone would run down to see who was killed."

The school trustees persuaded him to teach in the one-room school. This paid better than the store job, although he continued to work in the post office. However, he soon learned to regret the move he had made. The previous teacher had quit after two weeks, and the one before that had been run out of the district. But he was ashamed of failing. He was ashamed of having to go back and tell his father he was unable to stand up to it. He said he used to walk around nights praying that somehow the school would burn down so that he would have an honorable escape from the responsibility he had undertaken. But the Lord did not answer his prayers with a fire.

One day one of the boys whistled in class. Father reprimanded him. The boy, who was a big fellow, about the same size as his teacher, grabbed a hatchet near the stove and came after Father. The two wrestled, and Father finally got the hatchet. He told the boy to leave the school and not come back.

A few days later the boy's mother came to him to apologize for her son and to ask Father to take him back. He said he would do so only if the entire class voted for him. He then made a plea to the class to extend mercy.

The boy came, and all of the students voted to let him return. That changed the whole picture. That boy became a staunch friend. From that time on, Father had the respect and support of all the students. But the memory of that terrible event stayed with him throughout his life, and I heard him tell of it on several occasions.

But that is not the end of the story. As I remember, many years later Father was taking the train from Salt Lake to Los Angeles. A man came up to him in the Pullman car and asked if he were Bryant S. Hinckley. He then introduced himself as the belligerent boy from Frisco. He said he was now the chief security officer of the railroad. He thanked Father for turning him around, for saving his life from the course he was following, and for planting some ambition within him.

As you know, Karl G. Maeser was sent by Brigham Young to head the struggling Brigham Young Academy in Provo. Grandfather packed supplies in a wagon here in Fillmore and, taking the milk cow, which was tethered behind the wagon, drove some of his children from Fillmore to Provo. Some of them returned to live in Fillmore, but Father never did, although at one time he owned a farm in Hinckley. Karl G. Maeser was a man he came to love and respect. My father went on to teach at BYU, went east to school in New York, came back, and was asked by the First Presidency to head the business college in Salt Lake, in which they had great hopes. It was there he met my mother, who was teaching English and shorthand.

I am grateful for this city. I never lived here, but to this place I trace my roots. It was established as a frontier community. For 150 years now it has held its position as a choice place to live. Its best product has been its families, with children who have been reared here, and from this place they have gone to the ends of the earth, serving in positions of responsibility in the professions, in business, in education, in government, and in the Church. Some left here as young men and gave their lives in the wars that have involved this nation.

Only last Thursday I talked with Dan Bushnell in the Salt Lake Temple. Dan has been a very capable lawyer and litigator, and he is now retired. After retirement he served a mission in Europe and with great difficulty secured the permits to build the temple in Madrid, Spain. Without his skillful efforts and Millard County tenacity, that temple may never have been built. He told me that his grandfather and father lived in Meadow, and this county is the place to which he traces his ancestry and from which he gained his tenacity.

It is well, my dear friends, that on this 150th year you celebrate, remembering those who walked here long ago. This has been home to generations of men and women whose strong character, high values, significant accomplishments, and great faith were virtues planted within their hearts by wonderful parents who were pioneers of Fillmore and Millard County.

To you who are my fellow citizens of this great state, most of whom are of my faith, I salute you and invoke the blessings of the Almighty upon you.

May the future generations who come from this community ever be as strong as their noble forebears. May they hold high the torch of achievement and faith lighted by those pioneers who lived and struggled here a century and a half ago. I so pray with gratitude, invoking the blessings of heaven upon this lovely city and those who dwell here, and do so in the sacred name of Jesus Christ, amen.

# Mormon Tabernacle Choir Concert

## September 11, 2001

*The Mormon Tabernacle Choir was scheduled to give a concert for the National Association of Insurance and Financial Underwriters on this date. Earlier in the day, terrorists hijacked four commercial airplanes and flew two of them into the World Trade Center in New York City. Another plane was flown into the Pentagon in Washington, D.C., and another crashed in a field in Pennsylvania. Approximately 3,000 people died in the attacks. In light of these tragic events, the concert was changed to a memorial service.*

I AM GORDON B. HINCKLEY, President of The Church of Jesus Christ of Latter-day Saints.

Today has been a day that will be remembered always in the annals of our beloved nation. It has been a day when the ugly face of hatred has shown itself with terror, death, and destruction. It has been a day when uncounted numbers of the innocent have perished and their loved ones have been left to sorrow. Many have been wounded, and this, our nation, has been seriously injured and insulted.

Now we welcome you to this historic Tabernacle, a building dedicated to the gospel of peace. The choir and orchestra which make this building their home will entertain you. But in these circumstances we have taken the liberty of asking the choir to alter their program to make of this a sacred memorial service. We hope, dear friends, that you will accord with our request and that you will join with us in the spirit of this solemn occasion.

The choir opened with "The Star-Spangled Banner," our national anthem. The choir will sing other songs of America. But they will also sing songs of consolation, of comfort, of hope, and of assurance.

Our hearts are deeply touched, as are those of all Americans and of free people across the world. This has been a tragic, solemn, and dark day. We have been reminded that evil is still rampant in the world. Its insidious and dastardly hand has struck again in a most reprehensible manner.

The president of our nation has assured us that there will be detection and punishment. But that will not bring back the many whose lives have been taken or salve the pain of those who have been injured.

But dark as is this hour, there is shining through the heavy overcast of fear and anger the solemn and wonderful image of the Son of God, the Savior of the world, the Prince of Peace, the Exemplar of universal love, and it is to Him that we look in these circumstances. It was He who gave His life that all might enjoy eternal life.

May the peace of Christ rest upon us and give us comfort and reassurance, and particularly we plead that He will comfort the hearts of all who mourn, and we ask it in His holy name, even the name of Jesus Christ, amen.

# MEMORIAL SERVICE

## SEPTEMBER 14, 2001

*George W. Bush, president of the United States, declared this day a
national day of prayer and remembrance following the terrorist attacks of
September 11. This memorial service was held in the Tabernacle on Temple
Square and was broadcast to meetinghouses throughout the country.*

OUR HEARTS ARE BROKEN, our spirits subdued. We bow before
the Almighty in reverence and reach out to those who have lost
their lives, to their families, and to those who were wounded in the
attacks made against our beloved nation.

Our treasured land has been brought down into sorrow
through unbelievable acts of infamy. We cannot call back the dead
or ease the pains of the wounded, but at this solemn hour we call
upon our Eternal Father to bring comfort, solace, and reassurance
to those who have suffered much.

The Son of God came to earth and gave His life that all
mankind might have eternal life. It is to Him that we look on this
dark and somber occasion.

May the peace of the Redeemer rest upon us. May His healing
power mend the broken hearts and give strength to the wounded
bodies and minds of all who have paid so great a price because of
the evil acts of those who have injured us and betrayed the entire
civilized world. We also remember before Him those who at this
very hour search the ruins for any who may be alive.

We are profoundly grateful for this good land of America, a
land choice above all other lands. We are grateful for its Founding
Fathers, for its Constitution under which we live, and for the hand

of the Almighty upon this, our beloved country. May the sure hand of Providence guide the destinies of our nation, that it may remain a land of freedom, peace, goodwill, and yet a nation of power and strength, capable of striking its adversaries who would seek to destroy it.

May God bless us with an increased measure of outreaching love and that peace which comes alone from Him.

We pray that our Heavenly Father will hasten the day when men everywhere across this broad earth will "beat their swords into plowshares, and their spears into pruninghooks: nation shall not lift up sword against nation, neither shall they learn war any more" (Isaiah 2:4).

We so pray, in the name of Jesus Christ, amen.

# ANNUAL CONFERENCE OF THE INTERNATIONAL CITY/COUNTY MANAGEMENT ASSOCIATION

SEPTEMBER 23, 2001

*President Hinckley spoke at the opening session of this conference, held in the Tabernacle on Temple Square. In attendance were managers and administrators from cities, towns, and regional entities throughout the world.*

M Y DEAR FRIENDS, it is my genuine pleasure to welcome you to this unique and historic building. It was constructed in the pioneer days of our people as a house of worship. It is a wonderful structure with remarkable acoustic properties. For these many years it has been a gathering place for religious, cultural, and musical performances. It has been the home of this marvelous choir to which you have listened and which you will hear yet further.

A week ago Friday we held prayer and memorial services here. This building was filled to capacity, and the services were carried by satellite to our chapels across the nation. Again on Sunday prayer services were held in thousands of our chapels. We join the people of our beloved nation and civilized people everywhere in mourning, and we pray that the healing power of the Almighty may rest upon us all.

No one knows better than you the great problems which afflict our global society. The catastrophic events which occurred on September 11 remind us that something is seriously wrong in this old world. You are altogether too familiar with many of these problems—crime, pornography, drugs, fatherless homes, the whole litany of ills which have been tearing us apart. You know all about the expense of law enforcement. I am of the opinion—and I feel very strongly about it—that society's problems arise, almost without exception, out of the homes of the people. If there is to be a reformation, if there is to be a change, if there is to be a return to old and sacred values, it must begin in the home, where it can begin with us.

There is no place, no environment more conducive to the development and enactment of virtue than the family. The health of any society, the happiness of its people, their prosperity, and their peace all find their roots in the teaching of children by fathers and mothers.

I was sobered by the report of the Carnegie Task Force on meeting the needs of young children, which painted this dismal picture:

"Our nation's [infants and toddlers] and their families are in trouble. . . . Of the 12 million children under the age of three in the United States today, a staggering number are affected by one or more risk factors that [undermine] healthy development." One in four lives in poverty. One in four lives in a single-parent family. One in three victims of physical abuse is a baby under the age of one. (See *Starting Points: Meeting the Needs of Our Youngest Children* [1994], 3, 4.)

It is so plainly evident that both the great good and the terrible evil found in the world today are the sweet and the bitter fruits of the rearing of children. As we train a new generation, so will the world be in a few years.

We go to great lengths to preserve historical buildings and sites in our cities. We need to apply the same fervor to preserving and strengthening the most ancient and sacred of institutions—the human family!

We cannot effect a turnaround in a day or a month or a year. But with enough effort we can begin a turnaround within a generation and accomplish wonders within two generations—a period of time that is not very long in the history of humanity.

I would like to suggest some specific things we might do to help bring about such a turnaround.

1. Accept responsibility for our role as parents and fulfill our obligations to our children.

Every individual in the world is a child of a mother and a father. Neither can ever escape the consequences of parenthood. Inherent in the act of creation is responsibility for the child who is created. None can with impunity run from that responsibility.

Parents have a sacred duty to rear their children in love and, if you please, righteousness—to teach them to serve one another, to observe the basic commandments of God, and to be law-abiding citizens where they live.

These virtues must be learned at home. Churches can help immensely. Religion is the great conservator of values and teacher of standards. From the days of Sinai to the present, the voice of God has been an imperative voice concerning right and wrong. And when all is said and done, it is parents who have been admonished by God to bring up their children in an atmosphere of spiritual light and truth.

I quote from *U.S. News:* "Probably the best thing that society can do for its toddlers is to make 'parent' an honorable title again. No job is more important, yet no job is more often taken for granted. We teach work skills, but not life skills. . . . Becoming a parent should be . . . a sign of a lasting relationship, not just a passing infatuation; a source of pride, and not remorse. Only then will our children be safe" ("Neglecting Children—and Parents," *U.S. News & World Report,* Apr. 25, 1994, 11).

2. Get married and stay married.

After two years of intense study, the Council on the Family in America reached this conclusion, reported in the *Wall Street Journal:* "American society would be better off if more people got married and stayed married." What a remarkable finding! Nearly any clear-thinking person could have said that without a long and costly study. In support of its conclusion, the study stated that "children who don't live with both parents are more likely to grow up poor, have problems in school and get into trouble with the law." The editorial in the *Journal* concluded, "Marriage may be an imperfect institution, but so far in human history no one has come up with a better way to nurture children in a stable society" ("Married with Children," *Wall Street Journal*, Apr. 25, 1995, A20).

3. Put father back at the head of the home.

More than 40 years ago, the *Reader's Digest* carried an article written by Judge Leibowitz of New York City urging that we "put Father back at the head of the family." In his capacity as judge, the author spent his days listening to evidence and handing down sentences. Out of his vast experience he came to the conclusion that the easiest, the simplest way to reduce delinquency among the young was to put the father back as head of the family. (See Samuel S. Leibowitz, "Nine Words That Can Stop Juvenile Delinquency," *Reader's Digest*, Mar. 1958, 105–7.)

Far too many families have been denied the leadership and stabilizing influence of a good and devoted father who stands at the side of an able and caring mother in quietly training, gently disciplining, and prayerfully helping the children for whom they are both responsible.

4. Recognize and value the supreme importance of mothers.

The home produces the nursery stock of new generations. In that light, I must emphasize the importance, the value, the singular impact that women have within the fabric of our society and in the makeup of our homes. Mothers have no more compelling responsibility—nor any laden with greater rewards—than the nurture given their children in an environment of security, peace, companionship, love, and motivation to grow and do well.

The world needs the touch of women and their love, their comfort, and their strength. Our harsh environment needs their encouraging voices, the beauty that seems to fall within their natures, the spirit of charity that is their inheritance. The God in whom so many of us believe has endowed His daughters with a unique and wonderful capacity to reach out to those in distress, to bring comfort and succor, to bind up wounds and heal aching hearts, and, most of all, to rear children with love and understanding.

The decisions made by the women of this generation will be eternal in their consequences. The mothers of today have no greater opportunity and no more serious challenge than to do all they can to strengthen the homes of the nation.

5. Celebrate and treat children as our most priceless treasures.

The story is told that in ancient Rome a group of women were, with vanity, showing their jewels to one another. Among them was Cornelia, the mother of two boys. One of the women said to her, "And where are your jewels?" Cornelia responded, pointing to her sons, "These are my jewels." Under her tutelage, and walking after the virtues of her life, they grew to become Gaius and Tiberius Gracchus—the Gracchi, as they were known—two of the most persuasive and effective reformers in Roman history. For as long as they are remembered and spoken of, the mother who reared them after the manner of her own life will be remembered and spoken of with praise.

Jenkins Lloyd Jones penned sentiments that bespeak common sense. He said:

"The kid who isn't loved knows it. There is no trauma so excruciating as parental rejection. No other form of human cussedness can more efficiently wreck a human life. Yet there persists the superstition that 'advantages' are a substitute for affection. They aren't.

"The finest of the advantages a family can offer can't be found in a department store, a car dealer's show room or a prep school. The only priceless one is the sense of belonging. Otherwise, the family becomes a combination cafe and dormitory. There's no glue in it" ("Needed: Device to Point Out Unfit Parents," *Deseret News,* July 13, 1968, 12A).

6. Discipline and train children with love.

When I was a boy, our family lived in the city during the school season and on a fruit farm during the summer. On that farm we had a large orchard with a variety of fruit trees. When we were in our early teens, my brother and I were taught the art of pruning. Each holiday and Saturday in February and March, while snow was still on the ground, we would go out to the farm where, with our father, we pruned the trees. We learned that you could, in large measure, determine the kind of fruit you would pick in September by the way you pruned in February. The idea was to prune in such a way that the developing fruit would be exposed to air and sunlight, uncrowded as it occupied its place on the branch of the tree.

The same principle applies to children. An old and true proverb states, "As the twig is bent the tree's inclin'd" (Alexander Pope, *Moral Essays,* in *The Complete Poetical Works of Pope* [1903], 159). The primary place for building a value system is the home. Our children are never lost until we give up on them! Love, more than any other thing, will hold them in the family fold. Punishment is not likely to do it. Reprimands without love will not accomplish it. Patience, expressions of appreciation, and that strange and remarkable power that comes with love and prayer will eventually win through.

The example of wise, fair, honest, and loving parents will do more than anything else in impressing on the minds of children the important principles they need to adopt in their own lives.

7. Teach values to children.

Would not all of society benefit if parents could be counted on to teach time-honored principles and values that rear virtuous individuals and lead to a strong society? What, then, should we teach?

Teach children civility toward others. We have seen in the

barbaric terrorism of September 11 the horrible price of a lack of civility. We can protect America against conflict between ethnic groups or religious or diverse groups of any kind. Let it be taught in the homes of our people that we are all children of God and that as surely as there is fatherhood, there can and must be brotherhood. Conflict among the races and ethnic groups will fade when all of us recognize that we are all part of one great family, valued equally by the Almighty.

8. Teach children to work.

I have no idea how many generations ago someone first said, "An idle mind is the devil's workshop," but it is still true. Children need to learn to work. Ideally, they do this by working with their parents—mopping floors, if you please, mowing lawns, pruning trees and shrubbery, painting, and fixing up and cleaning up and doing a hundred other things whereby they learn that labor is the price of cleanliness, progress, and prosperity. Let children grow up with respect for and understanding of the meaning of labor, of working and contributing to the home and its surroundings, with some way of earning some of their own expense money. Hundreds of thousands of youth in this land are growing up with the idea that the way to get something is to steal it.

A little hard work breeds a greater respect for personal and public property. Graffiti would soon disappear if all those who sprayed it on had to clean it off.

9. Read to and with children.

Television is perhaps the greatest medium ever discovered to teach and educate and even to entertain. But the filth, the rot, the violence, and the profanity that spew from television screens into our homes is deplorable. A study by the American Psychological Association determined that a typical child who begins, at the age of 3 years, to watch 27 hours of TV a week, will view 8,000 murders and 100,000 acts of violence by the age of just 12 years.

I feel sorry for parents who do not read to their young children;

I feel sorry for children who do not learn the wonders to be found in good books. I once read that Thomas Jefferson's upbringing centered on the magnificent phrases of the King James Bible.

Emerson was once asked which of all the books he had read had most affected his life. His response was that he could no more remember the books he had read than he could remember the meals he had eaten, but they had made him. All of us are the products of the elements to which we are exposed.

10. Pray together.

Parents should teach children to pray while they are young. Is prayer such a difficult thing? Would it be so hard for parents to get on their knees with their little children and address the throne of Deity to express gratitude for blessings received and to pray for those in distress, as well as for their own needs?

Can we make our homes more beautiful? Yes, through addressing ourselves, as families, to the source of all true beauty. Can we strengthen our society and make it a better place in which to live? Yes, by strengthening the virtue of our family life through kneeling together and supplicating the Almighty.

Society's problems arise—and you know this more than anyone else—almost without exception, out of the homes of the people. Again, if there is to be a reformation, if there is to be a change, if there is to be a return to old and sacred values, it must begin in the home, with parents instilling within children the virtues that will make them into strong, contributing members of society.

That home may be simple, ever so poor. It may be in a poor neighborhood, but with a good father and a good mother, it can become a place of wondrous upbringing. Sam Levenson tells of growing up in a crowded New York slum where the environment was anything but good. Here his mother reared her eight precious children. He said, "The moral standard of the home had to be higher than that of the street." His mother would say when they acted inappropriately, "You are not on the street; you are in our home. This is not a cellar nor a poolroom. Here we act like human beings" (*Everything But Money* [1966], 145).

It is within families that respect for others is best learned, integrity is cultivated, self-discipline is instilled, and love is nurtured. It is at home that we learn the values and the standards by which we guide our lives. It is at home that we come to determine what we will stand for.

You are those who deal with the bitter fruits that come of broken and anchorless homes. You have in your positions of influence the capacity and the opportunity to bring about a change. I challenge you to try. God bless you, my dear friends, I pray in the name of my Lord, even Jesus Christ, amen.

# Los Angeles World Affairs Council

JUNE 12, 2002

*This was the third time President Hinckley was invited to address the Los Angeles World Affairs Council. More than 2,000 people were in attendance, including diplomats, professors, government officials, media representatives, and religious leaders of many faiths. A question- and-answer session followed, with questions submitted by the audience.*

THANK YOU SO MUCH. Ladies and gentlemen, it is a wonderful pleasure to be with you again. I have been here twice before. I do not know why you invited me back. I am getting so old I feel like an antique. This is a very competitive evening, with the Lakers playing. I do not know the score, or I would give it to you. Well, you honor me with your presence, and I am very, very grateful.

I have wondered what to say to you. I have thought about it a great deal. I have concluded that I would talk about two groups which we in this Church are trying to help and put to work.

The first is the elderly.

Life is stressful. It is so highly competitive. As people move along, they look to retirement. They yearn for an escape from the dreadfully demanding regimens of their vocational pursuits. They get weary of the fight.

Fortunately, for most there are retirement plans, the benefits of which, when coupled with Social Security, provide the means whereby they can rest when they reach 60 or 65. Those who have never traveled dream of going to faraway places with strange-sounding names. Others envision a motor home or some such arrangement under which they can get about and see the country. Yet others may be inclined to sit and think—or to just sit. In any event, we now have great numbers who are retiring. They have skills and capacity. But they are tired of what they have been doing. For a short time, they may enjoy following their dreamed-of pursuits. But they quickly discover that these are not very satisfying. What is there to do? Join a bridge club and endlessly pass the hours? No. Let me tell you of some of the great and challenging opportunities we are offering to such people and of literally thousands who are taking advantage of these opportunities.

Recently on a trip to Brazil we stopped overnight in Jamaica to meet with our people there. I think it was the first time a President of the Church had ever been there. At the airport, as we came through customs and immigration, were two wonderful women. One is from Los Angeles. Each is a widow. Each has reared a family to maturity. Each volunteered for missionary service without indicating where she might go or what she might do. They were assigned to Jamaica, and there they are performing a marvelous work. They are teaching, lifting, encouraging those who have felt they had very small opportunity in the world.

As I shook hands and conversed with Norma Hall and Erva Fredericksen, I asked them if they were having a good time. They said they were having the time of their lives. They have found that they are needed. They have discovered that they can help. They have learned that someone depends on them. They have come alive in their declining years. They love what they are doing. About the only fear they have is that all of this will come to an end before too long. When that happens, there can be a short time of rest and relaxation and then another opportunity. Their health is better because they are actively engaged. They had never known one another before, but they have become fast friends. They are making a contribution.

About four years ago I went to Ho Chi Minh City, formerly Saigon, where I went many times during the war. I then traveled up to Hanoi and there had a meeting with a few of our people who are there. Among them were two retired doctors—brothers. One was from Utah, the other from Idaho. After long and busy careers, they had closed their practices and set aside their instruments. But idleness soon became boring. They volunteered for missions. They must have felt a little uneasy when they received calls to go to Vietnam. But they went and were doing a remarkable service, one of them using his specialty in establishing a neonatal clinic and the other in general practice. They were now lost in the problems of their patients, using all of their energy and resources to heal broken bodies and fractured minds.

In Bangkok we were honored at a delightful dinner at the Hyatt Hotel, as guests of the mayor of Bangkok. The public schools are run by the city. That evening he wished to pay respect to some 20 or so older people who were serving missions for this Church in teaching English to the Thai children. This knowledge will be of priceless benefit to those children as they grow and move into the world of commerce. The mayor could not say enough for these capable and devoted women who, for the most part, had been public school teachers and who were now giving of themselves to the teaching of English as a second language to the young people of Thailand.

We talked with these women. At home they had little or nothing to do. Some lived in rest homes. They had been members of sports clubs and physical-fitness groups. Now, responding to calls from the Church, they were serving in that distant land among a strange people whom they had come to know and love. They bubbled over with enthusiasm. They were useful. They knew they were accomplishing good.

We now have altogether some 5,300 retired men and women serving in a meaningful missionary capacity for this Church throughout the world. The number is growing. They go where they are called. They serve where they are needed. Friendships are established; skills are shared; opportunities are opened for those who will never forget the men and women who have come among them in a spirit of entire unselfishness to teach and do good. They receive no money. They go at their own expense. The measure of their devotion is unlimited. The fruits of their efforts are beyond calculation.

We maintain in Salt Lake City a tremendous family history resource. This organization has satellite facilities throughout the nation and abroad. Such a facility is right here in Los Angeles. Some 424 volunteers work in these institutions to assist those who desire to know of their family roots.

Volunteer service is the genius of this Church. We now have over 26,000 congregations scattered over the world. Every one is presided over by a man who serves with two counselors on a volunteer basis. This same spirit, this work, reaches out to the elderly and brings a feeling of security, of usefulness, of service that brightens their lives and gives them a sense of making a great contribution.

On the way home from South America the other day, we stopped at Trinidad to meet with some of our people. A couple had come over from the island of Grenada. The man is a very successful Idaho farmer. He cultivates some 30,000 acres. He runs a tremendous operation. But he was tired and decided to slow down and let his brothers and his boys see what they could do with the farm. He volunteered for a mission call and today presides over our work in Grenada under the direction of a mission president, who also serves on a volunteer basis as head of the work, with headquarters in Trinidad.

Another retired Idaho potato farmer was sent to Minsk, Belarus, a part of the former Soviet empire. He was surprised at the low potato yield. He asked for a piece of ground. He used the fertilizer available to all other farmers in the area. He used the same equipment. And with his knowledge he produced a harvest 11 times greater than that of neighboring farmers. They could not believe it.

When he returned home, he sent, at his own expense, potato harvesting equipment such as they had never seen before. It was a gift of love for the people among whom he had served.

Now, I know, of course, that there are many other volunteer groups doing a great service in the world. There is the Peace Corps, and there are other organizations like it. But I know of no other organization which so harnesses the abilities, the capacities, and the willingness of retired men and women in an organized program of Christian service in many areas of the world.

These people are experiencing in a very real way the promise of their Master, the Lord Jesus Christ, who said, "Whosoever shall lose his life for my sake and the gospel's, the same shall save it" (Mark 8:35).

Some years ago I was in the Philippines, down in Cebu. We had convened a conference. I saw in the congregation an American and his wife. I had known them previously when he was a stake president, a leading officer of the Church, in New York City. At that time he worked for Union Carbide. He was a well-paid chemist and, as I understand, largely responsible for the discovery of Prestone. At the close of the meeting in Cebu, I said, "What are you doing here?"

He said, "We are having the time of our lives." They told me their story.

When he was about to retire, they said to themselves, "What are we going to do? We still have our health. We still have some ability. Let's make ourselves available to the Church to use us wherever they wish." They received a call, and then, as they related, "We sold our home. We gave our children what furniture they wanted and gave away the rest. We found ourselves left with a few clothes, some private records, and our retirement income. We even gave away our car.

"The Church called us to come here, and here we are." They were living in a small apartment, altogether about the size of their New York living room. They had previously known nothing of the Filipinos. Now they were working among them, lifting their sights, giving them understanding, building their faith in a great cause and faith in themselves. They were doing a wonderful work and having a wonderful time.

They have since served in other areas in various parts of the world. They are now growing old and somewhat handicapped, but they have rich and wonderful and nurturing memories—not just of the days when he was a great chemist, but of more recent years when they have been out serving among those who needed their help so urgently.

These volunteers include retired medical doctors, educators, farmers, business executives, and the garden variety of ordinary good people.

My dear friends, I speak to you of a reality. Caring for the elderly has become one of the great social problems of our time. Of course they reach an age when they cannot do very much. I can testify of that. But there are years between retirement and that age when they can play around doing things that really lead nowhere or they can give their great talents, the fruits of many years of marvelous experience, to lift and help people. They become concerned with others less fortunate and work to meet their needs. And they say, "What a great time we are having!" They finish one duty and volunteer for another, time after time. I know of one couple now on their eighth such mission. God bless them for their great and dedicated service.

I could go on a long time with you concerning this wonderful program which touches for good the lives of people in a hundred different ways and a thousand different circumstances. But I shall leave it and speak to you of another group facing serious challenges: some of the world's poverty-ridden young people.

By way of introduction, let me share a bit of our history. In the pioneer days of our Church, when our people were gathering from the lands of Europe and the British Isles, many of them were poor. The journey across the ocean was long, then all the way to the Salt Lake Valley in the Rocky Mountains. It was difficult, and it was costly. Many wanted to come, thousands. The Church organized what came to be known as the Perpetual Emigration Fund. It established an endowment, the earnings from which provided funds to those wishing to gather with their people. When they arrived, they went to work. As they were able to earn, they repaid the loan, and this money was used to make it possible for others to emigrate. It was a perpetual revolving fund that brought some 30,000 people to gather in the western area of the United States.

There were some failures; of course there were. There were some who did not repay the loans. But on balance, it was a tremendous success. The forebears of some of the strongest families in the Church today came to their Zion by means of this Perpetual Emigration Fund.

Now we come down a century and a half to our day. We found a problem existed. We have many young men and women in third-world countries, in the underprivileged nations of the earth. They are good and able and bright, but they live in poverty, as have generations of their people before them. Many of these young people have served missions for the Church. While doing so they have learned to speak English. As they served as companions of young men and women from the United States and Canada, their ambitions were awakened. Their sights were raised. Then they were released after 18 months or two years, and they soon found themselves back in the same condition of poverty out of which they had originally come.

We pondered this problem. We prayed about it. A year ago April, in our general conference, I announced that we were undertaking a new program patterned after the Perpetual Emigration

Fund of our forebears. We would call it the Perpetual Education Fund. We would invite our people to make contributions to this fund on a strictly volunteer basis. Hopefully we would establish a substantial corpus and set up a simple organization under which loans would be made to deserving young men and women by which they could acquire an education. We knew that education is the key to unlock opportunity.

We would not give them money. Growth seldom comes of handouts. We all value that which comes of effort and sacrifice.

These young people would not be brought to the United States for training. They would go to educational institutions in their own lands—in fact, in their own communities. Research had shown that there were good schools available right in their own backyards.

I sent out an invitation in our conference, to Church members who wished to do so, to voluntarily contribute to this fund. We started with nothing. Contributions have been received from a quarter of a million people, ranging from very small donations to donations in five figures.

Many donations have come from children. One family donated money they had worked all year to earn with the intent of purchasing snowmobiles. The five children each earned $1,000, but when they heard about this program, they donated it all to the Perpetual Education Fund. They concluded that they could get along without snowmobiles and that greater good would come from such a contribution.

Some whose ancestors were helped by the Perpetual Emigration Fund, after which this fund was patterned, have tried to pay what they thought their ancestors in the 19th century borrowed. A substantial number who are not members of the Church have also contributed to this fund.

In the little more than a year that has elapsed since the first announcement, we have, without touching the corpus, earnings enough to provide loans to more than 3,000 individuals.

We placed in charge of the program a very able California lawyer with extensive business experience who was ready for retirement. He gladly shouldered the burden and indicates he has never had a more challenging responsibility or one which has made him happier.

Assisting him is a retired Ford Motor Company financial executive with broad international experience. He too is having a wonderful time.

And so today, only 14 months after that first announcement, we have made loans to 720 young people in Brazil, 696 in Chile, 338 in Peru, 194 in Mexico, 523 in the Philippines, and 634 in other countries, making a total of 3,105 as of the first of June. I am confident the number will rise dramatically.

The interesting thing is this costs the Church nothing. Everyone who is working on it is doing so on a volunteer basis. It is soundly financed and operating in a businesslike way.

What will be the result? A boy from Mexico, for instance, whose forebears have lived in poverty for generations, will be enabled to rise out of that quagmire. He will become skilled. He will have good employment. He will marry and rear a family. He will go on and serve in positions of leadership in the Church. He and the generations after him will be blessed beyond measure, and the Church of which he is a member will be assured of generations of strong and able leaders in that land.

I was recently in Mexico and met with President Vicente Fox of Mexico, who expressed deep concern for those of his people in poverty. What a wonderful thing, what a marvelous thing to be able to light a candle by which to brighten the way of those with intellectual capacity to move out of the darkness when given an opportunity. As that happens, they will return that money to assist another, and so it will go on in perpetuity.

Let me give you, in their own words, two or three expressions. This from a young man in Concepción, Chile:

"I have felt frustrated and inadequate to provide my future family a better economic state and at the same time a spiritual surrounding. All my life I have fought mediocrity. My feelings for the Perpetual Education Fund are those of gratitude to the Lord. This is a great blessing for so many of us, not only from Chile but in all Latin American countries. Today I can change the future and give something better to my children. Thanks to all who have made this possible."

This from a young man in Colombia who is studying to become a computer systems network technician:

"When I was serving my mission, many of the members and even the investigators would ask me about my goals after my mission. Without hesitating I would always respond, 'I'll go to school, work, and get married.' Then, when I was in the apartment with my companion, the truth would come out. I told my companion that it would be too difficult for me, that I could never have the money to do it. My good companion would try to encourage me by saying that the Lord would help me somehow if I were just patient. Still, it seemed hopeless.

"The Perpetual Education Fund was an answer to my companion's faith and the prayers of many others. Now I am achieving that dream. I am attending one of the best schools in my city. My desires and motivation are higher than ever. I can see how I will be able to help my family, the Church, and others, and I will return in many ways the assistance given me. I am so grateful once again to see the fulfillment of the Lord's promise to always protect His sheep."

This from a young man in Brazil. He is now 27.

"I came home from my mission six years ago and eventually found a wonderful wife. However, all my efforts to gain an education were frustrated. The free courses I took were ineffective, and the good courses were expensive and therefore totally inaccessible. When the Perpetual Education Fund was announced, it gave me new hope about becoming self-reliant, about having a promising career. Today I am in training to become a radiology technician thanks to a loan from the fund. After my graduation I will find a job that will give me the time and money to take care of my family and serve better in the Church."

The list of educational programs for which loans were approved in the last meeting of the loan committee includes auto mechanic, banker, clothing maker, computer network systems engineer, computer maintenance, computer programmer, electronic technician, environmental technician, foreign commerce, hair stylist, hotel administration, marketing and sales specialist, Microsoft certified systems engineer, natural-gas technician, nurse, nutritionist, pathology-lab technician, pilot, Portuguese translator, radiology technician, secretary, telecom technician, Web technician.

I know my time is up. But can you get the wonderful vision of this thing?

I have spent much time in the Philippines, in the nations of South America, Central America, Mexico. I have seen the poverty, the utterly hopeless condition of so very many who are born, live, and die without rising above the level of those who have gone before them for generations.

I am profoundly grateful for what we are able to do. I am excited. I am optimistic. The pattern of that success was established 150 years ago. It is now being repeated, with a different application, in our day and time.

Of course, it is necessary to hand out food to those in need. They are in distress. They need help, and we are extending a great deal of help through our humanitarian services program. But it is an even greater thing to strike fire in the minds of the coming generation to walk out of the swamp of the past into a new day and a great future. The Lord being our Helper, we are making it happen.

Thank you very much, ladies and gentlemen.

*Question:* There are several questions here on your position or the Church's position on what is going on in the Middle East. What position do you believe the United States should take in the conflict between Israel and Palestine? Do you have any special insight into it? How does the Church feel about its Jewish neighbors and its Islamic neighbors?

*President Hinckley:* Well, of course, we regret very seriously what is going on in that part of the world. We have a wonderful facility in Jerusalem, the BYU Center for Near Eastern Studies. We have had to shut it down because of the conflict there. I hope, I pray with all my heart that something might come to pass to bring about a reconciliation of those two warring, quarreling neighbors. Both want a place to live. Both want peace. Both want to be able to live their lives without disturbance. I am convinced of that. I have been there, walked with both sides. I have great respect for them and hope and pray that somehow, somehow, with the help of the United States and anybody else in this world who can do so, there might come greater understanding and a greater desire to live together in peace. I think it will happen. I hope it will happen. I have confidence that it will happen, and hasten the day is the only thing I can say to that.

*Question:* Questions generally concerning the war on terrorism—would you please give us your thoughts. Also, has the terrorist activity throughout the world affected the missionary activities of the Church in any way?

*President Hinckley:* Of course, we are all affected. Our lives are changed because of what happened September 11. It is just amazing to me what has taken place in this country as a result of that dastardly act. We all regret it; of course we do. We mourn with those whose lives were lost. We stand behind the government in its effort to reduce entirely in this land any terrorist acts. It will not change, I am afraid, until a change comes in the hearts of men. And that is our job; that is our responsibility—to do everything we can. This spirit, this destructive spirit, comes of ignorance, of misunderstanding, of poverty and want and such factors as that. We have a great challenge, every one of us, regardless of our religious inclinations. We all have a challenge to do everything that we can to spread understanding and education and goodwill—as I have indicated, something to lift people out of poverty so that we might live together as peoples of the earth, all sons and daughters of God who treasure and love life.

Now, you ask if it has affected our missionary program? No, not noticeably in any way to date.

*Question:* The Roman Catholic Church has been rocked by the allegations of sex abuse—child sex abuse—by members of its leadership. Last week there was an allegation made against your Church. How does the LDS Church deal with child abuse cases amongst its leadership?

*President Hinckley:* Well, I suppose any large body has some such problem. We have done everything we know how to do. We have established a help line. We ask every local Church officer—bishop, stake president, whatever—if he runs across a case of this kind to immediately call that help line so that we can get professional help wherever it is needed. We have put out literature. We have never had, so far as I know, any officer of the Church involved in this practice, but we have had a few members of the Church. In most cases, they have been excommunicated from the Church long before any action was brought against us. And we are trying to do everything we know how to. But when all is said and done, our problem is really minor compared to the problem which our friends the Catholics are facing these days. Tomorrow, particularly, they will be in Dallas to consider this matter. It is a very, very serious thing.

Why cannot we live together more peaceably? Why cannot we respect one another? Why cannot we live up to the faith of our fathers? Why cannot we follow the dictates of the gospel of Jesus Christ or in the highest ideals of Jewry? Why cannot we live better than the way we live? We are trying to do everything we know how to do to achieve that.

*Question:* Several questions regarding temples—would you comment on the unique significance of the rededication of the Nauvoo Temple? Would you also talk about Kirtland? Could you talk about Jerusalem?

*President Hinckley:* I could talk a very long time about that, but I have a meeting at seven o'clock tomorrow morning. As you know, we are a temple-building people. When our people in Nauvoo constructed the Nauvoo Temple, it was a beautiful building. It has been classed time and time again as the finest structure then in the state of Illinois. They were driven out of that city by intolerant neighbors, and they had to leave that temple. It was set on fire by an arsonist. It was later blown down in a storm and destroyed. But it had been the great achievement of their efforts, the great thing to which they had looked forward.

Now we are 150 years past, and we are going to build some temples. It was my desire to get a temple within reachable condition of all of our people throughout the world, so we have built them everywhere—12 of them in Mexico and several in South America and other places. At the close of our October conference in 1999, I simply announced that we would rebuild the Nauvoo Temple, and somehow the whole Church went wild with that announcement. Well, the temple is now complete. It has been open to visitors. The last count that they had was a week ago that 170,000 people had passed through that temple. I think before we close it to public showing that there will be some 300,000 who will have the opportunity of going through it and seeing it. We will dedicate that temple on the 27th of June, the end of the month. It will then become to us the sacred house of the Lord to be used by members of the Church in their services. It will no longer be open to the public, but until then anyone who wishes to see it, to examine it, to ask questions about it may go in every part of it and is welcome to do so. As I indicated, so very many have done so.

This will be the 113th working temple of the Church. It is a beautiful building. No expense has been spared in constructing it. And the marvelous and wonderful thing is that a very, very substantial part of the cost of that reconstruction has come of contributions made by members of the Church who wish to see that building constructed and built and in service. It will be a wonderful thing. Nauvoo is an out-of-the-way place now, so it is hard to get to. But people will go there; we are satisfied of that. I am sure they will. They go wherever we do things. They will go there. We are happy that it is there. I repeat, it is a magnificent building. Now, what else do you want to know about temples?

*Question:* We'll change just a little bit. We have several again here on missionary work and the Church's presence primarily in Asia, with questions on China, India, Pakistan, in particular, and for good measure, someone also asked about Cuba.

*President Hinckley:* We are a proselyting Church. We send out missionaries. This is a volunteer service. We have 60,000 plus missionaries laboring all over the world in about 150 nations, in many languages. And they give service of 18 months for young women, two years for young men. They are doing a tremendous job. We have training centers in various parts of the world, some 16 of them, where they may go and receive a short time of training before they actually go into the field. It represents a tremendous program, even outside of the religious purpose which we are trying to serve. It does something very remarkable. At a time when a young man is most likely to think only of himself, in a selfish way, he loses himself in the service of others. And that transformation is a remarkable and wonderful thing.

As a young man I served a mission in the British Isles. I have never lost my love for Britain. I know the British are stuffy and difficult—is anybody from Britain here?—but nobody could ever sell me short on the British. I love the British because I worked among them—not as a tourist, but in their homes and among good people whom I came to love and treasure and admire very highly. I have a son who served in Germany. I have another son who served in Argentina and then went to Spain.

And so it goes. They learn languages. One of the great assets we have that contributed to the 2002 Winter Olympics in Salt Lake City was the capacity of many returned missionaries to speak so many languages and to speak them with fluency. Without hesitation our people responded in a remarkable and wonderful way. Now, there were others who were not members of the Church who also responded; I want to make that clear. But I think it can be said without any controversy that our contribution because of the language knowledge of these people and their acquaintance with the nations across the world rendered a tremendous volunteer service which helped make the Winter Olympics as highly successful as they were.

*Question:* Questions here on humanitarian aid by the Church—have you been able to get humanitarian aid into Afghanistan and also into the other areas of the Middle East?

*President Hinckley:* Yes. We have sent materials to Afghanistan. We try to send humanitarian aid wherever it is needed. We have a shipment of material on its way right now to Central America, where they have had such terrible flooding. We are sending emergency supplies by air and a great quantity of other goods by ship in order to alleviate the suffering. To help people across the world in the last few years, we have given more than $90 million of humanitarian aid, sent by this Church to people who are not members of this Church in many parts of the earth—Africa, Central America, Mexico. Out of the generosity of our people have come the funds necessary to do this. I think I can say that we have done our part and done it in a very free-handed way for the blessing of thousands and tens of thousands across the earth who find themselves in distress.

We work with the Catholics. We work with whatever agency is doing the best job in order to get it there in a most expeditious manner, because time is of the essence when people are in need.

*Question:* What is the difference between The Church of Jesus Christ of Latter-day Saints and the other churches in the Christian world?

*President Hinckley:* Of course not everybody agrees with us. We know that. We accept that. We do not try to push our religion down the throats of people. I say this: If you and your church have something of good, bring it with you, and let us see if we can add to it. That is the principle under which we operate.

Let me put it this way. This is our belief: We believe there was an apostasy in the Middle Ages. That is why the Protestants broke away and did everything that they did to protest against those practices. And out of that came the various Protestant churches, for the most part. We say that ours is not a reformation but a restoration. That is the difference—a restoration of the ancient Church as established by the Lord, restored to earth in our day and time.

*Question:* As the President of the Church, does your relationship with God differ from that of other Mormons, and does your position of authority supercede any of the previous prophets?

*President Hinckley:* I do not think so. I just want to say this: I think we are a great democratic people. I love my friends in this Church. I think I can say that I love humanity. I have been around the world time and again. I have been in nation after nation on every continent. I have served for a long time. I think I can say that I love a family in Africa as dearly as I love a family in Salt Lake or Los Angeles. I believe that with all my heart. I do not consider myself superior to anyone. I think I have a unique calling, but in furthering that calling, I hope I do not appear to be standoffish, above everybody else, or anything of the kind. I have appreciated this evening these people who came up in large numbers and wanted to shake hands and to take pictures. There are altogether

531

too many cameras in the world. But I hope that I can consider my people as my friends, my brothers and my sisters, my equals before the Lord in carrying forth His program. The great genius of this Church is work. Everybody works. You do not grow unless you work. Faith, testimony of the truth is just like the muscle of my arm. If you use it, it grows strong. If you put it in a sling, it grows weak and flabby. We put people to work. We expect great things of them, and the marvelous and wonderful thing is they come through. They produce.

*Question:* President Hinckley flew in here from Salt Lake just before tonight's meeting and is going back to Salt Lake immediately after the meeting because he does have a seven o'clock meeting tomorrow morning. So before we close the program, let me ask this two-part question. These are the hardest of the evening, President Hinckley.

*President Hinckley:* Are they really? Why don't you say amen right now?

*Question:* Where is Sister Hinckley? Or is she a Laker fan?

*President Hinckley:* Sister Hinckley is home. I hope she is asleep. Well, she is 90 years of age, and I am 92, practically. So I thought I had better just come down here very quickly and find out what the Lakers did, have some chicken, talk to you a little, try to answer your questions, and go back home. My daughter is with her tonight, so she is in good hands.

Thank you. Thank you very, very much.

# University of Denver,
## "Bridges to the Future"

APRIL 22, 2003

*This address was part of the inaugural year of "Bridges to the Future,"
which has become an annual series of lectures and other events
at the University of Denver and Colorado State University.
The theme for the series in 2002–2003 was "American History
and Values in Light of September 11th."*

I AM GRATEFUL FOR THE opportunity to be with you. I hope I can measure up to the challenge to express a few thoughts on the mammoth undertaking of building bridges to the future.

I am an old man now. I will be 93 on my next birthday. You ask, "What future is there for you?"

I live in a downtown apartment. But I have a little hideaway, a small house in the country surrounded by trees. I planted a number of Colorado blue spruce last week. They are very small now, but in 20 years they will be magnificent. There is something within me that makes me plant trees each spring. That impulse has been with me since I was a boy and lived on a fruit farm in the summer. Now, I think of what someone said: "A society grows great when old men plant trees in whose shade they will never sit."

I hope I can assist in building bridges—bridges I will likely never walk across but which will be crossed and appreciated by many.

I lived in Denver long ago. I worked for the Denver and Rio Grande Western Railroad, the D&RGW. Using those initials, people sometimes called it "Delayed and Rapidly Growing Worse." But it was really a great institution. We operated two lines westbound out of Denver. The first went from Denver down to Pueblo and then turned west and followed the Arkansas River. At one place where there was a deep and narrow gorge, there was no room for a railroad track. The construction engineers supplied one by literally suspending a bridge from the sheer walls of the steep canyon. It was an engineering feat of great wonder. The trains stopped here to permit the passengers to get out and look at this marvel. That bridge became a bridge to the future of the railroad.

The other line, which came along later, went up through the Moffat Tunnel and from there on to Grand Junction. That too was an engineering marvel.

I learned some very important and meaningful lessons when I worked for the railroad. That was in the days of steam locomotives, and those great, thunderous, and marvelous machines pulled long trains through the night. Those engines were hard-riding giants of power whose headlights combed the canyons of the Arkansas and Colorado Rivers, permitting the engineer to see the 500 or 600 feet of track that were constantly ahead of his engine all through the dark night. He did not have to worry about reaching his final destination. He had only to worry about that which lay in the light of his headlamp.

There is a great lesson in that for all of us as we think of building bridges for the future. We can have great dreams, wonderful concepts. But in the actual process of achieving those dreams we are limited in our foresight. However, for every foot that we move we extend our reach another foot beyond, out into the unknown.

I learned another great lesson. One day a freight train derailed in a very narrow gorge of the Colorado River. The line was blocked. There was no room to run a track around the wreck. Loaded cars filled with valuable freight were scattered along the right of way.

There was only one solution: push the derailed cars into the river. Sacrifice the freight, repair the tracks, and open the line. Otherwise, you simply shut down the railroad. I learned that a wreck can become a very costly thing, but it will be more costly to do nothing but wring your hands. You will soon find yourself out of business. You make the best of the situation, no matter the cost, and move forward.

One of my treasured possessions is a beautiful brass bell from a D&RG locomotive, presented to me in 1995 by the president of the railroad as an expression of appreciation.

Now the D&RG is gone. The Union Pacific has it all. It is the survivor in the history of railroads in this western country.

Events of history have always led to significant change. Such an event was the terrible tragedy of September 11, 2001, which must ever be remembered as a day of infamy. It was a mean and devilish attack on the United States. I think the people of a majority of the nations of the world sympathized with us on that occasion.

There followed the war on the terrorists, chiefly in Afghanistan. And out of that conflict grew the present conflict—war on Iraq against a tyrannical regime. The cities of Iraq have now been occupied. But terrible problems remain. We have won the war, and we now face the perplexing challenge of winning the peace.

This conflict has brought anger against America from those who have been our allies and our friends. As a nation we must build bridges to cross these rivers of bitterness. There will be a need for great statesmanship, magnanimous trust, and absolute integrity on our part.

But there are bridges which we must build not only outside but also within our nation—important bridges, without which there will be increasing national decay.

I love this great land of which we are a part. My work has taken me all over this world. I have flown across the seas—south, west, and east. I have worked on every continent. I love the beauties of the earth in all their diversity. I likewise love the peoples of the world. I believe this world and its people to be the creations of Jehovah, and I delight in their diversity.

I love them all, but most of all I love America, on whose soil I was born.

I love the people of this land and particularly the youth. I have met with them across the continent—hundreds of thousands of them. They are bright and beautiful. They have a certain vitality and strength. They have foresight and ambition. They have goals and objectives. What a wonderful generation they are, so very, very many of them.

And yet there are so many millions of others who have fallen between the cracks and whose lives are like smoking candles from which the flame has been blown. Many in this gathering tonight are scarcely aware of them. But they are out there, millions of them all about us. They have lost their dreams. They seem to have no purpose. Their lives lead to a dead end. They are the bitter fruit of broken families and fractured homes. Most of them have no fathers of whom they know.

In my judgment, the greatest challenge facing this nation is the problem of the family, brought on by misguided parents and resulting in misguided children. Though it did not begin with 9/11, the events of that day spoke to all of us of the necessity of strong and supportive families. The strengthening of the home is of paramount importance in building bridges for the future.

The family is the primary unit of society. I believe it was designed by the Almighty. A nation will rise no higher than the strength of its families.

The children of broken homes look for identity. They want to be a part of something. In their quest, so many of them turn to gangs. Here they swagger and fight. They steal and plunder. They kill and are killed. The spectacle of children killing children is an abhorrent and terrible thing. It leads inevitably either to death or the dead end of incarceration.

America now has two million of its citizens in prisons—more than any other nation on earth. The cost of building facilities, of maintaining them, of feeding and clothing and guarding the inmates is staggering. All of those inmates are the products of homes—the place where behavior is learned, where standards are taught, where values are established. The path that led to incarceration in so very many cases began in childhood.

It isn't the place, the real estate, that determines the quality of the home. It isn't the opulence of the dwelling or the race or the brilliance of the occupants. In most cases it's the parents that make the difference. It's the man and the woman who are responsible for the children. And to put it bluntly, too many of them are cop-outs.

As we contemplate the future, I see only a small chance of improving our values system unless we can strengthen the sense of responsibility and acceptance of the vital truth that fatherhood and motherhood carry with them tremendous and lifelong obligations. Let us begin to teach with increasing sincerity and skill the wondrous beauty of parenthood, the joy of bringing new life into the world, and the imperative of guiding and sustaining that life to make it meaningful and productive. One of my great predecessors was wont to say, "No other success can compensate for failure in the home" (David O. McKay, quoting J. E. McCulloch, *Home: The Savior of Civilization* [1924], 42; in Conference Report, Apr. 1935, 116).

Much of what happens in life is a matter of attitude. There is no greater responsibility on this earth than that of being parents to children. It is a responsibility that comes from the God of heaven Himself. As is apparent, it can be an experience of infinite beauty.

The divorce rate in our country is alarming. Today 43 percent of all first marriages end in divorce or separation within 15 years (see Matthew D. Bramlett and William D. Mosher, "First Marriage Dissolution, Divorce and Remarriage: United States," Advance Data from Vital and Health Statistics, May 31, 2001, 5, table 3). The father or the mother—usually the father—simply gets tired of marriage and walks out. In all too many cases he totally abandons the family. He often does not contribute to their maintenance.

I deal with the matter of divorce every week. I am convinced that some cases are justified. But many could be avoided. In most cases the problem begins with selfishness. We need to teach more effectively that happiness in marriage is not so much a matter of romance but rather an anxious concern for the comfort and well-being of one's companion and children. When a man begins to think less about himself and more about those for whom he is responsible, his entire outlook changes. No one can doubt the blessing that comes of a good father. He should stand as the provider, the defender, the teacher, the dearest friend of his wife and children.

I clipped the following from the *Wall Street Journal* some years ago. It recounts the experience of an African American youth who became a prominent lawyer. He says:

"One of my happiest childhood memories is of a ride with my father in our old clunker of an automobile. A shiny red Cadillac whizzed past and daddy remarked how pretty and expensive it was. 'Why do Cadillacs cost so much money?' I asked. 'Is it the name?'

" 'Well,' he responded deliberately, 'that's part of it. But it's also what that name means. It's like your name. It says that you are a [product] of the Chesses, and the Taylors and the Kings, and that you are so very, very special.'

"Ever since, I've carried that praise with me. And I've never looked to another human being for my worth. My father convinced me that I didn't need to. Even in my lowest times, I believed I was special" (Michael L. King, "Fatherhood and the Black Man," June 6, 1988, 20).

That's what makes the difference. A parent who runs away from family responsibility teaches irresponsibility to his children. A parent who stays with the family, nourishes them, loves them, teaches them pride in their name regardless of their economic circumstances, does something for the family, the community, and the nation that cannot be done in any other way or by anyone else.

Then there is the man—so very, very many of them—who, only to satisfy lustful desire, impregnates a girl and then abandons her. There is so much of this. The *New York Times Almanac* reports that "births out of wedlock represented 31 percent of all births in 1998, and 86 percent of all births to teenagers. . . . Every year in the U.S. almost 500,000 teenagers give birth" ([2002], 285).

Every case is a tragedy. It is a lifelong tragedy for the girl who becomes a single mother. It is a lifelong tragedy for the child who grows up without a father. It is a lifelong tragedy for society on whose ledger that child so often becomes a liability.

A writer in the *Wall Street Journal* observed:

"Boys raised outside of intact marriages are, on average, more than twice as likely as other boys to end up jailed. . . . Each year spent without a dad in the home increases the odds of future incarceration by about 5%.

" . . . A child born to an unwed mother is about 2½ times as likely to end up imprisoned, while a boy whose parents split during his teenage years was about 1½ times as likely to be imprisoned" (Maggie Gallagher, "Fatherless Boys Grow Up into Dangerous Men," Dec. 1, 1998, A22).

This situation led one observer to conclude, "America has become the most dangerous country in the world into which a child is born—the richest and the most dangerous" (Patrick Fagan, in George Archibald, "Diplomats Urged to Back Families, Teen Abstinence," *Washington Times,* May 5, 2002, A1).

What has brought us to this condition? It is not the result of some ruinous event such as the horror of 9/11. It has been a gradual process, the slow but corrosive abandonment of values once cherished and observed. We have lost much of a sense of civility. All of us who have watched television in recent days have wondered about the terrible looting that has taken place in Iraq. We say to ourselves, "What in the world has gone wrong with those people that they wantonly steal everything loose they can carry away?" And then I go back to the televised images of rioting in some of our own urban centers, when stores were broken into by lawless mobs and looted of merchandise and fixtures. Neither subjugation nor celebration justifies such behavior, no matter where it takes place.

The tragedy of gunfire in our schools bespeaks an absence of simple civility. It is seen in the phenomenon called "road rage." If something disappoints, if there is a grudge developed, we cannot settle it by shooting or solve it by looting. No, there can and must be some discipline in our lives. That discipline can be taught, and it can be learned, and that process happens best in the home.

There are many factors that have brought us to this point. You are familiar with them.

Pornography is one. It is rampant. It has become a huge industry whose producers grow rich while those who constitute its market sink lower and lower in a slough of debauchery.

We are all familiar with the problem of illegal drugs. It is a problem that seems to be impossible to control. We have an army of enforcement agents. But the traffic continues. I am satisfied that only education will turn the tide. I was amazed to read that in many instances parents were responsible for the introduction of their children to the use of drugs. How could a parent see any good in introducing illegal drugs to his or her child?

The fruits of unbridled sex we have already mentioned. The attitude that results in this comes in a very substantial measure from the entertainment world. I think none of us would wish to return to a code of extreme puritanism. But I honestly believe that most people would welcome an uplift, a great improvement in the products of Hollywood. I am told that the motion picture which recently won the top award is laden with sex and filled with profanity.

I believe that you cannot build an attitude of love for God in an environment where His name is constantly profaned—profaned and gagged over.

I heard Margaret Thatcher, former prime minister of Great Britain, say, "You use the name of Deity in the Declaration of Independence and in the Constitution of the United States, and yet you cannot use it in the schoolroom." Her words are a rebuke and an indictment.

And so I might go on. Do I sound like someone out of the Old Testament? I suppose so. But I do know this: you cannot destroy the family, with the values on which it must be based, without undermining the strength of the nation. There is no more important foundation stone on which to build a bridge for the future than the family—that simple but wonderful organization that the God of heaven put together, where there is a father who loves and takes responsibility, where there is a mother who nurtures and rears her children with pride, and where there are children who look to parents with love and respect and appreciation.

The Church which I am pleased to represent has for nearly 90 years encouraged families—mother, father, and children—to set aside one night a week in what we call family home evening. Here we talk and laugh, sing and learn, led by caring parents.

Let me tell of one such family in whose home I have been. They live in a small town in Wyoming. It is a large family, with seven children. At the head of that household stands a good father and a loving mother. A prominent lawyer in this city of Denver had as a client the father of that family. They worked together for months in a large international lawsuit. Of that father the Denver lawyer told me, "I have never met an individual with higher moral or ethical standards than [this man]."

That father practices in his house what he exemplifies in his career. As the children have grown, there has been no day that has passed without family prayer, without kneeling before the Almighty in reverence. There has been no week in which that father and mother have not gathered their children around them to read together, to plan together, to talk of the things of life together, to sing and pray together. Those now grown occupy positions of responsibility, and the younger ones are well on their way. Knowing that family, I believe I can predict that they will never become a liability to the society of which they are a part.

I submit that if we will work to turn the families of America to God, if they will recognize Him as our divine Father, as the Ruler of the universe, as the Giver of all good, something wonderful will happen. Think of what it means to know that each of us is actually a child of God and that He is our Father, to whom we may go in prayer. If we will use our energies to bring about a practice in the homes of America of good reading, including the reading of scripture; of a desire for education; of an attitude of civility one to another; then, and only then, will our nation truly become not only the military leader but also the moral light of the entire world.

I have seen such homes, very many of them. They are represented in large numbers in this audience. The children of your homes are growing up to be responsible, contributing citizens.

But there is a great underworld out there—a jungle, if you please—that needs our attention. We can and must do something.

Since 9/11 we have established in America a large agency entitled Homeland Security to deal with any present or future threat. May I say that it is likewise urgent that we work at home and family security.

As we do so, America will be strong not only in her arms and military affairs, she will be invincible in her moral values and in the integrity of her citizens.

I urge each of you to work at it, to become involved, to reach out to lift those who stand in need of help. We will not entirely solve the problem, but we can reduce it. If we do this, we shall in very deed begin to build bridges that will endure and carry this nation forward to better and nobler heights among the people of the earth.

God bless America, and may she be worthy of His blessing.

Thank you, ladies and gentlemen.

# University of Utah, Gordon B. Hinckley Endowment for British Studies

JULY 12, 2003

*The College of Humanities of the University of Utah established the Gordon B. Hinckley Endowment for British Studies in 1999. This address was given at a gala event at which it was announced that an additional five million dollars had been contributed to the endowment.*

W HAT A GREAT EVENING. What a deep sense of gratitude I feel to all of you for what you have done to make all of this possible, for these very generous contributors, and to all who put together this program, for the wonderful meal that we have had, and for your presence, my dear friends.

I brought with me tonight my old Shakespeare text, and I want to read a word or two of his to express my gratitude. He has Macbeth saying, "And that which should accompany old age, as honour, love, obedience, troops of friends" (*Macbeth,* act 5, scene 3). I have all of these: love, honor, obedience, troops of friends. To each of you I express my deep and affectionate gratitude, my dear ones.

This has stirred a thousand memories in my mind. I remember the day, 75 years ago, when I first walked to the Park Building on the university campus to register as a freshman. I was late in registration; I do not know why, except I have been late all my life. Freshman English was required, and all of the freshman English classes were filled. So the department created a special section headed by three old men, the senior men of the department: B. Roland Lewis, a Shakespeare scholar; George Marshall, a very distinguished grammarian; and Sherman Brown Neff, the head of the department. They had not taught freshman English for a long time, and they were not going to start over.

So they did not bother with freshman English. They taught us according to their love and their specialty. That awakened in me something of a desire. The next two years I filled the groups that are common to all such students: physics, geology, economics, whatever. Then came my junior year, when I had to make a decision as to what I would major in. I determined that I would like to do some writing. No degree was offered at the time in journalism. The only place you could take any writing classes was in English. So I majored in English and for the next two years studied under some great and wonderful men who shaped my life in many respects.

I had taken some Latin in high school, and I continued with that Latin and then picked up Greek. There were four of us in the university taking Greek. I think I had the distinct honor of perhaps being something of a classical scholar as an undergraduate. I had read the original Latin version of Virgil's *Aeneid* and other works and a good deal of the New Testament in the original Greek. It has all left me now, but I had a wonderful and instructive time in the process.

I then had the great fortune of going on a mission to the British Isles for the Church. I began in Lancashire among the poor, the very poor. It was the bottom of the Depression, and there was poverty everywhere. I learned to appreciate the British character, even in adversity. Then I was transferred to London, where I had a rich and rewarding and wonderful experience.

I have since had the opportunity of going to England many, many times. I have been all up and down that land, from Plymouth to Glasgow and from Edinburgh down to Brighton and on both sides of the island, including Wales and Ireland—the whole area of the UK. There is something tremendous about Britain. There is something wonderful about the British.

We are indebted to them as a people, not only for the language which we speak, which is becoming the language of the world, if there is such a thing, but also for the great English law, which began at Runnymede and progressed through the years to incorporate into its canon freedom of speech, freedom of religion, freedom of worship, freedom to do whatever we please in good citizenship.

There also has been bequeathed to us by this remarkable people the great English Bible, which has so influenced people across the world. We owe a debt of gratitude to Britain. We owe a tremendous debt of gratitude to the English people. We are inheritors of their past, and that which they had came to these shores and became incorporated in our way of life.

I know you are all familiar with these words, but I want to take the liberty of reading them again—the tremendous remarks of Gaunt in *Richard II:*

> *This royal throne of kings, this scepter'd isle,*
> *This earth of majesty, this seat of Mars,*
> *This other Eden, demi-Paradise;*
> *This fortress built by Nature for herself*
> *Against infection and the hand of war;*
> *This happy breed of men, this little world;*
> *This precious stone set in the silver sea,*
> *Which serves it in the office of a wall,*
> *Or as a moat defensive to a house,*
> *Against the envy of less happier lands;*
> *This blessed plot, this earth, this realm,*
> > *this England.*
> > > *[act 2, scene 1]*

What a great land it is. How grateful I am for the tremendous generosity of those who have given so much to establish this endowment and this chair, which will make it possible for others to enjoy what I have enjoyed in visits to this great and beautiful part of the earth.

I would just like to conclude by reading something that I heard Rudyard Kipling give in 1934, when I attended, as a young man, the Pageant of Parliaments at the Royal Albert Hall, and Kipling was asked to write a poem for this great occasion. I read it to you.

> *Non nobis Domine!—*
> *Not unto us, O Lord!*
> *The Praise or Glory be*
> *Of any deed or word;*
> *For in Thy Judgment lies*
> *To crown or bring to nought*
> *All knowledge or device*
> *That man has reached or wrought.*
> *And we confess our blame—*
> *How all too high we hold*
> *That noise which men call Fame,*
> *That dross which men call Gold.*
> *For these we undergo*
> *Our hot and godless days,*
> *But in our hearts we know*
> *Not unto us the Praise.*
> *O Power by Whom we live—*
> *Creator, Judge, and Friend,*
> *Upholdingly forgive*
> *Nor fail us at the end:*
> *But grant us well to see*
> *In all our piteous ways—*
> *Non nobis Domine!—*
> *Not unto us the Praise!*
>
> *[*"Non nobis Domine!*" in Rudyard*
> *Kipling's Verse [1946], 511]*

My dear friends, I am now an old man. I have had the opportunity of traveling around this world again and again. I have been on every continent, and I have spoken up and down in the nations of the earth. Our people reach out to 160 nations now, and I think I have been just about everywhere where they are. I still love this part of the world—home, Utah. I love the land I came closest to being adopted a part of—that is the great land of England, for which I feel profoundly grateful.

Thank you. Thank you, my dear friends. I cannot thank you enough for your generosity, your kindness, and your love. Thank you, and God bless you, everyone.

# NATIONAL FORENSIC LEAGUE
# AWARD CEREMONY

## JUNE 18, 2004

*The National Forensic League gave President Hinckley its 2004 Communicator of the Year Award and invited him to address participants of the 2004 National High School Speech Tournament. Over 3,000 student debaters and other distinguished guests were in attendance.*

THANK YOU FOR THE HONOR you have paid me. I am deeply grateful. I feel a tremendous challenge in speaking a few words to this talented group.

Those who have gathered here, young men and women from the high schools of this and other nations, I congratulate you most warmly. You are developing your capacity to communicate. There is nothing more important. It is the basic element of leadership.

In the United States we have just laid to rest one who was known as "The Great Communicator." It was a title that came of a remarkable capacity. He knew how to talk to people, both his friends and his enemies. We can never forget the look of defiance on his face as he said, "Mr. Gorbachev, tear down that wall."

Our nation had appeared as one in decline when he came into office. His predecessor had said, "The symptoms of [a] crisis of the American spirit are all around us" (*Public Papers of the Presidents of the United States: Jimmy Carter, 1979*, 2 vols. [1980], 2:1237).

Then, in 1981, in his inaugural address, President Ronald Reagan said: "The crisis we are facing today [requires] our willingness to believe in ourselves and to believe in our capacity to perform great deeds. . . . After all, why shouldn't we believe that? We are Americans" (in *The Inaugural Addresses of the Presidents of the United States, 1789–1985* [1985], 182).

The people rallied to his leadership. The next eight years saw very many serious problems, but it was his capacity to speak with radiance and hope, with assurance and confidence that lifted the spirit of the entire land. It was his ability to communicate that made him the leader that he was.

Ideas are so very important. Most people have ideas. But those ideas become realities only as they are clearly spoken and acted upon.

Winston Churchill's power came of his remarkable capability to communicate and galvanize people into action. We have just celebrated the 50th anniversary of D-day, June 6, 1944. That unforgettable event in human history was the outgrowth of what Churchill had said following the debacle at Dunkirk in 1940: "We shall fight on the beaches, we shall fight on the landing grounds, we shall fight in the fields and in the streets, we shall fight in the hills; we shall never surrender" ("Wars Are Not Won by Evacuations," *Winston S. Churchill: His Complete Speeches,* ed. Robert Rhodes James, 8 vols. [1974], 6:6231). It was that tremendous capacity to communicate that built resolve within the people of Britain which saved them from disaster.

The venue in which we meet tonight, this historic and unique Tabernacle, might have remained only a largely unrecognized and curious building were it not for the weekly network broadcasts of *Music and the Spoken Word.* For 75 years now there has gone from this great hall the music of a wonderful choir, together with a brief but stimulating message. This longest network broadcast in history is a remarkable phenomenon. There is nothing to compare with it. It has entertained, inspired, and motivated millions upon millions during these three-quarters of a century. And all of this has been an expression of the human voice.

The transfer of ideas from one man to the masses is really the magic by which people are persuaded to act. The words of Jesus have touched generations of mankind for 2,000 years and caused us to respect and ponder, to think and do. They are as meaningful today, if not more so, than when they were first spoken. Listen to them as I read an excerpt from the 1611 King James Bible.

> And seeing the multitudes, he went up into a mountain: . . .
> And he opened his mouth, and taught them, saying,
> Blessed are the poor in spirit: for theirs is the kingdom of heaven.
> Blessed are they that mourn: for they shall be comforted.
> Blessed are the meek: for they shall inherit the earth.
> Blessed are they which do hunger and thirst after righteousness: for they shall be filled.
> Blessed are the merciful: for they shall obtain mercy.
> Blessed are the pure in heart: for they shall see God.
> Blessed are the peacemakers: for they shall be called the children of God.
> Blessed are they which are persecuted for righteousness' sake: for theirs is the kingdom of heaven. [Matthew 5:1–10]

Marvelous and stirring words are those!

Who can discount the beauty and the wonder of Abraham Lincoln's words? These lines have become immortal: "With malice toward none, with charity for all, with firmness in the right as God gives us to see the right, let us strive on to finish the work we are in, to bind up the nation's wounds, to care for him who shall have borne the battle and for his widow and his orphan, to do all which may achieve and cherish a just and a lasting peace among ourselves and with all nations" (in *The Inaugural Addresses of the Presidents of the United States, 1789–1985* [1985], 77).

Power to communicate has also been used for evil purposes. It was Hitler's spellbinding oratory that led to the terrible Second World War. That war resulted in the death of more than 60 million people and in unspeakable misery for countless millions of others.

Looking back into history I can still see and hear Hitler, the demon of the gestapo, speaking with rare eloquence to the German people and leading them into the morass of that cataclysmic conflict.

The ability to speak to others is the ability to move individuals, masses, even nations and the world to action.

I recall these wonderful words written so long ago by Walt Whitman. Said he, "Surely whoever speaks to me in the right voice, him or her I shall follow, as the water follows the moon, silently, with fluid steps, anywhere around the globe" ("Vocalism," *Walt Whitman: Complete Poetry and Selected Prose and Letters,* ed. Emory Holloway [1938], 350–51).

And so it is. Wherever we go, whatever we do, we are inclined to follow the leader. And we will discover that the leader is one who knows how to communicate to others the principles or the plan in which he or she believes.

An old Arabic proverb states, "An army of sheep led by a lion will defeat an army of lions led by a sheep." The roar of a lion is far more persuasive than the bleating of a sheep.

And so I compliment you most warmly tonight as you have come together in this great gathering. What you do today will prepare you for leadership tomorrow. May God bless you that your dreams may become realities, that your vision may become a plan for action. Thank you.

# PRESS CONFERENCE, PRESENTATION OF PRESIDENTIAL MEDAL OF FREEDOM

### JUNE 23, 2004

*George W. Bush, president of the United States, presented President Hinckley with the Presidential Medal of Freedom at a ceremony in the White House in Washington, D.C. The Presidential Medal of Freedom is the nation's highest civilian honor and recognizes achievement in public service and other fields. Others receiving the award in 2004 were Pope John Paul II, golfer Arnold Palmer, and actress Doris Day. A press conference followed the ceremony.*

THIS IS QUITE A GATHERING—a lot of cameras, a lot of wasted film. We received today this very outstanding award and appreciate it very much. The group who received it are extremely able people, and to be counted among their number is a great privilege and a great honor.

This is an honor to my Church more than it is to me, because the Church has afforded me all of the opportunities and all of the responsibilities which have led to this occasion. It is a special thing to me because this is my 94th birthday. That is a wonderful birthday present, isn't it? It is tremendous.

This is the Medal of Freedom, and I think where it really belongs is to those men and women who are engaged in the battle for freedom in other parts of the world. They are carrying the torch and carrying the brunt of responsibility under the most difficult circumstances. As I think of the word *freedom*, which is embodied in this award, I think of them and the great, distinguished service which they are rendering.

Thank you very, very much.

Any questions?

*Question:* President Hinckley, what did President Bush say to you when he shook your hand and put that medal around your neck?

*President Hinckley:* I don't remember. I was so awestruck I can't remember what he said.

*Question:* It looks like all five of your children are here on the stage.

*President Hinckley:* Yes, all five of our children are here. We brought them with us this morning, and we'll go home tonight. All in one day.

*Question:* President Hinckley, when did you find out about receiving this honor, and how did you find out?

*President Hinckley:* The White House telephoned my secretary about a week ago, and we made arrangements to come.

*Question:* You've been here a number of times to visit a number of presidents.

*President Hinckley:* I think this is the fifth time I have been to the White House, yes.

*Question:* How would you contrast this day with Joseph Smith's visit with Martin Van Buren in 1839?

*President Hinckley:* Yes, of course, that brings back memories of that occasion when he came here from Nauvoo, riding a horse much of the way. He said he rented the cheapest accommodations they could find. They came here to plead the case of our people, who had been despoiled and persecuted and driven. He was turned down by President Van Buren, who rebuffed him and said, "If I help you, I'll lose the state of Missouri." Joseph went home without gaining anything for which he had come. Now to have this invitation from the president of the nation is a very signal and significant honor.

*Question:* When the pope received his medal, he said he was troubled by the war in Iraq. You mentioned today that you thought the medal belonged to those men and women.

*President Hinckley:* Well, we cannot discount the bravery of the men and women who at the behest of the commander in chief are there in the cause of freedom.

*Question:* President Hinckley, we miss Sister Hinckley on a day like this. What would she say about this day?

*President Hinckley:* She'd say, "What a wonderful thing. What a great thing." She'd say, "Am I going with you?" And I would say, "Of course." I am just so sorry that she isn't here. She would have enjoyed this very, very much. She liked to mingle with people and have a good time wherever she went. Thank you.

*Question:* President Hinckley, I had one more question. You said several times lately that the Church is doing very well and that you have barely scratched the surface. What do you see as its possibilities for the future?

*President Hinckley:* This work will spread across the earth. When you look at what has happened thus far, we have to realize that if we keep going, it will grow exponentially, and wherever it goes, it will touch for good the lives of people across this whole broad world. Thanks so much.

# Interview with Suzanne DeVoe of Catholic Community Services

## August 16, 2004

*Suzanne DeVoe was the public relations specialist of Catholic Community Services of Utah. The purpose of this interview was to prepare for an award dinner in October 2004, during which Catholic Community Services gave President Hinckley its Humanitarian of the Year Award.*

*Suzanne DeVoe:* What are some of the major needs that you see in our community?

*President Hinckley:* Well, we have people in trouble; of course we do. There are people in trouble everywhere. There are those who are homeless. There are those who are hungry. There are those who are sick. There are those who are abused. There are those who have difficulties of a variety of kinds, and we all have an obligation to help those in distress and need.

*Suzanne DeVoe:* In your view, what is a humanitarian?

*President Hinckley:* Well, a humanitarian is one who reaches out to assist someone who is in distress and needs help, who can lift him and give him encouragement, put him on his way. The Savior set the example in the parable of the good Samaritan. He said to us, "Inasmuch as ye have done it unto one of the least of these my brethren, ye have done it unto me" (Matthew 25:40). That is the spirit of the thing, and we who are followers of the Christ have an obligation to obey His commandments and follow His example. We are trying to do that—not always to the extent or the degree that we would like to, but we certainly make an effort.

*Suzanne DeVoe:* Do you see a difference between a humanitarian and a neighbor?

*President Hinckley:* Oh, I don't know that there is any substantial difference. I don't think so.

*Suzanne DeVoe:* What benefits do people receive when they help each other?

*President Hinckley:* Anybody who forgets and loses himself in the service of others magnifies himself. He gains the satisfaction of doing what he ought to be doing. When he sets aside his selfishness and reaches out to others, something happens within himself.

*Suzanne DeVoe:* How did you in your life learn to serve others?

*President Hinckley:* Oh, I don't know. We just try to do what we can here and there, not only locally, but our Church reaches across the world to help those in distress. Wherever there has been a great catastrophe, we have tried to assist and help. We do that on a local basis recognizing the need here, working with others such as the Catholic Community Services, and reaching out to others wherever they may be in need to the extent we can.

*Suzanne DeVoe:* How do you see your role in the community—you personally?

*President Hinckley:* I am a member of the community. As a member of the community, I have an obligation; of course I do. It is my role to speak up in defense of those who are defenseless and to give encouragement to those who are down and out and lend aid. James reminds us that we should be "doers of the word, and not hearers only" (James 1:22). And that is the position in which we find ourselves.

*Suzanne DeVoe:* Do you feel that we are getting better about helping others, or is it in kind of a standstill? How do you feel about that?

*President Hinckley:* Oh, I am an optimist. I hope we are getting better. There is a need. The Savior said, "The poor always ye have with you" (John 12:8). Of course we do. There has always been a need. I suppose there always will be need. I would hope that we are getting better at meeting that need.

*Suzanne DeVoe:* So then, it will always be there.

*President Hinckley:* We have always had them; I suppose we always will have them.

*Suzanne DeVoe:* What do you think the general world society or our community of Utah or Salt Lake, the whole society, should be doing to help those in need?

*President Hinckley:* Well, I hope we are already doing it. We join hands one with another, reach down to lift those who are in distress and need. That is an obligation incumbent upon us. We must work at it constantly and work one with another cooperatively to meet the needs of those who are in terrible need, who are hungry, who are sick, who are lonely, who are afraid, who walk in troubled ways. Those of us who have been blessed have an obligation to reach out to those who have not been so blessed. I hope that we are trying to do it and that we are doing it effectively.

*Suzanne DeVoe:* Do we need to wait for a big disaster to help others?

*President Hinckley:* Of course not. We do not have to wait for a big disaster, but if a big disaster comes, you have to face it and meet it. But at the same time, you have to work at those continuing needs—small in scale, perhaps, but very real—which confront us daily in every community, I suppose in all the world, and certainly right here where we are trying to work together to aid those who need help.

*Suzanne DeVoe:* So you see no difference between anyone in the community, their obligation is the same?

*President Hinckley:* Oh, surely—to reach out to all of them who are in need, to supply them with food, to help them. The resources of this Church are made available to other organizations, as well, including the Catholic Community Services, to feed those in need who come and are hungry and are in sore distress. We want to be of assistance, and we have been and will continue to be.

# INTERNATIONAL LAW AND RELIGION SYMPOSIUM*

## OCTOBER 6, 2004

*President Hinckley gave these remarks at the conclusion of the
11th Annual International Law and Religion Symposium, which was
sponsored by groups from Brigham Young University, Catholic University
of America, Columbia University, and others. Legal scholars and
government officials from Africa, Asia, Europe, the Pacific, and
North and South America were invited to the symposium.*

IT IS VERY DIFFICULT to speak after that wonderful performance
by those beautiful and delightful children. Children are beautiful all
over the world. I have never seen children anywhere who were not
beautiful, and they set a pattern for all of us.

Now, I want to thank every one of you who have come from
afar to be here. Thank you for the effort you have made. Thank you
for the promise that goes with your attendance here.

I have been thinking of what a different world this would be if
men's hearts all over the world would turn to the principles of true
religion and exemplify them in their lives and in their actions.
Where religion finds its finest expression, there is no conflict, really.
And if there is anything this world needs, it is the peace that comes
of understanding, of worship of one's God, and of loyalty to
principles of religious life.

I call your attention to the fact that you are meeting here in Salt
Lake City, a place that was founded by our people more than a century and a half ago. This was all wilderness then. Our people came
here seeking peace, and as they established themselves, they welcomed others. The result is that we have today all of the major religions represented here: the Catholics, the Protestants, the Muslims,

*delivered extemporaneously

the Greek Orthodox—everything, I think, and we get along together.

Only last night I was honored with a humanitarian award by the Catholics here in this valley. I greatly appreciate it because it was indicative of our peaceful relationships and working together to try to build one another.

So we congratulate you and wish for you success in your great undertaking in trying to establish freedom of religion in your lands. When we are all together, we may have different theological understanding, but we all have a common obligation and privilege, and that is to reach out, to assist those in need wherever they may be or whatever their problem may be.

One of our Articles of Faith of the Church says we believe in "worshiping Almighty God according to the dictates of our own conscience, and allow all men the same privilege, let them worship how, where, or what they may" (Articles of Faith 1:11). It is in that spirit that we carry on here. We do not fear competition in our religion, no. We simply say to people, "You see what we have. See if we can offer something better than you have. And if we can, then we extend the hand of fellowship to you. But whatever your religion, we will respect you and honor you and try to assist you as you walk the road of life."

I want to congratulate Dr. W. Cole Durham for all he has done to make this great symposium possible. This is no small undertaking. It is a tremendous thing to get a group of this kind together. I do not know where you would find a group like this outside the United Nations anywhere. You come together to reach a greater understanding.

Well, I think I have been to almost every nation from which you come. I would like to go again, but I am getting so old. My Chinese friends have sent me some of their ancient medicine to try to help me live to be 100. If I make it, I will come to your countries again.

Well, I just want to repeat my appreciation. I have been all over this world, and I have not been anywhere that I have not met good people. I mean that. There are good people everywhere, and there is goodwill everywhere. There are a few bad people, unfortunately, but I hope the good outnumber the bad.

It was a delightful thing to sit at our table here with our dear friends from Spain and converse with them. I was with them last spring in their native land. And I was so grateful to see our friend, Brother San Ngoc Nguyen here, who comes from Vietnam. This nation was at war once in that land. If we had had better understanding, I do not think we would have had that kind of war. I was in Vietnam many times during the war, and I have been there recently since the war. I am so glad to sit down and sup with Brother San. The same thing goes for all of you wherever you come from—from the many lands of the world.

God bless you, my dear brothers and sisters, for that is what you are. We all have a common Father—God, our Eternal Father, the Almighty Ruler and Governor of the universe. And if we have a common Father, we are all brothers and sisters. That is a fact of life. And so I can shake your hand and look you in the eye and say, "Brother, Sister, how nice to know you."

Now, when I was here last year, people crowded around and wanted some autographs and my card. This time I have a little book that I wrote that sets forth my views on various things *[Standing for Something]*. It is published by a national publisher, Random House, with an introduction by Mike Wallace. If you will accept that little volume with my kind regards, along with a copy of the Book of Mormon, one of our scriptures which testifies of the Lord Jesus Christ, I will be greatly obliged.

And so to each of you, thank you so very, very much. I used to be able to say *thank you* in about 30 languages. I cannot remember that many anymore. But anyway, thank you very much. God bless you. I wish you a safe journey home, and please know that we love you. We reach out with affection in our hearts to every one of you. Our prayers go with you. Please come again. We will count it a wonderful privilege if we get to see you where you live. Thank you.

# INDEX

# H

Haight, David B., 245

Hall, Norma, 516

Happiness: and children, 30–31, 35–36, 38; cultivating, 164; in marriage, 261–62; in Church callings, 389–90

Harbertson, Robert, 32–33

Harold B. Lee Library, 305

Hatch, Orrin, 478

Hinckley, Bryant S., 497, 498–500

Hinckley, Ed, 497

Hinckley, Gordon B. (GBH): and Conference Center pulpit, 7; calls stake president, 10–12; evolution of testimony of, 19–21; testifies of Jesus Christ, 21–24, 90–91, 141, 449; high school experience of, 63; classmates of, 64–66; carries cane, 89; testifies of Joseph Smith, 141; testifies of the First Vision, 158; testifies of the Restoration, 161–62; marriage of, 173; desires beneficial policy, 175; feelings of, about war, 180–81; unknown influence of, for good, 190; conversation of, with portrait of Brigham Young, 208–9; heritage and posterity of, in Church, 273–74; and Singapore, 278–80; Primary experiences of, 382–83; testimony of, 397–98, 428–29, 443; and family home evening, 402; finds site for Manhattan New York Temple, 419–22; and the North Star, 431–32; and forgiveness for unethical business dealing, 441; *Standing for Something,* book by, 474–75, 561; health of, 477; education of, 477–78; life experiences of, 485–86; pruning trees, 511; mission of, 529–30, 545; love of, for humanity, 531–32, 535; railroad experiences of, 533–35; Endowment for British Studies

named for, 544; University of Utah experiences of, 544–45; receives Presidential Medal of Freedom, 553–54; receives Catholic Community Services Humanitarian of the Year Award, 556

Hinckley, Ira Nathaniel, 495, 496–98, 500

Hinckley, Marjorie Pay: marriage of, 173; motherhood of, 189; companionship of, 193; illness of, 243; death of, 257–58; funeral for, 414–15; and Radio City Music Hall, 424; influence of, 452–53; and aging, 532; personality of, 555

Hitler, Adolf, 551–52

Holbrook, Lafayette, 498

Holy Ghost: reality of promptings from, 314, 315; receiving knowledge through, 315; and missionary work, 364–65, 366; following promptings of, 381–82

Holy nation, 360

Homes, 213

Honesty: consequences of lack of, 35; and peace, 44–45; and priesthood power, 126; of bishops, 202; with employer, 378; importance of, 489

Hong Kong Temple, 281–82, 422–23

Hosanna Shout, 53–54

Humanism, 315

Humanitarian aid, 231–33; and immunizations, 197–98; recognition of, 229; donations for, 231, 530; drilling for water in Ghana, 231–32; medical, 232–33; and disaster relief, 233, 430–31, 487, 588; ongoing need for, 233; as part of gospel, 349; benefitting non-LDS, 465–66; worldwide efforts in, 465–66, 557; destinations for, 530. *See also*

# V

# W

Work: done by ordinary people, 487; teaching children about, 512; importance of, 532

World War II, 331–32, 551–52

Worthiness: and priesthood power, 97–98, 124–31; of bishops, 203

# Y

Young, Brigham: on temples, 5; on marriage, 45; and the arts, 121; on settling in Salt Lake area, 121–22; and Nauvoo Temple, 143; conversation with portrait of, 208–9; on staying in Utah, 320; on knowing the truth of God's principles, 400–401; and Fillmore, Utah, 495–96

Young women: divine nature of, 218–19; potential of, 219; education of, 219–20; respect of, for bodies, 221–22; reliance of, on the Lord, 222; "dropping the ball," 223–24

Youth: faithfulness of, 18–19; plea for mothers to guide, 30; parents' responsibility for, 38–39; challenges for, 39–42, 211–12; strength of, 167; faith of, 226; strengthening, against sin, 351–52; plea for leaders to get close to, 376–77; performing baptisms for the dead, 424; American, condition of, 536